Teen Health Resources

Students & Families

glencoe.com

New Student Edition Includes

- The latest health information
- Fitness Zone Handbook
- What Teens Think
- Health eSpotlight Videos
- Reading Skills Handbook

Cross-Curricular Activities

- Guide to Reading
- Building Academic Vocabulary
- Connect To… Science, Math, and Language Arts
- Write About It

Online Learning Center

- Online Student Edition
- Chapter Summaries in English and Spanish
- Interactive Study Guides
- eFlashcards
- Building Health Skills
- Student Web Activities
- Career Corner
- Podcasts
- Study-to-Go

Teen Health

COURSE 1

Mary H. Bronson, Ph.D.

Michael J. Cleary, Ed.D., C.H.E.S.

Betty M. Hubbard, Ed.D., C.H.E.S.

Contributing Authors
Dinah Zike, M.Ed.
TIME®

McGraw Hill **Glencoe**

Meet the Authors

Mary H. Bronson, Ph.D., recently retired after teaching for 30 years in Texas public schools. Dr. Bronson taught health education in grades K–12, as well as health education methods classes at the undergraduate and graduate levels. As Health Education Specialist for the Dallas School District, Dr. Bronson developed and implemented a district-wide health education program. She has been honored as Texas Health Educator of the Year by the Texas Association for Health, Physical Education, Recreation, and Dance and selected Teacher of the Year twice, by her colleagues. Dr. Bronson has assisted school districts through-out the country in developing local health education programs. She is also the coauthor of the *Glencoe Health* textbook.

Betty M. Hubbard, Ed.D., C.H.E.S., has taught science and health education in grades 6–12, as well as undergraduate- and graduate-level courses. She is a professor at the University of Central Arkansas, where, in addition to teaching, she conducts in-service training for health education teachers in school districts throughout Arkansas. In 1991, Dr. Hubbard received the university's teaching excellence award. Her publications, grants, and presentations focus on research-based, comprehensive health instruction. Dr. Hubbard is a fellow of the American Association for Health Education and serves as the contributing editor for the Teaching Ideas feature of the *American Journal of Health Education.*

Michael J. Cleary, Ed.D., C.H.E.S., is a professor at Slippery Rock University, where he teaches methods courses and supervises field experiences. Dr. Cleary taught health education at Evanston Township High School in Illinois and later served as the Lead Teacher Specialist at the McMillen Center for Health Education in Fort Wayne, Indiana. Dr. Cleary has published widely on curriculum development and assessment in K–12 and college health education. Dr. Cleary is also coauthor of the *Glencoe Health* textbook.

Contributing Authors

Dinah Zike, M.Ed., is an international curriculum consultant and inventor who has designed and developed educational products and three-dimensional, interactive graphic organizers for over thirty years. As president and founder of Dinah-Might Adventures, L.P., Dinah is author of over 100 award-winning educational publications. Dinah has a B.S. and an M.S. in educational curriculum and instruction from Texas A&M University. Dinah Zike's *Foldables®* are an exclusive feature of McGraw-Hill textbooks.

TIME® is the nation's leading news and information magazine. With over 80 years of experience, TIME® provides an authoritative voice in the analysis of the issues of the day, from politics to pop culture, from history-making decisions to healthy living. TIME® Learning Ventures brings the strength of TIME® and TIME® For Kids' editorial and photographic excellence to educational resources for school and home.

The **McGraw·Hill** Companies

Printed in the United States of America.

Send all inquiries to:
Glencoe/McGraw-Hill
21600 Oxnard Street, Suite 500
Woodland Hills, California 91367

ISBN-13: 978-0-07-877405-8 (Course 1 Student Edition)
MHID-10: 0-07-877405-5   (Course 1 Student Edition)

ISBN-13: 978-0-07-877406-5 (Course 1 Teacher Wraparound Edition)
MHID-10: 0-07-877406-3   (Course 1 Teacher Wraparound Edition)

2 3 4 5 6 7 8 9 043/071 12 11 10 09 08

Alia Antoon, M.D.
Chief of Pediatrics
Shriners Hospital for Children
Assistant Clinical Professor, Pediatrics
Harvard Medical School
Boston, Massachusetts

Elissa M. Barr, Ph.D., C.H.E.S.
Assistant Professor of Public Health
University of North Florida
Jacksonville, Florida

Beverly Bradley, Ph.D., R.N., C.H.E.S.
School Health Consultant
Retired Assistant Clinical Professor
University of California, San Diego
San Diego, California

Donna Breitestein, Ed.D.
Professor and Coordinator, Health Education
Appalachian State University
Boone, North Carolina

Roberta L. Duyff, M.S., R.D., C.F.C.S.
Food and Nutrition Consultant/President
Duyff Associates
St. Louis, Missouri

Kristin Danielson Fink, M.A.
National Director
Community of Caring
Salt Lake City, Utah

Kathryn J. Gust, M.A.
Instructional Technology Specialist
Freedom High School
Morganton, North Carolina

Christine A. Hayashi, M.A. Ed., J.D.
Attorney at Law, Special Education Law
Adjunct Faculty, Educational Leadership
and Policy Studies Development
California State University, Northridge
Northridge, California

Michael E. Moore, M.A., LCSW
School Psychologist
Speech Education Coordinator
Centerville/Abington Community Schools
Centerville, Indiana

Tinker D. Murray, Ph.D., FACSM
Professor of Health, Physical Education, and Recreation
Texas State University
San Marcos, Texas

Don Rainey, M.S., C.S.C.S.
Director, Physical Fitness and Wellness
Texas State University
San Marcos, Texas

John Rohwer, Ed.D.
Professor of Health Education
Bethel University
St. Paul, Minnesota

Michael Rulon, M.S.
Instructional Coach
Health Instructor
Albuquerque Public Schools
Albuquerque, New Mexico

Robin Scarcella, Ph.D.
Director, Academic English/ESL
University of California, Irvine
Irvine, California

Diane Tanaka, M.D.
Assistant Professor of Clinical Pediatrics
Keck School of Medicine
Attending Physician
Division of Adolescent Medicine
University of Southern California
Los Angeles, California

Robert Wandberg, Ph.D.
Staff Development
St. Paul Public Schools
St. Paul, Minnesota

Peter T. Whelley, M.S., N.C.S.P.
School Psychologist
Moultonborough School District
Adjunct Faculty
Plymouth State University
Plymouth, New Hampshire

David C. Wiley, Ph.D.
Professor of Health Education
Texas State University
San Marcos, Texas

Neile Bennett
Health Educator
Pierce County Middle School
Blackshear, Georgia

Kathy Bowman-Harrow
Supervisor, Health Education
Orange County Public Schools
Orlando, Florida

David Bryant
Health/Physical Education
Athletic Director
Greene County Middle School
Snow Hill, North Carolina

Mary Capaforte
Healthful Living Teacher
Department Chair
Lufkin Road Middle School
Apex, North Carolina

Jason S. Chandler
Physical Education/Health Teacher
Head Certified Athletic Trainer
Prince George County Public Schools
Prince George County, Virginia

Pamela Rizzo Connolly, M.E.
Curriculum Coordinator for Health
and Physical Education
North Catholic High School
Diocese of Pittsburgh
Pittsburgh, Pennsylvania

Audrey Maria Diamond
Science Teacher
Ellis G. Arnall Middle School
Newnan, Georgia

Allison Duckworth, M.A.
Physical Education Teacher
Head Athletic Trainer
Freedom High School
Morganton, North Carolina

Valerie Hernandez, BSN RN, M.S.
Registered Nurse/Health Educator
Escambia County School District
Pensacola, Florida

Andy Keyes
Health/Physical Education Teacher
Hastings Middle School
Upper Arlington, Ohio

April Lane
Health Teacher
Portland Middle School
Portland, Tennessee

Norma H. Lee, M.A.
Wellness Instructor
Jefferson County High School
Dandridge, Tennessee

Cindy Meyer, M.A.T.
Health Educator
South Oldham Middle School
Crestwood, Kentucky

Bobby Jean Moore, M.A.T.
Health Education Specialist
Creekland Middle School
Lawrenceville, Georgia

Dale Mueller
Health/Physical Education Teacher
New Holstein School District
New Holstein, Wisconsin

Tammy Smith
Administrator
Tulsa Public Schools
Tulsa, Oklahoma

Joan Gilger Stear, M.Ed
Health Education Instructor
West Clermont Institute of Performing Arts
Glen Este High School
Cincinnati, Ohio

Stacia K. Tatum
Physical Education Teacher
Westridge Middle School
Orlando, Florida

Jeanne Title
County Coordinator
Office of Safety and Wellness
Napa County Office of Education and Physical
Education
Napa, California

Lisa Ward
Health/Physical Education Teacher
Kernodle Middle School
Greensboro, North Carolina

Robert T. Wieselberg
Health Educator
Westridge Middle School
Orlando, Florida

Table of Contents

CHAPTER 2 Mental and Emotional Wellness

CHAPTER 3 Healthy Relationships

CHAPTER 6

Personal Health

CHAPTER 11

Preventing Diseases

CHAPTER 12

Safety and The Environment

Be Healthy and Active with Teen Health

Physical activity and fitness are important to good health. Use the Fitness Zone Handbook and Glencoe's Online Fitness Zone to develop personal fitness.

Fitness Zone Handbook

The Fitness Zone Handbook on pages xiv – 1 can help you create a personal fitness plan to balance your activities and build your overall fitness level. You'll also learn about the elements of fitness and discover fun group activities.

FITNESS ZONE Handbook

Physical Fitness Plan

Everyone should have a fitness plan. A personal plan can help you get started in developing your physical fitness. If you are already active or even athletic, a physical fitness plan can help you balance your activities and maintain a healthy level of activity.

Planning a Routine

When you're ready to start a fitness routine, it may be tempting to exercise as hard as you can for as long as you can. However, that approach is likely to leave you discouraged and even injured. Instead, you should plan a fitness routine that will let your body adjust to activity. Work up to your fitness goals slowly. Gradually increase both the length of time you spend exercising and the number of times you exercise each week. For example, you might start by doing a fitness activity for just 5 minutes a day, 3 days a week. Increase the amount of time you exercise, to say 7 minutes the next week and to 10 minutes during the third week of your plan. When you are exercising 20 minutes, 3 days a week, you're ready to add a fourth day to your fitness routine. Eventually, you will be exercising for 20 to 30 minutes, 5 days a week.

Warming Up

There's more to a physical fitness plan than fitness activities. It's important to prepare your body for exercise. Preparation involves warm-up activities that will raise your body temperature and get your muscles ready for your fitness activity. Easy warm-up activities include walking, marching, and jogging, as well as basic calisthenics.

When you're developing your own fitness plan, you should include warm-ups in your schedule. As you increase the time you spend doing a fitness activity, you should also increase the time you spend warming up.

This chart shows how you can plan the time you spend on warm-ups and fitness activities.

Sample Physical Fitness Plan

DAY	Monday		Tuesday		Wednesday		Thursday		Friday	
WEEK	Warm Up	Activity	Warm Up	Activity	Warm Up	Activity	Warm Up	Activity	Warm Up	Activity
1	5 min	5 min	—	—	5 min	5 min	—	—	5 min	5 min
2	5 min	7 min	—	—	5 min	7 min	—	—	5 min	7 min
3	5 min	10 min	—	—	5 min	10 min	—	—	5 min	10 min
4	5 min	12 min	—	—	5 min	12 min	—	—	5 min	12 min
5	7 min	15 min	—	—	7 min	15 min	—	—	7 min	15 min
6	7 min	17 min	—	—	7 min	17 min	—	—	7 min	17 min
7	10 min	20 min	—	—	10 min	20 min	—	—	10 min	20 min
8	10 min	20 min	10 min	20 min	10 min	20 min	—	—	10 min	20 min
9	10 min	20 min	10 min	20 min	10 min	20 min	10 min	20 min	10 min	20 min

xiv   Fitness Zone Handbook

Go Online

Get energized with Glencoe's *Fitness Zone Online* at *glencoe.com*

Fitness Zone Online is a multimedia resource that helps students find ways to be physically active each day.

The Nutrition and Physical Activity Resources include:

- Clipboard Energizer Activities
- Fitness Zone Videos
- Polar Heart Rate Monitor Activities
- Tips for Healthy Eating, Staying Active, and Preventing Injuries
- Links to additional Nutrition and Physical Activity Resources

Reading in the health classroom with
Teen Health

Review Key Terms
Complete the Building Vocabulary activity to become familiar with these terms before you read the lesson. Vocabulary terms are highlighted in yellow to make them easy to find.

Do the QuickWrite
This feature will help you start thinking about the information in the lesson.

Look at the Reading Checks
When you see a Reading Check, stop and answer the question to make sure that you understand what you have just read.

Preview the Lesson
Get a preview of what's coming by reading the lesson objectives in Focusing on the Main Ideas. You can also use this feature to prepare for quizzes and tests.

Strengthen Your Reading Skills
Complete the Reading Strategy activity to help you understand some of the information in the lesson.

Reading Skills Handbook
The Reading Skills Handbook on pages 328–337 offers strategies to help you become a faster, more effective reader. Strong reading skills can help you improve your grades, study skills, and writing skills.

Lesson 4

Managing Your Weight

Guide to Reading

Building Vocabulary
List each term below in your notebook. As you come across it in your reading, write the definition.
- body image (p. 109)
- eating disorder (p. 110)

Focusing on the Main Ideas
In this lesson, you will learn to
- **explain** how to maintain a healthy weight.
- **identify** problem eating behaviors.
- **demonstrate** decision-making skills to help a friend.

Reading Strategy
Predicting Look over the he___ in this lesson. Write a question that you think the lesson will an___ ___r reading, check to see if your question was answered.

Quick Write
In a few sentences, tell what you think the benefits are of maintaining a healthful weight.

Achieving a Healthful Weight
Knowing the weight that is right for you is tricky during the teen years. That's because your body is growing so fast. The only way to tell for sure is to see a health professional. This person can help you determine if your weight and body composition are within a healthy range. Your *body composition* is the fat, bone, muscle, and fluid that make up your body weight. Generally, a healthy body has more bone, muscle, and fluid than fat.

To keep your weight and body composition within a healthy range, choose healthy foods, control the amount of food you eat, and stay physically active to help you burn off some of the calories you take in. If you are concerned about your weight, talk to your doctor. He or she can help you create a healthful eating and physical activity plan.

Reading Check Explain How can you maintain a healthy weight?

Weight Problems and Teens
The number of overweight young people has risen dramatically in the past 20 years. Being overweight can make physical activity more difficult and tiring. Your self-esteem can be negatively affected, too. Some children and teens are

108 ___ter 4: Nutrition

Reading Skills Handbook

▶ **Reading: What's in It for You?**

What role does reading play in your life? There are many different ways that reading could be part of what you do every day. Are you on a sports team? Perhaps you like to read the latest news about your favorite team or find out about new ways to train for your sport. Are you interested in music or art? You might be looking for information about ways to create songs or about styles of painting. Are you enrolled in an English class, a math class, or a health class? Then your assignments probably require a lot of reading.

Improving or Fine-Tuning Your Reading Skills Will:
- Improve your grades
- Allow you to read faster and more efficiently
- Improve your study skills
- Help you remember more information
- Improve your writing

▶ **The Reading Process**

Good reading skills build on one another, overlap, and spiral around just like a winding staircase goes around and around while leading you to a higher place. This Reading Guide will help you find and use the tools you'll need before, during, and after reading.

Strategies You Can Use
- Identify, understand, and learn new words
- Understand why you read
- Take a quick look at the whole text
- Try to predict what you are about to read
- Take breaks while you read and ask yourself questions about the text
- Take notes
- Keep thinking about what will come next
- Summarize

▶ **Vocabulary Development**

Vocabulary skills are the building blocks of the reading and writing processes. By learning to use a number of strategies to build your word skills, you will become a stronger reader.

Use Context to Determine Meaning

The best way to increase your vocabulary is to read widely, listen carefully, and take part in many kinds of discussions. When reading on your own, you can often figure out the meanings of new words by looking at their **context**, the other words and sentences that surround them.

328 Reading Skills Handbook

Physical Fitness Plan

Everyone should have a fitness plan. A personal plan can help you get started in developing your physical fitness. If you are already active or even athletic, a physical fitness plan can help you balance your activities and maintain a healthy level of activity.

Planning a Routine

When you're ready to start a fitness routine, it may be tempting to exercise as hard as you can for as long as you can. However, that approach is likely to leave you discouraged and even injured. Instead, you should plan a fitness routine that will let your body adjust to activity. Work up to your fitness goals slowly. Gradually increase both the length of time you spend exercising and the number of times you exercise each week. For example, you might start by doing a fitness activity for just 5 minutes a day, 3 days a week. Increase the amount of time you exercise, to say 7 minutes the next week and to 10 minutes during the third week of your plan. When you are exercising 20 minutes, 3 days a week, you're ready to add a fourth day to your fitness routine. Eventually, you will be exercising for 20 to 30 minutes, 5 days a week.

Warming Up

There's more to a physical fitness plan than fitness activities. It's important to prepare your body for exercise. Preparation involves warm-up activities that will raise your body temperature and get your muscles ready for your fitness activity. Easy warm-up activities include walking, marching, and jogging, as well as basic calisthenics.

When you're developing your own fitness plan, you should include warm-ups in your schedule. As you increase the time you spend doing a fitness activity, you should also increase the time you spend warming up.

This chart shows how you can plan the time you spend on warm-ups and fitness activities.

Sample Physical Fitness Plan

DAY	Monday		Tuesday		Wednesday		Thursday		Friday	
WEEK	Warm Up	Activity	Warm Up	Activity	Warm Up	Activity	Warm Up	Activity	Warm Up	Activity
1	5 min	5 min	---	---	5 min	5 min	---	---	5 min	5 min
2	5 min	7 min	---	---	5 min	7 min	---	---	5 min	7 min
3	5 min	10 min	---	---	5 min	10 min	---	---	5 min	10 min
4	5 min	12 min	---	---	5 min	12 min	---	---	5 min	12 min
5	7 min	15 min	---	---	7 min	15 min	---	---	7 min	15 min
6	7 min	17 min	---	---	7 min	17 min	---	---	7 min	17 min
7	10 min	20 min	---	---	10 min	20 min	---	---	10 min	20 min
8	10 min	20 min	10 min	20 min	10 min	20 min	---	---	10 min	20 min
9	10 min	20 min	10 min	20 min	10 min	20 min	10 min	20 min	10 min	20 min

Five Elements of Fitness

When you're making a plan for your own fitness program, you should keep the five elements of fitness in mind.

Cardiovascular endurance is the ability of the heart and lungs to function efficiently over time without getting tired. Activities that improve cardiovascular endurance involve non-stop movement of your whole body or of large muscle groups. Familiar examples are jogging, walking, running, bike riding, soccer, basketball, and swimming.

Muscle endurance is the ability of a muscle or a group of muscles to work non-stop without getting tired. Many activities that build cardiovascular endurance also build muscular endurance, such as jogging, walking, and bike riding.

Muscle strength is the ability of the muscle to produce force during an activity. You can make your muscles stronger by working them against some form of resistance, such as weights or gravity. Activities that can help you build muscle strength include push-ups, pull-ups, lifting weights, and running stairs.

Flexibility is the ability to move a body part freely, without pain. You can improve your flexibility by stretching gently before and after exercise.

Body composition is the amount of body fat a person has compared with the amount of lean mass, which is bone, muscle, and fluid. Generally, a healthy body is made up of more lean mass and less body fat. Body composition is a result of diet, exercise, and heredity.

On the next pages, you'll find ten different fitness activities for groups. They can help you develop all five elements of fitness, with an emphasis on cardiovascular endurance. They can also help you add variety and fun to your fitness plan.

Group Fitness Activities

Activity 1: Fitness Day

Fitness Elements Muscle strength and endurance, flexibility

Equipment With a group of other students, make a set of exercise cards. Each card should name and illustrate an exercise. You can include some or all of the exercises shown here.

Formation Stand in two lines facing each other, or stand in a large circle.

Directions Take turns leading the group. The leader picks a card, stands in the center of the formation, and leads the group in the exercise on that card.

Reach for the Sky

Hold for a count of 10, rest, and repeat.

Plank

Hold for a count of 10, rest, and repeat.

Leg Raise

Hold for a count of 10, rest, and repeat.

Pointer

For each side, hold for a count of 10, rest, and repeat.

Donkey Kick

Start

Finish

Kick up 5 times, rest, and repeat.

Open/Closed Pike

Open

Closed

Hold for a count of 10, rest, and repeat.

Single Knee Hug

Hold for a count of 10, rest, and repeat.

Crab

Hold for a count of 10, rest, and repeat.

Flyer (half)

Raise legs. Hold for a count of 10, rest, and repeat.

Flyer (whole)

Raise arms and legs. Hold for a count of 5, rest, and repeat.

Activity 2: Fitness Circuit

Fitness Elements Muscle strength and endurance, flexibility, and cardiovascular endurance

Equipment 2–4 jump ropes, 2–4 aerobic steps, signs or posters naming each station spread throughout the activity area (see diagram.)

Formation Set up stations as shown in the diagram. Form pairs, so that each student has a partner.

Directions With your partner, move through the stations: plank, jump rope, seated toe touches, sit-ups, push-ups, jump in place, leg raises, jumping jacks, arm circles, step-ups. Each pair can start at any station. If your group is large, two pairs may use the same station. At each station, perform as many repetitions as you can in 30 seconds. After 30 seconds, have a teacher or a student volunteer signal the end of the time. With your partner, move in a clockwise direction to the next station.

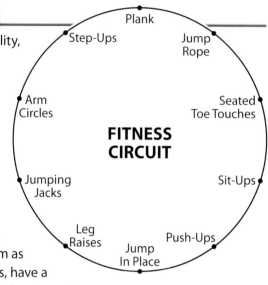

FITNESS CIRCUIT — Plank, Jump Rope, Seated Toe Touches, Sit-Ups, Push-Ups, Jump In Place, Leg Raises, Jumping Jacks, Arm Circles, Step-Ups

Activity 3: Multi-Ball Crab Soccer

Fitness Elements Muscle strength and endurance

Equipment 3–6 crab soccer balls or other large balls

Formation Mark a goal line at each end of the playing area, and divide the players into two teams. All the players on both teams get into the crab position and remain in that position throughout the game.

Directions Put the crab soccer balls in the middle of the playing area. Members of both teams kick the balls past the other team's goal line to score. Remember, all players have to stay in the crab position all the time. The game continues until all the balls have been scored.

Activity 4: Crab Relay

Fitness Elements Muscle strength and endurance

Equipment 4–5 flying disks

Formation Mark two lines 15–25 feet apart, depending on the fitness level of group members. One is the starting line, and the other is the turn-around line. Divide the group into four or five single-file lines behind the starting line. The first player in each group is in the crab position with a flying disk resting on his or her abdomen.

Directions Have a teacher or a student volunteer give a signal to start the relay. The first player in each line crab-walks to the turn-around line and back to the starting line. The players have to move in the crab position and must keep the disks on their abdomens. If the disk falls off, the player has to stop, pick the disk up, and place it back on his or her abdomen. When players return to the starting line, they hand their disks to the next player in line. The next player follows the same procedure. Continue playing until all the members of each team have participated. If you want to play again, reorganize the teams by having the first player in each line move to the team on his or her right.

Activity 5: Piranha River

Fitness Elements Cardiovascular endurance and flexibility

Equipment None

Formation Mark a line at each end of the activity area. One is the starting line and the other is the finish line. Mark two more lines, about ten feet apart, between the starting line and the finish line. The space between these two lines is the "river." Let two volunteers stand in the "river." They are the "piranhas." All the other players stand behind the starting line.

Directions Have a teacher or a student volunteer give the signal to begin. The players behind the starting line run down the river. As they run, the "piranhas" try to tag them. Players who reach the finish line without being tagged are safe. Players who are tagged stay in the "river" and become "helper piranhas." "Helper piranhas" must keep their feet in one place but can bend and stretch to tag the players running down the "river."

Activity 6: Partner Walk Tag

Fitness Element Cardiovascular endurance

Equipment None

Formation Form pairs, so that each player has a partner. With your partner, decide which one of you will begin as the tagger and which will begin as the walker.

Directions Have a teacher or a student volunteer give the signal to begin. If you are the tagger, chase and try to tag your partner. If you are the walker, walk to stay away from your partner. You must both walk at all times, not run. Once the tagger tags the walker, change roles with your partner. Continue until the teacher or student volunteer signals the end. You can vary this activity by hopping, skipping, or using another movement instead of walking.

Activity 7: Scarf Tag

Fitness Element Cardiovascular endurance

Equipment Scarves (one for each player)

Formation Each player should tuck one end of a scarf into the back of his or her waistband or into a rear pocket. Then players should scatter over the activity area.

Directions Have a teacher or a student volunteer give the signal to start. Each player moves throughout the activity area, trying to grab and pull out other players' scarves. Students who pull a scarf must say, "I got a scarf," bend down on one knee, and place the new scarf in their waistbands or pockets. They are "safe" while they are doing this. Players who lose their scarves continue playing, trying to capture other scarves. Players may pull only one scarf at a time. They may not hold onto their own scarves, and they may not push, pull, or grab other players. Play continues until the teacher or student volunteer gives the signal to stop.

Activity 8: Alien Invaders

Fitness Element Cardiovascular endurance

Equipment None

Formation Mark a goal line at each end of the playing area, and divide the players into two teams. One team is the "aliens," and the other team is the "soldiers." Form pairs, so that each player has a partner. Throughout the game, partners have to remain together, with their arms locked. All the players on the "aliens" team stand behind one goal line, and all the players on the "soldiers" team stand behind the other.

Directions The "aliens" stand with their backs to the playing area. The "soldiers" walk quietly toward the "aliens." When the "soldiers" are close to the "aliens," a teacher or student volunteer calls out "There are soldiers in your galaxy!" The "aliens" turn around and chase the "soldiers." All the "soldiers" who are tagged, or whose partners are tagged, become "aliens." "Soldiers" who reach their own goal line are safe.

Activity 9: Par Course

Fitness Elements Cardiovascular endurance, muscle strength and endurance

Equipment 4 jump ropes, 4 cones, signs or posters naming each station on the par course (See diagram.)

Formation: Set up stations as shown in the diagram. Mark each station with a cone and identify it with a sign or poster. Form groups of four.

Directions With the three other members of your group, start at one station on the course. Perform the activity identified there. Then jog to the next station, and perform that activity. Continue around the course until you have completed each activity at least once. If you're participating with a large class, you might work in two shifts, with half the groups completing the full par course and then giving the other groups a turn.

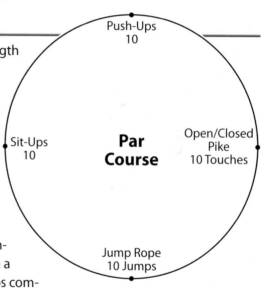

Activity 10: Intervals

Fitness Element Cardiovascular endurance

Equipment Whistle, 5-8 cones (optional)

Formation If possible, use a running track for this activity. If no track is available, use cones to mark a large circle on a gym floor or a field. All the players stand around the circle, not too close together, and all facing the same direction.

Directions Have a teacher or a student volunteer serve as the leader. The leader uses a whistle to signal how players should move. One blast on the whistle means walk, two blasts mean jog, and three blasts mean run. The leader varies the whistle commands, paying attention to the players' energy and to the temperature.

CHAPTER

1

Your Health and Wellness

Chapter Preview

▲ *Working with the Photo*

Regular physical activity is a good health habit to develop. **What are some other good health habits?**

Start-Up Activities

Before You Read What do you do to take care of your health? Find out by taking the short health inventory on this page. Keep a record of your answers.

HEALTH INVENTORY

1. I try to stay physically active.
(a) always   (b) sometimes   (c) never

2. I am aware of what influences my health.
(a) always   (b) sometimes   (c) never

3. I think about my health before making decisions.
(a) always   (b) sometimes   (c) never

4. I set realistic goals for myself.
(a) always   (b) sometimes   (c) never

FOLDABLES Study Organizer

As You Read   Make this Foldable® to help you organize the main ideas on health and wellness in Lesson 1. Begin with a plain sheet of 8½″ × 11″ paper.

1 Line up one of the short edges of the sheet of paper with one of the long edges to form a triangle. Fold and cut off the leftover rectangle.

2 Fold the triangle in half; then unfold. The folds will form an X dividing the paper into four equal sections.

3 Cut along one fold line; and stop at the middle. This forms two triangular flaps. Draw an X on one tab, and label the other three as shown.

4 Fold the X flap under the other flap, and glue together to make a three-sided pyramid.

Write the main ideas about the three parts of health on the back of the appropriate side of the pyramid.

Go Online   Visit **glencoe.com** and use the eFlashcards to preview vocabulary terms for Chapter 1.

3

Lesson 1

Your Total Health

Guide to Reading

● **Building Vocabulary**

As you read this lesson, write each highlighted term and its definition in your notebook.

■ health (p. 4)
■ wellness (p. 7)
■ habit (p. 7)

● **Focusing on the Main Ideas**

In this lesson, you will learn to

■ **identify** the three parts of the health triangle.
■ **describe** the relationship between health and wellness.
■ **explain** how to balance your physical, mental/emotional, and social health.

● **Reading Strategy**

Classifying Using the diagram to the right as a guide, create a concept map that gives examples of each of the three types of health.

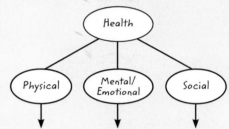

FOLDABLES Study Organizer Use the Foldable® on p. 3 as you read this lesson.

uick Write

Write an explanation of what the word *health* means to you.

What Is Health?

What sports and other activities do you participate in? What kinds of foods do you eat? What kind of people do you spend time with? Your answers to these and similar questions reflect your total health. **Health** is *a combination of physical, mental/ emotional, and social well-being.* These parts of your health work together to build good overall health.

Often, good health is pictured as a triangle with equal sides. As shown in **Figure 1.1,** one side of the triangle is your physical health. Another side is your mental/emotional health, and the third side is your social health. Like the sides of a triangle, the three "sides" of health meet. They are connected. If you ignore any one side, your total health suffers. By the same token, if you make improvements to one side, the others benefit. For example, when you participate in physical activities, you improve your physical health. This helps you feel good about yourself, benefiting your mental health. Activities can also improve your social health when you share them with family and friends.

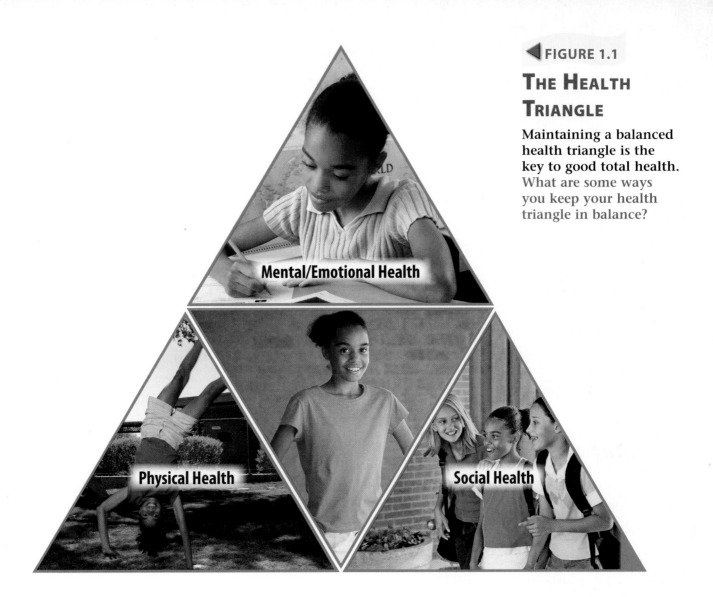

THE HEALTH TRIANGLE

Maintaining a balanced health triangle is the key to good total health. What are some ways you keep your health triangle in balance?

Mental/Emotional Health

Physical Health

Social Health

Physical Health

Do you exercise for about an hour on most days of the week? Do you get plenty of rest each night? Do you eat healthy snacks? Your answers to these questions will tell you something about your physical health. Physical health is the condition of your body.

Physical health is measured by what you *do* as well as what you *don't* do. Teens who want to be healthy avoid harmful substances such as tobacco, alcohol, and other drugs. They balance the amount of time they spend watching TV or playing computer games with physical activity. Physical activity includes things such as playing sports, hiking, aerobics, swimming, dancing, or taking a walk. By avoiding harmful substances and being physically active, you can stay physically healthy. In other words, being physically healthy means taking care of your body.

ACTIVITY

G⊙ Online

Topic: Creating Healthy Habits

Visit **glencoe.com** for Student Web Activities on creating healthy habits.

Activity: Using the information provided at the link above, make a checklist of five activities you can do for 60 minutes every day to maintain your health.

Physical activity is a good choice for improving your health. **What other parts of the health triangle are these teens working on?**

Mental/Emotional Health

Do you feel good about who you are? Do you know how to handle stressful situations? Do you have a positive attitude about life? Your answers to these questions will tell you something about your mental/emotional health. Mental/emotional health is measured by the way you think and express your feelings.

You can develop good mental/emotional health by learning to think positively and to express your feelings in healthy ways. Positive thinking is a good strategy to use when you are feeling sad or down. Try focusing your attention on all of the good things in your life, such as your friends, family, and activities you enjoy. Then the cause of your sadness might not seem so bad. Likewise, recognizing and building your strengths will help you feel good about yourself. When negative thoughts and feelings come up, look to express them in ways that won't hurt you or others. You should also recognize that it is normal to feel sad from time to time. If problems feel overwhelming, don't be afraid to talk to adults you trust. Knowing when to ask for help is a sign of good mental/emotional health.

Social Health

How well do you get along with others? Can you work through problems with others peacefully? Are you a good listener? Can your friends count on you when they have a problem or need advice? Your answers to these questions will help you measure your social health. Good social health means communicating well with and having respect for family, friends, and acquaintances. It also means building relationships with people you can trust and who can trust you in return. You might build a relationship with a counselor, coach, or someone you trust and can go to when you have a problem. A close friend at school may need you to listen to him or her if he or she has a problem or needs advice. Think about the people in your life. With whom do you feel the most comfortable and why? Can you imagine reaching out to them to offer or ask for support?

Go Online

Visit **glencoe.com** and complete the Interactive Study Guide for Lesson 1.

Reading Check

Identify What are the three sides of total health? Name a trait or characteristic found on each of the three sides.

Healthy Habits and Wellness

When you are taking care of your health triangle and all three sides are balanced, wellness is achieved. **Wellness** is *a state of well-being, or total health.* You can improve your wellness by developing good health habits. A **habit** is *a pattern of behavior that you follow almost without thinking.* Good health habits include

- choosing healthy foods.
- participating in regular physical activity.
- learning how to handle stress.
- getting along with others.

By taking a look at your health habits, you can get a snapshot of how healthy you are right now. Take a look at **Figure 1.2**. It shows how habits can contribute to peak health or poor health. The pages ahead will help you develop positive health behaviors that will aid in the prevention of injury, illness, disease, and other health problems.

 Reading Check **Define** What is *wellness*?

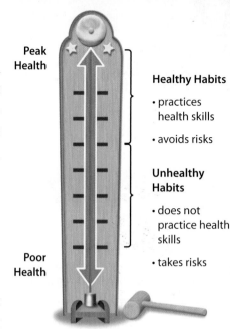

▲ FIGURE 1.2

THE WELLNESS SCALE

Your health habits affect your wellness. Where do you fit in on the wellness scale?

Lesson 1 Review

 After You Read

Review this lesson for new terms, major headings, and Reading Checks.

What I Learned

1. **Vocabulary** What is *health*?

2. **List** What are two measures of good social health?

3. **Recall** Identify three positive health habits.

Thinking Critically

4. **Hypothesize** Jordan spends most of his time getting together with friends. They play video games and skateboard. Jordan is not doing very well in school. What do you think his health triangle would look like?

5. **Evaluate** Alexandra is feeling upset because she didn't do well in her piano recital. Does this mean that she does not have good total health? What can she do to keep her mental/emotional health in balance?

Applying Health Skills

6. **Analyzing Influences** Name a positive health habit that you recently started practicing. Who or what influenced you to begin this health habit?

Go Online For more Lesson Review Activities, go to **glencoe.com**.

Lesson 1: Your Total Health **7**

Influences on Your Health

Guide to Reading

● Building Vocabulary
Read the terms below. Define each in your notebook as best you can. As you read the lesson, make changes where needed.

- heredity (p. 8)
- environment (p. 9)
- culture (p. 9)
- peers (p. 9)
- media (p. 10)
- technology (p. 10)
- behavior (p. 11)
- attitude (p. 11)

● Focusing on the Main Ideas
In this lesson, you will learn to

- **identify** factors that influence your health.
- **explain** the role that your behavior and choices play in your health.
- **describe** how your attitude affects your health.

● Reading Strategy
Skimming Look over the major and minor headings in this lesson. Write a brief paragraph explaining what you think the lesson is about.

*Q*uick Write

Make a list of your likes and dislikes. Explain which of these are shared by your family and which are shared by your friends.

Factors that Affect Your Health

What foods do you like to eat? What are your hobbies and favorite activities? Your answers to these questions reflect your personal tastes and your likes and dislikes. Your health is influenced by your personal tastes. It is also influenced by outside factors. These include heredity, environment, family, culture, peers, the media, and technology.

Heredity

Heredity is *the process by which biological parents pass traits to their children.* These include physical traits, such as eye, hair, and skin color, and body type and size. You may also inherit a musical or athletic ability. The risk of developing certain diseases such as diabetes or allergies can also be passed along through heredity.

◀ The ability to run fast is sometimes passed along through heredity. **What health choice might you make based on inheriting this ability?**

Environment

Where you live and where you go to school are part of your environment. **Environment** (en·VY·ruhn·muhnt) is *the sum total of your surroundings*. It also includes the air you breathe, the water you drink, the neighborhood you live in, and the people around you.

Your environment can both positively and negatively affect your personal health. If you live in a warm climate, you may have more opportunities to participate in outdoor activities. You will also have to be extra careful in the sun. How does the environment where you live affect your health?

▲ Your tastes in food may be a reflection of your family's preferences and your culture. **What other factors might influence your food choices?**

Family and Culture

Two related influences on your health are your family and your culture. **Culture** is *the collected beliefs, customs, and behaviors of a group*. Family and culture can influence your future decisions about your health including eating habits, physical activity, and the use of health services. Some cultures, for example, eat special foods on special occasions. Some eat no food at all during religious celebrations. Bessem's family observes the holiday of *Ramadan*. During this holiday, members of the family fast until sundown. Your family might also celebrate certain holidays and observe special cultural traditions. These traditions might include dances, foods, ceremonies, songs, and games.

Peers

Peers are an especially important influence during your teen years. **Peers** are your *friends and other people in your age group*. Peer pressure can influence healthful choices. For example, Dena's friend Shawn began volunteering at the animal shelter. Shawn invited Dena to go with him one day, and now they volunteer at the animal shelter together.

Peers can also have a negative influence on your health. If your friends take part in risky behaviors, such as smoking or drinking, you might feel pressure to join in.

Academic Vocabulary

factors (FAK terz) *(noun)* something that leads to a result. *One of the factors of lifelong health is getting plenty of exercise most days of the week.*

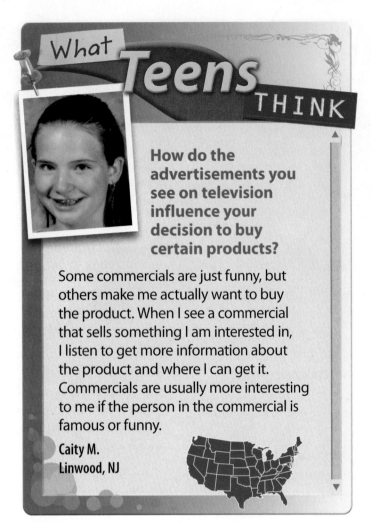
Media

Troy realized how much the media could influence him when he saw a TV ad for a video game. As soon as he saw it, he knew he wanted the video game for his birthday. Have you had an experience similar to Troy's? The **media** include *the various methods of communicating information, including newspapers, magazines, radio, television, and the Internet.* These are often used by companies to encourage us to buy their products, such as the video game Troy saw on TV.

Messages from the media and other sources influence health behavior. Media messages may make us curious about a product. Through the media, it's possible to quickly find information on almost any health topic. The media also provide us with advertisements for health products and services. However, not all media sources are equally reliable. Later in this chapter, you will learn how to judge whether a source is reliable.

Technology

Technology is *the use of scientific ideas to improve the quality of life.* The use of computer technology in planes has made it easier and safer to fly. A variety of technologies for health information are now available. E-mail and the Internet are only two examples. These resources influence your health because they can provide you with fast and easy access to valid health information that can easily be shared within a community. The control of diseases is another area that technology has impacted.

One area in which technology has had a huge impact is in detecting illnesses. For example, MRI machines give a view of the inside of any area of the body. Finding early evidence of diseases can help doctors treat them successfully. Can you give another example of technology that has made your health and life better?

Reading Check

List Name four factors that affect your health. Give an example of each.

Your Health Choices and Behaviors

Some of the factors that influence your health, such as heredity, are out of your control. You do, however, have control over your behavior and the choices you make. Your **behavior** is *the way you act in the many different situations and events in your life.* Many of the choices you make affect your health. For example, choosing to eat healthy foods will affect your physical health. Knowing the consequences of your choices and behaviors can help you take responsibility for your health.

Personal Attitudes

An **attitude** is *what you believe or feel about someone or something.* Individual, family, community, and cultural attitudes play a role in your health. For example, if you have a positive feeling about wearing safety belts, you'll probably wear one when riding in a car. Teens who have positive attitudes toward healthy habits usually encourage others to do the same.

 **Reading Check** **Recall** Give one example of a choice that can affect your health.

 **Go Online**

Visit **glencoe.com** and complete the Interactive Study Guide for Lesson 2.

Lesson 2 Review

 After You Read

Review this lesson for new terms, major headings, and Reading Checks.

What I Learned

1. *Vocabulary* Define *culture* and *media*. Explain how each influences health.

2. *Describe* How has medical technology improved life?

3. *Explain* How does your attitude affect your health?

Thinking Critically

4. *Synthesize* Which side of the health triangle do you think is most affected by outside influences?

5. *Apply* What family influences have shaped your personal values and beliefs? How will your family's influences affect your future decisions?

Applying Health Skills

6. *Analyzing Influences* Our country has people from many different cultures living within its borders. Identify cultures in your own community. With a group, discuss how these cultures enrich and challenge people in the community. Think about celebrations, food, music, and the like.

Go Online For more Lesson Review Activities, go to **glencoe.com**.

Lesson 2: Influences on Your Health **11**

Building Health Skills

Guide to Reading

● Building Vocabulary
Write each term in your notebook. As you read the lesson, add each term's definition.
- prevention (p. 12)
- health skills (p. 12)
- communication (p. 15)
- advocate (p. 15)

● Focusing on the Main Ideas
In this lesson, you will learn to
- **identify** skills that can help you stay healthy.
- **explain** why health skills are skills for life.
- **demonstrate** how to analyze media influences.

● Reading Strategy
Comparing Identify similarities and differences between two of the skills mentioned.

Quick Write

Preview the lesson. Choose one health skill. Write about ways you could use it in your life.

Skills for a Healthy Life

One of the keys to good health is the prevention of illness and injury. **Prevention** means *practicing health and safety habits to remain free of disease and injury.* You can prevent illness and injury in many ways. Wearing protective gear during certain activities, such as bike riding or playing baseball, can help you prevent injury to your body. You can help prevent common illnesses such as colds by washing your hands often.

These examples demonstrate health skills. **Health skills** are *skills that help you become and stay healthy* (see **Figure 1.3**). Health skills can help you improve your physical, mental/emotional, and social health. Like reading, math, and sports skills, health skills can have a positive effect throughout your life.

◀ Wearing goggles when swimming in a pool is one way of maintaining physical health. **What are some other examples of protective gear you should wear during sports or activities?**

THE HEALTH SKILLS

These ten skills affect your physical, mental/emotional, and social health.
Why are these skills important throughout your entire life?

Health Skill	What It Means to You
Accessing Information	You know how to find valid health information and health-promoting products and services, including medical resources on the Internet.
Practicing Healthful Behaviors	You take action to reduce risks and protect yourself against illness and injury.
Stress Management	You find healthy ways to reduce and manage stress in your life.
Analyzing Influences	You recognize the many factors that influence your health, including family, culture, media, and technology.
Communication Skills	You express your ideas and feelings and listen when others express theirs.
Refusal Skills	You can say no to risky behaviors.
Conflict Resolution	You work out problems with others in healthful ways.
Decision Making	You think through problems and find healthy solutions.
Goal Setting	You plan for the future and work to see your plans through.
Advocacy	You take a stand to work for the common good and make a difference in your home, school, and community.

Staying Informed

Knowing how to *access*, or get, reliable health information is an important skill. A main source of information is adults you can trust. Parents and guardians, teachers, and your school nurse are reliable sources. They can help you find accurate books, articles, and Web sites on a variety of health topics. Community resources provide other ways to get reliable information. These resources include government health agencies and organizations such as the American Red Cross.

Taking Care of Yourself

Practicing healthy behaviors and managing stress are two skills that all teens should learn. When you eat healthy foods and get enough sleep, you are taking actions that promote good health. Stress management is learning to cope with challenges that put a strain on you mentally or emotionally. Strategies for managing stress can help you deal with stress in a healthy way.

Health Skills Activity

Analyzing Influences

Too Good to Be True?

Trevor was excited when he first saw an infomercial for a new acne medicine. It promised to make pimples vanish overnight. This health claim sounded too good to be true. He knew the importance of considering

- **the source.** Infomercials are TV ads made to look like programs. There are few rules that control the kinds of claims advertisers can make. Trevor knew infomercials were not reliable health sources.

- **the motive.** When you hear a suspicious health claim, ask yourself, "What am I being encouraged to do?" If the answer is "buy something," beware.

As a Group

Analyze an ad from a magazine, a newspaper, or TV. Determine the source and motive behind the ad. Notice the kinds of words the ad uses to try to influence you. Talk about whether the ad is a reliable health source. Share your findings with other groups.

Analyzing Influences

Learning how to analyze health information, products, and services will help you act in ways that protect your health.

The first step in analyzing an influence is to identify its *source*. A TV commercial may tell you a certain food has health benefits. In this case, the source is an advertiser who is trying to get you to buy the food.

Next, you should think about the *motive*, or reason, for the influence. Does the advertiser really take your well-being into consideration? Does the ad make you curious about the product? Does it try to scare you into buying the product?

Visit **glencoe.com** and complete the Interactive Study Guide for Lesson 3.

 **Reading Check** **Identify** What is the first step in analyzing an influence?

Communicating with Others

Three of the ten health skills involve the way you communicate with other people. **Communication** is *the clear exchange of ideas and information.* Good communication skills include telling others how you feel. They also include listening to others and understanding how *others* feel. You will learn more about communication skills in Chapter 3.

Sometimes you have to say no to others. An example is when you are pressured to do something you believe is wrong. *Refusal skills* help you say no in an effective way. When you have conflicts, or disagreements with others, *conflict-resolution skills* can help you find a solution that is fair to everyone involved.

Advocacy

To advocate something means to support it or speak out in favor of it. When you **advocate** for health, you *encourage other people to live healthy lives.* You influence others to make positive choices. Advocacy also includes keeping others informed. By sharing health information, you enable others to make healthful choices.

▲ Talking through disagreements is a healthful way of dealing with them. **Can you think of another healthful way to handle a disagreement?**

Lesson 3 Review

 After You Read

Review this lesson for new terms, major headings, and Reading Checks.

What I Learned

1. *Vocabulary* Define *prevention.* Use the word in an original sentence.

2. *Recall* What are two steps you can use to analyze influences?

3. *Explain* Why are health skills important for good health?

Thinking Critically

4. *Apply* Imagine that you overhear two teens talking about a great new CD that everyone "has to have." Analyze the possible sources of this influence.

5. *Hypothesize* Danielle has noticed that many traffic accidents appear at one intersection in her community. How can she use the health skill of advocacy to help correct this problem?

Applying Health Skills

6. *Communication Skills* Practice having a conversation with a classmate. Think about ways of showing you are listening. Why is it important to let the other person know you are listening?

Go Online For more Lesson Review Activities, go to **glencoe.com**.

Lesson 3: Building Health Skills **15**

Making Responsible Decisions

Guide to Reading

● **Building Vocabulary**
Find the highlighted terms in the lesson. Write the definition of each in your notebook.

- decisions (p. 16)
- consequences (p. 16)
- risk (p. 16)
- cumulative risk (p. 17)
- values (p. 18)

● **Focusing on the Main Ideas**
In this lesson, you will learn to

- **identify** how to make responsible decisions.
- **explain** why values are important when making decisions.
- **practice** the decision-making process.

● **Reading Strategy**
Sequencing Create a concept map showing the order of the steps in decision making. Use the diagram to the right as a guide.

Step 1
↓
Step 2
↓
Step 3

Quick Write

Identify a problem that you faced recently. Write a brief paragraph explaining how you went about solving it.

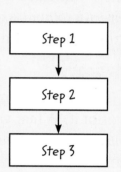

Your Decisions Count

What are some decisions you made today? **Decisions** are *choices that you make.* Some decisions are small, such as what to eat for breakfast. Other decisions are tougher. They can have serious **consequences,** or *results.* During your teen years, you will have many important decisions to make, some of which can affect your personal wellness. You will want to consider the alternatives of such choices. For some decisions, you also may want to seek help from your parents, guardians, or other trusted adults.

Risk Factors

Some decisions involve risks. **Risk** is *the chance of harm or loss.* Any decision that involves a risk to your health is an important one. When making decisions, you should understand the short-term and long-term consequences of safe, risky, and harmful behaviors.

◀ Decisions can sometimes be difficult to make. **What are some decisions that affect your health?**

The Decision-Making Process

Big decisions are a little like math problems. They should be broken down into smaller parts before they can be solved. Using the following six-step process can help you make healthy and responsible decisions.

Whenever possible, it's a good idea to write down your answers as you work through each step. That way, you won't leave out important details. You can also go back and review the steps.

Step 1: State the Situation.

Before you can make a decision, you should understand the situation. Ask yourself the following: What are the facts? Who else is involved?

Step 2: List the Options.

Once you have analyzed the situation, think of your **options**. Try to cover all the possibilities. You may want to ask other people for suggestions. An adult whom you trust is a good person to ask for advice when making an important decision.

Step 3: Weigh the Possible Outcomes.

Consider your options carefully. Remember the word H.E.L.P. when working through this step:

- **H (Healthful)** What health risks, if any, will this option present?

- **E (Ethical)** Does this choice reflect what you and your family believe to be *ethical*, or right?

- **L (Legal)** Does this option violate any local, state, or federal laws?

- **P (Parent Approval)** Would your parents approve of this choice?

For some decisions, you should think about cumulative risks. **Cumulative** (KYOO·myuh·luh·tiv) **risk** is *the addition of one risk factor to another, increasing the chance of harm or loss.* For example, riding in a car without wearing a safety belt is one risk factor. Riding in a car that is going over the speed limit is another. When combined, the two behaviors increase your risk of harm.

Academic Vocabulary

options (OP shuhnz) (noun) choices. *Jake and Maggie like the diner down the street because it offers many lunch options.*

Step 4: Consider Values.

Values are *beliefs you feel strongly about that help guide the way you live.* Values reflect what is important to you and what you have learned is right or wrong. Your values should guide any important decision you make.

Step 5: Make a Decision and Act on It.

You've weighed your options. You've mapped out the risks and consequences. Now you're ready for action. Choose the course that seems best and that supports your values. Make sure you are comfortable with your decision. If not, look at other options or ask a trusted adult for help.

Step 6: Evaluate the Decision.

After you've acted on your decision, look at the results. Were they positive or negative? Were there any unexpected outcomes? Was there anything you could have done differently? What have you learned from the experience? If the action you took wasn't as successful as you'd hoped, try again. Use the decision-making process to find another way to deal with the situation.

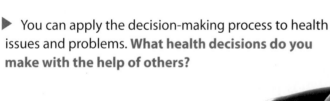

Reading Check **List** What are the six steps in the decision-making process?

▶ You can apply the decision-making process to health issues and problems. **What health decisions do you make with the help of others?**

Go Online

Visit **glencoe.com** and complete the Interactive Study Guide for Lesson 4.

Health Skills Activity

Decision Making

A Test of Friendship

Kris's family moved to a new town. Almost from the first day, Lisa became her best friend. Lisa showed Kris around the town and introduced her to other teens. At school Lisa asked Kris to help her pass an English test. "All you need to do," Lisa explained, "is move your hand so I can see your paper." Kris was taught to always help out a friend. Yet what Lisa was asking Kris to do was help her cheat. Kris was also taught that cheating is wrong. What should Kris do?

What Would You Do?

Apply the six steps of decision making to Kris's problem. When you've finished, share the decision you would make with the class.

1. State the situation.
2. List the options.
3. Weigh the possible outcomes.
4. Consider values.
5. Make a decision and act on it.
6. Evaluate the decision.

Lesson 4 Review

 After You Read

Review this lesson for new terms, major headings, and Reading Checks.

What I Learned

1. *Vocabulary* Use the terms *decisions* and *consequences* in a sentence.

2. *Explain* What are two questions you might ask yourself when stating the situation in the decision-making process?

3. *Recall* Why are values important when making a decision?

Thinking Critically

4. *Analyze* Choose one of the six steps in the decision-making process, and describe its importance to the process.

5. *Apply* Lena is supposed to spend the weekend with a younger cousin from out of town. A friend calls offering an extra ticket to a concert for that Saturday night. How should Lena decide what to do?

Applying Health Skills

6. *Decision Making* With a partner, write a skit in which a teen is faced with a tough choice. Show how the teen uses the decision-making process to arrive at a good solution.

Setting Health Goals

📖 Guide to Reading

● Building Vocabulary
Examine the terms below. Look for relationships among them. As you come across these terms in the lesson, write them in your notebook.

- goal (p. 20)
- short-term goal (p. 21)
- long-term goal (p. 21)

● Focusing on the Main Ideas
In this lesson, you will learn to

- **explain** why having goals is important.
- **describe** how to set goals.
- **develop** a strategy to reach your goals.

● Reading Strategy
Comparing and Contrasting What do you think is the difference between a short-term and long-term goal? Give an example of each.

🇶uick Write

Write about a goal you would like to achieve. Tell why it is important to you, and how you plan to achieve it.

Setting Goals

What do you dream of achieving in your lifetime? What are your ambitions? Your answers to these questions reflect your goals. A **goal** is *something you hope to accomplish*. Some goals are broad, such as wanting to be happy or successful. Other goals are specific, such as getting a good grade on a test. Goal setting is an important skill that will help you achieve and maintain good health.

▶ Achieving your goals requires planning. **What dreams do you hope to achieve? What can you do now to start on the road to achieving them?**

Types of Goals

Goals may be short-term or long-term. A **short-term goal** is *a goal that you plan to accomplish in a short time*. An example of a short-term goal is getting your homework done in time to watch a certain TV program. A **long-term goal** is *a goal that you hope to achieve within a period of months or years*.

Often, short-term goals lead to long-term goals. Inez's long-term goal is to be a veterinarian, an animal doctor. Her short-term goals include doing well in science and earning money for college. To achieve her short-term goal, Inez walks neighbors' dogs. This also gives her experience running a business and being around animals. Notice that goals such as these form a chain (see **Figure 1.4**). How would you fill in the fourth link of Inez's chain?

By setting clear goals for herself, Inez has taken charge of her life. Have you taken charge of yours?

Reading Check

Identify What are the two types of goals? How are they related?

Inez studies hard to achieve the goal of passing her science test.

She earns good grades to achieve the goal of getting into college.

Inez started her own dog-walking business. This helps her achieve the goal of paying for college.

Toward Inez's future

▶ **FIGURE 1.4**

THE GOAL CHAIN

The goal chain illustrates how short-term goals can help you achieve a long-term goal. How will Inez's short-term goals help her become a veterinarian?

DEVELOPING
Good Character

Setting Goals in a Group

Setting goals can be challenging, especially when a whole group is involved. Sara's soccer team needed to raise money for new equipment. One team member insisted that a yard sale was the answer. Another argued that they should hold a raffle. A third student suggested doing both, and everyone agreed. By working together, the team reached its goal.

Describe a group goal-setting experience you have been involved in. How did you choose your goal? How did you go about reaching it?

Choosing Goals

The goals that are right for you depend on your interests, skills, and abilities. Priorities, changing abilities, and responsibilities also influence setting goals. What do you do well? What would you like to improve? Answering questions such as these will help you choose goals you will want to work toward. Being aware of your skills and interests will help you choose goals you can achieve. Here are a few other *do's* and *don'ts* when setting a goal:

- *Do a reality check.* Ask yourself whether your goal is realistic. Is it something you can really achieve?

- *Don't sell yourself short.* Select goals that are challenging for you. Don't be afraid to aim high. Believe in yourself, and use all of your abilities.

 **Recognize** Identify three tips for choosing a goal.

Reaching Your Goals

All goals, big and small, have one thing in common. To achieve them, you should have a plan. How do you get from where you are now to where you want to be? Here are some tips:

▶ Following a logical plan can help you achieve many goals. **What realistic goal can you achieve?**

- **Make your goals specific.** Don't just say, "I want to be a better piano player." Say, "I want to be able to play a certain piece without making any mistakes at my next recital."

- **List the steps to reach your goal.** Break big goals down into smaller tasks. For example, to play piano in the recital, you will need to practice. Set a practice schedule, maybe half an hour each day.

- **Get help from others.** Identify people who can help you achieve your goals. Seek the input of parents, teachers, and other trusted adults. Also, identify sources of information, such as books and magazine articles.

- **Evaluate your progress.** Check periodically to see how well you're progressing toward your goal. In the case of the piano piece, you might record and play back your performances. Your teacher can also give you any necessary feedback. Should you be doing anything differently? Is one part giving you more trouble than others? If necessary, adjust your plan, or seek help.

- **Reward yourself.** Treat yourself in a special way, and celebrate your accomplishments.

Visit **glencoe.com** and complete the Interactive Study Guide for Lesson 5.

Lesson 5 Review

After You Read

Review this lesson for new terms, major headings, and Reading Checks.

What I Learned

1. *Vocabulary* Define *short-term goal* and *long-term goal*. Use each term in an original sentence.

2. *Describe* Why is it important to set a realistic goal?

3. *Recall* Describe each step in the goal-setting process.

Thinking Critically

4. *Apply* Seth's long-term goal is to be a professional baseball player.

What short-term goals could Seth set for himself to help him reach this goal?

5. *Hypothesize* Sometimes goals need to be changed. What are some reasons a goal might need to be changed?

Applying Health Skills

6. *Goal Setting* Choose a personal health goal. Discuss strategies and skills needed to attain a personal health goal.

What Does Analyzing Influences Involve?

Analyzing influences involves recognizing the factors that affect your health choices. These factors include:

- Family and culture
- Friends and peers
- Messages from the media
- Your likes, dislikes, fears, curiosities, values, and beliefs

Evaluating Influences on Your Health

Follow the Model, Practice, and Apply steps to help you master this important health skill.

① Model

Read how Darrol uses the skill of analyzing influences when shopping for new shoes.

Darrol went to the mall to buy new sneakers. He planned to buy the same kind of shoes he already owned. In the store, the saleswoman showed him a different style. "These just came in, and they're going to be very popular," the saleswoman said. She pointed to a large colorful poster. It showed a teen about Darrol's age wearing the new sneakers. Suddenly, Darrol couldn't decide what he wanted.

Darrol told the saleswoman he needed to think about his choice. At home, Darrol made a list of influences that were affecting his decision. This list helped him decide which shoes to get. He went back to the store and bought the shoes he had planned to buy.

Decision: Which shoes should I buy?

Influences	
Likes/dislikes	1—The shoes I've owned are comfortable.
	2—I like the way my shoes look.
Peers	3—The new sneakers might be popular at school.
Media	4—The poster in the store looked really cool.

② Practice

Use the skill of analyzing influences to help Andy decide which friend he should hang out with.

Andy has made a new friend, Brock. Brock's friends are different from those Andy usually hangs out with. Andy has eaten lunch with Brock several times and has enjoyed getting to know some of the kids in his group. Today, Brock invited Andy to hang out at his house with a few of his friends. Andy really wants to go, but he has already promised to go to his friend Chris's house. List the influences that would affect Andy's decision. Assign a number value to each influence, with number one being the most important.

③ Apply

Use what you have learned about analyzing influences to complete the activity below.

Imagine you are choosing which after-school club to join. Think about the different influences that would affect your decision. Make a list like the one that you made for Andy in the Practice section. Decide which influences are most important to you and assign a number value to each one. Write a paragraph to explain how your health triangle could be affected by joining an after-school club.

Self-Check
- Did I list influences?
- Did I assign number values?
- Did I explain how my health triangle would be affected?

HANDS-ON HEALTH

Your Personal Health

Do you have a clear picture of your own health triangle? Take this personal health inventory to identify factors that affect your physical, mental/ emotional, and social health.

What You Will Need

- Pencil or pen
- Paper

 ### What You Will Do

On your paper, write the numbers 1 to 6 for each health area. Think about each of the following statements and respond with yes or no.

Physical Health

1. I eat at least three well-balanced meals each day and snack on healthful foods such as fruits and vegetables.
2. I get at least 60 minutes of physical activity daily.
3. I sleep at least eight hours a night.
4. I avoid the use of tobacco, alcohol, and other drugs.
5. I have good personal hygiene habits.
6. I follow safety rules.

Mental/Emotional Health

1. I feel good about myself.
2. I can name several things I do well.
3. I generally keep a positive attitude.
4. I ask for help when I need it.
5. I am able to handle stress.
6. I try to improve myself.

Social Health

1. I get along well with my family.
2. I try to work out any differences I have with others.
3. I express my feelings in positive ways.
4. I treat others with respect.
5. I have at least one friend I can talk to.
6. I listen when someone is speaking to me.

Wrapping It Up

Give yourself 1 point for each yes. A score of 5–6 in any area reflects good health. A score of 3–4 indicates you're doing well but can still improve. If you score 0–2 in any area, try to improve that part of your health triangle.

Reading Review

STUDY TO GO   Visit **glencoe.com** to download quizzes and eFlashcards for Chapter 1.

FOLDABLES® Study Organizer

Foldables® and Other Study Aids Take out the Foldable® that you created for Lesson 1 and any graphic organizers that you created for Lessons 1–5. Find a partner, and quiz each other using these study aids.

Lesson 1 Your Total Health

Main Idea Your total health is a state of well-being, or wellness.

- The three parts of the health triangle are physical health, mental/emotional health, and social health.
- You can balance your physical, mental/emotional, and social health by developing good health habits.

Lesson 2 Influences on Your Health

Main Idea Your health is influenced by outside factors and by your behavior.

- Outside factors include heredity, environment, family and culture, peers, the media, and technology.
- Maintaining a positive attitude will help you choose health-promoting behaviors.

Lesson 3 Building Health Skills

Main Idea Health skills help you become and stay healthy throughout your life.

- There are ten health skills: accessing information, practicing healthful behaviors, stress management, analyzing influences, communication skills, refusal skills, conflict resolution, decision making, goal setting, and advocacy.
- All teens should learn to practice healthful behaviors and manage stress.

Lesson 4 Making Responsible Decisions

Main Idea You can make good, responsible health decisions by learning and practicing the six-step decision-making process.

- The six steps of the decision-making process are: state the situation, list the options, weigh the possible outcomes, consider values, make a decision and act on it, and evaluate the decision.
- H.E.L.P. stands for **H**ealthful, **E**thical, **L**egal, and **P**arent Approval.

Lesson 5 Setting Health Goals

Main Idea Goal setting will help you achieve and maintain good health.

- Goals may be short-term or long-term. Short-term goals often lead to long-term goals.
- You can reach goals by making your goals specific, listing the steps to reach your goal, getting help from others, evaluating your progress, and rewarding yourself when you reach your goal.

Assessment

After You Read

HEALTH INVENTORY

Now that you have read the chapter, look back at your answers to the Health Inventory on the chapter opener. Is there anything that you should do differently?

Reviewing Vocabulary and Main Ideas

On a sheet of paper, write the numbers 1–6. After each number, write the term from the list that best completes each sentence.

- attitudes
- consequences
- culture
- decisions
- habit
- health
- health skills
- media
- prevention
- wellness

Lesson 1 | Your Total Health

1. _____ is a state of well-being, or total health.
2. _____ is a combination of physical, mental/emotional, and social well-being.
3. A(n) _____ is a pattern of behavior that you follow almost without thinking.

Lesson 2 | Influences on Your Health

4. The collected beliefs, customs, and behaviors of a group is its _____.
5. TV and the Internet are two methods of communicating information grouped together as the _____.

6. Feelings and beliefs, or _____, can play a role in how well you take care of yourself.

*On a sheet of paper, write the numbers 7–14. Write **True** or **False** for each statement below. If the statement is false, change the underlined word or phrase to make it true.*

Lesson 3 | Building Health Skills

7. <u>Wellness</u> is keeping something bad from happening to your health.
8. Two parts to the skill of <u>analyzing influences</u> are identifying the source and the motive.
9. Parts of the skill of <u>advocacy</u> are being a good listener and telling others honestly how you feel.

Lesson 4 | Making Responsible Decisions

10. Every decision you make has <u>risks</u>, or results.
11. Stating the situation is the <u>first</u> step in the decision-making process.
12. When considering options, remember the word H.E.L.P., whose letters stand for Healthful, Ethical, Legal, and <u>Permission</u>.

Lesson 5 | Setting Health Goals

13. It is important to ask yourself whether a goal is <u>realistic</u>, or something you can achieve.
14. Breaking down big goals into smaller tasks is a step in <u>goal setting</u>.

Go Online Visit **glencoe.com** and take the Online Quiz for Chapter 1.

Thinking Critically

Using complete sentences, answer the following questions on a sheet of paper.

15. **Synthesize** Write a plan that breaks down the long-term goal of achieving physical fitness into several short-term goals that can be reached one at a time.

16. **Describe** Identify a cumulative risk. How can this affect your health?

Write About It

17. **Narrative Writing** Write a short story in which a teen becomes a positive role model for a younger child. Show how the teen influences the child by making healthful choices and displaying healthful behaviors.

↗ Applying Technology

Healthy Habits

In pairs, use GarageBand™ or Audacity® to create a recording that demonstrates a clear understanding of how to develop healthy habits in order to stay well. Follow the steps below to complete the project.

- Write a five-minute script about a school situation highlighting some of the good health habits mentioned in this chapter.
- Use GarageBand™ or Audacity® to record your script.
- Edit the track for clarity and content. Make sure your message is clearly delivered.
- Save your track.

Standardized Test Practice

Reading

Read the passage and then answer the questions.

Information on good health habits has been around for a long time. In the 1100s, a physician named Moses Maimonides published a book titled *Rules for Physical Health*.

Rules for Physical Health suggests that people need eight hours of sleep a night to maintain their health. It also encourages its readers to exercise or play sports regularly. It even contains specific suggestions about the kinds of food a person should eat.

The book is not just about what individuals could do to improve their health. It also stresses the importance of breathing clean air. In other words, it recognizes that a healthy environment is an important part of staying healthy.

TEST-TAKING TIP

Read the passage carefully once to find out what information it contains. After you read each question, look back at the passage to find the answer.

1. As described in the passage, *Rules for Physical Health* gives suggestions on all of the following EXCEPT
   - **A.** healthful eating habits.
   - **B.** ways of improving social health.
   - **C.** making physical activity a regular habit.
   - **D.** getting enough sleep at night.

2. What suggestion in the book relates the environment to personal health?
   - **A.** the importance of sealing garbage bags
   - **B.** the importance of drinking clean water
   - **C.** the importance of recycling
   - **D.** the importance of breathing clean air

2 Mental and Emotional Wellness

Chapter Preview

▲ *Working with the Photo*

Good health includes physical fitness, but there is more to being healthy than that. **What signs of good emotional health do these teens exhibit?**

Start-Up Activities

Before You Read Do you know how to gain self-confidence? Answer the Health eSpotlight question below and then watch the online video. Keep a record of your answers.

Health eSpotlight

Your Self-Concept

A healthy self-concept is a trait that all teens can achieve. One of the best ways to gain self-confidence is by setting realistic goals and participating in group activities. Have you ever encouraged a friend to sign up for an event or try out for a team? Explain your answer in detail.

Go to **glencoe.com** and watch the health video for Chapter 2. Then complete the activity provided with the online video.

FOLDABLES Study Organizer

As You Read Make this Foldable® to record what you learn about positive self-concept in Lesson 1. Begin with a plain sheet of 8½″ × 11″ paper.

1 Fold the sheet of paper in half along the long axis.

3 Unfold and cut the top layer along both fold lines. This makes three tabs.

4 Draw two overlapping ovals, and label as shown.

2 Turn the paper and fold it into thirds.

Under the appropriate tab, take notes on what you learn about positive self-concept and positive self-esteem. Under the middle tab, write down what the two have in common.

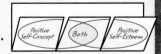 Visit **glencoe.com** and complete the Health Inventory for Chapter 2.

A Healthy Self-Concept

Guide to Reading

● Building Vocabulary

Two of the terms below share a common word part. In your notebook, write a definition for each based on what you believe the term means. Revise your definitions as you read the lesson.

- self-concept (p. 32)
- reinforce (p. 33)
- self-esteem (p. 34)
- resilience (p. 34)

● Focusing on the Main Ideas

In this lesson, you will learn to

- **explain** what your self-concept is.
- **identify** influences on your self-concept.
- **describe** how you can build a positive self-concept.

● Reading Strategy

Analyzing a Graphic Using the diagram to the right as a guide, create a concept map that shows influences on your self-concept.

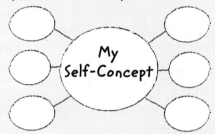

My Self-Concept

FOLDABLES Study Organizer Use the Foldable® on p. 31 as you read this lesson.

uick Write

Imagine that you are applying for a job. Write a brief letter to the employer describing your strengths.

What Is Self-Concept?

"Is *that* what I sound like?" Theo asked. He was listening to a recording of his voice. Have you ever heard your own voice played back? Other people hear us differently from how we hear ourselves. The same is true of how we see ourselves.

Each of us has a different self-concept. Your **self-concept** is *the view you have of yourself.* It may or may not mirror the way other people see you. This much is clear: having a positive self-concept is an important part of good mental/emotional health.

◄ Also known as self-image, self-concept is your view of your abilities, skills, and talents. **Why is having a positive self-concept important?**

How Does Self-Concept Develop?

Your self-concept starts forming when you are very young. Parents or guardians are your first and greatest **influence**. How they speak to you and treat you has a lasting effect. Grandparents, sisters, brothers, and relatives have an effect, too.

Your skills and abilities also shape your self-concept. You may see yourself as a good basketball player or a good singer. You may feel you are good at writing stories but average in math. How you view your talents and abilities influences your overall self-concept. Focus on your strengths rather than your weaknesses. When you focus on your weaknesses, you may begin to feel that you are not good at anything. Instead, identify what you do well and what you enjoy doing. This will help you develop a positive self-concept. Seeing yourself in a positive way will help you feel good about yourself.

Family members, friends, and teachers **reinforce,** or *support*, your self-concept through messages. Some of the messages from people around you are spoken or written. Others take the form of looks or gestures. "Way to go!" is an example of a positive word message. Can you think of a look or gesture that carries the same idea?

Positive messages help you develop a positive self-concept. You may think you did well on a school project. Having your parent or teacher tell you that you did a good job reinforces your belief. Keep in mind that sending positive messages is a two-way street. When you support others, they are likely to support you, too.

Academic Vocabulary

influence (IN floo entz) *(noun)* an effect on a person or object. *Her well-behaved, older brother was a good influence on her.*

▶ Messages from others influence your self-concept. These messages may be spoken, written, or communicated through looks or gestures. **What is the message being sent by the gesture pictured here?**

33

Health Skills Activity

Analyzing Influences

How Does the Media Influence Your Self-Concept?
One factor that affects your self-concept is the media. Think about the images you see on television or in movies. They often show attractive people having fun. Some teens try to look and act like the people they see on-screen. They may feel this will improve their self-concept. It's important to recognize the ways in which media messages influence the way you feel about yourself.

With a Group
Collect pictures, video clips, or descriptions of images from the media. Analyze the message each sends.

Self-Concept and Self-Esteem

Do you like and respect yourself? Do you have the confidence to try new things? If you do, you have high self-esteem. Your **self-esteem** is *a measure of how much you like and respect yourself.* Your self-esteem is closely related to your self-concept. Having a positive self-concept will help you build a high level of self-esteem. When you have high self-esteem, you feel good about yourself. You have confidence in what you do and have a positive outlook. You come to new challenges with a "can-do" attitude. You can rely on yourself to solve problems. When things go wrong, you are resilient. **Resilience** is *the ability to work through and recover from disappointment.* Being resilient helps you cope with failure in a positive way. For example, imagine that you try out for one of the lead parts in the school play. You are disappointed when you find out you didn't get the part. If you are resilient, you won't let this disappointment stop you. Instead of getting angry or frustrated, try out for a smaller part or even volunteer to help backstage.

◀ Resiliency is your ability to bounce back from difficulties. **Why is this an important ability? How does being resilient help you cope with failure?**

Developing a Positive Self-Concept

Developing a positive self-concept is an important part of emotional health. To develop a positive view of yourself, list your strengths and weaknesses. Focus on what you do well. This gives you the confidence you need to try new things. Here are some other suggestions:

- Have confidence in yourself and your abilities.
- Accept encouragement; use it to recognize your strengths.
- Set a goal and work to reach it. This will give you a sense of accomplishment.
- Develop realistic expectations. Remember that no one is perfect.
- Find friends that support and encourage you.
- Avoid worrying about hurtful remarks or looks. Put them behind you and move on.

 Reading Check **Explain** Give one suggestion for improving your self-concept.

Visit **glencoe.com** and complete the Interactive Study Guide for Lesson 1.

 **Lesson 1 Review**

After You Read

Review this lesson for new terms, major headings, and Reading Checks.

What I Learned

1. *Vocabulary* Define the terms *self-concept* and *self-esteem*. Write a sentence that includes both terms.

2. *Identify* What is resilience?

3. *Give Examples* Name three ways to improve your self-concept.

Thinking Critically

4. *Analyze* How might having a high level of self-esteem help you set goals for the future?

5. *Apply* Yolanda didn't make the soccer team. She was disappointed but decided to try out again next season. Does Yolanda have a positive self-concept? Why or why not?

Applying Health Skills

6. *Goal Setting* List three things you do well. Set a goal to improve one of these strengths during the next week. Follow your plan carefully. Then write a paragraph describing the results.

Your Character Counts

Guide to Reading

Building Vocabulary
List each term below in your notebook. As you come across it in your reading, write the definition.

- character (p. 36)
- advocacy (p. 38)
- role model (p. 39)

Focusing on the Main Ideas
In this lesson, you will learn to

- **identify** the traits of good character.
- **explain** how character develops.
- **list** ways of showing good character.

Reading Strategy
Predicting Look over the headings in this lesson. Write a question that you think the lesson will answer. After reading, check to see if your question was answered.

Quick Write

Make a list of the good deeds you did this month. Then describe two of them in a paragraph.

What Is Character?

Do you help out with chores at home? Are you honest? Do you help others when you can?

If you truthfully answered yes to these questions, you probably have good character. **Character** is *the way you think, feel, and act*. Your character is reflected in your attitudes, views, and words. Do you recall reading about values in Chapter 1? Your character is an outward expression of your inner values. It's an important part of your relationships and the choices you make.

◀ Keeping an open mind helps you grow as a person. It gives you a chance to see the world through someone else's eyes. **How can being open-minded positively affect your health?**

People with good character are loyal to their friends. They respect others and their property. They try to keep an open mind to ideas, cultures, and views different from their own. People with good character do not cheat or lie. They do not help others cheat or lie. They do not take credit for someone else's work.

Your character affects your physical, mental/emotional, and social health. Taking care of your body shows that you have respect for your physical health. When you act responsibly and follow safety rules, you are protecting your physical health. When you are kind to others, you feel good about yourself. This strengthens your mental/emotional health. Good character also improves your social health. Being fair and honest helps you get along well with others. You can build strong relationships by treating others with respect and understanding.

 **Reading Check** **Explain** How does having good character affect your health?

Traits of Good Character

There are six main traits of good character. They are *trustworthiness, respect, responsibility, fairness, caring,* and *citizenship.* Developing these character traits now will help you communicate care, consideration, and acceptance of self and others throughout your life.

Trustworthiness

People who are trustworthy are reliable—they keep the promises they make. For example, if a teen promises his parents that he will be home on time, he keeps his word. People who are trustworthy are also honest. They always tell the truth.

Respect

Demonstrating respect means showing regard for other people, for property, and for authority. This involves treating others the way you'd like them to treat you.

Responsibility

Accepting responsibility means being willing to take on duties or tasks. It also means being willing to accept blame for mistakes you have made. A responsible person accepts the consequences of his or her actions and decisions.

Fairness

When you were young, you were taught to take turns and share your toys. You were taught fairness. Being fair means treating everyone equally and honestly. A fair person judges a contest on the basis of talent. She or he doesn't just award first prize to a friend in the contest.

Fairness also includes being a good sport and playing by the rules. It means knowing how to accept defeat when you lose and not showing off when you win.

Caring

Caring means treating others with understanding. Caring people are kind and consider the feelings of others. They help others when they can. Show that you care about others. Make an effort to welcome new students to your school. Listen to a friend who needs you.

▲ Helping to keep your community clean is an example of good citizenship. **What are some other examples of good citizenship?**

Citizenship

Being a good citizen means following rules and obeying laws. Good citizens also take action to make their community better. This is called advocacy. **Advocacy** is *taking a stand to make a difference.*

 **Reading Check** **Recall** Name and define three traits of good character.

How Does Character Develop?

Your character is shaped by your family and others around you. It is also influenced by your experiences in life and your values.

Family members are often the first teachers of character. Through their words and actions, they help you develop your own values. For example, your family may volunteer to help others in need. This teaches you to be a good citizen. You also learn responsibility at home. Doing chores or helping younger siblings with homework teaches responsibility. Being kind and helpful are ways that family members show they care about each other.

As you grow older, you learn from experience. Sports and games teach the importance of fairness and of following rules. At school you learn responsibility. You are responsible for getting your work done and in on time. School also teaches respect for authority.

 Reading Check Explain Who are the first teachers of character?

Role Models

One of the most important ways in which you learn character and values is by watching and listening to others. You learn by their examples. Some of these people may become positive role models for you. A **role model** is *a person whose success or behavior serves as a good example for others*. Parents or guardians are among the most important role models for their children.

Connect To...
Language Arts

The Idea of Character

The word *character* comes from a Greek word meaning "to mark or engrave." Look up the word *character* in a dictionary.

What other meanings do you find? How are they related?

▼ Team players demonstrate character through good sportsmanship. **What are some ways that team sports help build character?**

Character in Action

Good character is not something you feel or show once in a while. It is part of who you are. It is a way of living. By having good character, you promote your own health and the health of others. You feel good about yourself and are able to make responsible decisions. At the same time, you set a good example for others to follow.

At home, you can demonstrate good character by showing respect for your parents and other family members. Be honest with them. Listen when they talk to you. Show responsibility by getting up on time for school and by doing your chores. Let your family members know that you care about them. Work out your differences calmly and peacefully.

At school or during other activities, you can show you have good character by being a good citizen. Work together with others to advocate for healthy individuals, families, and communities. Follow school or other rules. Help to keep your school and community clean. Show respect for teachers, other adults, and students. Don't act out of hate or frustration. Be honest—don't cheat on your schoolwork. In sports, play fair and responsibly.

Lesson 2 Review

 After You Read

Review this lesson for new terms, major headings, and Reading Checks.

What I Learned

1. *Vocabulary* Define *character*. What are the six character traits?

2. *Recall* What is advocacy?

3. *Explain* Tell how role models can shape a person's character.

Thinking Critically

4. *Evaluate* Give an example of how good character might influence your health.

5. *Analyze* How is making responsible decisions related to good character?

6. *Synthesize* Give two examples of how life experiences might have a positive influence on character.

Applying Health Skills

7. *Decision Making* Write a short story about a teen faced with a difficult choice. Tell how he or she demonstrates good character in making a decision.

Go Online For more Lesson Review Activities, go to **glencoe.com**.

Expressing Emotions

Guide to Reading

Building Vocabulary

Read each of the words below. If the word is familiar, write down what you think its meaning is. If it's not, guess at its meaning using word clues. These include word parts, such as *ab-*, meaning "from."

- emotions (p. 41)
- hormones (p. 41)
- abstinence (p. 44)

Focusing on the Main Ideas

In this lesson, you will learn to

- **explain** what causes the emotions you experience.
- **express** strong feelings healthfully.
- **discuss** why abstinence is important for teens.

Reading Strategy

Identifying Cause and Effect As you read, think about examples of each emotion described. Identify a possible cause of this emotion in your daily life.

Your Emotions

What are you feeling right now? Maybe you are feeling happy about some good news that you got today. Maybe you are feeling down. You may even be feeling several different emotions at once. **Emotions** are *feelings such as joy, love, anger, or fear.* Your emotions affect all sides of your health triangle.

What Causes Emotions?

Emotions are often triggered by daily events. You are passed over for a part in the school play and feel sad. Your friend returns a borrowed jacket with a rip and you feel angry.

During your teen years, another emotional trigger is at work. It is deep inside you and beyond your control. Have you had days lately where you feel "up" one minute and "down" the next? These mood shifts are related to your body's release of hormones (HOR·mohnz). **Hormones** are *powerful chemicals, produced by glands, which regulate many body functions.* These hormones are preparing your body for adulthood. The emotional swings hormones cause can be confusing or even scary. If you've had these feelings, relax. Mood swings are part of growing up.

Quick Write

List five ways you show you're happy. Now list five ways you show you're angry. Which feelings do you find easier to express? What does this tell you?

Explain What are hormones? How do they affect emotions during the teen years?

► Mood swings can make you feel as if you are riding an emotional roller coaster. **What is the cause of mood swings during the teen years?**

Types of Emotions

Some emotions, such as happiness, are pleasant to experience. Other feelings, while less enjoyable, are still normal. Every person feels angry or afraid at one time or another. These emotions aren't good or bad—they just *are*. An important part of good mental/emotional health is learning how to handle your emotions in healthy ways.

Understanding Your Emotions

The first step in responding healthfully to a strong or difficult emotion is understanding what you're feeling. Sometimes, you know exactly what you are feeling and why. Other times, it's easy to confuse one emotion with another. This is especially true of anger. Strong words like "I hate you!" often mean "I'm angry with you." When you feel a strong emotion, take a moment to stop and think about what you are feeling and why. Try to focus on what is bothering you or making you angry. Ask yourself: What am I really reacting to? Am I angry because I feel hurt or disappointed? Once you understand your feelings, you can learn to manage them in healthy ways.

Expressing Your Emotions

Expressing your emotions healthfully is an important strategy for dealing with strong feelings. It is also important to effectively express feelings and opinions on health issues. Holding emotions inside can harm all sides of your health triangle. It can lead to stomachaches and headaches. It can make it hard to focus on what you are doing. Keeping your feelings inside can also have a negative effect on your relationships. It is better to let emotions out, especially strong ones. For instance, suppose you are angry or upset with someone. Pause for a moment and take a deep breath. Think of words that will express your true feelings without being hurtful. Then calmly tell the other person how you feel. For example, Cara was angry when her friend Jen called to cancel their plans. Cara took a moment to breathe slowly and deeply. She realized that she felt hurt because she and Jen hadn't been spending much time together lately. She called Jen back and they talked calmly about the situation. Cara felt much better afterward.

There are many other healthful strategies for dealing with strong or difficult feelings. These include the following:

- Engage in physical activity. This can help relieve tension.

- Talk with family members or friends. They can provide help and support.

- Create something, such as a drawing or poem.

- Listen to music. This can help you relax.

Reading Check **Explain** Is keeping feelings inside a good idea? Why or why not?

Go Online

Topic: Managing Strong Emotions

Visit **glencoe.com** for Student Web Activities on identifying and expressing your emotions.

Activity: Using the information provided at the link above, write down four healthful ways you can manage strong emotions.

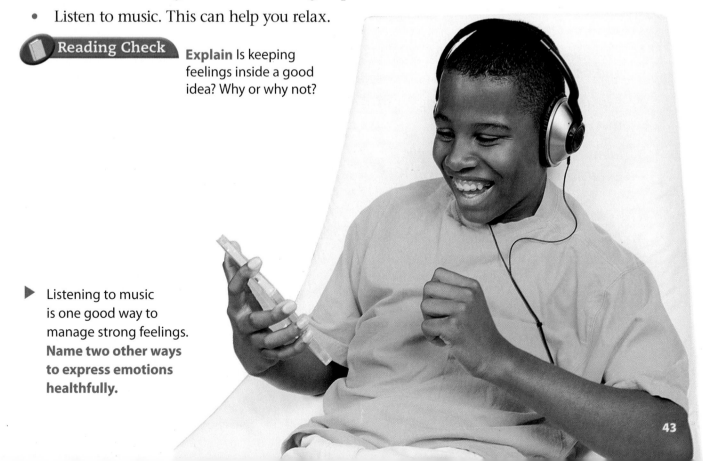

▶ Listening to music is one good way to manage strong feelings. **Name two other ways to express emotions healthfully.**

Practicing Abstinence

Everyone has basic emotional needs. These include the need to be loved and accepted. Some teens try to fill their emotional needs by participating in risky behavior. They may join gangs. Some may use tobacco, alcohol, or illegal drugs. Others become sexually active. These behaviors do not really meet emotional needs. Dealing with emotions in healthy ways includes saying no to high-risk behaviors like these.

Abstinence (AB·stuh·nuhns) is *not participating in high-risk behaviors.* Abstinence is a strategy for avoiding harmful situations. It protects your health and the health of others. Being abstinent tells others that you refuse to take part in unsafe behaviors. It also shows you have self-control. You will learn more about the value of abstinence in Chapter 3 and Chapter 8.

Go Online

Visit **glencoe.com** and complete the Interactive Study Guide for Lesson 3.

Reading Check   **Discuss** How is abstinence related to making good decisions?

Lesson 3 Review

After You Read

Review this lesson for new terms, major headings, and Reading Checks.

What I Learned

1. *Vocabulary* Define the word *emotion,* and use it in a sentence.

2. *Explain* Why are mood swings common during the teen years?

3. *Identify* What are two strategies for expressing emotions healthfully?

Thinking Critically

4. *Analyze* How might expressing emotions affect your social health?

5. *Apply* You are angry because your brother or sister has borrowed your headphones without asking. Explain how you will deal with your emotions.

6. *Summarize* What might you say to someone who tried to fill his or her emotional needs by participating in high-risk behaviors?

Applying Health Skills

7. *Practicing Healthful Behaviors* Describe how abstinence can help you avoid harmful situations.

Coping with Stress

Guide to Reading

Building Vocabulary

As you read this lesson, write each new highlighted term and its definition in your notebook.

- stress (p. 45)
- anxiety (p. 46)
- adrenaline (p. 47)

Focusing on the Main Ideas

In this lesson, you will learn to

- **explain** what stress is.
- **describe** how your body responds to stress.
- **list** ways to manage stress.

Reading Strategy

Finding the Main Idea Copy each main heading in the lesson. For each, write one sentence that states the main idea.

Quick Write

Write about a stressful situation you have been in and how you dealt with the stress.

What Is Stress?

Sonya has to give an oral report in class. Her mouth feels dry, and her palms are sweaty. Her stomach feels like butterflies are fluttering around inside it. Alex is on the soccer team. The championship game is coming up, so he's been at practice every night this week. He also has a big test to study for and a major project due. Lately Alex has been having trouble sleeping. He's been lying awake thinking about all the things he has to do. Whenever he worries about how he's going to get everything done, his heart starts to race. Sonya and Alex are feeling stress. **Stress** is *your body's response to changes around you.* Everyone feels stress from time to time—it's a normal part of life. Stress can give you energy and help you get things done. However, stress that continues over a long period of time can harm your physical, mental/emotional, and social health. While you can't always avoid stress, you can learn strategies for managing stress. This is an important part of staying healthy.

▶ Stress is a part of life. **What are some examples of stressful events?**

► Positive stress gives athletes the motivation they need to perform. **How can you use positive stress to your own benefit?**

Sources of Stress

Many different things can cause stress. It can result from small events, like forgetting your locker combination. Stress can also come from major events. These include life-changing situations—for example, moving to a new city or starting a new school. People sometimes respond to stressful events with anxiety. **Anxiety** is *feelings of uncertainty or worry over what may happen.*

People may view different events as stressful. You may feel stress when trying out for a part in the school play. Your friend may find this situation exciting rather than stressful. What has happened to you in the past may affect your views on what is stressful. For example, maybe you forgot some of your lines when performing in the school play. This might make you more anxious in similar situations. Your beliefs, attitudes, and values also influence what you think of as stressful.

Types of Stress

Stress can be positive or negative. For example, Jay was really excited about the race. When the signal to start sounded, he felt a burst of energy and took the lead. Jay was experiencing what is known as *positive stress*. Positive stress has many benefits. It can help you reach goals and accomplish tasks. It also provides needed energy to help you escape danger.

Negative stress gets in your way and holds you back. Sources of negative stress are often out of your control. They may include problems at home or school. Too much negative stress can be unhealthy.

 **Analyze** Compare and contrast positive and negative stress. What are their causes and effects?

The Stress Response

The stress response is how nature prepares the body to deal with threats of harm. This is also known as the *fight-or-flight response*. Your body is preparing to *fight* the threat or take *flight* from it. During the stress response, your body undergoes a series of physical changes, which are summarized in **Figure 2.1.**

 **Recall** Name two physical changes that occur during the fight-or-flight response.

▼ FIGURE 2.1

THE FIGHT-OR-FLIGHT RESPONSE

This illustration shows some of the physical changes stress can cause. What does stress do to the heart and blood vessels?

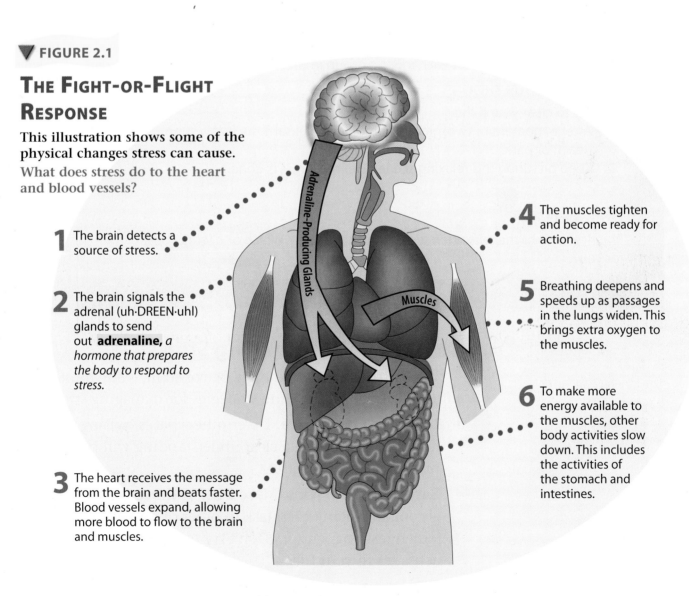

1 The brain detects a source of stress.

2 The brain signals the adrenal (uh·DREEN·uhl) glands to send out **adrenaline,** *a hormone that prepares the body to respond to stress.*

3 The heart receives the message from the brain and beats faster. Blood vessels expand, allowing more blood to flow to the brain and muscles.

4 The muscles tighten and become ready for action.

5 Breathing deepens and speeds up as passages in the lungs widen. This brings extra oxygen to the muscles.

6 To make more energy available to the muscles, other body activities slow down. This includes the activities of the stomach and intestines.

Adrenaline-Producing Glands

Muscles

Health Skills Activity

Stress Management

Relaxation Exercises

When you're feeling stress, your whole body is affected. You may feel stiffness in your shoulders or neck. Your mind may be cluttered with troubling thoughts. One strategy for dealing with stress is to use relaxation exercises.

There are three main types of relaxation exercises:

DEEP BREATHING

1. Close your eyes and inhale deeply.
2. Hold the breath for a moment, then slowly exhale.
3. Repeat these steps several times.

MUSCULAR RELAXATION

1. Picture the muscles in your body.
2. Working one at a time, tighten a muscle group.
3. Hold the position for a moment, then relax.
4. Repeat these steps for each muscle group in the body.

DIRECTING YOUR THOUGHTS

1. Try to clear your mind.
2. After a moment or two, picture someplace pleasant, such as a sunny beach or park.
3. Keep picturing this relaxing scene until the stress is gone.

On Your Own

Practice each of the relaxation techniques described. Which one works best for you?

Strategies for Managing Stress

When stress levels are high or constant, your health can suffer. Fortunately, there are strategies for managing stress.

- **Identify the source.** Determine what is causing you to feel stressed. Having a clear understanding will help you manage the stress better.

- **Set your priorities.** Make a list of things you want to accomplish. Rank each task in order of importance. Decide which task to focus on. Don't try to include too many activities in your life.

- **Budget your time.** Set aside regular times for homework and chores. That way you won't have to rush to get them done at the last minute.

- **Redirect your energy.** Stress increases your energy. Use that energy for something positive. Learn a hobby. Offer to help a family member with a project.

- **Talk to someone.** Talking about stress can reduce it. A parent, friend, or school counselor may give you some useful advice.

- **Put things in perspective.** Remember that you are not alone. Everyone experiences failure and disappointment. Don't make your problems bigger than they are.

- **Increase physical activity.** Becoming more active releases built-up energy from stress. Vigorous physical activity naturally relaxes the body.

 Reading Check   **Identify** How can budgeting your time help you manage stress?

Visit glencoe.com and complete the Interactive Study Guide for Lesson 4.

Lesson 4 Review

After You Read

Review this lesson for new terms, major headings, and Reading Checks.

What I Learned

1. *Vocabulary* Define the term *stress*.

2. *Describe* What does adrenaline do during the stress response?

3. *Give Examples* Name a major event and a minor event that might cause stress.

4. *Identify* List two strategies for managing stress.

Thinking Critically

5. *Hypothesize* Do you think it's possible to have too much positive stress? Explain why or why not.

6. *Synthesize* Name some negative ways of dealing with stress. How would these actions affect your health triangle?

7. *Apply* How can setting priorities help a teen manage stress?

Applying Health Skills

8. *Stress Management* Jamal is anxious about starting a new school. What are some ways that Jamal could manage his stress?

Lesson 5

Emotional Problems

Guide to Reading

● Building Vocabulary

Two of the terms below contain the word *disorder*. Look up this word in a dictionary. See if you can guess the meaning of the two terms.

- anxiety disorder (p. 51)
- mood disorder (p. 51)
- depression (p. 51)
- suicide (p. 51)

● Focusing on the Main Ideas

In this lesson, you will learn to

- **describe** types of emotional problems.
- **recognize** the warning signs of suicide.
- **identify** sources of help for emotional problems.

● Reading Strategy

Analyzing a Graphic Using the diagram below as a guide, create a chart that lists and describes different types of emotional disorders.

Mental Health Problems	
Name of Problem	Symptoms

Quick Write

Imagine a friend writes you to say she or he has been feeling sad for weeks. Write a paragraph describing what positive action you could take.

What Are Emotional Problems?

Cindy's friend Jon seemed sad, but she figured he would soon bounce back from whatever was bothering him. Then a month went by and Jon still rarely smiled or spoke to anyone. Cindy began to worry that something was really wrong.

▶ When sadness or other emotions last for weeks or months, action is needed. **How might you show your concern for someone who is dealing with an emotional problem?**

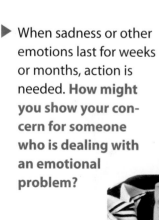
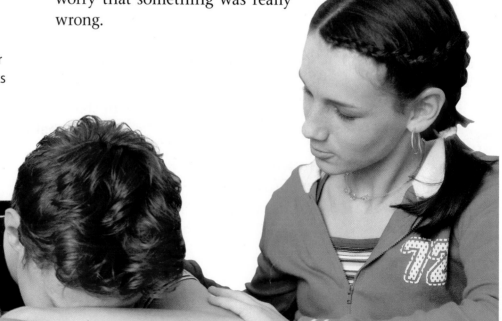

It's normal to feel sad or afraid from time to time. However, when such feelings last for weeks, it can be a sign of an emotional problem. Help is needed to reduce risks related to emotional problems of adolescents. Some common emotional problems are described below.

Anxiety Disorders

An **anxiety disorder** is *a serious emotional problem that keeps a person from functioning normally.* An anxiety disorder is not the same thing as anxiety, or worry, mentioned in Lesson 4. Anxiety disorders prevent people from leading normal lives.

One type of anxiety disorder is *phobia* (FOH·bee·uh). Phobias are unreasonable fears of objects or ideas. Some people, for example, have a phobia about being in high places. Others have an unreasonable fear of spiders. Another anxiety disorder is *obsessive-compulsive disorder (OCD).* People with OCD can't keep certain thoughts or images out of their minds. They may repeat behaviors, such as washing their hands, over and over. In the person's mind, this helps relieve anxiety.

 **Reading Check** **Recall** Name and describe two anxiety disorders.

▲ Some people have an intense fear of spiders. **What type of anxiety disorder would such a person have?**

Mood Disorders

Another type of emotional problem is mood disorders. A **mood disorder** is *a serious emotional problem where a person's mood goes from one extreme to another.* These changes are far more extreme than the mood swings typical in teens. A person may "cycle" between feelings of deep sadness and extreme happiness. In some people, both moods happen at once. In others, the happiness is replaced by anger or rage.

Depression

Sometimes when they're feeling down, people will say they "feel depressed." **Depression** is *an emotional problem marked by long periods of hopelessness and despair.* It is different from ordinary sadness. Depression can make it hard for a person to function.

Suicide

Sometimes, the effects of emotional problems are so severe the person considers suicide. **Suicide** is *the deliberate act of taking one's own life.* Suicide is the third leading cause of death in people ages 10 to 14. Most of the time, these young people don't want to die. They just want their problems to go away.

Suicide is not the answer. If someone you know is talking about suicide, go for help immediately. Urge the person to talk to a concerned adult. Tell an adult about the situation yourself. Never promise to keep the person's plan a secret. Suicide is one secret no friend should keep.

Warning Signs of Suicide

Sometimes, a person planning suicide doesn't use the word *suicide*, but there are other signs that a person may be thinking about it. If you notice any of the following behaviors, remember to tell a trusted adult right away.

- Avoiding activities that involve family or friends
- Taking greater risks than usual
- Losing interest in hobbies, sports, or school
- Giving away prized possessions

 **Reading Check** **Explain** What should you do if someone you know talks about suicide?

Help for Emotional Problems

Emotional problems have many causes. Some come from chemical changes in a person's brain. Others may be passed on through heredity.

It's important to know that emotional problems can be treated. Some are treated with medication, others with counseling, still others with both. Having an emotional problem is no different from having any other illness. Being able to ask for help shows you are taking responsibility for your health.

Sources of Help

There are many **sources** of help and support for emotional problems. Some are in your home or at school. You might talk to a parent or other family member. A teacher or a school counselor is another good person to turn to. Some people find it helpful to talk to a religious leader.

Often, people with emotional problems see a mental health professional. These are people specially trained to deal with emotional problems. They can give the person the specialized care he or she needs.

 **Reading Check** **Recall** Name two sources of help for people with emotional problems.

▲ Caring adults can provide comfort when the going gets rough. **How would you comfort a close friend with a problem?**

Academic Vocabulary

sources (sohrs sez) *(noun)* where something comes from. *Spinach and milk are good sources of iron.*

Visit glencoe.com and complete the Interactive Study Guide for Lesson 5.

Health Skills Activity

Decision Making

Helping a Troubled Friend

Caitlin's best friend, Torry, has been acting moody lately. When Caitlin asked her about it, Torry shrugged. "There's nothing to talk about," she said. Caitlin is worried that her friend may have a serious emotional problem. She wishes she could get Torry to open up. She knows from experience, however, that Torry doesn't like to be pressured. What should Caitlin do?

What Would You Do?

Put yourself in Caitlin's position. Use the decision-making process to decide what you would do.

1. State the situation.
2. List the options.
3. Weigh the possible outcomes.
4. Consider values.
5. Make a decision and act on it.
6. Evaluate the decision.

Lesson 5 Review

 After You Read

Review this lesson for new terms, major headings, and Reading Checks.

What I Learned

1. *Vocabulary* Define the term *depression*.

2. *Give Examples* What is an example of a phobia?

3. *List* Name three warning signs of suicide.

Thinking Critically

4. *Analyze* Imagine overhearing someone saying he or she planned to commit suicide. What would you do?

5. *Synthesize* A friend says, "I've been depressed lately." What positive health behaviors could you take to help your friend?

Applying Health Skills

6. *Advocacy* Write an article for the school paper about emotional problems. Identify what students should do if they are feeling very stressed or unhappy. Tell how they can help a friend with those feelings.

Building Health Skills

What Is Stress Management?

Stress management includes activities and behaviors that help you deal with stress in a healthy way. When you experience stress, do one or more of the following:

- Get plenty of sleep.
- Think positive thoughts.
- Make time to relax.
- Be physically active.
- Talk to someone you trust.
- Manage your time wisely.

Stress and Teens

Follow the Model, Practice, and Apply steps to help you master this important health skill.

❶ Model

Read about how Victor uses the skill of stress management to deal with problems after moving to a new town.

When Victor's family moved to a new town, he was excited about going to a larger school. But after the first few weeks, Victor started feeling a lot of stress about school and he missed his old friends.

Victor knew that he had to deal with his stress. First, he identified the cause. He realized that his problems began with the move. **(Identify the source.)** He talked to his brother about how he felt and he went to see the school counselor. **(Talk to someone.)** The counselor helped Victor focus on things he liked about moving instead of concentrating on the things he didn't like. **(Put things in perspective.)** Victor decided to join the chess club where he could meet some new friends. **(Redirect your energy.)**

❷ Practice

Make a plan to help Tyra manage the stress in her life.

Life improved for Tyra once she adjusted to her new school. Now she feels that she is stressed out about trying to do too many things. She works in a diner to earn money. She also spends a lot of time studying. Tyra wants to do well in school, earn some extra money, and have time to hang out with her friends. It seems that when she isn't stressed about one part of her life, she's worrying about another.

On a sheet of paper, identify what's causing Tyra's stress. Make a plan to help her by listing at least four things Tyra could do to manage the stress that she feels.

❸ Apply

Apply what you have learned about stress management when completing the activity below.

With a small group, think about the causes of stress in your own life. Develop an eye-catching brochure that includes an interesting title and the following topics:

1. A definition of stress
2. Sources of stress
3. Healthful and harmful strategies to manage stress
4. Reasons to manage stress

Self-Check

- Is our brochure eye-catching with an interesting title?
- Did we include a definition and sources of stress?
- Did we show healthful and harmful strategies and reasons to manage stress?

Building Health Skills

Developing Good Character

Character is formed every day by your thoughts and actions. Developing good character is important to your health. It will help you develop positive relationships and behaviors. A person of good character is trustworthy; treats people with respect; is responsible, fair, caring, and a good citizen. In this activity, you will create a poster with examples of how to develop one of the six traits of character.

What You Will Need

- Poster board
- Markers or crayons

What You Will Do

1 Your teacher will divide the class into six small groups and assign each group one of the six traits of character: trustworthiness, respect, responsibility, fairness, caring, or citizenship.

2 In your group, brainstorm and list examples of how teens can develop the assigned character trait. For example, if your group was assigned trustworthiness, you might list telling the truth and keeping promises.

3 Now, create a colorful poster featuring the examples you listed in Step 2. Use your group's character trait as the title for your poster. As a group, explain to the class how your examples can help a teen develop good character.

Wrapping It Up

After all the groups have presented their posters, discuss these questions as a class: How can teens help other teens develop good character? How can good character affect your physical, mental/emotional, and social health?

Display your posters where your classmates can see them. This will help other students learn about the six traits of good character.

Visit **glencoe.com** to download quizzes and eFlashcards for Chapter 2.

FOLDABLES Study Organizer

Foldables® and Other Study Aids Take out the Foldable® that you created for Lesson 1 and any graphic organizers that you created for Lessons 1–5. Find a partner, and quiz each other using these study aids.

Lesson 1 A Healthy Self-Concept

Main Idea Developing a positive self-concept is an important part of emotional health.

- Your self-concept is the view you have of yourself. It is influenced by parents, guardians, and those around you.
- You can build a positive self-concept by thinking positive thoughts, accepting encouragement, and finding friends who support you.

Lesson 2 Your Character Counts

Main Idea Having good character promotes your health and the health of others.

- Traits of good character include trustworthiness, respect, responsibility, fairness, caring, and citizenship.
- You develop character by learning from role models, your environment, and your understanding of right and wrong.

Lesson 3 Expressing Emotions

Main Idea It is important to learn how to handle your emotions.

- Emotions and mood swings are caused by events around you and by your hormones.

- Strategies for dealing with strong or difficult feelings include physical activity, talking with family and friends, creating something, or listening to music.
- Choosing abstinence protects your health and the health of others.

Lesson 4 Coping with Stress

Main Idea Managing stress is an important part of staying healthy.

- Stress can be positive or negative.
- The fight-or-flight response is one way your body responds to stress.
- You can manage stress by identifying the source, setting priorities, budgeting your time, redirecting your energy, talking to someone, keeping perspective, and increasing physical activity.

Lesson 5 Emotional Problems

Main Idea It's important to recognize the signs of emotional problems and seek help for them.

- Emotional problems include anxiety disorders, mood disorders, and depression.
- Warning signs of suicide include avoiding activities that involve family and friends, taking risks, losing interest in hobbies or school, and giving away prized possessions.

CHAPTER 2 Assessment

 After You Read

Health eSpotlight **VIDEO**

Now that you have read the chapter, look back at your answer to the Health eSpotlight question on the chapter opener. What are some other ways that you can boost self-confidence or help a friend set positive, realistic goals?

Reviewing Vocabulary and Main Ideas

On a sheet of paper, write the numbers 1–8. After each number, write the term from the list that best completes each statement.

- abstinence
- advocacy
- character
- confidence
- emotions
- encouragement
- hormones
- role model
- self-concept

Lesson 1 A Healthy Self-Concept

1. The view you have of yourself is known as your _____.
2. When you have high self-esteem, you have _____ in what you do.
3. Accepting _____ is one way to develop a positive self-concept.

Lesson 2 Your Character Counts

4. The way you think, feel, and act is known as your _____.
5. Taking a stand to make a difference is known as _____.
6. A person whose success or behavior serves as an example for others is a _____.

Lesson 3 Expressing Emotions

7. _____ are powerful chemicals that regulate many body functions.
8. Refusing to participate in high-risk behaviors is called _____.

Lesson 4 Coping with Stress

*On a sheet of paper, write the numbers 9–11. Write **True** or **False** for each statement below. If the statement is false, change the underlined word or phrase to make it true.*

9. Your body's response to changes around you is known as <u>stress</u>.
10. Anxiety refers to feelings of <u>happiness</u> over what may happen.
11. Adrenaline is a hormone that <u>stops the body from responding</u> to stress.

Lesson 5 Emotional Problems

On a sheet of paper, write the numbers 12 and 13. After each number, write the letter of the answer that best completes each statement.

12. A disorder in which a person has an unreasonable fear of an object or idea is known as
   a. depression.
   b. phobia.
   c. obsessive-compulsive disorder.
13. Signs that a person might be thinking about suicide include
   a. avoiding activities with friends.
   b. taking greater risks than usual.
   c. both of the above.

G **Online** Visit glencoe.com and take the Online Quiz for Chapter 2.

Thinking Critically

Using complete sentences, answer the following questions on a sheet of paper.

14. **Interpret** How do messages from those around you affect your self-concept?

15. **Analyze** What are three events that have caused stress in your life.

Write About It

16. **Expository Writing** Imagine you are writing an article on self-esteem for the school newspaper. In your article, explain what factors might affect a teen's self-esteem.

Courageous Character

You and a partner will use Comic Life or Microsoft Word® to create a poster advertising an event that builds teamwork while modeling good character.

- Open a new Comic Life template that has image and text boxes.
- Locate clip art or digital images that show teens with good character.
- Import the images into your template.
- Add titles or captions for the images. Make sure to explain how your images show good character.

Standardized Test Practice

Math

Use the table to answer the questions.

Percentage of Schools Teaching Suicide Prevention, by Topic		
Topic	Middle School	High School
How to handle stress in healthy ways	90.0	96.5
Recognizing types of stress and signs of depression that might be associated with suicide	64.8	86.5
What to do if someone is thinking about suicide	60.3	82.1

TEST-TAKING TIP

When questions use tables, read the title of the table. This will help you figure out its subject. Read each column heading and the label of each row.

1. What percentage of middle school students learn what to do if someone is thinking about suicide?
   - **A.** 60.3
   - **B.** 64.8
   - **C.** 90.0
   - **D.** 96.5

2. Which statement is *true*?
   - **A.** More middle school students learn healthful ways of handling stress than high school students.
   - **B.** More than 90 percent of high school students learn what to do if someone is thinking about suicide.
   - **C.** Nearly 65 percent of middle school students learn to recognize the types of stress associated with suicide.
   - **D.** Less than 60 percent of middle school students learn what to do if someone is thinking about suicide.

Chapter Preview

▲ *Working with the Photo*

This group of friends enjoys spending time at a local landmark. **What places do you and your friends like to visit?**

Start-Up Activities

Before You Read What do you know about healthy relationships? Take the short quiz below. Keep a record of your answers.

HEALTH QUIZ Answer *True* or *False* to each of the following questions.

1. Communication is important in healthy relationships.

2. Every family has two parents and one or more children.

3. Good friends are honest with each other.

4. Saying no to friends isn't always easy.

ANSWERS: 1. True.; 2. False.; 3. True; 4. True

FOLDABLES Study Organizer

As You Read Make this Foldable® to help you organize what you learn about good communication skills in Lesson 1. Begin with four plain sheets of 8½″ × 11″ paper.

1 Place the sheets of paper ½″ apart.

2 Roll up the bottom edges, stopping them ½″ from the top edges. This makes all tabs the same size.

3 Crease the paper to hold the tabs in place. Staple along the fold.

4 Label the tabs as shown. Use your Foldable® to describe several rules for effective communication listed in **Figure 3.1**.

Effective Communication
Ask questions
Use "I" messages
Make clear statements
Use appropriate body language
Listen actively
Mirror thoughts & feelings
Wait your turn

Go Online Visit **glencoe.com** and complete the Chapter 3 crossword puzzle.

Communication Skills

Guide to Reading

Building Vocabulary
Copy the terms below into your notebook. Guess the meaning of each. As you read, see how many terms you got right.

- communication (p. 62)
- relationship (p. 62)
- body language (p. 63)

Focusing on the Main Ideas
In this lesson, you will learn to

- **explain** different ways people communicate.
- **describe** how you can be a better speaker and listener.
- **identify** the three styles of communication.
- **develop** skills to communicate safely online.

Reading Strategy
Organizing Information Copy the major and minor headings from the lesson onto a sheet of paper. Leave space beneath each. Write a sentence beneath each heading that summarizes the ideas under that heading.

FOLDABLES Study Organizer Use the Foldable® on p. 61 as you read this lesson.

Quick Write

Think of someone you like talking with. In a short paragraph, explain why you enjoy talking with this person.

What Is Communication?

Each day you communicate with people. **Communication** is *the clear exchange of ideas and information.* When you communicate, you send or receive a message. Successful communication is at the root of healthy relationships. A **relationship** is *a connection you have with another person or group.* Good communication helps people understand each other and get along.

◀ Talking is the main way people communicate. **What are some other forms of communication?**

Body language can be a powerful communication device. **What message is being sent by the teen leaning in?**

Good communication requires special skills. Both the sender of the message and the receiver should have them. In this chapter, you will learn about these skills and how to use them.

 Reading Check **Define** What is *communication*?

Different Ways to Communicate

The main way people communicate is through language. On one end of the communication, there is a speaker or writer. On the other end, there is a listener or reader.

Communication, however, runs much deeper than just words. One way to demonstrate attentive communication is through body language. **Body language** refers to *facial expressions, eye contact, gestures, and posture.* Shrugging your shoulders at a question you can't answer is an example of body language. So is leaning in toward someone who's speaking about something you find interesting. People are often unaware of their body language. Sometimes, without knowing it, they send *mixed messages*. This means that their words don't match what their body is saying. For example, a friend might say, "That is a good idea," but roll her eyes. Mixed messages are confusing for listeners.

You can communicate with others in several different ways. You can speak face-to-face or by telephone. You can send written messages using e-mail, text messaging, or mail services. You can also give someone a written note or letter in person. For people with hearing loss, sign language is an effective way to communicate face-to-face.

Health Skills Activity

Practicing Healthful Behaviors

Safety Online

Instant messaging (IM) is a great example of how technology improves communication in our lives. So is e-mail. When using these technologies, it is important to play it safe. Here are some tips:

- Make sure that a parent or guardian gives you permission to communicate with others online.
- Never give out any information about yourself or your family. That includes your address, phone number, age, passwords, or family members' names.
- Stay out of unsupervised chat rooms.
- Never agree to meet anyone in person you have met online, without asking a parent or guardian.
- If an online conversation makes you feel uncomfortable, exit and tell a parent or other adult right away.

On Your Own

These are good rules for all members of the family. Make a copy and post it near your home computer.

There are advantages and disadvantages to different kinds of communication. Talking on the phone, for example, allows you to communicate your feelings, exchange ideas and information, and get an immediate response. However, when you speak on the telephone, visual clues such as facial expressions are absent. Communicating by e-mail gives you a chance to think and make corrections before you hit the send button. E-mail also gives you the ability to communicate information that needs to be remembered. You might e-mail directions to a birthday party or a list of supplies you should bring to school. Sometimes it is easier to express feelings or difficult emotions in writing than face-to-face or on the phone. In written messages, your reader can't see your facial expressions or hear the tone of your voice. All forms of communication allow you to communicate successfully.

 **Reading Check** **Give Examples** Give two examples of body language.

Using Good Communication Skills

Figure 3.1 summarizes effective verbal and nonverbal communication skills for both sending and receiving messages. Whether you are speaking or listening, it is important to use good communication skills.

Communication Styles

In addition to the variety of ways we can communicate, there are also different *communication styles*. Tom is *aggressive* in his communication. When he wants something, he will say, "Give me that!" in a threatening tone. His sister Abby is the opposite. If she wants something, she'll ask for it in a low, timid voice. Her meek and shy style of communication is *passive*.

▼ **FIGURE 3.1** **COMMUNICATION SKILLS**

Giving and getting messages each have their own "skill set." How do these skills relate to each other? What rules could you add for communication that is not face-to-face?

Careers for the 21st Century

Family Counselor

When a family has a problem that they cannot solve on their own, they might seek the help of a family counselor. A family counselor is a trained professional who teaches members of a family to listen to and speak to each other with respect. Family counselors are in demand because families can't always solve problems on their own. If you would like to become a family counselor, you should practice your communication skills.

What skills does a family counselor need? Go to *Career Corner* at **glencoe.com** to find out.

Outbound ("Sending")	Inbound ("Receiving")
■ **Think, then speak.** Don't just blurt out the first words that come into your mind. Plan what you're going to say. Think it through.	■ **Listen actively.** Recognize the difference between hearing and listening. Hearing is just being aware of sound. Listening is paying attention to it. Use your mind as well as your ears.
■ **Use "I" messages.** Express your concerns in terms of yourself. You'll be less likely to make others angry or feel defensive.	■ **Ask questions.** This is another way to show you are listening. It also helps clear up anything you don't understand. It prevents misunderstandings, which are a roadblock to successful communication.
■ **Make clear, simple statements.** Be specific and accurate. Stick to the subject. Give the other person a chance to do the same.	
■ **Be honest with thoughts and feelings.** Say what you really think and feel, but be polite. Respect the feelings of your listener.	■ **Mirror thoughts and feelings.** Pay attention to what is being said. Repeat what someone says to show that you understand.
■ **Use appropriate body language.** Make eye contact. Show that you are involved as a speaker. Avoid mixed messages. Beware of gestures, especially when speaking with people of different cultural backgrounds. Some gestures, such as pointing, are considered rude in certain cultures.	■ **Use appropriate body language.** Even if you disagree, listen to what the other person has to say. Make eye contact, and don't turn away.
	■ **Wait your turn.** Don't interrupt. Let the person finish speaking. You'll expect the same courtesy when it's your turn.

Neither Tom's nor Abby's approach to communication is very effective. Speaking aggressively can cause arguments or hurt feelings. People who communicate in a passive tone may not clearly express their needs to others. They risk not being heard or taken seriously. To communicate effectively, you must learn to use an *assertive* style. Assertive communication means you aren't shy or hesitant about expressing yourself. It is making your wants or needs known in a positive, active manner. A positive approach means the tone and feeling of your words are calm and pleasant. Suppose someone sitting near you at the movies is talking. An aggressive person might say something rude. A shy person might say nothing at all. But an assertive communicator would politely but firmly ask the person to stop talking.

Go Online

Visit **glencoe.com** and complete the Interactive Study Guide for Lesson 1.

 Reading Check   **Identify** What are three styles of communication?

Lesson 1 Review

 **After You Read**

Review this lesson for new terms, major headings, and Reading Checks.

What I Learned

1. *Vocabulary* Define *body language*.

2. *Identify* List four speaking skills a good communicator uses.

3. *Recall* What is assertive communication?

Thinking Critically

4. *Evaluate* Max was wrapped up in a TV show. His mother said something to him but got no response. When she scolded him for not listening, he replied, "I heard every word you said." What communication skills could Max have used to show his mother he was listening?

5. *Apply* "I'd love to come," Karen said when her friend called to invite her to a party. Karen's voice sounded uncomfortable. Did Karen's words match her voice? What kind of message was she giving her friend?

Applying Health Skills

6. *Communication Skills* You and two classmates are having a conversation. Demonstrate attentive communication skills. Make eye contact and use appropriate hand and body gestures.

Go Online For more Lesson Review Activities, go to **glencoe.com**.

Your Family

📖 Guide to Reading

🔴 Building Vocabulary
As you read this lesson, write each new highlighted term and its definition in your notebook.

- family (p. 67)
- nurture (p. 69)
- abuse (p. 71)
- physical abuse (p. 71)
- sexual abuse (p. 71)
- neglect (p. 71)

🔴 Focusing on the Main Ideas
In this lesson, you will learn to

- **recognize** different types of family units.
- **identify** your role within your family.
- **explain** how family members care for each other.
- **develop** effective communication skills for family meetings.

🔴 Reading Strategy
Organizing Information Make two lists. One list should contain types of family units. The other should list roles people play within a family.

Family Relationships

Think of the different relationships you have in your life. You have relationships with family, friends, classmates, teachers, and others in the community. Relationships are an important part of your social health. Good relationships make you feel loved, wanted, safe, and secure.

Family relationships are some of the most important. The **family** is *the basic unit of society*. A family includes two or more people brought together by blood, marriage, adoption, or a desire for mutual support.

There are many different kinds of families. Some families have two parents, others one. Trevor lives with his father, stepmother, and half-sister. Trevor's is a *blended family*. Can you guess what an *extended* family might be? Extend means "to reach out or make bigger." What kinds of people might be in an extended family? **Figure 3.2** shows several different family types. Which type is your family?

Quick Write

List some activities you do regularly with your family. Choose one activity and explain how it brings your family closer together.

▶ Extended families include members from more than one generation. This family, for example, is made up of a mother, child, and grandfather. **What are some other types of family units?**

FAMILY TYPES

There are many different types of family units. Are there examples of each type of family in your community?

Academic Vocabulary

role (ROHL) *(noun)* a person's job or responsibility. *One of Adam's roles in his family is helping his brother and sister with their homework.*

Family Type	Makeup
Couple	A husband and a wife who do not have children
Nuclear family	Two parents and one or more children
Extended family	A nuclear family plus other relatives such as grandparents
Single-parent family	One parent and one or more children
Blended family	Two people, one or both with children from previous marriages
Foster family	Adults caring for one or more children born to different parents
Adoptive family	A couple plus one or more adopted children
Joint-custody family	Two parents living apart, sharing custody of their children
Single-custody family	Two parents living apart and one or more children living with only one parent

ACTIVITY DEVELOPING Good Character

Teaching Character

One of the biggest responsibilities parents have is to help their children develop good character. They do this through both their words and actions. For example, Nikki's father talks to her about the importance of honesty. He also demonstrates honesty in his own life, giving her a good example to follow.

Which character trait do you think would be hardest to teach? Try teaching it to a younger sibling or friend.

Roles and Responsibilities in the Family

Every family member has a **role** to play. Parents and other adults are responsible for making sure the basic needs of the family are met. Their jobs also include teaching and practicing good health habits. They have a responsibility to model good communication and other health skills.

Not all responsibilities in the family fall on parents and other adults. Children have special jobs, too. In many families, for example, children share the household chores. Helping around the house is one way to demonstrate that you are responsible. Another way to contribute to the health and happiness of your family is by showing appreciation. To appreciate means to value someone or something. Saying "thank you" to the person who cooked dinner, for example, is a good way to show appreciation. You could also help with the dishes, volunteer to carry groceries, or do other tasks. Practicing positive behaviors such as showing appreciation for other family members helps maintain a healthy family relationship. As a teen, your role may also include helping other family members. You may be asked to spend time with a grandparent who has trouble getting around, or help a brother or sister with homework. However you choose to help, it's important to realize that your support helps make your family healthier.

Reading Check

List Name and describe three types of families.

Building Strong Families

The main job of any family is to meet the needs of its members. A strong family nurtures its members. To **nurture** is *to fulfill physical, mental/emotional, and social needs.* Nurturing families meet each other's needs on all three sides of the health triangle.

Some of the physical needs your family should provide include a place to live, food, and clothing. Healthy families go beyond these basics. They show concern for one another's safety and well-being.

Emotional support from the family includes love, but it's more than that. Strong families provide an atmosphere of warmth and security. Members make each other feel welcome and accepted. Members also help shape the values and beliefs of each other. They celebrate one another's successes and help each other deal with disappointments and challenges.

Socially, strong families understand the importance of sharing. Members willingly pitch in with tasks or chores. Strong families spend time together. They may watch television, attend school functions, or participate in physical activities together.

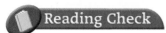 **Reading Check** **List** What are three kinds of support that strong families provide?

Coping with Family Changes

Just as individuals go through changes, so do families. Some changes, such as a job promotion or graduation, are positive. Other changes can be difficult, for example, when a family member becomes ill or loses a job. These events can be stressful for the whole family.

Two especially difficult changes are separation and divorce. A split in the family can bring on feelings of anger, sadness, or guilt. It can make you feel uncertain about the future. Children are never the cause of divorce or separation. It is an adult problem. If your family is going through a separation or divorce, share your feelings with your parents or another trusted adult. They can help you understand how these changes will affect you and other

G Online

Showing Appreciation

Visit **glencoe.com** for Student Web Activities that will give you more information on how to show appreciation.

Activity: Using the information from the link above, make plans to show three people in your life how much you appreciate them.

▼ Spending time together helps build strong family relationships. **What are some qualities of a strong, healthy family?**

Health Skills Activity

Communication Skills

Family Meetings

The behavior of family members and peers affects interpersonal communication. One way of improving communication among family members is through *family meetings*. In family meetings, all members meet to discuss problems and find solutions. Each family member should be encouraged to share opinions and offer suggestions.

It is important during family meetings to speak respectfully to one another. Each family member should have a chance to speak. It is also important for each member to listen carefully while others are speaking.

With a Group

Discuss how you think a family meeting should be run. Make a list of rules and guidelines to follow during a family meeting. Discuss behaviors that are helpful and unhelpful. When should people speak? Should all members vote on decisions to be made?

family members. Remember that parents, whether together or apart, love and care about their children.

Among the hardest changes to cope with is the death of a family member. Strong emotions are common and include sadness, grief, fear, and even anger. Expressing these feelings is an effective communication strategy for managing grief caused by disappointment, separation, or loss. Share your thoughts and feelings with people you can trust. Comforting others may also help you deal with your own feelings. It takes a long time to manage all the feelings caused by loss. Don't hesitate to ask for help. You might want to talk to a counselor who specializes in helping people manage grief.

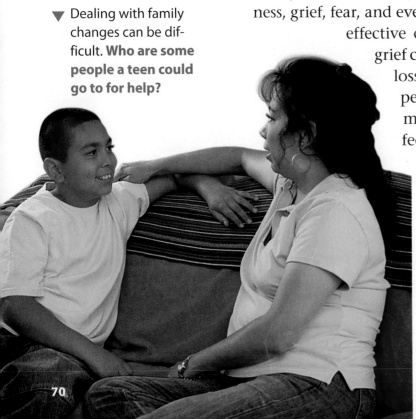

▼ Dealing with family changes can be difficult. **Who are some people a teen could go to for help?**

Reading Check   Give Examples

What are some changes that can affect the health of a family?

Serious Family Problems

We all have our ups and downs, good days and bad. The same is true of families. A healthy family manages to get over the bumps. Sometimes, however, the situation is more serious. It is beyond the family's ability to handle. One such problem is abuse (uh·BYOOS). **Abuse** is *a pattern of mistreatment of another person.* An adult or a child can be the target of abuse. Abuse is a serious problem that can have long-lasting effects on all family members. A family with an abuse problem needs to get help immediately.

Abuse can take several different forms. **Physical abuse** *involves the use of physical force.* A physically abused person often shows signs such as bruises, burns, or broken bones.

Emotional abuse is harder to spot. It often involves yelling and putting a family member down. Although there may be no physical harm, emotional abuse is just as serious. An emotionally abused person often feels worthless and angry.

Sexual abuse is *any mistreatment of a child or adult involving sexual activity.* Sexual abuse includes any type of unwanted or forced sexual activity. This can include touching one's private body parts or being forced to touch someone else's. Showing sexual material to a child is another act of sexual abuse. It is often difficult to see that a person is being sexually abused.

Parents are responsible for taking care of their children. When parents fail to do so, they are neglecting their children. **Neglect** is *the failure of parents to provide their children with basic physical and emotional care and protection.* Physical neglect involves not providing enough food, clothing, shelter, or medical care. Emotional neglect involves not giving love, respect, and other forms of emotional support.

Another serious problem for a family is when a family member is addicted to alcohol or drugs. You will learn strategies for coping with addiction in Chapter 10.

▲ Some victims of abuse are afraid to talk to someone. Talking to a trusted adult, however, is the first step in getting help. **What are some sources of help for families with problems of abuse or neglect?**

Help for Troubled Families

If you ever feel you are in danger from a family member, you must be brave enough to get help right away. Families where there is abuse need help. Start by speaking with an adult you feel you can trust. This might be a teacher or school counselor. The abuser needs help, too. He or she must understand the reasons behind his or her behavior and why it must change. If the danger is immediate, the police should be called. Abusing others is never acceptable.

Situations involving abuse or neglect often require professional health services. Social workers are professionals trained to help families with problems. Religious leaders and crisis centers can also help. You can call hot lines listed under "crisis intervention" in your telephone book. Still other resources to turn to are school counselors and doctors. They can suggest support and self-help groups. Some support groups are for those who are abused. Others are for the abusers. Both types try to help all the people involved.

 Go Online

Visit **glencoe.com** and complete the Interactive Study Guide for Lesson 2.

Reading Check **List** Name two forms of abuse, and tell what steps you would take to get help in an abusive situation.

 **Lesson 2 Review**

 After You Read

Review this lesson for new terms, major headings, and Reading Checks.

What I Learned

1. **Give Examples** Name two roles a person can have in a family.

2. **Vocabulary** Define *nurture*, and use it in a sentence.

3. **List** What are two forms of neglect?

Thinking Critically

4. **Apply** Al lives in an extended family that includes a grandparent and a younger cousin. What are some ways in which Al could show he cares about the members of his family?

5. **Synthesize** Kelly just found out her parents are getting divorced. How would you suggest that Kelly get help dealing with her concerns and fears?

Applying Health Skills

6. **Accessing Information** Use the phone book to access the names of community agencies that advocate healthy individuals, families, and communities. Make a list of these agencies.

Go Online For more Lesson Review Activities, go to **glencoe.com**.

Lesson 3

Your Friends and Peers

Guide to Reading

● Building Vocabulary

How are the terms below related? Are there words that have similar or related meanings? Define each term as best you can.

- friendship (p. 73)
- reliable (p. 74)
- loyal (p. 74)
- empathy (p. 74)
- cooperation (p. 75)
- peers (p. 76)
- peer pressure (p. 76)

● Focusing on the Main Ideas

In this lesson, you will learn to

- **identify** the qualities of a good friend.
- **recognize** character traits found in friends.
- **understand** the two kinds of peer pressure.

● Reading Strategy

Organizing Information As you read the lesson, make two lists. One should contain a list of the positive character traits of good friends. The second should list the ways peers can be negative influences.

● Quick Write

What changes and challenges have you noticed in your relationships with your friends? Write a paragraph explaining your answers.

Who Are Your Friends?

Friendships are important relationships. A **friendship** is *a special type of relationship between people who enjoy being together.* There are many reasons people become friends. When you are young, location is a factor. Most of your current friends are probably from the same neighborhood or school. Another reason for choosing friends is shared interests, such as hobbies or activities. Personality traits, such as a sense of humor, may also lead people to each other so that they become friends.

Sometimes making new friends can be tough, especially when you move to a new school or city. Here are some tips to help you build friendships.

▶ Participating in activities helps you make friends with similar interests. **What are some activities and hobbies you enjoy?**

- *Get to know yourself.* Make a list of your own interests and talents. What are your positive qualities? What would make you a good friend to others?

- *Break the ice.* Start a conversation with a classmate you think you'd like to know better. Ask a question, or give a compliment. Talk about sports, movies, or whatever else interests you. If the other person shares the same interests, a friendship may develop.

- *Join a club, sports team, or community group that interests you.* You will be able to meet people with shared interests.

- *Offer a helping hand.* Help a classmate or neighbor with homework or other projects. When you reach out, you let others know you're a good friend to have.

Character Traits of Good Friends

It is important to choose friends who have positive values and attitudes. Good friends often have the same views of what is right and wrong. They may share common character traits such as trustworthiness and caring.

Do you have friends you can share your thoughts and feelings with? People who fit this description are trustworthy. Good friends should also be **reliable,** or *dependable.* They keep their promises. If they say they'll meet you at 4:00, they show up at 4:00. They don't arrive 30 minutes late. Good friends are also **loyal,** or *faithful.* A loyal friend will not allow others to say untrue or mean things about you.

Good friends care about each other and support each other, through good and difficult times. Good friends look out for each other when faced with hard times or harassment. They display **empathy,** *the ability to identify and share another person's feelings.* When you're feeling sad or disappointed, a good friend shares your pain.

▶ Friendships are relationships that you actively seek out. **What are some qualities you and your friends share?**

◀ Friends often help each other improve their skills. **How does this benefit both of you?**

Does being friends with someone mean the two of you will always agree? Of course not. It is only natural for the two of you to have occasional disagreements. Accepting views and opinions that are different from your own is a sign of respect and a healthy relationship. It is also a measure of maturity, a sign that you're growing up.

 **Reading Check** **Give Examples** Give one example each of reliability and empathy.

Building Strong Friendships

Building and maintaining positive friendships is important. You can build stronger friendships through cooperation. **Cooperation** means *working together for the common good.* Eduardo and Ben help each other prepare when one of them has a test. Ben will ask Eduardo questions, and vice versa. As members of the same Little League team, the two also practice fielding together. When Ben and Eduardo play sports together, they play fairly and follow the rules.

Another way of making friendships stronger is through mutual respect and support. This means that friends listen and respect each other's opinions. Talking together about problems or concerns is a form of support. Supporting each other will help you and your friend make more healthful decisions. This includes saying no to negative peer pressure.

► When your peers see you doing good work, they may feel motivated themselves. **What are some other examples of positive peer pressure?**

Peer Pressure

Peers, as noted in Chapter 1, are *friends and other people in your age group.* During the teen years, your expanding abilities, independence, and responsibilities can influence personal behavior. Peers can give you support and confidence during this *transition*, or move, toward adulthood.

During this time, peer pressure can influence healthful choices. **Peer pressure** is *the influence that people your age may have on you.* Peer pressure can be something you feel indirectly. You see classmates wearing a certain type of clothing. Without a word from anyone else, you go out and buy the same item or something similar. At other times, peer pressure is direct. A peer may tell you what you should do to blend in or be accepted. Sometimes, this may come in the form of a demand or threat. Because it influences your decisions, peer pressure can affect your health in many ways.

Positive Peer Pressure

Academic Vocabulary

positive (PAH zi tiv) *(adjective)* helpful. *My sister gave me positive reinforcement after listening to my speech.*

Peer pressure can be either **positive** or negative. Positive peer pressure can inspire you to improve yourself or do something worthwhile. For example, you may be encouraged to study for a test by studying together with friends or other peers. They are having a positive influence on you.

Inspiring you to improve your health and appearance, or to perform well on a team, are other ways to be positive influences. Maggie joined the yearbook staff partly because of encouragement from her friends. In what ways do your friends positively influence your behavior?

Negative Peer Pressure

"I dare you!" When Shauna heard these words, she knew it was time to walk away. Daring someone to behave in dangerous or illegal ways is an example of negative peer pressure. The same is true of challenges that go against your beliefs and values. Here are some examples:

- Urging a peer to use tobacco, alcohol, or other drugs
- Talking a peer into being unkind to someone who is different
- Persuading a peer to do something illegal such as shoplifting
- Encouraging a peer to be disrespectful to parents or other adults
- Urging a peer to fight or get involved in gangs

Standing up to negative peer pressure can be difficult. It is, nevertheless, an important skill to learn. In the next lesson, you'll learn ways to say no to negative peer pressure.

 Reading Check **Explain** What is the difference between negative and positive peer pressure?

Visit glencoe.com and complete the Interactive Study Guide for Lesson 3.

Lesson 3 Review

 **After You Read**

Review this lesson for new terms, major headings, and Reading Checks.

What I Learned

1. *Vocabulary* Define *friendship.*

2. *Identify* What are two characteristics of a good friend?

3. *List* Give two examples of negative peer pressure.

Thinking Critically

4. *Apply* How do you show empathy to a friend who has just lost a pet?

5. *Analyze* What are some positive and negative effects of peer pressure?

Applying Health Skills

6. *Decision Making* Write a story in which a teen chooses to volunteer time because of positive peer pressure. In your story, show how the teen uses the six decision-making steps.

Refusal Skills

Guide to Reading

● Building Vocabulary
Write the terms below in your notebook. Define each term as you read about it in the lesson.

- refusal skills (p. 78)
- abstinence (p. 80)

● Focusing on the Main Ideas
In this lesson, you will learn to

- **identify** how to use refusal skills to resist peer pressure.
- **demonstrate** refusal skills to resist negative peer pressure.
- **explain** the importance of abstinence during the teen years.

● Reading Strategy
Identifying Problems and Solutions After reading this lesson, give examples of peer pressure. Tell how you might say no in each situation.

*Q*uick Write

List as many ways as you can of saying no when someone pressures you to do something dangerous or unhealthy.

What Are Refusal Skills?

Lance worked in the school store. Stan, another student, asked Lance to let him have a notebook without paying. "Come on, no one will notice," Stan said. Lance knew he was being asked to do something wrong. He could get into trouble. Even if he didn't get into trouble, his conscience would bother him.

When you are pressured to do something wrong, tension can build. You may worry what will happen if you don't go along with the group. Will your friends still like you? Will you still be a part of the group? It is at these times that refusal skills can help. **Refusal skills** are *ways of saying no.* They are communication strategies for avoiding potentially harmful situations.

Using Refusal Skills

You may find yourself in a situation in which you feel pressure to participate in unsafe behaviors. One way of refusing effectively is to use the S.T.O.P. strategy. Each of the letters stands for a different step:

◄ When pressure builds, something has to give. **What is a method for resisting pressure without having a situation get out of control?**

Health Skills Activity

Refusal Skills

Saying No

Apply the S.T.O.P. strategy to Lance's problem in the lesson opener. Role-play the story with a classmate. One of you is to take the role of Lance. The other will play the classmate pressuring Lance. Prepare a script for your story. Show how Lance uses the four steps to say no to his classmate.

With a Group

Be prepared to perform your role-play for classmates. What is another situation in which you could use the S.T.O.P. strategy to avoid negative peer pressure?

- **Say no in a firm voice.** Sometimes, saying no is enough. Friends who respect you will take no for an answer. People are more likely to believe you if you speak firmly. Show self-confidence without being insulting to others.

- **Tell why not.** Explain your reasons for saying no. Let your peers know that you value your health and safety. It's also a chance to show your good character traits.

- **Offer other ideas.** Change the subject by coming up with something else to do instead.

- **Promptly leave.** If people continue to put pressure on you, walk away. If certain people always put pressure on you whenever you see them, avoid them.

Remember that you are not alone when you face a difficult situation. You can always get help from a trusted adult. A parent, older brother or sister, or counselor will listen to your problem. They can help you decide the best course of action to take. They might even suggest some options you hadn't thought about.

▼ Saying no to risky behaviors can be tough. **What are some ways to say no to risky behaviors?**

 **Reading Check** **Explain** How do refusal skills protect your health and safety?

What Is Abstinence?

Some of the negative pressures you face as a teen are relatively minor. Others can be major. Among these are pressures to take part in high-risk behaviors such as using tobacco, alcohol, or illegal drugs. Becoming sexually active is another high-risk behavior. When you say no to high-risk behaviors, you are practicing abstinence (AB·stuh·nuhns). **Abstinence** is *not participating in high-risk behaviors*. Abstinence protects your health and that of others. It shows you have self-control.

Choosing Abstinence

When you choose abstinence, you protect the three sides of your health triangle. Abstaining from tobacco, for example, protects your lungs and heart. Abstaining from alcohol and illegal drugs protects your body and mind. Abstaining from sexual activity protects you against pregnancy and sexually transmitted diseases. Teens who abstain from high-risk behaviors understand the importance of practicing positive health behaviors.

 Reading Check **List** Name three benefits of choosing abstinence.

 Go Online

Visit **glencoe.com** and complete the Interactive Study Guide for Lesson 4.

Lesson 4 Review

After You Read

Review this lesson for new terms, major headings, and Reading Checks.

What I Learned

1. *Vocabulary* What are *refusal skills*?

2. *Identify* Describe the relationship between peer pressure and refusal skills.

3. *Recall* Why is abstinence important during the teen years?

Thinking Critically

4. *Explain* Tell how positive peer pressure can make a friendship stronger.

5. *Analyze* Hannah told her friend that smoking harms a person's lungs and heart. Her friend continues to urge Hannah to smoke a cigarette. What must Hannah do next? Explain.

Applying Health Skills

6. *Advocacy* Create a poster that colorfully explains the S.T.O.P. strategy. With permission from school administrators, place your poster on a hallway wall.

Go Online For more Lesson Review Activities, go to **glencoe.com**.

Resolving Conflicts

Guide to Reading

● Building Vocabulary

Arrange the terms below in two columns: problems and solutions. Match each problem with a solution.

- conflicts (p. 81)
- prejudice (p. 82)
- tolerance (p. 82)
- compromise (p. 83)
- negotiation (p. 83)
- peer mediation (p. 83)
- violence (p. 84)
- gang (p. 84)

● Focusing on the Main Ideas

In this lesson, you will learn to

- **explain** why conflicts occur.
- **describe** ways of protecting yourself from violence.
- **identify** a strategy to resolve conflicts through negotiation.

● Reading Strategy

Sequencing Create a flow chart to show the steps that lead up to violence. Then add steps that show how to prevent conflicts from turning violent.

What Are Conflicts?

"Give that back to me! It's mine." The twins Jenny was babysitting were at it again. It seemed they couldn't go more than a few minutes without arguing. Luckily, Jenny had learned about conflicts in health class. **Conflicts** are *disagreements in ideas, beliefs, or interests.* The first step in preventing conflicts is understanding what causes them.

● Quick Write

Do you think schools with violence problems should install video cameras? Why or why not? Explain in a brief paragraph.

◀ When conflict arises, it is no game. **What are some healthy ways to resolve conflicts?**

Causes of Conflict

When you understand the possible causes of conflict, you can develop positive communication strategies for preventing conflict. Most conflicts can be traced back to an act or event. A difference of opinion, or jealousy, can create a conflict. For example, a group of students working on a school project might disagree over the jobs each person should do.

Sometimes conflicts are started *because of* prejudice (PREH·juh·dis). **Prejudice** is *an opinion or fear formed without having facts or firsthand knowledge.* Disliking a person because of his or her skin color or culture is an example of prejudice. Prejudice can cause both emotional and social health risks within a community.

 **Reading Check** **Identify** Name some common causes of conflict.

Preventing Conflicts

The first step in preventing conflict is using good communication skills. When you disagree with someone, state your case clearly and calmly. Use "I" statements that do not accuse or blame. An example of an "I" statement is "I feel like I am being left out of the group." Compare this with the more aggressive "You are ignoring me!"

Another valuable tool in preventing conflicts is tolerance. **Tolerance** is *the ability to accept other people as they are.* Accepting people who are different from you can help you build and maintain positive interpersonal relationships.

Resolving Conflicts

When a conflict occurs, conflict-resolution skills can help you resolve it in a positive way. One skill is knowing when to walk away. Sometimes the right response to a possible conflict is no response. Often, the disagreement will end quickly if you walk away.

No matter what the disagreement, refuse to fight. If a conflict appears to be turning physical, just walk away. This does not make you a coward or chicken. It makes you wiser and more mature than the other person.

If a conflict is brewing between two other people, don't get in the middle or take sides. If a fight breaks out, don't get between the fighters. Instead, go get help from an adult right away.

DEVELOPING Good Character

The Myth of Positive Prejudice

Some kinds of prejudice can seem positive. For example, saying all French people are good cooks may sound like a compliment. However, it is really a form of prejudice. Prejudices assume things about people based on their race, their culture, or the groups they belong to. Don't assume anything about a person until you get to know him or her.

Imagine hearing a prejudiced remark at school. What would you say to correct the prejudice without creating conflict?

Reaching a Compromise

One important conflict-resolution skill is compromise. **Compromise** is *a skill in which each side gives up something in order to reach an agreeable solution.* Suppose that you and your friends go to the schoolyard to play soccer. Unfortunately, you arrive at the exact same time as a girl from your class and you both try to grab the only ball left. Instead of fighting over the ball however, you reach a compromise. You all join in a game together. Compromise is a great way to resolve conflicts, as long as it does not go against your values.

Reaching a compromise sometimes requires negotiation (neh·GOH·shee·AY·shuhn). **Negotiation** is *the process of talking about a conflict and deciding how to reach a compromise.* The T.A.L.K. strategy is an effective way of resolving conflict through negotiation. The steps are as follows:

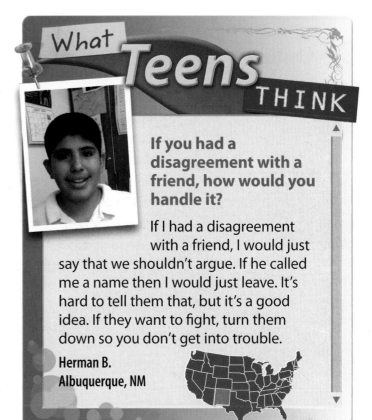

If you had a disagreement with a friend, how would you handle it?

If I had a disagreement with a friend, I would just say that we shouldn't argue. If he called me a name then I would just leave. It's hard to tell them that, but it's a good idea. If they want to fight, turn them down so you don't get into trouble.

**Herman B.
Albuquerque, NM**

- **Take a time-out.** Wait at least 30 minutes before you talk over the situation. This will give both of you a chance to calm down and think more clearly.

- **Allow each person to tell his or her side.** Each person should have the chance to explain his or her feelings without interruption. Always listen carefully, and show respect for the other person.

- **Let each person ask questions.** Each person should have the chance to question the other. Stay calm and respectful. Also, stay focused on one problem. Don't bring up other problems at this time.

- **Keep brainstorming.** Try to see the situation from the other person's point of view. Work to find a solution that will satisfy you both.

When all else fails, get help from a school counselor, parent, or other adult. An option in some schools is peer mediation (mee·dee·AY·shuhn). **Peer mediation** is *a process in which a specially trained student listens to both sides of an argument to help the people reach a solution.*

 **Reading Check** **List** Identify two steps in the T.A.L.K. strategy. Tell what happens in each.

Go Online

Visit **glencoe.com** and complete the Interactive Study Guide for Lesson 5.

When Conflicts Get Out of Hand

When conflicts are not dealt with, they can get out of hand. This in turn can lead to violence. **Violence** is *the use of physical force to harm someone or something.* Violence is a growing problem in the United States. It can lead to injury and even death.

In some communities, there is gang violence. A **gang** is *a group whose members often use violence or take part in criminal activity.* Some teens join gangs because of peer pressure. Many teens who join gangs come from troubled families. They seek a sense of belonging that is missing in their lives. Gang membership is never an answer to life's problems. Belonging to a gang only makes problems worse. Teens in gangs have a higher school dropout rate than nonmembers. They are arrested more often, too. Because gangs often use weapons, these teens have a higher risk of getting seriously injured or of dying.

Avoiding Violence

There may be times when conflict or violence finds you. For example, someone may try to bully you or pull you into a fight. Fortunately, there are techniques for avoiding threatening situations.

For starters, learn and practice self-control. Do not fight or threaten others. Don't wear any clothing that could be mistaken for gang clothing. If you use a purse, carry it with the strap across your chest. Whenever you can, steer clear of harmful situations. If you know a party might include alcohol or drugs, don't go. If you know or suspect someone has a weapon, report it immediately to a parent or another trusted adult.

Avoid violence by becoming an advocate for peace. Let others know you are a nonviolent person. Serve as a positive example. Use good communication skills. Being polite and showing respect for others are also good ways to avoid violence.

Protecting Yourself from Violence

Observing safety rules is another way of protecting yourself from violence. If you're home alone, do not open the door to anyone you don't know. Keep doors and windows locked. Never tell visitors or callers you are alone. Instead, say your parents are busy or can't come to the phone.

▼ This teen is wearing her handbag in a way that lessens her risk of becoming a victim of violence. **What are some other injury-prevention strategies for personal and family health?**

If you are going out, tell your family where you are going and how you will get there. Make sure they also know when you expect to return. When walking home, try to walk in pairs or with a group. Stay in familiar neighborhoods; avoid deserted streets and dangerous shortcuts.

Avoid strangers. Never get into or go near a stranger's car or hitchhike. Do not enter a building with a stranger. Don't agree to run errands or do other tasks for strangers. Finally, if someone tries to grab you, scream and run away. Go to the nearest place with people. Ask them to call 911 or your parents.

▲ Remember that there is safety in numbers. Bullies are less likely to pick on a group. **What are some other ways of protecting yourself against violence?**

 Reading Check   **Identify** What are some ways of avoiding violence?

Lesson 5 Review

After You Read

Review this lesson for new terms, major headings, and Reading Checks.

What I Learned

1. *Vocabulary* Use *prejudice* and *tolerance* in a sentence.

2. *List* Name two ways in which you can help prevent conflicts from occurring.

3. *Recall* When should you not be willing to compromise?

Thinking Critically

4. *Evaluate* When Seth walks away from a fight, he hears his bully call him "chicken." What should Seth do? Explain.

5. In a conflict, why is it important to understand how the other person feels? How can conflicts be settled with respect to the feelings of others?

Applying Health Skills

6. *Communication Skills* With a partner, practice changing "you" sentences into "I" sentences. How does the use of "I" sentences help prevent conflict?

Building Health Skills

What Is Conflict Resolution?

Conflict resolution involves finding a positive solution to a disagreement or preventing it from becoming a larger conflict. The T.A.L.K. strategy can help you resolve conflicts in a positive way.

T Take a time-out, at least 30 minutes.

A Allow each person to tell his or her side uninterrupted.

L Let each person ask questions.

K Keep brainstorming to find a good solution.

Working Things Out

Follow the Model, Practice, and Apply steps to help you master this important health skill.

❶ Model

Read about how Kari and Samantha use the T.A.L.K. strategy to resolve a conflict.

Kari's friend Samantha borrowed her new sweater without asking. Kari took 30 minutes to calm down and think about what she should say to Samantha (**Take a time out.**). Kari told Samantha why she was mad. Samantha said she thought that because they were friends, they shared their clothes (**Allow each person to tell her side.**). Samantha asked Kari if she wanted her sweater back right away. Kari said that she didn't need it. She asked Samantha if they could make a rule about borrowing each other's clothes in the future (**Let each person ask questions.**). Kari said that the next time either friend wanted to borrow something from the other, they should ask first. Samantha liked this idea, but wondered what they would do if the other friend wasn't home when they wanted to borrow something. Kari and Samantha continued to talk about their problem (**Keep brainstorming.**).

❷ Practice

***Read how Kelly and Anne use the skill of
conflict resolution.***

Kelly: Anne, I need the CD you borrowed last
month.

Anne: I think that I left it at Sara's.

Kelly: That's my favorite CD! I need to go for a
walk and think about this. I will meet up with
you later.

Kelly: Anne, can you please find the CD or pay
for a new one?

Anne: I didn't mean to lose it, so I don't think I
should have to pay for it.

Kelly: I know you didn't lose it on purpose,
but you promised to return the CD.

Anne: Will you wait until I ask Sara if she has
the CD?

Kelly: When would you ask her?

Anne: I'll send her a text message. I'll get the CD from Sara or bring
the money on Friday.

1. Identify the T.A.L.K. steps in this conversation.

❸ Apply

***Apply what you have learned about conflict resolution to complete
the activity below.***

Conflict-resolution skills promote social health through positive
communication. On a piece of paper, write a paragraph that discusses
causes of conflict and ways to prevent it. Then list several situations
that lead to conflict for teens. Choose one of these situations, and
write a script showing your conflict-resolution skills.

Self-Check

- Did my paragraph discuss causes of conflict and ways to
  prevent it?
- Did my script show how to use the T.A.L.K. steps for conflict
  resolution?

Building Health Skills

Schoolroom
TORMENT

Do you have the wrong idea about bullies?

Many people think that bullies don't have any friends and are lonely. If you know a bully, you probably know that isn't always true. According to psychologist Dorothy Espelage, the typical bully is not a loner at all. Instead, bullies are popular and athletic. Bullies know how to get their way with adults while bullying their schoolmates at the same time.

Here's how Dr. Espelage answered some of our questions about bullies.

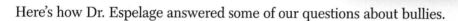

Q: How do you define "bully"?

A: A bully is a kid who teases and intimidates other students. Bullies spread rumors about other kids. Bullies form social groups that keep many kids out.

Q: What's behind bullying behavior?

A: First of all, with some teens, you can fit in and be cool if you bully others. Second, bullies don't feel that great about themselves, and bullying can block some of those feelings. Lastly, some teens don't always have the skills to tolerate differences in other kids. So when bullies see people who are different, they lash out and make fun of them.

Q: Are bullies usually from single-parent homes?

A: We find bullying just as often where there is a mom and a dad at home. It's all about parental supervision. If kids are unsupervised, they're more likely to become bullies.

Q: What can young people do about bullies and bullying?

A: Kids shouldn't be easy targets for bullies. Look the bully in the eye and walk away confidently. Bullies want to hurt your feelings. Even if they're being really mean, act as if they're not succeeding and don't get into a fight.

Also, tell a parent or a teacher. They want to know what is happening and how you feel about it. If the bullying happened at school, have a parent talk it over with your teacher. Parents shouldn't call the parents of the bully.

Reading Review

 Visit **glencoe.com** to download quizzes and eFlashcards for Chapter 3.

FOLDABLES® Study Organizer

Foldables® and Other Study Aids Take out the Foldable® that you created for Lesson 1 and any graphic organizers that you created for Lessons 1-5. Find a partner, and quiz each other using these study aids.

Lesson 1 Communication Skills

Main Idea Communication is necessary for good, healthy relationships.

- People communicate with each other in many ways, including body language, face-to-face conversation, the telephone, and e-mail.
- A good communicator thinks before he or she speaks, listens actively, and makes statements that are easy to understand.
- The three styles of communication are assertive, passive, and aggressive.

Lesson 2 Your Family

Main Idea The family is a small-scale version of society.

- Different types of families include nuclear, blended, extended, and single-parent families.
- Every member of a family has a role.
- Families care for each other by showing love, appreciation, and support.
- Good communication is crucial to help families grow and change together.

Lesson 3 Your Friends and Peers

Main Idea Friendship is an important kind of relationship between two people who enjoy being together.

- Good friends often share similar interests.
- Character traits found in good friends include reliability, loyalty, and willingness to show empathy.
- Cooperation means working together for the common good.
- Peer pressure is either positive or negative.

Lesson 4 Refusal Skills

Main Idea You can use refusal skills to help avoid harmful situations.

- You can resist negative peer pressure by using the S.T.O.P. strategy.
- Abstinence is the refusal to participate in high-risk behaviors.

Lesson 5 Resolving Conflicts

Main Idea Conflicts happen when people disagree about an idea, belief, or interest.

- Conflicts occur for a number of reasons, including jealousy and competition.
- Prejudice is an opinion or fear formed without having facts or firsthand knowledge.
- Conflict-resolution skills include compromise and negotiation.
- You can protect yourself from violence by avoiding dangerous situations.

Assessment

 After You Read

HEALTH QUIZ

Now that you have read the chapter, look back at your answers to the Health Quiz in the chapter opener. Would you change any of them? What would your answers be now?

Reviewing Vocabulary and Main Ideas

On a sheet of paper, write the numbers 1–5. After each number, write the term from the list that best completes each statement.

- abuse
- body language
- communication
- empathy
- loyal
- neglect
- nurture
- relationship

Lesson 1 Communication Skills

1. _____ includes facial expressions, eye contact, gestures, and posture.

2. _____ is the sharing of thoughts and feelings between two or more people.

Lesson 2 Your Family

3. Healthy families _____ their members, or fulfill physical, mental/emotional, and social needs.

4. A pattern of mistreatment of another person is known as _____.

5. _____ is the failure of parents to provide their children with basic physical and emotional care and protection.

*On a sheet of paper, write the numbers 6–11. Write **True** or **False** for each statement. If the statement is false, change the underlined word to make it true.*

Lesson 3 Your Friends and Peers

6. When you can depend on a person to keep promises, that person is <u>reliable</u>.

7. <u>Cooperation</u> is the influence to take on behaviors and/or beliefs of your peers.

Lesson 4 Refusal Skills

8. The <u>T.A.L.K.</u> strategy can help you say no when you face a high-pressure situation.

9. The active choice not to participate in high-risk behaviors is <u>abstinence</u>.

Lesson 5 Resolving Conflicts

10. An opinion or fear formed without having facts or firsthand knowledge is known as <u>tolerance</u>.

11. The process of talking about a conflict and deciding how to reach a compromise is called <u>peer mediation</u>.

Thinking Critically

Using complete sentences, answer the following questions on a sheet of paper.

12. **Recognize** Mike and his sister Meg are having a dispute. Mike waits patiently for Meg to finish speaking before he speaks. What type of skill is Mike demonstrating?

Go Online Visit glencoe.com and take the Online Quiz for Chapter 3.

13. **Give Examples** What is an example of peer pressure that can positively affect your health?

Write About It

14. **Personal or Descriptive Writing** Write a letter of appreciation to someone in your family. In your letter, identify what he or she did, and tell how it made you feel.

15. **Descriptive Writing** Write a paragraph describing the positive character traits of a good friend. How can a good friend influence you in positive ways? Use specific examples in your paragraph.

Applying Technology

Teaching T.A.L.K.

Work in small groups to create an iMovie® clip that models how to deal with high-pressure situations using T.A.L.K.

- Create a script that shows ways to avoid harmful situations.
- Rehearse, videotape, and import the script to a new iMovie® file.
- Add titles that highlight conflict prevention and resolution.
- Edit the clip for accuracy of information and clarity.
- Save your clip.

Standardized Test Practice

Reading

Read the passage and then answer the questions.

Every culture of the world uses body language. In many cultures, people are not aware of their body's "messages." In some, however, people go to great lengths to "speak" through their bodies. In one culture, for example, people at work never smile. To outsiders, they may look angry. Actually, smiling on the job means you are not serious about your work.

Sometimes, misunderstandings arise over gestures and posture. Americans, for example, like to put space between themselves and those they're speaking with. In the Middle East, this posture is interpreted differently. It means you are not interested in what the speaker is saying.

Facial expressions can also have different interpretations. In the United States, it is rude to stare. In Greece, people feel ignored if they are not stared at in public. Europeans usually change their facial expression to show happiness, anger, boredom, and sadness. In Asia, facial expressions change less frequently.

TEST-TAKING TIP

Read the passage carefully once to find out what information it contains. After you read each question, look back at the passage to find the answer.

1. Which best sums up the author's purpose?
   A. To show that body language differs among cultures
   B. To show that Americans are viewed as rude worldwide
   C. To show that body language is meaningless
   D. To show that facial expression is less important than posture

2. If you stare at someone in Greece, he or she is likely to
   A. become angry.
   B. feel ignored.
   C. feel as though you are paying attention to him or her.
   D. feel as though you are being rude.

4 Nutrition

Chapter Preview

▲ **Working with the Photo**

Learning how to analyze the nutrition information on food labels can help you make healthy food choices. **What important nutrition information is provided on a packaged food label?**

Start-Up Activities

Before You Read Do you make healthy food choices? To find out, take the health inventory below. Keep a record of your answers.

HEALTH INVENTORY

1. I drink water every day.
(a) always   (b) sometimes   (c) never

2. I make sure to eat breakfast.
(a) always   (b) sometimes   (c) never

3. I try to limit the amount of fat I eat.
(a) always   (b) sometimes   (c) never

4. I try to maintain a weight that is healthy for me.
(a) always   (b) sometimes   (c) never

FOLDABLES Study Organizer

As You Read Make this Foldable® to help you organize the material in Lesson 1 on nutrients. Begin with a plain sheet of 8½″ × 11″ paper or one sheet of notebook paper.

1 Fold the sheet of paper along the long axis, leaving a ½″ tab along the side.

2 Turn the paper, and fold into thirds.

3 Cut the top layer along both folds. Then cut each tab in half to make six tabs.

4 Turn the paper vertically, and label the tabs as shown. Under the appropriate tab, write down major concepts, definitions, and food sources of each type of nutrient.

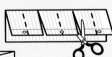

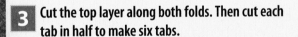
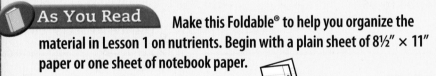

Go Online Visit **glencoe.com** and use the eFlashcards to preview Chapter 4 vocabulary terms.

Your Body's Nutrient Needs

📖 Guide to Reading

● Building Vocabulary
You may already know the meaning of some words in the list below. Write each word and what you think it means.

- nutrients (p. 94)
- nutrition (p. 94)
- carbohydrates (p. 95)
- fiber (p. 95)
- proteins (p. 95)
- fats (p. 95)
- vitamins (p. 96)
- minerals (p. 96)

● Focusing on the Main Ideas
In this lesson, you will learn to

- **identify** the six main classes of nutrients.
- **determine** what foods you can eat to obtain the nutrients you need.
- **recognize** foods high in fiber.

● Reading Strategy
Classifying Using the diagram to the right as a guide, create a concept map that identifies the main nutrient classes.

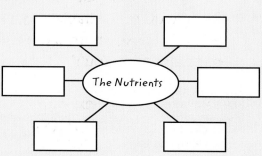

FOLDABLES Study Organizer Use the Foldable® on p. 93 as you read this lesson.

uick Write

Make a list of the foods you eat often. What do you think influences your food choices?

Nutrients and Nutrition

How is your body like a car? It needs fuel in order to run. The fuel your body uses comes from food, or more specifically from nutrients (NOO·tree·ents). **Nutrients** are *substances in food that your body needs to carry out its normal functions.*

Which nutrients does your body need? The answer to that question is the subject of nutrition (noo·TRIH·shun). **Nutrition** is *the process of taking in food and using it for energy, growth, and good health.* There are more than 40 kinds

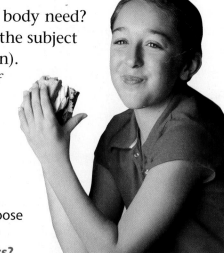

▶ The nutrients in the foods you choose give you energy. **What is another important role of these nutrients?**

of nutrients. A balanced nutrition program includes a variety of foods containing different nutrients, which help you maintain appropriate weight and energy levels, and contribute to your overall wellness.

All nutrients are grouped into one of six categories: *carbohydrates, proteins, fats, vitamins, minerals,* and *water.*

Carbohydrates

The fuel your body gets the best mileage from is carbohydrates (kar·boh·HY·drayts). **Carbohydrates** are *sugars and starches contained in foods.* Carbohydrates are your body's primary energy source.

There are two main types of carbohydrate. *Simple carbohydrates,* or sugars, are found in fruits, milk, and table sugar. *Complex carbohydrates,* or starches, are found in bread, rice, pasta, beans, and other vegetables. Your body cannot use these nutrients directly. First, it must break them down through the process of *digestion.* You'll learn more about digestion in Chapter 7.

Another type of complex carbohydrate, fiber, cannot be digested. **Fiber** is *the tough, stringy part of raw fruits, raw vegetables, whole wheat, and other whole grains.* Fiber helps carry wastes out of your body.

Proteins

Proteins (PROH·teenz) are *nutrients that provide the building blocks your body needs for growth.* Proteins promote healing and aid in the repair of tissues. Protein sources include fish, chicken, beef, eggs, milk, and most other dairy products. You can also get protein from beans, nuts, and most soy-based products.

Fats

This may surprise you, but did you know your body needs some fat? **Fats** are *nutrients found in fatty animal tissue and plant oils.* Fats carry certain vitamins in your bloodstream and help keep your skin healthy. Fats are a source of energy for your body. They also help you feel full after a meal.

Although fats are important, you only need small amounts in your diet. Eating too many foods that are high in fat can contribute to health problems, such as heart disease and some kinds of cancer. These conditions usually appear later in life. Yet, they can often be traced to unhealthy habits developed earlier in life. Salad dressings, cookies, and fried foods are often high in fat. Eat only small amounts of these foods.

▼ Eating a variety of different nutrients is important to good health. **Which of these foods do you enjoy eating?**

Vitamins

Vitamins (VY·tuh·muhnz) are *nutrients that help regulate body functions.* Your body needs only tiny amounts of these nutrients. Vitamins help your body use other nutrients and some help fight disease.

Many foods are naturally rich in vitamins. This includes many fruits and vegetables, such as oranges, carrots, and broccoli. Whole-grain breads and meats are also excellent sources of some vitamins.

Some vitamins, such as vitamin C and the B-complex vitamins, need to be replaced daily. Other vitamins—including Vitamins A, D, E, and K—are stored in your body. Vitamin A is important for good vision. Vitamin D promotes strong bones and teeth.

Minerals

Minerals (MIN·uh·ruhlz) are *elements in foods that help your body work properly.* Like vitamins, minerals are needed only in small amounts. Calcium is a mineral that helps build strong bones and teeth. Calcium is important during the teen years but also throughout your life. So is the iron found in red meats, beans, and other foods. Iron carries oxygen to your cells, which produces energy for your body.

Some people take supplements to get extra vitamins and minerals. However, food sources are best. Eating a variety of foods will help you get the nutrients you need. Always check with a parent or guardian before taking any vitamin or mineral supplements. **Figure 4.1** provides additional information on vitamins and minerals important to teens.

▼ **FIGURE 4.1**

Most teens don't get enough of the nutrients shown. **Which foods in the chart are part of your regular eating plan?**

	Vitamins	Minerals	Food Sources
✓	**Vitamin A**		Dark green leafy vegetables (such as spinach), milk and other dairy products, carrots, apricots, eggs, liver
✓	**Vitamin B$_{12}$**		Eggs, meat, poultry, fish, dairy products, some soy products
✓	**Vitamin C**		Oranges, grapefruits, cantaloupe, strawberries, mangoes, cabbage, broccoli
✓	**Vitamin E**		Fortified ready-to-eat cereals, peanut butter, almonds
✓		**Calcium**	Milk, fortified ready-to-eat cereals, oatmeal, canned salmon
✓		**Potassium**	Baked potato, peaches, bananas
✓		**Magnesium**	Pumpkin seeds, cashews, almonds

Water

Did you know that about 45 to 75 percent of the body is water? Water is essential to life. It carries other nutrients around your body. It helps with digestion, removes waste, and cools you off. The amount of water you need to drink depends on how much water you are getting from food, and other liquids, and how much you sweat from physical activity. Drink when you are thirsty and with meals to help your body get enough water. You can also get water from many foods and from beverages such as milk. See **Figure 4.2** for some examples of foods with a high water content.

 Reading Check **Explain** Why is water important for your body?

▼ FIGURE 4.2

WATER, WATER EVERYWHERE

Most of the weight of the foods shown is from water. **What other nutrients do you think these foods contain?**

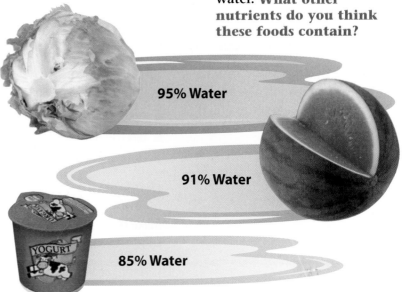

95% Water

91% Water

85% Water

Lesson 1 Review

After You Read

Review this lesson for new terms, major headings, and Reading Checks.

What I Learned

1. *Vocabulary* Define the term *nutrition*. Use it in an original sentence.

2. *Identify* Name the six categories of nutrients.

3. *Recall* Why is calcium important to your body?

Thinking Critically

4. *Hypothesize* How might your knowledge of nutrients influence your snack food choices?

5. *Analyze* Record what you eat for one day. Remember to count the cups of water you drink. What nutrients have you eaten? What improvements, if any, can you make?

Applying Health Skills

6. *Accessing Information* Use the Internet to research foods that are high in fiber. Identify three examples of whole grains, fruits, and vegetables that are high in fiber. Then, find all of the high-fiber foods in your house. How many foods did you find? Is your family eating enough high-fiber foods?

Following a Healthful Eating Plan

In a paragraph, explain why you think it is important to eat a variety of foods.

The MyPyramid Food Guidance System

Have you ever been inside a mega-supermarket? These giant food warehouses have thousands of foods and food products to choose from. How do you know which foods give your body the nutrients it needs?

The United States Department of Agriculture (USDA) publishes information to help you make the best food choices for your health. One source of information appears in **Figure 4.3.** This is the **MyPyramid food guidance system,** *a system designed to help Americans make healthful food choices.* Where do the foods you eat fit on the MyPyramid system?

◀ Food supermarkets offer many choices. **How can product labels help you tell which foods will help your body meet its nutrient needs?**

MyPyramid is a colorful graphic, meant to provide healthful reminders. One is that you should eat a variety of foods. Each color band stands for a different food group. The bands are different widths, meaning that you need more of some types of food than others. Another reminder appears in the form of the figure going up the stairs. This is to remind you to make regular physical activity part of your lifestyle.

 **Reading Check**   **Identify** What does the MyPyramid graphic remind people to do?

▼ **FIGURE 4.3**

MYPYRAMID FOOD GUIDANCE SYSTEM

The MyPyramid food guidance system can help you make healthful food choices. **Why are some color bands wider than others?**

MyPyramid
STEPS TO A HEALTHIER YOU

| GRAINS | VEGETABLES | FRUITS | MILK | MEAT & BEANS |
| Make half your grains whole | Vary your veggies | Focus on fruits | Get your calcium-rich foods | Go lean with protein |

Academic Vocabulary

gender (JEN der) *(noun)* the condition of being male or female. *Gender, weight, and age are three components to consider when determining your daily caloric intake.*

Go Online

Topic: MyPyramid

Visit glencoe.com for Student Web Activities that will help you develop a personal eating plan using MyPyramid.

Activity: Using the information from the link above, create a personal eating plan based on your age, gender, and activity level.

A Closer Look at MyPyramid

The idea behind MyPyramid is not to avoid certain foods. Rather, it is a tool designed to help each person develop a personal eating plan based on calorie needs. A **calorie** is *a unit of heat that measures the energy available in foods.* Your body converts the calories it receives from the foods you eat into energy. The amount of calories your body needs is based on your age, **gender**, and how physically active you are.

If you are physically active on most days, your body needs more calories than it would if you were not physically active. MyPyramid estimates that females between the ages of 9 and 13 need 1,600 to 2,200 calories per day, based on activity level. Males in the same age group need 1,800 to 2,600 calories per day.

Your main source of calories should come from nutrient-rich foods. MyPyramid lets you know how much of which foods to eat in order to stay healthy. The diagonal color bands on the pyramid represent the different food groups that you should be eating. These foods are shown by the broad color bands: orange, green, red, blue, and purple. Figure 4.3 shows examples of foods for each color group. These represent just a few of the many foods that can help you meet your daily food group recommendations.

The following is an example of what a moderately active teen should eat. If you are very active most days, you may need to eat a little more. Likewise, if you are less active or not at all active, you may need to eat less.

- **Grains—the Orange Group:** Girls should have five to seven 1-ounce equivalents of grain products each day. Foods in the grain group are high in fiber, an important nutrient. Boys should have six to nine 1-ounce equivalents. In general, 1 slice of bread, 1 cup cold cereal, or ½ cup cooked rice, pasta, or cooked cereal is equal to 1 ounce from the grains group. Half of these choices should come from whole-grain foods such as whole wheat bread.

- **Vegetables—the Green Group:** Most boys need 2½ to 3½ cups of vegetables a day, girls 2 to 3 cups. When eating leafy greens such as lettuce, 2 cups is equal to 1 cup of vegetables.

- **Fruits—the Red Group:** Most girls and boys should have 1½ to 2 cups from this group daily. When eating dried fruit such as raisins, ½ cup is equal to 1 cup from the fruit group.

- **Milk—the Blue Group:** Boys and girls should have 3 cups of milk or other foods made from milk. In general, 1 cup of yogurt, 1½ ounces of natural cheese, or 2 ounces of processed cheese is equal to 1 cup from the milk group.

- **Meats and Beans—the Purple Group:** Most girls should have 5 to 6 ounces from the meat or beans group every day. Most boys should have 5 to 6½ ounces. In general, 1 egg, 1 tablespoon of peanut butter, ¼ cup of cooked beans, or ½ ounce of nuts is equal to 1 ounce from the meat and beans group.

Notice the narrow yellow color band in MyPyramid. This group represents oils and other fats you should eat in only very small amounts. Examples include vegetable oil, salad dressing, and mayonnaise. In the next lesson, you will learn how to include high-fat foods in a healthy eating plan.

 **Reading Check** **Explain** How can MyPyramid help you develop a healthy eating plan?

 **Go Online**

Visit **glencoe.com** and complete the Interactive Study Guide for Lesson 2.

Lesson 2 Review

 After You Read

Review this lesson for new terms, major headings, and Reading Checks.

What I Learned

1. *Vocabulary* What is the *MyPyramid food guidance system*?

2. *Explain* Why does your level of activity affect how many calories your body needs?

3. *Recall* How many cups of fruit should a moderately active 12-year-old eat per day? How many cups of vegetables?

Thinking Critically

4. *Synthesize* Use MyPyramid to compare and contrast different food options. Consider ethnic, vegetarian, and holiday foods.

5. *Analyze* Stacy had a cup of milk at breakfast and a cup of yogurt after school. How many more cups from the milk group does she need to meet her daily recommendation?

Applying Health Skills

6. *Analyzing Influences* As you watch television, describe an advertisement you see about food. What does the advertisement tell you about the food? Does it make you want to try the food? Use your findings to discuss how television influences eating habits.

Lesson 3

Making Healthful Food Choices

Guide to Reading

● Building Vocabulary
How are the terms below related? As you read the lesson, write the definitions in your notebook.

- saturated fats (p. 106)
- cholesterol (p. 106)
- trans fats (p. 106)
- sodium (p. 107)

● Focusing on the Main Ideas
In this lesson, you will learn to

- **recognize** influences on your food choices.
- **identify** guidelines to make healthy food choices.
- **analyze** key nutrients in a food product.

● Reading Strategy
Identifying Cause-and-Effect Identify three factors that you think cause people to be overweight. As you read, notice which of these factors is or is not mentioned.

Quick Write

Write about your current eating habits. What kind of foods do you eat most often? What kind of snacks do you usually eat?

Your Food Choices and You

What does the statement "You are what you eat" mean to you? The foods you choose to eat affect your health. Eating too much of certain foods can lead to health problems. As a teen, you need a variety of foods that give your body nutrients to grow and be healthy. Eating a variety of foods helps your body work better and gives you energy for school and other activities.

Your Eating Habits and Influences

As a teen, your body is growing rapidly. Your nutrient needs right now are great. To make sure you're meeting those needs, look closely at your eating habits. This includes being aware of what you eat and when. When you are hungry, do you reach for a piece of fruit or a bag of potato chips? Do you snack, for example, while watching TV?

Have you ever thought about why you eat the foods you do? There are several factors that influence your food choices, including the taste, texture, and appearance of food. Your appetite also influences the foods you choose. *Appetite* is an emotional desire for certain foods or flavors.

Other influences include friends, family, **culture**, and the need for convenience. One big influence on many people's food choices is the media. Advertisers often use health claims on food labels to get you to buy a product. However, these claims may not accurately represent the nutritional value of the product. A product that claims to be "made with whole grains" may have only a small amount of whole-grains. You can evaluate a health claim on a fool label by reading the ingredient list and the Nutrition Facts panel. Complete the Health Skills Activity on page 104 to learn more about the Nutrition Facts panel.

Reading Check **List** Name four factors that influence a person's eating habits.

Guidelines for Healthy Teens

How can you make sure you're getting the nutrients you need? One way that you've already read about is the MyPyramid food guidance system. MyPyramid reflects the scientific advice in the *Dietary Guidelines for Americans*. These guidelines encourage people ages two and up to develop a healthy lifestyle. The *Dietary Guidelines* give the following advice on choosing healthy foods and staying active.

Eat a Variety of Foods

Adding variety to your eating plan is one way to make eating more fun. It can also help you get the nutrients your body needs. Use your imagination or try ethnic foods and vegetarian dishes. Ask a parent or guardian for help.

Control the Amount You Eat

Pay attention to the portion sizes and calories that you are eating. Remember that one slice of bread is equal to 1 ounce. If you eat a sandwich with two slices of bread, you are eating 2 ounces and double the calories. Only consume as many calories as your body needs. Healthy teens will normally gain weight as they grow and develop. However, if you take in more calories than your body needs, you could gain more weight than is healthy for your body.

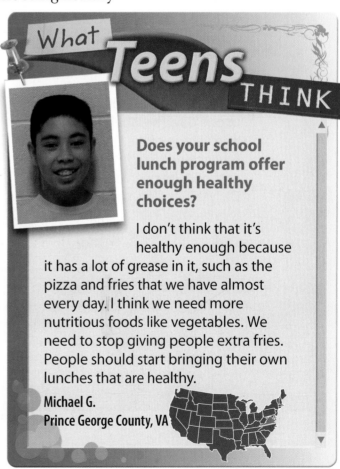

What **Teens** THINK

Does your school lunch program offer enough healthy choices?

I don't think that it's healthy enough because it has a lot of grease in it, such as the pizza and fries that we have almost every day. I think we need more nutritious foods like vegetables. We need to stop giving people extra fries. People should start bringing their own lunches that are healthy.

Michael G.
Prince George County, VA

Academic Vocabulary

culture (KUHL chur) *(noun)* the beliefs and traditions of a group of people. *Sinaz and Karmel talked about Persian culture during their history presentation.*

Health Skills Activity

Accessing Information

Mastering Nutrition Facts

How can you tell how many calories a packaged food has? The answer is to look at the Nutrition Facts label on the product's package. This will tell you how many calories are in a label serving, which nutrients, and how much of those nutrients the product contains. Some common terms used on food labels are:

- **Serving Size** is the amount of food in one label serving. How many cups are in one serving of this product?

- **Servings per Container** is the number of servings the package contains. How many servings are in this product?

- **Calories** shown on the label reflect the number of calories in one serving. If the product contains two servings and you ate the whole product, you would consume twice the number of calories.

- **Daily Values** is the amount of a nutrient a person needs in one day. The label shows a percentage of the Daily Value for each nutrient in a serving of food. What percent of the Daily Value of Vitamin A does this product contain, based on a 2,000-calorie diet?

Nutrition Facts	
Serving Size 1 cup (226g)	
Servings Per Container 2	
Amount Per Serving	
Calories 250	Calories from Fat 110
	% Daily Value*
Total Fat 12g	18%
Saturated Fat 3g	15%
Trans Fat 3g	
Cholesterol 30mg	10%
Sodium 470mg	20%
Potassium 700mg	20%
Total Carbohydrate 31g	10%
Dietary Fiber 0g	0%
Sugar 10g	
Protein 5g	
Vitamin A 4%	Vitamin C 2%
Calcium 2%	Iron 4%

*Percent Daily Values are based on a 2,000 calorie diet. Your Daily Values may be higher or lower depending on your calorie needs.

	Calories	2,000	2,500
Total Fat	Less than	65g	80g
Sat Fat	Less than	20g	25g
Cholesterol	Less than	300mg	300mg
Sodium	Less than	2,400mg	2,400mg
Total Carbohydrate		300g	375g
Dietary Fiber		25g	30g

With a Group

Analyze the Nutrition Facts label shown above. Which nutrients does this product contain? If you ate this entire food product, how many calories would you consume? How much of each nutrient would you consume, based on a 2,000-calorie-per-day diet?

Be Physically Active

To maintain a healthy weight, you should balance the food you eat with physical activity. Teens should be physically active for at least one hour on most days. Physical activity helps you burn off some of the calories you consume. It also builds strength and helps you feel good about yourself. What are some ways you can add physical activity into your day?

Keep Foods Safe to Eat

"Wait, you better use another cutting board!" Gail warned Philip. Her brother was about to cut up vegetables on a board he had just used for cutting raw meat.

Gail was right. Using the same cutting board or even the same knife, without washing them first, can spread germs. This is one rule of food safety. Here are some others:

- Wash your hands before handling food. Wash them again if you are about to handle a different kind of food.

- Separate raw, cooked, and ready-to-eat foods while shopping for, preparing, or storing them.

- Cook meat, chicken, turkey, and fish to safe internal temperatures. Use a meat thermometer to check internal temperatures. Refrigerate leftovers right away after meals. Both these actions will help stop the growth of germs. See **Figure 4.4** for safe food temperatures.

- Make sure reheated foods are at least 140°F.

Choose Foods Wisely

The *Dietary Guidelines for Americans* contains additional tips for making wise food choices. Some of these tips are explored in the following sections.

Eat More Fruits, Vegetables, and Whole Grains. Try "coloring" your plate with green, orange, red, and yellow vegetables and fruit at mealtimes. As for grains, here is a tip to remember: make at least half your grains whole. These include whole wheat breads and crackers, oatmeal, and brown rice.

▼ FIGURE 4.4

FOOD TEMPERATURES

Foods should be cooked and stored at safe temperatures. **How does this help keep foods safe to eat?**

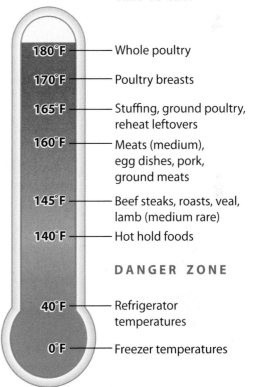

180°F	Whole poultry
170°F	Poultry breasts
165°F	Stuffing, ground poultry, reheat leftovers
160°F	Meats (medium), egg dishes, pork, ground meats
145°F	Beef steaks, roasts, veal, lamb (medium rare)
140°F	Hot hold foods
	DANGER ZONE
40°F	Refrigerator temperatures
0°F	Freezer temperatures

► Some of the calories you take in are burned off during physical activity. If you take in more calories than you burn, you gain weight. **What happens if you take in fewer calories?**

Careers for the 21st Century

Dietetic Technician

Dietetic technicians assist dietitians to educate patients on proper nutrition. They often use computer programs to help them track and assess patients' dietary needs. Many nursing homes employ dietetic technicians to develop nutrition plans for residents. Dietetic technicians will be in greater demand as more is learned about improving health through diet. You can prepare for this career by taking biology, chemistry, and nutrition courses.

What skills does a dietetic technician need? Go to *Career Corner* at glencoe.com to find out.

Know Your Fats. Did you know that some fats are more healthful than others? A fatty oil found in salmon and other fish may actually promote heart health; so does olive oil when used in reasonable amounts. These fats are mostly unsaturated. Saturated (SAT·chur·ay·tuhd) fats, on the other hand, should be limited. **Saturated fats** are *fats found in many animal products such as butter, meat, and cheese.* Eating too much saturated fat may increase your body's level of cholesterol (kuh·LES·tuh·rawl). **Cholesterol** is *a waxy chemical our bodies produce and need in small amounts.* Too much, however, can lead to heart disease and stroke. Another fat to limit is trans fats. **Trans fats** *start off as oils and are made solid through processing.* Like saturated fats, trans fats are linked to heart problems.

Limit Added Sugars. You already know that foods like soda, cookies, and cake have added sugar. But, did you know that sugar is also added to salad dressing and bread? Foods with added sugar often have little nutritional value. So, it's better to reach for a piece of fruit when you want something sweet to snack on, because fruit is high in nutrients. If you are thirsty, it's better to reach for a glass of water or some fruit juice than a sugary soda. However, if you are going to drink fruit juice, remember to choose 100 percent fruit juice. Fruit-flavored drinks that are not 100 percent juice can be high in added sugars.

Reading Check

Compare What is the difference between a nutritious and nonnutritious beverage? Give an example of each.

Limit Salt. Watch your intake of salt. Salt contains **sodium,** *a mineral that helps control the amount of fluid in your body.* Too much sodium can promote high blood pressure in some people. You can find out how much sodium is in a given amount of food by reading the label.

 Reading Check **Identify** Give two pieces of advice from the *Dietary Guidelines for Americans.*

Tips on Snacks

Snacks are an important part of eating for teens on the go. Just try to keep them healthy. Peanuts or other nuts provide protein. They can give you more nutrients than a candy bar. Tuck a small box of dried fruits, such as raisins, into your backpack. Fresh fruit or frozen juice bars made from 100 percent juice also make great snacks. Healthy snacks will provide some of the nutrients your body needs.

 Reading Check **Give Examples** What is one example of a healthy snack?

Visit **glencoe.com** and complete the Interactive Study Guide for Lesson 3.

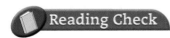 **Lesson 3 Review**

 After You Read

Review this lesson for new terms, major headings, and Reading Checks.

What I Learned

1. *List* Name two foods that contain saturated fats.

2. *Recall* Why is limiting salt and fat important?

3. *Identify* Briefly explain the advice given by the Dietary Guidelines for Americans. How do these guidelines affect eating behaviors?

Thinking Critically

4. *Analyze* Using advertisements found in newspapers, magazines, or on television, create a list of terms used in food advertisements and write a definition for each term. How do you think these terms affect a shopper's decision to buy a food item?

5. *Hypothesize* Todd, who is active in sports, burns 2,500 calories a day. He eats about 2,500 calories a day. His diet is nutritionally balanced. How will Todd benefit now and in the future if he keeps up this routine?

Applying Health Skills

6. *Analyzing Influences* Research common health claims found on food labels. Look at the food items you have at home and try to find one that contains at least one of the health claims you have identified. Evaluate the health claim as accurate and valid, or true, by reading the ingredient list and the Nutrition Facts label. Write a paragraph on your evaluation.

Managing Your Weight

Guide to Reading

● **Building Vocabulary**
List each term below in your notebook. As you come across it in your reading, write the definition.

■ body image (p. 109)
■ eating disorder (p. 110)

● **Focusing on the Main Ideas**
In this lesson, you will learn to

■ **explain** how to maintain a healthy weight.
■ **identify** problem eating behaviors.
■ **demonstrate** decision-making skills to help a friend.

● **Reading Strategy**

Predicting Look over the headings in this lesson. Write a question that you think the lesson will answer. After reading, check to see if your question was answered.

Quick Write

In a few sentences, tell what you think the benefits are of maintaining a healthful weight.

Achieving a Healthful Weight

Knowing the weight that is right for you is tricky during the teen years. That's because your body is growing so fast. The only way to tell for sure is to see a health professional. This person can help you determine if your weight and body composition are within a healthy range. Your *body composition* is the fat, bone, muscle, and fluid that make up your body weight. Generally, a healthy body has more bone, muscle, and fluid than fat.

To keep your weight and body composition within a healthy range, choose healthy foods, control the amount of food you eat, and stay physically active to help you burn off some of the calories you take in. If you are concerned about your weight, talk to your doctor. He or she can help you create a healthful eating and physical activity plan.

 Reading Check **Explain** How can you maintain a healthy weight?

Weight Problems and Teens

The number of overweight young people has risen dramatically in the past 20 years. Being overweight can make physical activity more difficult and tiring. Your self-esteem can be negatively affected, too. Some children and teens are becoming *obese* (oh·BEES), which means they are significantly overweight. People who are obese have a very high amount of body fat. This puts them at risk for developing other diseases such as diabetes and heart disease. You will learn more about these diseases in Chapter 11.

Treatment for Obese Teens

Obesity is a serious disease. Teens who are obese should be under a doctor's care, because the extra weight they carry around puts them at risk for developing other health problems. These teens should reach a healthy weight slowly. Sometimes, the best approach is to keep from gaining more weight as your body grows.

 **Reading Check** **Explain** How is obesity a risk factor for other diseases?

Body Image and the Teen Years

Do you see yourself as overweight? Underweight? Just right? Maybe you feel some parts of you are too wide or too narrow. Feelings like these are tied to your body image. **Body image** is *how you view your body*. Like your self-concept, your body image may differ from how others see you. You may feel you are too thin or not thin enough. You might compare yourself to people in the media. Making this comparison leads some teens to develop a negative body image. It is important to know that most people do not look like the people you see on television or in magazines. Instead of comparing yourself to others, try to be realistic about your body. No two people have the exact same body composition. Remember that bodies come in all shapes and sizes. Take care of your body by following a balanced nutrition program and staying active. Following a balanced nutrition program will ensure you receive the nutrients that are essential to staying healthy. These habits will help you look and feel better.

 **Reading Check** **Define** What is body image?

▶ Weight problems in teens can lead to other health problems. **What are some health problems that can develop from being overweight?**

ACTIVITY
DEVELOPING
Good Character

Respect for Others' Bodies and Feelings

Some teens tease peers who are overweight or underweight. They may make hurtful comments or use impolite nicknames. This type of behavior shows a lack of respect. It is a form of bullying or bias, or acting cruelly to those who look different. A person who does this is not demonstrating good character. **What advice would you give a person who was behaving this way?**

Eating Disorders

Some teens, and even some adults, become overly concerned with their body weight. They may have a negative body image. They may feel they need to lose weight, even when they don't. These people are at risk for developing an eating disorder. An **eating disorder** is an *extreme eating behavior that can seriously damage the body.* Eating disorders are most common among teen girls and young women. However, males can develop them as well. Two of the most common eating disorders are *anorexia nervosa* (an·uh·REK·see·uh ner·VOH·suh) and *bulimia* (boo·LEE·mee·uh) *nervosa.*

People with anorexia are overly concerned with weight gain. They may starve themselves. They eat far fewer calories than they need to stay healthy. They may exercise excessively. Even after they have become dangerously thin, they still see themselves as overweight.

People with bulimia eat large amounts of food, then "purge" themselves, which means they rid their bodies of food by vomiting or taking *laxatives.* These are medicines meant for people who have trouble moving their bowels. Victims of bulimia also may exercise excessively to burn off the calories from the foods they eat. They often stay the same weight, so it can be difficult to tell if someone has bulimia

▲ Having a healthy body image is important to good mental/emotional health. **What are some ways you can develop a healthy body image?**

Go Online

Visit **glencoe.com** and complete the Interactive Study Guide for Lesson 4.

Treatment for Eating Disorders

Eating disorders are mental health problems. They are often associated with a negative body image. Eating disorders can affect normal growth and development. They can lead to serious health problems, such as nervousness, hair loss, heart and kidney failure, and even death. If you are concerned that you or someone you know may have an eating disorder, talk to a trusted adult. A person with an eating disorder should get help right away. The sooner a person gets treatment, the better his or her chances are of recovering.

 **Reading Check**

Compare How are anorexia nervosa and bulimia nervosa similar? How are they different?

Health Skills Activity

Decision Making

Help for a Friend with an Eating Disorder

Kara and Rachel have been friends since kindergarten. Lately, Rachel has begun to notice some changes in Kara. During lunch, Kara hardly eats anything. She claims she is not hungry. She also seems to be getting very thin. Rachel is beginning to worry that Kara may have an eating disorder. Rachel isn't sure whether she should talk to Kara about her concerns or tell someone else.

What Would You Do?

Apply the six steps of decision making to Rachel's problem. Tell what decision you would make if you were Rachel, and why.

1. State the situation.
2. List the options.
3. Weigh the possible outcomes.
4. Consider your values.
5. Make a decision and act on it.
6. Evaluate the decision.

Lesson 4 Review

After You Read

Review this lesson for new terms, major headings, and Reading Checks.

What I Learned

1. *Vocabulary* What is the difference between being obese and just being overweight?

2. *Recall* Name two eating disorders.

3. *Explain* Why is it important to develop a realistic body image?

Thinking Critically

4. *Analyze* What are the physical and mental consequences of a poorly balanced diet?

5. *Apply* Ryan has created an exercise plan to help him achieve a healthy weight. Why is it important for Ryan to start exercising slowly?

Applying Health Skills

6. *Analyzing Influences* Explain how images in the media might play a role in a teen's body image.

What Steps Can You Take To Make Healthy Decisions?

The decision-making process can help you make healthy and responsible choices. The six steps of the decision-making process are:

- State the situation.
- List the options.
- Weigh the possible outcomes.
- Consider your values.
- Make a decision and act on it.
- Evaluate the decision.

Choosing Health-Promoting Foods

Follow the Model, Practice, and Apply steps to help you master this important health skill.

Model

Read about how Teri uses decision making when deciding whether to buy a salad or a burger.

Teri was having lunch at the mall with friends. She wanted a salad, but the line was long. "You need to hurry so we can get to our movie on time, Corey said." Teri decided to use the decision-making process to help her choose.

Step 1. State the Situation.

I want a salad, but the line is long. My friends are bugging me to get something quickly.

Step 2. List the Options.

I could wait and meet my friends at the movie theater. I could have a burger and do something more healthful tomorrow.

Step 3. Weigh the Possible Outcomes.

I'm having pizza for dinner with my family. I want something for lunch that has less fat.

Step 4. Consider Your Values.

Eating right is important to me.

Step 5. Make a Decision and Act on It.

I will wait in the salad line and ask my friends to save me a seat at the movie theater.

Step 6. Evaluate the Decision.

I feel good about my choice.

② Practice

Read about the problem Dana faced when she wanted a quick snack before soccer practice.

Dana had to be at soccer practice by 4:00 p.m. It was now 3:45 p.m. Dana wanted something that would give her a quick energy boost. She studied the choices in the school vending machine. She knew the snack cake was a source of energy but had added sugar and could also be high in fat. The other choices included peanut butter crackers, potato chips, and candy bars. Write out the decision-making steps to help Dana choose a snack.

③ Apply

Apply what you have learned about decision making to complete the activity below.

Think of a situation in which you need to decide what to eat. One possibility might be choosing what to eat for breakfast. Think about the type of food you generally choose in this situation. Is your usual choice healthy? Are there healthier foods you could choose? Show your decision by using the six-step decision-making process. Explain how your choice enhances your health.

Self-Check
- Did I list several food choices?
- Did I use each step in the decision-making process?
- Did I explain how my choice enhances my health?

Jars of Sugar

Do you know how much sugar you consume when you grab a quick drink or snack? The following table lists the amount of sugar, in grams, that you might find in several popular foods.

Food	Grams of Sugar
Cola (12 oz.)	42
Fat-free, fruit yogurt (8 oz.)	35
Light popcorn (1 c.)	0
Fruit punch drink (8 oz.)	27
Sweetened breakfast cereal (¾ c.)	15
Three reduced-fat chocolate sandwich cookies	14
Chocolate candy bar (1.55 oz.)	40

What You Will Need

- Seven empty baby food jars
- Container of sugar
- Set of measuring spoons

What You Will Do

1 Note that 5 grams of sugar is equivalent to 1 level teaspoon of sugar; 1 gram is just under ¼ teaspoon; 2 grams is a little under ½ teaspoon.

2 Calculate how many teaspoons of sugar each listed product contains.

3 Using the spoons, measure the amount of sugar in each product. Place that amount in a jar and label the jar.

Wrapping It Up

Evaluate your findings.

Take time out to determine the nutrient content of the foods in each list. Which foods offer the best nutritional value?

Reading Review

Visit glencoe.com to download quizzes and eFlashcards for Chapter 4.

FOLDABLES® Study Organizer

Foldables® and Other Study Aids Take out the Foldable® that you created for Lesson 1 and any graphic organizers that you created for Lessons 1–4. Find a partner, and quiz each other using these study aids.

Lesson 1 Your Body's Nutrient Needs

Main Idea Nutrients are a vital part of maintaining good health.

- Nutrition is the process of taking in food and using it for energy, growth, and good health.
- The six categories of nutrients are carbohydrates, proteins, fats, vitamins, minerals, and water.
- Eating a variety of nutrients is important to a balanced diet.

Lesson 2 Following a Healthful Eating Plan

Main Idea The MyPyramid food guidance system is a helpful reminder for making healthy food choices.

- Each of us should develop personal eating plans based on how many calories we need.
- Grains, vegetables, fruits, milk, and meat and beans are the food groups that make up MyPyramid.

Lesson 3 Making Healthful Food Choices

Main Idea Making healthful food choices helps you feel better and gives you more energy.

- Eating a variety of foods is fun and ensures your body gets the nutrients it needs.
- Pay attention to the amount you eat. Eating more calories than your body needs could cause weight gain that may be unhealthy for your body.
- Physical activity is another healthful choice. It burns off extra calories and builds strength and confidence.

Lesson 4 Managing Your Weight

Main Idea Managing your weight in your teen years can be tricky, but having a balanced eating plan and staying active can help.

- Your body image may differ from how others see you, but remember to be realistic. Bodies come in all shapes and sizes, and a healthy body is always best.
- Obesity can lead to many other health problems.
- An eating disorder is a distortion of body image. The most common eating disorders are anorexia nervosa and bulimia nervosa.

Assessment

 After You Read

HEALTH INVENTORY
Now that you have read the chapter, look back at your answers to the Health Inventory on the chapter opener. Is there anything you should do differently?

Reviewing Vocabulary and Main Ideas

On a sheet of paper, write the numbers 1–5. After each number, write the term from the list that best completes each sentence.

- body image
- calorie
- eating disorder
- minerals
- MyPyramid
- nutrients
- proteins
- saturated fats

Lesson 1 Your Body's Nutrient Needs

1. Nutrients that provide the building blocks your body needs for growth are called _____.

2. _____ are elements in foods that help your body work properly.

3. Substances in food that your body needs to carry out its normal functions are called _____.

Lesson 2 Following a Healthful Eating Plan

4. A _____ is a unit of heat that measures the energy available in foods.

5. _____ is a system designed to help Americans make healthful food choices.

On a sheet of paper, write the numbers 6–9. After each number, write the letter of the answer that best completes each statement.

Lesson 3 Making Healthful Food Choices

6. According to MyPyramid, nutrients provided by the grain group include the following:
   a. complex carbohydrates **c.** fiber
   b. vitamins **d.** all of the above

7. How many cups per day from the milk group is recommended for most teens?
   a. 2 cups **c.** 3 cups
   b. 2½ cups **d.** 4½ cups

Lesson 4 Managing Your Weight

8. Which of the following is true about obesity?
   a. It can make physical activity more difficult and tiring.
   b. It is a health problem that can be corrected quickly.
   c. The number of obese teens has been dropping steadily.

9. Which of the following is true both of people with anorexia and people with bulimia?
   a. They "purge" after eating large amounts of food.
   b. They are overly concerned with weight gain.
   c. They eat far fewer calories than their body needs.

Go Online Visit glencoe.com and take the Online Quiz for Chapter 4.

Thinking Critically

Using complete sentences, answer the following questions on a sheet of paper.

10. **Identify** Why is it important to use a product's Nutrition Facts label to guide your eating habits?

11. **Predict** What are some short- and long-term benefits of healthy eating?

Write About It

12. **Descriptive Writing** Write a paragraph describing how influences can affect your food choices.

13. **Narrative Writing** Write a story about a teen who is concerned about his or her body image. What advice might you give this teen?

Applying Technology

Healthful Eating

You and a partner will use GarageBand™ or Audacity® to create a podcast on nutrition and healthful eating habits. Follow the steps below to complete your project.

- Write a three-minute script in dialogue format explaining the building blocks of nutrition. Include tips on how to make healthful eating habits part of your daily life.
- Open a new podcast project with two audio tracks.
- Record your script. Include lead-in music.
- Edit the track for clarity and content. Make sure your message is clear and effective.
- Save your work.

Standardized Test Practice

Math

The graph below helps you determine which foods give you the most fiber without adding excess calories. Use the graph to answer the questions.

TEST-TAKING TIP

Questions about graphs sometimes rely on outside knowledge. If an answer is not stated directly, try eliminating choices that are clearly wrong.

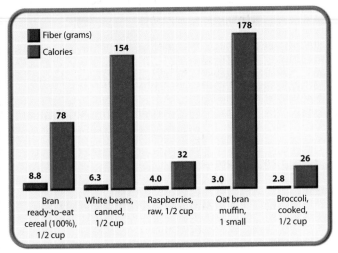

1. How many calories are there in the food with the second highest amount of fiber?

   A. 32   **C.** 178

   B. 154   **D.** None of the above

2. To get the ratio of fiber to calories, you would divide the number of calories by grams of fiber. For example, ½ cup of cooked broccoli has 26 calories and 2.8 grams of fiber. 26 ÷ 2.8 = 9.3, or a ratio of 1 to 9.3. What is the ratio of fiber to calories for ½ cup of raspberries?

   A. 1 to 17   **C.** 1 to 60

   B. 1 to 25   **D.** 1 to 8

Chapter Preview

▲ **Working with the Photo**

Finding something you are good at helps you feel good about yourself. **Can you name some other physical activities?**

Start-Up Activities

Before You Read Is exercise part of your daily routine? Answer the Health eSpotlight questions below and then watch the online video. Keep a record of your answers.

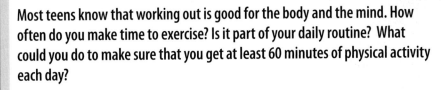

Health eSpotlight

Daily Fitness

Most teens know that working out is good for the body and the mind. How often do you make time to exercise? Is it part of your daily routine? What could you do to make sure that you get at least 60 minutes of physical activity each day?

Go to **glencoe.com** and watch the health video for Chapter 5. Then complete the activity provided with the online video.

FOLDABLES® Study Organizer

As You Read Make this Foldable® to help you organize information about the importance of physical activity. Begin with a sheet of plain 8½" × 11" paper.

1 Fold the sheet of paper along the long axis, leaving a ½" tab along the side.

2 Fold in half, then fold again into fourths.

3 Unfold and cut along the three fold lines on the front flap. Label as shown.

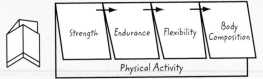

Strength | Endurance | Flexibility | Body Composition

Physical Activity

Record information about strength, endurance, flexibility, and body composition under the appropriate tabs. Give examples of ways to build each element of physical fitness.

Go Online Visit **glencoe.com** and complete the Chapter 5 crossword puzzle.

Physical Activity and Your Health

Guide to Reading

● Building Vocabulary
Some terms below are related or have similar meanings. Can you tell which ones?

- physical activity (p. 120)
- lifestyle activities (p. 121)
- physical fitness (p. 121)
- endurance (p. 123)
- stamina (p. 123)
- strength (p. 123)
- flexibility (p. 124)
- exercise (p. 125)

● Focusing on the Main Ideas
In this lesson, you will learn to

- **explain** the benefits of regular physical activity.
- **identify** the elements of physical fitness.
- **recognize** the two main types of exercise.
- **practice** healthful behaviors with your family.

● Reading Strategy
Organizing Information Create a concept map that captures the main ideas in the lesson. Use the diagram below as a guide.

Physical Activity	
Type of Activity	Builds Endurance, Stamina, Strength, or Flexibility
1. running	1. endurance
2.	2.
3.	3.
4.	4.

FOLDABLES Study Organizer Use the Foldable® on p. 119 as you read this lesson.

uick Write

Write a paragraph about ways you can participate in physical activity at school and in the community.

What Is Physical Activity?

Shannon swims at the community pool every chance she gets. Matt is really into rock climbing. Kate and her friends have started an inline skating club. What do all these teens have in common? They all make physical activity a part of their lives. **Physical activity** is *any kind of movement that causes your body to use energy.*

How about you? Do you participate in regular physical activity? If not, it is never too late to start. Health experts recommend that teens get 60 minutes of physical activity daily. This hour can be done all at once or in moderate to vigorous 10- to 15-minute bursts. What are some ways you could fit 60 minutes of physical activity into your daily routine?

Lifestyle Activities

Do you have daily chores you do at home, such as raking leaves or shoveling snow? Do you enjoy outdoor activities, such as hiking or skateboarding? These are examples of life-style activities. **Lifestyle activities** are *physical activities that are part of your day-to-day routine or recreation.* They can become part of a lifelong commitment to fitness.

The Benefits of Physical Activity

Physical activity helps you use, or burn, calories from the foods you eat. See **Figure 5.1** for examples of how many cal-ories are burned during a variety of activities. Burning calo-ries means your body won't store extra calories as fat. This will help you maintain a healthy weight. Physical activity also contributes to physical fitness. **Physical fitness** is *the ability to handle everyday physical work and play without becom-ing tired.* Being physically fit can reduce your risk of develop-ing certain diseases like diabetes, obesity, and heart disease.

Academic Vocabulary

commitment (kuh MIT muhnt) *(noun)* a promise. *You should make a lifelong commitment to good health.*

▼ FIGURE 5.1

CALORIES BURNED DURING VARIOUS ACTIVITIES

The graph shows how many calories a 100-pound person burns during 60 minutes of different activities. Which activity burns the most calories? Which activity burns the fewest?

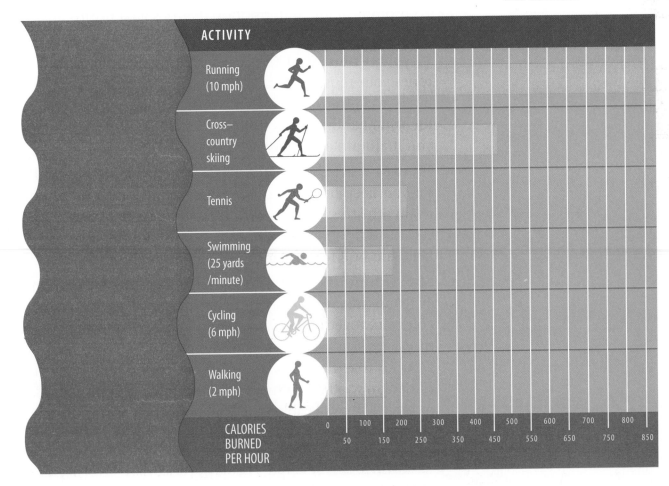

ACTIVITY

- Running (10 mph)
- Cross—country skiing
- Tennis
- Swimming (25 yards /minute)
- Cycling (6 mph)
- Walking (2 mph)

CALORIES BURNED PER HOUR

0   100   200   300   400   500   600   700   800
  50   150   250   350   450   550   650   750   850

Health Skills Activity

Practicing Healthful Behaviors

Fun for the Family

Kiara's family skis every winter. Louis and his family go camping whenever they can. These kinds of outings give family members a chance to spend time together and be physically active. Take camping, for example. Carrying a backpack, finding and carrying wood, and setting up tents all work the body's muscles.

Of course, not all family activities need to take place away from home. Tossing a Frisbee in the backyard, weeding the garden, or taking a walk are all excellent ways to combine physical activity with family time.

On Your Own

Think of an activity you could get your family involved in.

Your physical, mental/emotional, and social health all benefit when you are physically active and fit.

- **Physical benefits.** Physical activity strengthens and tones your muscles. It also strengthens your heart and lungs and builds strong bones. You will have more energy for school and other activities. Physical activity also helps you maintain a healthy weight.

- **Mental/Emotional benefits.** When you are physically fit, you sleep better. You can concentrate longer in school, deal with stress more easily, and get along better with others. In addition, developing new skills and interests can help you build confidence and self-esteem.

- **Social benefits.** Physical activities that involve partners or teams are a great way to make friends. They also help you work together as a group and learn about other cultures. Physical activity brings people from diverse backgrounds together. Max, for example, learned the rules of Canadian football from a classmate from Alberta. Thanks to Jorge, Greg was able to learn about the Latin sport of *pelota*. This sport is played similarly to tennis.

 **Reading Check** **Identify** Name two health benefits of physical activity.

▲ Swimming improves heart and lung endurance. Raking leaves contributes to flexibility. **What activities promote other elements of fitness, such as muscle endurance and strength?**

Elements of Fitness

There are five elements of fitness: *muscle endurance, heart and lung endurance, strength, flexibility,* and *body composition.* These elements help you find out how physically fit you are.

Endurance (en·DER·uhns) is *the ability to keep up a physical activity without becoming overly tired.* There are two kinds of endurance. *Muscle endurance* is how long your muscles can perform a task without getting tired. Activities that build muscle endurance are dancing, jumping rope, or biking. *Heart and lung endurance* is how well these organs can provide your body with oxygen. This type of endurance is important in many physical activities, including running, swimming, and playing team sports. Both kinds of endurance help build stamina (STA·mih·nuh). **Stamina** is *your ability to stick with a task or activity for a long period of time.* Building stamina will help you be active for longer periods of time without getting tired or out of breath.

Strength is *the ability of your muscles to exert a force.* Muscles help support your bones and make your joints stronger. You build muscle strength by pushing or pulling against a force such as gravity. Pull-ups, for example build muscle strength in your arms. The more strength you have, the more efficiently you can complete physical tasks.

Go Online

Topic: Get Moving

Visit **glencoe.com** for Student Web Activities that will help you choose an exercise or other physical activity.

Activity: Using the information provided at the link above, choose an exercise to do for 60 minutes most days. Keep a journal, recording how you feel on the days you exercise and the days you don't. For example, do you feel more energetic on the days you exercise?

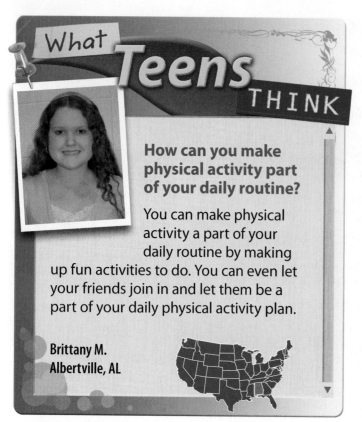
Flexibility is *the ability to move body joints through a full range of motion.* For the joints to be able to move easily, the muscles, tendons, and ligaments around them can't be too tight. Flexibility helps you with everything from stopping and turning to throwing a ball. Being flexible also helps prevent injuries. You build flexibility by stretching your muscles and joints. Activities that promote flexibility include yoga, swimming, karate, and gymnastics.

The last element of fitness is *body composition.* Body composition is the fat, bone, muscle, and fluid that make up body weight. A healthy body generally has more bone, muscle, and fluid than fat. Your body composition is the result of how you eat, how much you exercise, and the genes you inherited from your parents. You can improve your body composition by eating healthy foods and increasing your physical activity.

 **Reading Check**   **List** Name and explain two elements of fitness.

Fitness for Life

Fitness is a result of regular, ongoing activity. It is an important goal for a healthy life. If you are currently physically active, stay active. If you are not, make physical activity part of your daily routine. Walk or ride your bike to school if it's not too far. Take a walk with your family or with a friend. Even cleaning your room is a way to get your body moving.

When it comes to activities and sports, think *variety.* In the same way mixing up your diet makes eating more fun, varying activities adds enjoyment. Set fitness goals for yourself, and explore a variety of ways to achieve them so you don't get bored. Try different sports. Sign up for a dance class or karate. Shoot baskets, or skateboard in your neighborhood. You're more likely to stick with something you like doing.

Exercise

In the last section, we talked about the important role physical activity plays in your overall health and well-being. One of the best ways to ensure that you get enough physical activity is

 **Online**

Visit **glencoe.com** and complete the Interactive Study Guide for Lesson 1.

to exercise. **Exercise** is *planned, structured, repetitive physical activity that improves or maintains physical fitness.*

There are two main types of exercise: *aerobic* (ah·ROH·bik) and *anaerobic.* Aerobic exercise is a nonstop, moderate to vigorous activity. It strengthens the heart and lungs, allowing you to breathe in more oxygen. Strengthening your heart and lungs can lower your risk of heart disease and diabetes. Aerobic exercise should be done at least five times a week at a comfortable pace. Swimming, bike riding, running, and walking are great aerobic exercises. You should do them for at least 20 to 30 minutes at a time to get their full aerobic benefits.

Anaerobic exercises build muscle strength and endurance through intense physical activity that does not use large amounts of oxygen. Examples include push-ups and pull-ups. Weight lifting, gymnastics, and hiking build muscle strength, too. Anaerobic exercises should be done two to three times per week.

▲ Push-ups build muscle strength in the upper arms and shoulders. **Which type of exercise are push-ups: aerobic or anaerobic?**

 Reading Check **Compare** Explain the difference between aerobic and anaerobic exercise.

Lesson 1 Review

 After You Read

Review this lesson for new terms, major headings, and Reading Checks.

What I Learned

1. *Vocabulary* What are *strength, endurance,* and *flexibility*?

2. *Identify* Name an activity that builds muscle endurance. Name an activity that builds heart and lung endurance.

3. *Recall* What are the benefits of aerobic exercise?

Thinking Critically

4. *Apply* Why should endurance be a goal even for a weight lifter?

5. *Evaluate* What aerobic activities might you recommend for a teen who doesn't have access to a bicycle?

Applying Health Skills

6. *Advocacy* Write and perform a skit for your classmates that explains why it is important to play sports by the rules. After the skit, have your classmates write a short reflection on the skit. Ask what they liked most about the performance.

Creating a Personal Fitness Plan

Guide to Reading

● Building Vocabulary
Find each term below in the lesson. Write its definition in your notebook.

- F.I.T.T. principle (p. 128)
- resting heart rate (p. 129)
- target heart rate (p. 130)
- recovery heart rate (p. 130)
- warm-up (p. 130)
- cooldown (p. 131)

● Focusing on the Main Ideas
In this lesson, you will learn to

- **identify** the parts of a fitness plan.
- **develop** fitness goals.
- **describe** the benefits of warm-ups and cooldowns.
- **create** a schedule to achieve fitness goals.

● Reading Strategy
Organizing Information Copy the major and minor heads from the lesson onto a sheet of paper. As you read, write one sentence or phrase next to each that captures the main point.

Quick Write

Think about an activity in your life that required developing a plan. Write a brief description of how you got started.

Setting Fitness Goals

You wouldn't build a house without a blueprint, or plan. The same goes for starting a physical fitness program. Before you begin, you need a plan. Like any good plan, yours should start with a statement of your goals. What do you eventually hope to accomplish? Would you like to find a new aerobic exercise or improve flexibility? Maybe you want to become stronger or to have more stamina. If you're not sure, talk to your physical education teacher or coach. Students with weight problems should check with their doctors before starting a new fitness plan.

▶ Pickup games are a great way to stay active and meet people. **What are some physical activities that are offered by your school or in your community?**

Healthy Fitness Zones for Ages 11 and 12			
Test	Sex	Age 11	Age 12
Curl-ups	Boys	15–28	18–36
	Girls	15–29	18–32
1-mile run (in minutes and seconds)	Boys	11:00–8:30	10:30–8:00
	Girls	12:00–9:00	12:00–9:00
Pull-ups	Boys	1–3	1–3
	Girls	1–2	1–3
Sit and Reach (inches)	Boys	8	8
	Girls	10	10

◀ FIGURE 5.2

HEALTHY FITNESS ZONES FOR AGES 11 AND 12

Some fitness assessments, such as the 1-mile run, are formal. Others, such as walking a flight of stairs, are informal. **Can you think of other informal assessments to test your fitness levels?**

Measuring Your Fitness Level

Once you've identified your goals, you will need to test your current fitness level. **Figure 5.2** shows several tests, called fitness assessments, commonly used to determine fitness. The chart shows typical results for teens your age. The assessments shown in the chart are formal assessments, but you can use informal assessments to measure your fitness level, too. For example, can you walk up a flight of stairs without feeling short of breath? If you've already begun a fitness program, you can use the results of these fitness assessments as guides for making changes to your program.

Choose Activities

Now that you know your fitness level and have set some goals, it's time to choose activities that will help you meet those goals. Start by making a list of the activities you like or would consider doing. The list can include anything from team sports and exercise classes to activities you can do at home, such as sit-ups and push-ups. Here are some questions to think about when choosing an activity:

- Will I need a partner or teammates?
- Are there special skills I'll need to learn?
- Will I need special equipment?
- Where will I practice?
- How much will I need to practice?
- If it's a team sport, is there a team nearby that I can join?
- How much, if anything, will it cost?

Careers for the 21st Century

Athletic Trainer

Athletic trainers work with people to help prevent and heal injuries that result from physical activities. There is a growing demand for these health care professionals, and many of them enjoy working with professional athletes. You can prepare for a career as an athletic trainer by studying muscles, bones, and the types of injuries they can have.

What skills does an athletic trainer need? Go to *Career Corner* at **glencoe.com** to find out.

FITNESS RATINGS FOR DIFFERENT ACTIVITIES

Different activities promote different areas of fitness. What are your fitness goals? Which activities can best help you achieve those goals?

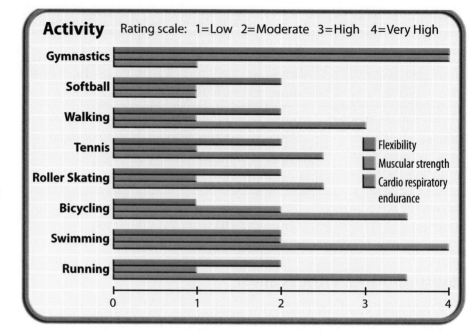

Activity   Rating scale: 1=Low   2=Moderate   3=High   4=Very High

Gymnastics, Softball, Walking, Tennis, Roller Skating, Bicycling, Swimming, Running

Flexibility
Muscular strength
Cardio respiratory endurance

The chart in **Figure 5.3** lists some other common activities. It also shows the fitness rating of each.

Reading Check   **Identify** What are two questions you should ask when choosing a fitness activity?

Achieving Your Goals

Whatever activity you choose, start small. If you've never run before, you're probably not ready to run a 5-kilometer race. Begin by running short distances. For example, you might run one block and walk two. Increase your distance slowly.

As you increase the amount of activity in your life, keep the F.I.T.T. principle in mind. The **F.I.T.T. principle** is *a method for safely increasing aspects of your workout without injuring yourself.*

The **F** in F.I.T.T. stands for "frequency." This is how often you work muscles of the body. Frequency depends on your fitness goals.

I stands for "intensity." This is how hard you work different muscle groups. Begin slowly and increase over time.

The first **T** stands for "time," meaning the length of time you spend exercising. Gradually increase your workout time.

The last **T** stands for "type," the type of activity you choose to do. Your type of activity should match your goals.

As a teen just beginning to exercise, pay close attention to the F.I.T.T. aspects of your fitness plan. If you're not sure how to determine the F.I.T.T. level that is best for you, ask a coach or physical education teacher for help. This is especially important before you increase your intensity level. Overdoing it can be harmful.

ACTIVITY

DEVELOPING

Good Character

Good Sportsmanship

Good sportsmanship means following the rules and playing fairly. If your team wins, don't try to make the other team feel bad about its loss. If your team loses, don't get angry at the winners or your teammates. Know that you all did the best that you could. Accept decisions made by officials, communicate with teammates, and respect the other players so that everyone can have a safe and fun time.

In what other ways can you show good sportsmanship?

Fitness Log Week 1		
Aerobic Activity	**Day**	**Minutes**
Running	Monday	30
Basketball	Tuesday	60
Strength Training		
Push-ups	Monday	10
Sit-ups	Tuesday	10
Weight Training	Wednesday	20
Flexibility		
Stretching	Monday	15
Karate	Friday	60

◀ FIGURE 5.4

SAMPLE FITNESS LOG

A fitness log will show your progress in the different areas of fitness. **How does a fitness log help you achieve your fitness goals?**

Creating a Schedule

Before beginning your program, you will need to make a fitness log. A fitness log is a record of your physical activities that lets you keep track of your progress. **Figure 5.4** shows a sample log. A complete fitness program should include a balance of aerobic, strength training, and flexibility activities. Your goal should be to spend 60 minutes a day, four to five days a week, on physical activity. If you have been inactive, you may need to work up to this goal. For aerobic workouts, it is best to spend at least 20 to 30 minutes at a time. On days in which time is limited, try working in 10- to 15-minute bursts of moderate to vigorous activity.

Checking Your Heart Rate

One way of measuring fitness is to check your *heart rate*. This is the number of times your heart beats per minute. **Figure 5.5** on the next page, gives information on how to measure your heart rate. There are three heart rate readings you need to take. The first is your resting heart rate. **Resting heart rate** is *the number of times*

▼ FIGURE 5.5

MEASURING YOUR HEART RATE

Measure your resting heart rate. **What is another name for heart rate?**

Your heart rate is also known as your pulse. There are several ways to take your pulse. One of the easiest is shown in the picture.

1. Place two fingers on your neck at the point shown in the picture. Find the throb in your neck. This is your pulse. Your heart is pumping blood through an artery in your neck. *NOTE:* Do not use your thumb for this activity.

2. Use a watch or clock with a second hand. Time the number of throbs, or pulses, that take place in 10 seconds.

3. Multiply the number you get by 6. This gives you your pulse.

Measure your resting pulse. What number did you arrive at?

Health Skills Activity

Practicing Healthful Behaviors

Exercise with "Eye Appeal"

There's a lot more to physical activity than setting goals and working up a sweat. It's also a lot of fun to develop and test your skills, not to mention express your creativity. Just think of the satisfaction an ice skater gets when she lands a double axel. What about the thrill of sinking a basket during a close game? Many physical activities such as dance, gymnastics, and cheerleading are also a pleasure to watch.

On Your Own

Think of two other activities that are fun to watch as well as play. What are some activities that allow you to express your creativity?

Connect To... Math

Hitting the Target

To find your target heart rate, you first need to find your *maximum heart rate*. To do this, subtract your age from 220. Then determine 60 to 80 percent of that number to get your *target heart rate*. For example, using a factor of 70 percent, the target rate of a 12-year-old would be figured like this: 220 − 12 = 208. 70 percent of 208 is 145.6, so you should shoot for a target heart rate of 146.

your heart beats per minute when you are relaxing. You should take this measurement before you begin working out.

Once you have worked out for a while, you should take your target heart rate. **Target heart rate** is *the level at which your heart and lungs receive the most benefit from a workout.* A 12-year-old's target heart rate is 125 to 167 beats per minute. This is the number you should aim for during your workout. To gain aerobic benefits from an exercise or activity, you need to maintain your target heart rate for 20 to 30 minutes. You should measure your target heart rate twice during a standard workout.

The third heart measurement is your recovery heart rate. **Recovery heart rate** is *how quickly your heart rate returns to normal right after exercise is stopped.* The higher your fitness level, the faster the drop in heart rate. An aerobic fitness goal should be to achieve a lower recovery heart rate.

 **Reading Check** **Compare** Explain the differences between your resting heart rate and target heart rate.

Warm Up and Cool Down

Before beginning any workout or exercise session, you need to warm up. A **warm-up** is *gentle activity that prepares your body for exercise or sport.* The warm-up prevents injuries to muscles, joints, and connective tissue. A good warm-up usually includes an easy exercise to get your heart pumping a little faster and blood flowing into the muscles. Walking or jogging in place for five to ten minutes are good examples of warm-up activities. Warm-ups can also include practicing skills for the activity you will be doing. For example, you might warm up before playing basketball by shooting baskets, passing the ball, or dribbling.

After you have warmed up your body, you can do some basic stretches. Stretching loosens your muscles, tendons, ligaments, and joints. Only stretch muscles that have been warmed up. Stretching muscles that have not been warmed up could cause injury.

At the end of your workout, you need to cool down. A **cooldown** consists of *gentle activity to slow down after exercise.* The cooldown gradually returns your body to its resting state. Stretching is an important part of a cooldown. Stretching builds flexibility and helps ease your muscles back into their resting state. Be sure to drink water before, during, and after your workout.

In addition, many activities and sports have their own *training techniques.* These include exercises you should do off the playing field. They help prepare your body for the next event or competition.

 Reading Check   **Give Examples** Provide a detailed, step-by-step description of a proper stretching exercise.

 **Go Online**

Visit **glencoe.com** and complete the Interactive Study Guide for Lesson 2.

Lesson 2 Review

 After You Read

Review this lesson for new terms, major headings, and Reading Checks.

What I Learned

1. *Vocabulary* Define *target heart rate.*

2. *List* What are the parts of a fitness plan?

3. *Describe* Describe what you need to do in order to warm up before physical activity.

Thinking Critically

4. *Analyze* Calvin would like to bowl as a fitness activity. How can he determine whether this activity will provide fitness benefits?

5. *Apply* Dana plans to swim to achieve fitness. She claims that because you stretch during swimming, there is no need to cool down. How would you respond?

Applying Health Skills

6. *Goal Setting* Choose two activities that you can do to meet a fitness goal. Create a fitness log to track your progress before, during, and after reaching your goal. Measure the frequency, intensity, and length of time you can perform the activities. Be sure to monitor your heart rate.

Safety in Sports and Physical Activities

 Guide to Reading

● **Building Vocabulary**

Some of the terms below may seem familiar. Write down what you think they mean. Check your answers as you come across them in the text.

- sports gear (p. 132)
- P.R.I.C.E. (p. 134)
- dehydration (p. 134)
- heat exhaustion (p. 134)
- frostbite (p. 135)

● **Focusing on the Main Ideas**

In this lesson, you will learn to

- **identify** types of proper sports gear.
- **describe** treatment for sports-related injuries.
- **apply** the skill of advocacy to inform other teens about exercise.

● **Reading Strategy**

Identifying Problems and Solutions As you read the lesson, list health problems or injuries that are described. Next to each, identify a solution.

 *uick Write*

Write about a time when you became overly hot or tired while playing. Explain what you did to feel better.

Academic Vocabulary

techniques (TEK neeks) *(noun)* how activities are done. *The coach asked Sheila to show her passing and kicking techniques to the rest of her teammates.*

Playing It Safe

Physical activity, as you have seen, can be fun. It should also be free of injury. You have already learned two ways to make your workouts safe: warming up and cooling down. In this lesson, you'll learn **techniques** for making them even safer. You'll also learn how to treat some sports injuries if they should occur.

The Right Stuff

A first step to injury-free exercise is proper sports gear. **Sports gear** includes *sports clothing and safety equipment.* Depending on the sport or activity, safety equipment can include helmets, mouth guards, protective pads, and goggles. **Figure 5.6** shows several activities and the types of gear needed.

Note that some activities call for "approved" helmets. Be aware that different activities have different helmet requirements. For example, bicycle helmets should be certified by the Snell Memorial Foundation. Make sure you know which type is right for your activity.

Safety Gear by Sport or Activity

The chart below lists some of the safety gear needed for different activities. **What safety gear do you wear when playing your favorite sport?**

Sport or Activity	Safety Gear
Skating, skateboarding, scooter riding	Helmet, wrist pads, knee pads, elbow pads
Bicycling	Bike helmet, pads
Contact sports, including wrestling and volleyball	Mouth guard, knee pads
Racquetball and snowboarding	Eyeguards for racquetball; goggles and helmet for snowboarding
Hockey, football, and baseball	Pads, helmet, mouth guard, chest guard

Choose athletic clothing that is comfortable. Tight clothing doesn't allow your skin to breathe. However, clothing should not be so loose that it can snag or get caught on objects. It should be loose enough to allow free movement. Also, wear light-colored clothing when you excercise outdoors. Light colors will keep you cool. Dark colors absorb heat from the sun. As you grow older, your body, hands, and feet will grow. It is important to update your sports gear to meet these changes.

Drink Water

During moderate to vigorous activity, your body can lose a lot of water through *perspiration*, or sweat. It is important to replace this lost fluid. The solution is to drink plenty of water. Before beginning your activity, give your body a head start. Drink at least 8 ounces of water. Take small sips from time to time during a workout or game. You should drink about 8 ounces of water for every 30 minutes of heavy exercise. This is true even in cold weather. If there is no source of drinking water at the field or park, bring some from home.

▼ Getting plenty of fluid during vigorous activity is important. **Explain why this is so.**

Treating Injuries

Sometimes, even when you are careful, injuries happen. Scrapes, cuts, and muscle soreness are common in sports. When a muscle is stiff or aches, remember *P.R.I.C.E.* The letters in **P.R.I.C.E.** stand for *protect, rest, ice, compress, and elevate.* The sooner the treatment is applied, the better. You should:

- **Protect** the injured part from further injury by keeping it still. Moving it may make the pain worse.
- **Rest** the injured part.
- **Ice** the part using an ice pack.
- **Compress**, or put pressure on, the part using an elastic bandage. This will keep the injury from swelling. Just be careful not to wrap the bandage too tightly. This could cut off the flow of blood.
- **Elevate** the injured part above the level of the heart.

Weather-Related Injuries

Some activities are done in very cold or very hot temperatures. Both carry health risks. When you exercise or play during very hot weather, your temperature rises. Sweating increases to try to cool you down. Unless this water is replaced, dehydration can result. **Dehydration** is *a condition caused by too much water loss.* It can lead to other, more serious health problems. One of these is **heat exhaustion.** This is *an overheating of the body that can result from dehydration.* People with heat exhaustion often feel dizzy and have a headache. Their skin feels clammy when touched. If someone you know has these symptoms, find a cool, shady spot. Give the person plenty of fluids. If the person doesn't start to feel better, call for help right away.

Similar precautions need to be taken in cold weather. Winter activities, such as ice-skating, skiing, and snowboarding, require protection against snow and cold. To stay warm, dress

◀ When an injury occurs, the P.R.I.C.E. formula can be used to treat them. **What do the letters in P.R.I.C.E. stand for?**

in several layers of clothing. Layered clothing will trap warm air next to your body. A windproof jacket should be the outermost layer. Always wear a hat and gloves.

In the coldest weather, be alert to signs of **frostbite,** or *freezing of the skin.* Frostbite usually affects the nose, ears, fingers, and toes. The area will be numb, pale, and stiff. Frostbite is a serious injury. Get the person inside right away. Treat the affected area by soaking it in warm, not hot, water. Get medical help as soon as possible.

Wearing proper clothing can protect you during winter activities. **What are some health risks you face when participating in cold-weather sports or activities?**

Reading Check **Explain** What causes dehydration?

G **Online**

Visit glencoe.com and complete the Interactive Study Guide for Lesson 3.

Lesson 3 Review

After You Read

Review this lesson for new terms, major headings, and Reading Checks.

What I Learned

1. *Vocabulary* What is heat exhaustion?

2. *Recall* Why is replacing lost water important during physical activity?

3. *List* Name two types of protective sports gear.

Thinking Critically

4. *Apply* Rey wants to play hockey, but he doesn't want to wear the face mask that players need to wear. What advice might you give Rey about the importance of sports gear?

5. *Apply* Maintain a three-day activity and exercise diary. How much time did you spend playing sports? How much time did you spend participating in activities? What changes do you need to make to your routine?

Applying Health Skills

6. *Advocacy* Create a pamphlet titled *Five Things Teens Should Know Before Exercising.* Include five pieces of advice from the lesson, and put each in your own words.

What Is Goal Setting?

Goal setting is a five-step plan for improving and maintaining your personal health. Some goals are easy to reach while others may be more challenging.

The Five Steps of the Goal-Setting Plan:

Step 1: Choose a realistic goal and write it down.

Step 2: List the steps that you need to take to reach the goal.

Step 3: Find others, like family, friends, and teachers, who can help and support you.

Step 4: Set checkpoints along the way to evaluate your progress.

Step 5: Reward yourself once you have reached your goal.

Developing a Personal Fitness Plan

Follow the Model, Practice, and Apply steps to help you master this important health skill.

❶ Model

Read about how Enrique uses goal setting to create a fitness goal and a plan to reach his goal.

Step 1. Make your goal specific.

Enrique wants to build up his endurance.

Step 2. List the steps to reach your goal.

Enrique decides to play soccer as a way of achieving his goal. He is joining a local soccer team.

The team practices two weekdays for an hour. They have games on weekends.

Step 3. Get help from others.

When Enrique feels discouraged, his father and brother are there to cheer him on.

Step 4. Evaluate your progress.

Enrique is able to play for longer periods of time. He is also improving his soccer skills.

Step 5. Reward yourself.

Enrique bought himself a new soccer jersey.

② Practice

Read about how Hector uses goal setting to become a better soccer player.

Hector's goal is to become a more limber soccer player. He learned in health class that yoga is an excellent exercise that increases flexibility. Hector decides to give yoga a try. He writes down his new goal. "Take a yoga class three times a week." Now that Hector has set a specific goal, use these questions to help him reach it.

1. What steps can Hector take to reach his goal?
2. Who could help Hector reach his goal?
3. How can Hector evaluate his progress?
4. How could Hector reward himself when he succeeds?

③ Apply

Apply what you learned about goal setting to complete the activity below.

Working in small groups, set a fitness goal in a cooperative or competitive activity. Perhaps you want to perform a team sport better or play a game with another team and win. As a group, write down your goal. Use the goal-setting steps to help you reach it. Share your goal with the class. Explain the physical, mental/emotional, or social benefits you will get from achieving this goal.

Self-Check

- Did I use each of the goal-setting steps?
- Did I explain the benefits of reaching this goal?

Building Health Skills

How to Stay FIT FOR LIFE

Getting the right amount of exercise is key to staying healthy.

Kids are busier than ever before. They feel pressure to do well in school and to keep up with music lessons and other activities. But most kids' hectic schedules leave out one of the most important activities: exercise.

Nearly half of all young people in the United States are not active on a regular basis. This trend is a big factor in the rising rate of obesity among kids. School budget cuts and more emphasis on preparing for tests have led many schools to cut down on gym and recess time. So it's up to you to make sure you stay fit.

GOOD FOR YOUR MIND AND BODY

Along with building muscle and preventing health problems, staying fit can give you more energy to keep up with your packed daily schedule. Experts suggest that young people get a total of 60 minutes of exercise most days. Exercise can help you relax, respond better to stress, and boost your self-confidence.

You don't need to play competitive sports to stay in shape. Riding a bike or inline skating with your friends will provide results, too. Choose activities that are fun—you'll be more likely to keep doing them in the future!

A FORMULA FOR STAYING FIT

To stay strong and flexible, different parts of our bodies require different types of exercise.

EXAMPLE	BENEFIT	AMOUNT
Aerobic Exercise Running, basketball, jumping rope, dancing	Aerobic exercise increases your heart rate and makes you breathe harder. This strengthens your heart and lungs.	Thirty minutes of aerobic exercise most days
Strength Training Pull-ups, sit-ups, push-ups	Muscle strength is the ability of your muscles to exert a force. Muscle endurance is the ability to keep up a physical activity without becoming overly tired. Building both improves overall fitness.	Two or three days a week
Flexibility Training Sit and reach, yoga, gymnastics, Tai Chi	Jog or warm up for five to 10 minutes before you do light stretching. After exercise, do more stretching. This helps protect you from injury.	Before and after any workout

Reading Review

 Visit **glencoe.com** to download quizzes and eFlashcards for Chapter 5.

FOLDABLES Study Organizer

Foldables® and Other Study Aids Take out the Foldable® that you created for Lesson 1 and any graphic organizers that you created for Lessons 1–3. Find a partner, and quiz each other using these study aids.

Lesson 1 Physical Activity and Your Health

Main Idea Physical fitness is an important goal for a healthy life.

- Physical activity is any kind of movement that causes your body to use energy.
- Health experts recommend that teens get 60 minutes of physical activity daily. This hour can be done all at once, or in 10-15 minute bursts.
- Lifestyle activities are physical activities that are part of your day-to-day routine or recreation.
- Good physical fitness benefits every side of your health triangle.
- The five elements of fitness are muscle endurance, heart and lung endurance, strength, flexibility, and body composition.
- Set fitness goals for yourself, and explore a variety of ways to achieve those goals. Variety adds enjoyment and will keep you from getting bored.

Lesson 2 Creating a Personal Fitness Plan

Main Idea A fitness plan includes setting and achieving goals, measuring your fitness level, choosing activities, creating a schedule, checking your heart rate, warming up, and cooling down.

- Fitness assessments are fitness tests commonly used to determine fitness levels.
- Keep the F.I.T.T. principle in mind: **F**requency, **I**ntensity, **T**ime, and **T**ype of your physical activity.
- Your heart rate is the number of times your heart beats in a minute. When you exercise, measure your heart rate three times: before you workout (resting heart rate), during your workout (target heart rate), and when you just finish your workout (recovery heart rate).
- A complete fitness program should include a balance of aerobic, strength training, and flexibility activities.
- Remember to warm up and cool down to reduce the risk of injury.

Lesson 3 Safety in Sports and Physical Activities

Main Idea Sports and other physical activities should be safe as well as fun.

- When exercising, wear comfortable athletic clothing and proper protective gear.
- Dehydration is often a consequence of exercise. Drink plenty of water before, during, and after your activity.
- When a muscle is stiff or aches, remember P.R.I.C.E.: **P**rotect, **R**est, **I**ce, **C**ompress, and **E**levate the injury.
- Dehydration is a condition caused by too much water loss. It can cause heat exhaustion, or the overheating of the body.

 After You Read

Health eSpotlight **VIDEO**

Now that you have read the chapter, look back at your answers to the Health eSpotlight questions on the chapter opener. What are some additional ways you could make being active a fun part of your daily schedule?

Reviewing Vocabulary and Main Ideas

On a sheet of paper, write the numbers 1–6. After each number, write the term from the list that best completes each sentence.

- dehydration
- heat exhaustion
- lifestyle activities
- physical activity
- physical fitness
- recovery heart rate
- resting heart rate
- target heart rate

Lesson 1 **Physical Activity and Your Health**

1. _____ is the ability to handle everyday physical work and play without becoming tired.

2. Forms of physical activity that are part of your day-to-day routine or recreation are known as _____.

3. Any kind of movement that causes your body to use energy is called _____.

Lesson 2 **Creating a Personal Fitness Plan**

4. Your _____ is the number of times your heart beats per minute when you are relaxing.

5. The level at which your heart and lungs receive the most benefit from a workout is your _____.

6. Your _____ is how quickly your heart rate returns to normal right after exercise is stopped.

On a sheet of paper, write the numbers 7–10. Write True *or* False *for each statement below. If the statement is false, change the underlined word or phrase to make it true.*

Lesson 3 **Safety in Sports and Physical Activities**

7. Depending on the sport or activity, <u>safety equipment</u> can include helmets, protective pads, and goggles.

8. To replace water your body loses through sweat, you should drink about <u>20 ounces</u> of water every 30 minutes.

9. The <u>F.I.T.T. principle</u> can be used to treat muscle soreness and other sports-related injuries.

10. Symptoms of <u>frostbite</u> include dizziness and clammy skin.

Thinking Critically

Using complete sentences, answer the following questions on a sheet of paper.

11. **Compare and Contrast** In what ways are warming up and cooling down similar? How are they different?

12. **Synthesize** Imagine you are playing softball on a hot day. One of your teammates becomes ill. There is no shade or water nearby. What should you do?

Go Online Visit **glencoe.com** and take the Online Quiz for Chapter 5.

Write About It

13. **Persuasive Writing** Write a paragraph explaining the benefits of physical activity. In your paragraph, persuade other teens to be physically active by stating facts, using supporting evidence, and giving examples.

14. **Expository Writing** Choose a physical activity or sport that you enjoy. Write a safety guide for players to refer to that tells them how to stay safe and prevent injury.

Standardized Test Practice

Reading

Read the passage and then answer the questions.

A moderate to high level of flexibility has many health benefits. It helps reduce muscle strains and lower-back problems. It also improves performance in most sports and activities.

Many different stretches can be used to improve flexibility. There are stretching exercises for all major joints of the body. A complete workout should include stretches for each.

While flexibility is important, you should know your limits. It is possible to overdo stretching. A joint that is overly stretched can become injured easily. It can also cause injuries in nearby muscles. An overly stretched shoulder joint, for example, can lead to a dislocated shoulder. This is a painful condition in which the entire shoulder moves out of its normal location.

TEST-TAKING TIP

Find the main idea in a reading passage. Then look for details that support this idea.

1. Which statement best sums up the main idea of the passage?
   A. Flexibility is important but impossible to measure.
   B. Flexibility helps reduce muscle strains and lower-back problems.
   C. Maintaining flexibility by stretching is important, but know your limits.
   D. A dislocated shoulder is a painful condition that can be prevented by stretching.

2. Which of the following is *not* included in the passage?
   A. An example of an injury that can occur when a joint is made overly flexible
   B. Examples of stretching activities for all the different joints of the body
   C. Support for the claim that flexibility has many health benefits
   D. A warning that you should not overdo it when it comes to stretching

6 Personal Health

Chapter Preview

▲ *Working with the Photo*

Taking care of your personal health includes brushing your teeth. **What are some other ways to care for your personal health?**

Start-Up Activities

 Before You Read What do you know about personal health? Take the short quiz below. Keep a record of your answers.

HEALTH QUIZ Answer *True* or *False* to each of the following questions.

1. It is important to get annual physical checkups.
2. The media has no influence on what health products I buy as a consumer.
3. I should only use medicines that are prescribed specifically for me.
4. Loud sounds are not harmful to my ears.

ANSWERS: 1. True; 2. False; 3. True; 4. False

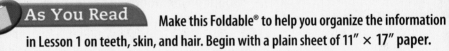

FOLDABLES Study Organizer

As You Read Make this Foldable® to help you organize the information in Lesson 1 on teeth, skin, and hair. Begin with a plain sheet of 11" × 17" paper.

1 Fold the sheet of paper into fourths along the short axis. This forms four columns.

2 Open the paper and refold it into fourths along the long axis. This forms four rows.

3 Unfold and draw lines along the folds.

4 Label the chart as shown.

Chapter 6	Form	Function	Care
Teeth			
Skin			
Hair			

Record information about teeth, skin, and hair in the appropriate sections of the chart. Then use the chart to compare different types of personal care.

G Online Visit **glencoe.com** and complete the Health Inventory for Chapter 6.

Lesson 1

Your Teeth, Skin, and Hair

Guide to Reading

● Building Vocabulary

In your own words, write definitions for the following terms. Check to make sure your definitions are correct as you read the chapter.

- hygiene (p. 144)
- plaque (p. 145)
- fluoride (p. 146)
- epidermis (p. 147)
- dermis (p. 147)
- sunscreen (p. 147)
- acne (p. 148)
- dandruff (p. 149)
- cuticle (p. 150)

● Focusing on the Main Ideas

In this lesson, you will learn to

- **recognize** ways to keep your teeth and gums healthy.
- **identify** ways to take care of your skin.
- **describe** how to care for hair and nails.
- **apply** the skill of advocacy to inform others about proper tooth and gum care.

● Reading Strategy

Predicting Read the major and minor headings throughout the lesson. Write a sentence about the kind of advice you think will be given for each heading.

FOLDABLES Study Organizer Use the Foldable® on p. 143 as you read this lesson.

Describe the steps you take in caring for your teeth, skin, and hair.

Looking Your Best

Think about your appearance. Are your clothes neat and clean? Is your hair combed? Did you brush your teeth this morning? Caring for your appearance includes paying attention to your personal hygiene (HY·jeen). **Hygiene** includes *the actions you take to improve or maintain your health.* Keeping your body clean is an example of good hygiene. Your hygiene and resulting appearance affect all three sides of your health triangle. When you look your best, you feel good about yourself. This improves your mental/emotional health. You are more confident around others, strengthening your social health. Good hygiene also keeps your body physically healthy. For example, washing your hands helps prevent illness.

 **Define** What is *hygiene?*

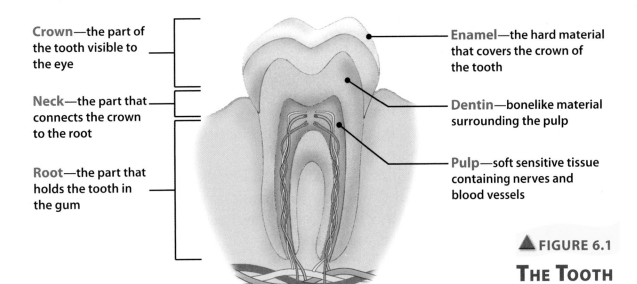

Crown—the part of the tooth visible to the eye

Neck—the part that connects the crown to the root

Root—the part that holds the tooth in the gum

Enamel—the hard material that covers the crown of the tooth

Dentin—bonelike material surrounding the pulp

Pulp—soft sensitive tissue containing nerves and blood vessels

▲ FIGURE 6.1

THE TOOTH

This figure illustrates the different parts of the tooth. **Which part of the tooth do you see when you look at your smile in the mirror?**

Healthy Teeth and Gums

Your teeth and gums have important jobs. Your teeth make it possible for you to chew and grind food. They aid in forming certain speech sounds. Your teeth help shape and give structure to your mouth.

Your gums anchor your teeth in your mouth and keep them in place. About three-fourths of each tooth is located below the gum line. **Figure 6.1** shows the parts of the tooth.

Tooth and Gum Problems

Proper care of your teeth and gums can prevent tooth decay. If this occurs and goes untreated, your teeth can fall out.

Tooth decay begins with the formation of plaque (PLAK). **Plaque** is *a soft, colorless, sticky film containing bacteria that grows on your teeth.* The germs in plaque cause bad breath. If left on the teeth, these germs combine with sugars to form an acid that causes tooth decay and gum disease. If plaque is not removed, it eventually hardens and becomes *tartar* (TAR·tuhr). Only a dentist or dental hygienist can remove tartar. **Figure 6.2** shows the stages in tooth decay.

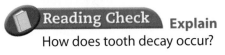 **Explain**
How does tooth decay occur?

▼ FIGURE 6.2

TOOTH DECAY

Tooth decay and gum disease can both be prevented. **What are some steps you can take to prevent these problems?**

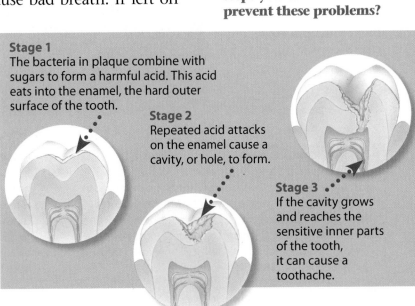

Stage 1
The bacteria in plaque combine with sugars to form a harmful acid. This acid eats into the enamel, the hard outer surface of the tooth.

Stage 2
Repeated acid attacks on the enamel cause a cavity, or hole, to form.

Stage 3
If the cavity grows and reaches the sensitive inner parts of the tooth, it can cause a toothache.

Keeping Teeth and Gums Healthy

You can help prevent tooth and gum problems by remembering to do three important things. Two of these, brushing and flossing, are illustrated in **Figure 6.3.** Brushing cleans the teeth, removes plaque, and stimulates the gums. Flossing removes food particles and plaque from between the teeth and under the gum line that the toothbrush cannot reach. Flossing also helps to clean underneath braces.

The third way you can maintain your dental health is by eating right. Choose foods that are high in the mineral calcium, such as yogurt and milk. You should also limit foods that are high in sugar, which can cause tooth decay. When you do eat sugary foods, brush your teeth as soon as you can.

▶ **FIGURE 6.3**

PROPER BRUSHING AND FLOSSING TECHNIQUES

To reduce plaque build-up, brush at least twice a day and floss once a day. **Why is it important to know how to brush and floss properly?**

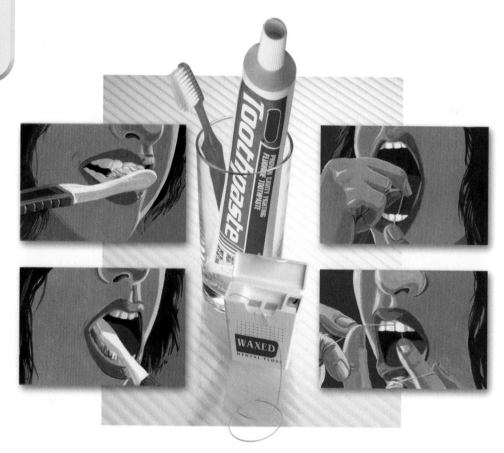

- You should brush using a soft-bristled brush. Use toothpaste that contains **fluoride** (FLAWR•ahyd), *a substance that fights tooth decay.* Brush the outer tooth surfaces first. Tilt the top of your toothbrush where your teeth and gums meet. Move your brush back and forth gently, using short strokes across your teeth. Then brush the inner tooth surfaces and your chewing surfaces. Finally, brush your tongue.

- Proper flossing begins with an 18-inch piece of dental floss. Wrap the ends around the middle finger of each hand. Hold the floss tightly between the thumb and forefinger. Now gently slide the floss between your teeth. Move it up or down to the gum line, using a gentle sawing motion. Rub the side of the tooth, and bring the floss back out gently. Repeat the process between all of your teeth.

Regular Dental Checkups

Another important way to protect your teeth and gums is to have dental checkups twice a year. The dentist or dental hygienist will clean your teeth to help prevent tooth decay and gum disease. The dentist will also examine your teeth for cavities or other problems.

If your teeth need straightening, your dentist may refer you to an *orthodontist.* This is a dentist who specializes in correcting irregularities of the teeth and jaw. The orthodontist may apply braces to straighten your teeth. This will make your teeth look better and easier to clean.

 **Reading Check** **List** Name three habits that promote healthy teeth and gums.

Healthy Skin

What's the biggest organ of your body? Believe it or not, the answer is your skin. The skin acts as a waterproof shield that defends your body against germs. It maintains your body temperature and allows you to feel and sense pressure and temperature.

The two main layers of the skin are shown in **Figure 6.4** on the next page. *The thinner outer layer of the skin* is called the **epidermis.** *The thicker inner layer of the skin* is the **dermis.**

Skin Care

The most important part of skin care is cleansing. As your body develops, sweat glands become more active. Bacteria can grow in areas where you sweat, such as under your arms. In large enough numbers, these germs give off an unpleasant odor. Washing sweat away keeps your skin clean and smelling fresh. You can also help control sweat and odor by using an antiperspirant or deodorant.

You should also protect your skin from the sun. The sun's ultraviolet (UV) rays can cause sunburn and wrinkles and can increase your risk of skin cancer. Avoid direct sunlight between the hours of 10:00 A.M. and 4:00 P.M. This is when the sun's UV rays are strongest. Whenever you do spend time in the sun, wear protective clothing and use a **sunscreen.** This is *a cream*

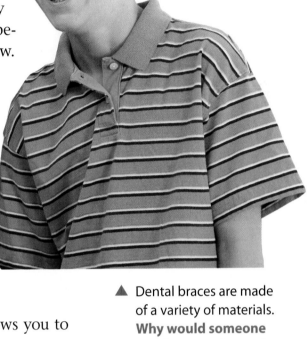

▲ Dental braces are made of a variety of materials. **Why would someone need to wear braces?**

Careers for the 21st Century

Dental Hygienist

Dental hygienists examine and clean patients' teeth and gums. Dental hygienists are in demand because everyone needs to have their teeth and gums cared for. You can prepare for a career as a dental hygienist by studying teeth, gums, and the problems they can have.

What skills does a dental hygienist need? Go to *Career Corner* at glencoe.com to find out.

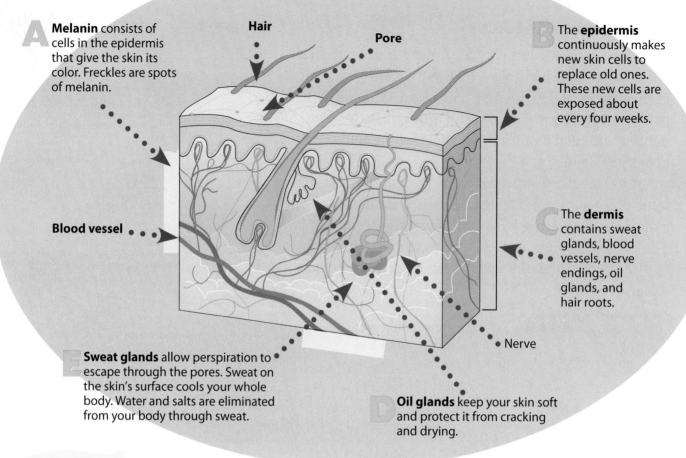

A **Melanin** consists of cells in the epidermis that give the skin its color. Freckles are spots of melanin.

Hair

Pore

B The **epidermis** continuously makes new skin cells to replace old ones. These new cells are exposed about every four weeks.

Blood vessel

C The **dermis** contains sweat glands, blood vessels, nerve endings, oil glands, and hair roots.

E **Sweat glands** allow perspiration to escape through the pores. Sweat on the skin's surface cools your whole body. Water and salts are eliminated from your body through sweat.

Nerve

D **Oil glands** keep your skin soft and protect it from cracking and drying.

▲ **FIGURE 6.4**

THE SKIN

Your skin is a very complex body organ. It has many parts. **What is the outer layer of skin called?**

G **Online**

Topic: Helping Troubled Skin

Visit **glencoe.com** for Student Web Activities to learn more about dealing with acne.

Activity: Using the information provided at the link above, create a one-page fact sheet that lists the causes, effects, myths, and treatment of acne.

or lotion that filters out some UV rays. Choose sunscreens with a sun protection factor (SPF) of 15 or higher. Reapply sunscreen about every two hours and after swimming.

Dealing with Acne

No matter how careful you are to keep your skin clean, some skin problems are hard to avoid. One of these problems is acne. **Acne** is *a skin condition caused by overly active oil glands.* This is due to increased hormone production during the teen years. The excess oil can clog pores, causing bumps on the skin's surface. Mild acne can usually be treated at home. Wash your face with mild soap, but do not scrub too hard. This can irritate skin and cause more acne. Also, avoid squeezing pimples, which can leave acne scars on your skin. For serious cases, you may need to see a *dermatologist* (DER·muh·TAH·luh·jist). This is a doctor who treats skin disorders.

Reading Check

Explain Why is it important to keep your skin clean?

Healthy Hair

Your hair is made up of a substance called keratin. The roots of the hair are in the dermis, the deep inner layer of skin. They are housed in small pockets called *follicles*. As new hair cells are formed, old ones are forced out.

The part of the hair that you can see is the *shaft*. The shape of the hair shafts determines whether your hair is wavy, curly, or straight. Like living skin, hair gets its color from the pigment melanin. The color of your hair is determined by heredity.

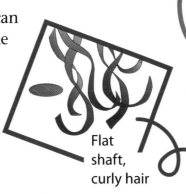

Round shaft, straight hair

Oval shaft, wavy hair

Flat shaft, curly hair

Hair Care

Keep your hair healthy by washing it regularly with a gentle shampoo and using a conditioner. If possible, let your hair dry by itself. If you use a blow dryer, use low heat. Styling irons and high heat from hair dryers can make hair dry, brittle, and faded. Brushing or combing daily removes dirt and helps spread natural scalp oils down the hair shaft.

Problem Hair and Hair Problems

Two conditions that can affect the health of your hair are dry or oily scalp. Either problem can be corrected by choosing the right shampoo. Read the label carefully. Different products are made for dry, oily, and normal hair. Chlorine in pool water can be another problem. Special shampoos can remove chlorine.

Another common scalp problem is **dandruff.** This is *flaking of the outer layer of dead skin cells*. Washing your hair regularly controls dandruff. If this does not work, try a dandruff shampoo.

Sometimes, an itchy scalp is caused by head lice. These tiny, wingless insects live in the hair. They are easy to catch from someone else. To prevent lice from spreading, avoid sharing hats, combs, and brushes. If you get lice, you can kill them with a medicated shampoo. You will also need to wash all your bedding, towels, combs, brushes, and clothing. Everyone else in your house will need to take these steps, too.

▲ No matter what kind of hair you have, it deserves proper treatment. **What are three steps you can take to keep your hair healthy?**

List Name two steps that are part of good hair hygiene.

 Proper nail care keeps your nails looking clean and healthy. **What are some steps you can take to improve the appearance of your nails?**

Your Nails

Like your hair, your fingernails and toenails are made of a tough substance called keratin. Around the nail is *a nonliving band of outer skin* called the **cuticle** (KYOO·ti·kuhl).

To keep nails healthy, soften your hands with warm water. Use a cuticle stick to push back the cuticle. Trim your nails using a nail clipper or small scissors. Cut your toenails straight across, so the nail is at or just beyond skin level. Use an emery board or nail file to round out the ends of your fingernails slightly and smooth out rough edges. Never bite your nails. Putting your fingers in your mouth can spread germs.

Reading Check **Explain** Describe how you should trim your fingernails and toenails.

Go Online

Visit **glencoe.com** and complete the Interactive Study Guide for Lesson 1.

Lesson 1 Review

After You Read

Review this lesson for new terms, major headings, and Reading Checks.

What I Learned

1. *Vocabulary* What is *plaque*?

2. *Recall* Between what hours are the sun's UV rays strongest?

3. *Explain* What are two ways to treat acne?

Thinking Critically

4. *Hypothesize* What can happen to your teeth and gums if you do not floss regularly?

5. *Compare* In what ways are hair and nails similar? How are they different?

Applying Health Skills

6. *Advocacy* Create a booklet that explains the importance of proper tooth and gum care. Include original art, if you like, with step-by-step instructions. Distribute copies to students in other classes.

150 Chapter 6: Personal Health

Go Online For more Lesson Review Activities, go to **glencoe.com**.

Lesson 2

Protecting Your Eyes and Ears

Guide to Reading

● **Building Vocabulary**
Write the terms below in your notebook. As you read, write a definition for each.

- farsightedness (p. 152)
- nearsighted (p. 152)
- astigmatism (p. 152)

● **Focusing on the Main Ideas**
In this lesson, you will learn to

- **describe** how to care for your eyes and ears.
- **explain** how to protect your hearing.

● **Reading Strategy**
Organizing Information Copy the headings from the lesson onto a sheet of paper. Use these to make an outline of the lesson.

Healthy Eyes

Your eyes are your windows to the world. They allow you to take in millions of bits of information, which are sent to your brain. There, the information is processed into shapes, colors, and movements. The many parts of the eye are shown in **Figure 6.5** on page 152.

Eye Care

The following tips can help you take care of your eyes:

- Take a break when using your computer, watching TV, and reading. Resting your eyes from time to time will help prevent eyestrain.

- Try not to sit too close to the TV or computer. The computer screen should be about two feet from your face.

- Read and watch TV in a well-lighted room. Light should come from above your reading material.

- Wear safety goggles during sports or science lab. Be especially careful when you are holding sharp objects.

- Wear sunglasses outdoors on sunny days. Buy sunglasses that have UV-approved lenses.

- If your eyes hurt or itch, don't rub them. You could have allergies or an infection. Tell a parent or guardian.

Quick Write

Write an original science fiction story about a visitor from another planet. The creature should have no ears or eyes. In your story, explain seeing and hearing to this visitor.

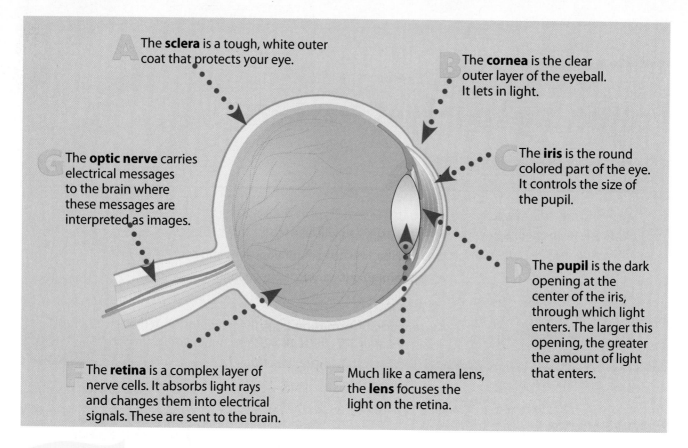

The **sclera** is a tough, white outer coat that protects your eye.

The **cornea** is the clear outer layer of the eyeball. It lets in light.

The **optic nerve** carries electrical messages to the brain where these messages are interpreted as images.

The **iris** is the round colored part of the eye. It controls the size of the pupil.

The **pupil** is the dark opening at the center of the iris, through which light enters. The larger this opening, the greater the amount of light that enters.

The **retina** is a complex layer of nerve cells. It absorbs light rays and changes them into electrical signals. These are sent to the brain.

Much like a camera lens, the **lens** focuses the light on the retina.

▲ **FIGURE 6.5**

THE EYE

The many parts of the eye work together to tell you about the world around you. **How do the various parts interact to make vision possible?**

- If you get something in your eye, try to blink to let tears wash it out. If this doesn't work, rinse the eye with water.

- Never share eye makeup or eye care products. Using someone else's products can spread germs.

- Get regular vision screenings and eye exams.

Vision Problems

Two common vision problems are farsightedness and nearsightedness. **Farsightedness** is *the ability to see objects at a distance while close objects look blurry.* For example, if you are farsighted, the words on this page may look unclear. However, if you look at a sign on the wall across the room, the words will be in focus. The opposite will be true if you are **nearsighted.** This is *the ability to see objects close to you while distant objects look blurry.* A third common condition is **astigmatism** (ah·STIG·muh·tizm), *a misshaped cornea or lens causing objects to look wavy or blurred.*

Eye problems are usually corrected by using eyeglasses or contact lenses. Both help the lens of the eye focus light on the retina. An eye doctor can determine if you need corrective lenses.

 Reading Check **Compare** What is the difference between *nearsightedness* and *farsightedness*?

Healthy Ears

Like your eyes, your ears allow you to receive information. Your ears also help you keep your balance. Balance is controlled by the *semicircular canals*, tubelike structures in the inner ear. The different parts of the ear and what they do are shown in **Figure 6.6.**

Ear Problems

Infections in the middle ear are the most common ear problems. Germs from colds in the nose or throat can spread through the eustachian tube into the middle and inner ear. Ear infections can be treated by a doctor.

The most serious ear problems are hearing loss and deafness. These can result from injury, disease, and birth defects. Very loud noise can also cause hearing loss. Have you ever had a ringing in your ears after exposure to noise for a long period of time? This is called *tinnitus* (TIN·uh·tuhs). For some people, tinnitus is ongoing; the ringing is always present. Frequent or ongoing tinnitus is an early warning sign of inner-ear nerve damage.

ACTIVITY
Connect To...
Science

Help for the Hearing Impaired

Medical science has developed a device that permits deaf and hearing-impaired people to communicate through sound. The device is called a *cochlear* (KOK·lee·ur) *implant* and is placed under the skin behind the ear. Unlike a hearing aid, which makes sound louder, the device allows the person using it to identify speech sounds.

Using online or print resources, learn more about this technology. Share your findings in a short report.

▼ FIGURE 6.6

THE EAR

The ears carry sound to the brain and help you stay balanced. Which parts of the ear are responsible for these two main functions?

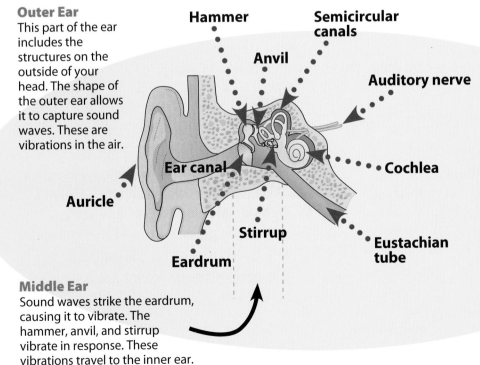

Outer Ear
This part of the ear includes the structures on the outside of your head. The shape of the outer ear allows it to capture sound waves. These are vibrations in the air.

Middle Ear
Sound waves strike the eardrum, causing it to vibrate. The hammer, anvil, and stirrup vibrate in response. These vibrations travel to the inner ear.

Hammer

Anvil

Semicircular canals

Auditory nerve

Ear canal

Auricle

Stirrup

Eardrum

Cochlea

Eustachian tube

Inner Ear
Sound
Tiny hair cells inside the cochlea move. This movement produces electrical messages in nerves deep inside the inner ear. These are sent to the brain along the auditory nerve. There, they are sorted out as speech sounds or nonspeech sounds. The sounds are then interpreted.

Balance
These canals are lined with tiny hairs and filled with fluid. When you move or change positions, the hairs and fluid also move. The brain senses these delicate movements. It tells your body which way to adjust your weight. This prevents you from falling over.

◄ People with hearing loss may wear hearing aids. These increase the loudness of sounds. **What are some ways people with hearing loss can communicate?**

Ear Care

The best way to care for your ears is to protect them from loud sounds. The loudness of sounds is measured in units called *decibels* (DES·ih·belz). Normal conversation measures about 60 decibels. Repeated exposure to sounds above 85 decibels is harmful. When listening to music, especially with headphones, keep the volume down.

Never use cotton swabs to clean the inside of your ear. Putting anything inside your ear opening can damage your ear. Instead, clean the outside of the ears with water. Allow the insides of the ears to dry on their own.

Go Online

Visit glencoe.com and complete the Interactive Study Guide for Lesson 2.

Reading Check

Explain Why is it important to limit your exposure to loud sounds?

Lesson 2 Review

After You Read

Review this lesson for new terms, major headings, and Reading Checks.

What I Learned

1. *Vocabulary* What is *astigmatism*? How is it treated?

2. *Describe* List three habits that you would recommend to promote eye health and protect vision.

3. *Recall* Name two jobs your ears perform.

Thinking Critically

4. *Apply* Frank is a drummer for a local band. As an advocate for hearing protection, what advice would you give to Frank?

5. *Evaluate* Why might a person living near an airport need to take special care of his or her ears?

Applying Health Skills

6. *Decision Making* Eileen has learned that she needs glasses for a vision problem. She tried on several pairs and doesn't like any of them. What are Eileen's choices?

 **Go Online** For more Lesson Review Activities, go to **glencoe.com.**

Choosing Health Products

Guide to Reading

● Building Vocabulary
Copy the terms below into your notebook. As you come across each term in the lesson, write its definition.

- consumer (p. 155)
- guarantee (p. 157)
- unit price (p. 157)
- coupons (p. 158)
- generic (p. 158)
- fraud (p. 158)

● Focusing on the Main Ideas
In this lesson, you will learn to

- **identify** factors that influence your consumer choices.
- **explain** ways to choose health products wisely.
- **analyze** how the media influences consumer choices.

● Reading Strategy
Predicting You probably make purchases already. Predict what kind of information would help you improve your shopping skills.

Consumer Skills

"I can't believe there are so many kinds of adhesive bandages," Marty remarked. He was finding it difficult to choose which product to buy. Having consumer skills would have made Marty's job easier. A **consumer** is *someone who buys products or services*. Consumer skills allow you to make informed choices when shopping.

Recognizing Influences

Many different factors influence your decisions as a consumer. Cost is likely to be a factor. Another is your likes and dislikes. You might prefer one shampoo brand over another because it makes your hair shinier. Environmental impact may also be an influence. You may prefer a product that is all-natural, organic, or recyclable.

Another factor that influences you is the media. This includes television, radio, the Internet, and newspapers. One important influence you may not always be consciously aware of is advertising. Without knowing it, you might be tempted to buy an item that has a catchy ad.

Quick Write

Make a list of health and beauty aids you use, such as shampoo and toothpaste. Explain how you decide what products to buy.

▶ There are many different health care products to choose from. **What influences your decisions as a consumer?**

Reading Product Labels

The first step in becoming a smart shopper is to understand what you're buying. With many products, this means reading the product label. Most product labels contain similar information. **Figure 6.7** shows a typical label on a health product. Take a moment to study the information on it.

Notice that the label tells you what the product is intended to do. This information appears first, under *indications*. What is the purpose of the product shown?

The label also gives directions. These tell you how much of the product to use and how often to use it. Use a product *only* as directed. If problems occur when you use the product, stop using it immediately and tell a trusted adult. There may be an ingredient in it that is causing the problem.

Comparison Shopping

When you compare two or more similar products by different manufacturers, you are comparison shopping. When comparing products, consider the benefits of one product over another. Which brand offers more of what you need and want? You should also consider the brand's reputation. Do you know anyone who has used and liked it? Finally, check to see if the

▼ FIGURE 6.7

WHAT PRODUCT LABELS CAN TELL YOU

Product labels contain important information. What do you think this product would be used for?

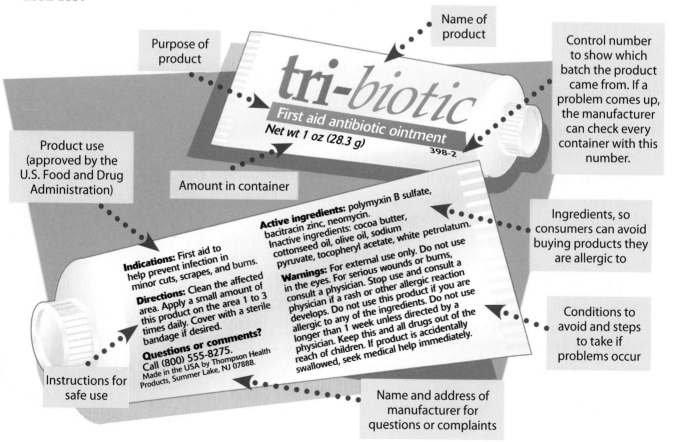

Name of product

Purpose of product

Control number to show which batch the product came from. If a problem comes up, the manufacturer can check every container with this number.

Product use (approved by the U.S. Food and Drug Administration)

Amount in container

Ingredients, so consumers can avoid buying products they are allergic to

Conditions to avoid and steps to take if problems occur

Instructions for safe use

Name and address of manufacturer for questions or complaints

tri-biotic
First aid antibiotic ointment
Net wt 1 oz (28.3 g)
398-2

Active ingredients: polymyxin B sulfate, bacitracin zinc, neomycin. Inactive ingredients: cocoa butter, cottonseed oil, olive oil, sodium pyruvate, tocopheryl acetate, white petrolatum.

Warnings: For external use only. Do not use in the eyes. For serious wounds or burns, consult a physician. Stop use and consult a physician if a rash or other allergic reaction develops. Do not use this product if you are allergic to any of the ingredients. Do not use longer than 1 week unless directed by a physician. Keep this and all drugs out of the reach of children. If product is accidentally swallowed, seek medical help immediately.

Indications: First aid to help prevent infection in minor cuts, scrapes, and burns.
Directions: Clean the affected area. Apply a small amount of this product on the area 1 to 3 times daily. Cover with a sterile bandage if desired.
Questions or comments? Call (800) 555-8275. Made in the USA by Thompson Health Products, Summer Lake, NJ 07888.

Health Skills Activity

Analyzing Influences

Persuasive Advertising

Advertisers often use the following positive and negative techniques to persuade you to buy their items.

- **Hidden messages.** Sometimes messages are in the form of pictures. A picture may show attractive people smiling when they use a product. This is telling you that the product will make you happier and healthier.
- **Comments by previous users.** These ads show people who claim to have used the company's product and gotten great results. These people may be paid actors.
- **Celebrity backing.** Popular actors, athletes, or celebrities promote some products making them seem glamorous. Remember that these people are paid to promote these products.

With a Group

Find an example of an ad that uses one of the techniques described above. How might these ads influence your decision to try the product? Discuss your findings with the class.

---

product has a guarantee. A **guarantee** is *a promise to refund your money if the product doesn't work as claimed.* It shows that the company that makes the product actually believes in their product and is willing to stand behind it.

When comparing the costs of health products, one important factor is **unit price.** This is the *cost per unit of weight or volume.* Often, a product's unit price appears on a tab on the shelf beneath it. You can compute it yourself, if necessary.

1. Find the weight or volume given on each product container. (Make sure that both products are measured in the same type of units.)
2. Divide the price of the product by its weight or volume.
3. The result is the unit price.

For example, an 8-fluid-ounce bottle of lotion costs $3.89. Dividing $3.89 by 8 equals 49¢. The unit price is 49¢ per fluid ounce. What's the unit price of each bottle of liquid soap in **Figure 6.8**? Which costs less per fluid ounce? Which is a better value?

▲ FIGURE 6.8

USING UNIT PRICING

Comparing unit price can help you save money. **Which of these products is a better value?**

Saving Money

Comparing unit prices can help you save money. So does buying personal products at discount stores. Clipping coupons is another way to save. **Coupons** are *slips of paper that save you money on certain brands*. Coupons are found in many daily newspapers and store flyers. Another way to save is by selecting the store, or **generic** (juh·NEHR·ik), brand. These are *products that imitate name-brand products but are sold in plain packages.* They cost less because the product maker spends less money on advertising.

Spotting False Claims

Some ads and product labels make claims that sound too good to be true. Some companies go beyond making misleading claims. They commit the crime of fraud. **Fraud** is *deliberately trying to trick consumers into buying a product or service.* Health fraud is a serious issue. You can report suspicious health products at the Food and Drug Administration (FDA) Web site. Helping fight fraud allows you to use your skill as a health advocate.

Visit glencoe.com and complete the Interactive Study Guide for Lesson 3.

 Reading Check

Explain What are two ways consumers can save money?

Lesson 3 Review

 **After You Read**

Review this lesson for new terms, major headings, and Reading Checks.

What I Learned

1. *Vocabulary* Define *consumer*.

2. *List* What are two kinds of information found on health product labels?

3. *Recall* What is the benefit of knowing a product's unit price?

Thinking Critically

4. *Apply* Jessica has poison ivy. She uses twice as much cream as the product label directs. Is this a good way of getting better faster?

5. *Synthesize* Why might a less expensive product not be the best product to buy? What other factors should you consider?

Applying Health Skills

6. *Analyzing Influences* Imagine that you are selecting a deodorant. Compare your wants and needs to the product's claims. What other factors would influence your decision?

Go Online For more Lesson Review Activities, go to **glencoe.com**.

Using Medicines Responsibly

Guide to Reading

● Building Vocabulary
Arrange the terms below in a word web. Place what you believe is the *main* term at the center.

- medicines (p. 159)
- prescription medicines (p. 159)
- over-the-counter (OTC) medicines (p. 159)
- vaccines (p. 160)
- antibiotics (p. 160)
- side effect (p. 160)
- tolerance (p. 160)
- drug misuse (p. 162)

● Focusing on the Main Ideas
In this lesson, you will learn to

- **explain** how medicines help you.
- **identify** information on medicine labels.
- **access** reliable health information on medicines.

● Reading Strategy
Organizing Information As you read the lesson, make notes about what medicines do and how to use them safely.

What Are Medicines?

Medicines are *drugs used to treat, cure, or prevent diseases or other medical conditions.* In earlier times, medicines were taken from plant leaves. People would eat the leaves or drink tea brewed from them. Today, most medicines are in the form of pills or liquids. Occasionally they are also injected into the bloodstream using needles, inhaled into the lungs, or rubbed into the skin.

There are two types of medicines. **Prescription** (prih·SKRIP·shuhn) **medicines** are *medicines sold only with a written order from a doctor.* **Over-the-counter (OTC) medicines** are *medicines available without a written order from a doctor.* These are also known as "nonprescription medicines." Prescription medicines require a doctor's supervision because they can carry more risks. However, OTC medicines should be used just as carefully.

Quick Write

Describe a TV commercial you have seen advertising a medicine. Tell what the medicine is supposed to do.

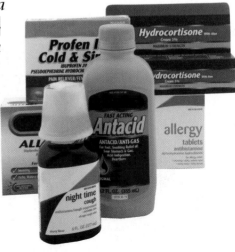

▶ Different medicines do different jobs. **Why do you think it is important to tell a new doctor what medicines you are taking?**

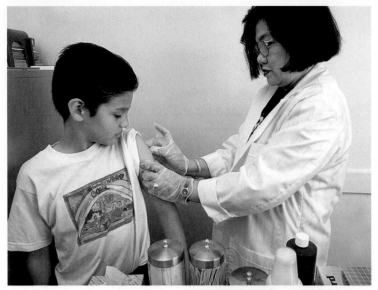

▲ Vaccines are medicines that prevent disease. **What are some common vaccines given today?**

Academic Vocabulary

interact (in ter AKT) (verb) to act with another person or object. *Team players interact well with others.*

What Medicines Do

Different medicines do different jobs. *Medicines that protect you from getting certain diseases* are known as **vaccines.** Some medicines cure diseases or kill germs. One type of germ-fighting medicine is **antibiotics** (an·tih·by·AH·tiks). These *kill or stop the growth of bacteria and other specific germs.* Still some medicines are used to manage *chronic,* or ongoing, conditions such as asthma. Other medicines relieve symptoms, such as itching or pain.

 **List** Name three different kinds of medicine, and tell what each does.

How Medicines Affect the Body

Because everyone's body is unique, medicines affect people in different ways. Factors that determine how a medicine affects you include age, weight, and general health. Combining medicines may also affect the way they work. Some medicines don't **interact** well with others and can cause harmful reactions. Some people are allergic to certain medicines and cannot take them at all.

Negative Reactions to Medicines

Even when used as directed, medicines can cause unwanted reactions. A **side effect** is *any reaction to a medicine other than the one intended.* Common side effects are drowsiness, dizziness, or upset stomach. Taking more than one medicine at a time can cause dangerous side effects if they are not supposed to be taken together. Make sure your doctor and pharmacist know *all* the medicines you are taking, including OTC medicines.

If you take a medicine for a long time, you may develop a **tolerance** (TAHL·ehr·uhns). This means *the body becomes used to the medicine and it no longer has the same effect.* Greater amounts of the medicine are needed to get the same results. This can become a dangerous problem. If a medicine you are taking no longer seems to be working, tell a parent or guardian, and speak to your doctor.

Reading Check **Define** What does *side effect* mean?

Using Medicines Safely

Before using OTC or prescription medicines, read the product label. The FDA requires makers of medicines to include certain information on medicine labels. Pharmacists are also required to include specific information on prescription labels. This includes the name of the patient and doctor, instructions for using the medicine, and the *dose*. This is how much of the medicine to take at one time. One especially important item on the label is the *expiration date of the medicine.* Find the expiration date on the sample prescription medicine label in **Figure 6.9.** All medicines have ingredients that can change over time and become less effective. The expiration date will tell you the date after which you can no longer use the medicine.

Over-the-counter (OTC) medicines have both front and back labels. The front label contains the name of the product and type of medicine. It also lists the main ingredient. The back label lists *directions* for use, which are similar to dosage information on a prescription label. If you have questions about an OTC or prescription medicine, talk to your pharmacist or doctor.

▼ FIGURE 6.9

LABEL ON A PRESCRIPTION MEDICINE

Medicine labels include instructions on how to use the medicine safely. **If you had questions about the use of this product, whom could you ask?**

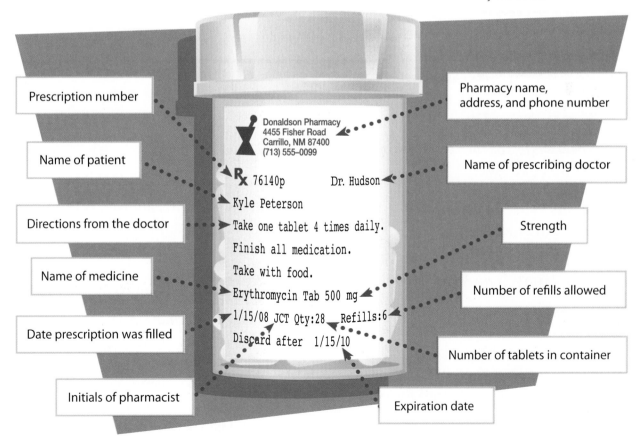

Prescription number

Name of patient

Directions from the doctor

Name of medicine

Date prescription was filled

Initials of pharmacist

Pharmacy name, address, and phone number

Name of prescribing doctor

Strength

Number of refills allowed

Number of tablets in container

Expiration date

Donaldson Pharmacy
4455 Fisher Road
Carrillo, NM 87400
(713) 555–0099

Rx 76140p   Dr. Hudson

Kyle Peterson

Take one tablet 4 times daily.

Finish all medication.

Take with food.

Erythromycin Tab 500 mg

1/15/08 JCT Qty:28   Refills:6

Discard after 1/15/10

DEVELOPING

Responsibility

You can show responsibility by sharing information about the dangers of drug misuse with your family. Urge parents or guardians to throw away any medicines that have expired.

What are some other steps you can take to demonstrate responsibility at home?

 Go Online

Visit **glencoe.com** and complete the Interactive Study Guide for Lesson 4.

Improper Use of Medicines

Medicines can do serious harm as well as good. This is why they should be taken with great care. *Taking medicine in a way that is not intended* is **drug misuse.** Taking more medicine than a doctor instructs is one example of drug misuse. To avoid misusing drugs, follow these guidelines.

- Talk to your doctor or pharmacist if you are not sure how to use a medicine.

- In the case of prescription medicines, take only medicines prescribed specifically for you.

- Use all medicines only as instructed. Make sure you understand the dose and how often it should be taken. Use exactly the amount indicated on the label.

- Don't use a medicine that was prescribed for an earlier illness without a doctor's approval.

- Don't use a medicine that has expired.

Using medicines in ways that are unhealthy is a form of drug abuse. You will learn more about drug abuse in Chapter 10.

Reading Check

Give examples What are three ways of avoiding drug misuse?

Lesson 4 Review

After You Read

Review this lesson for new terms, major headings, and Reading Checks.

What I Learned

1. *Identify* What are three ways that medicines can enter the body?

2. *Recall* Name two items on an over-the-counter (OTC) medicine label.

3. *Vocabulary* Define *tolerance*.

Thinking Critically

4. *Hypothesize* Why might a doctor prescribe different medicines for two people with the same illness?

5. *Synthesize* Why do you think the number of refills allowed is important information to include on a medicine label?

Applying Health Skills

6. *Accessing Information* The Internet makes it easier than ever to get information about medicines. Under your teacher's supervision, visit a Web site that contains information about medicines. List the kinds of facts provided.

 For more Lesson Review Activities, go to **glencoe.com**.

Lesson 5

Health Care in Your Community

Guide to Reading

Building Vocabulary

Define the familiar terms below in your notebook. Define the unfamiliar terms as you read the lesson.

- health care (p. 163)
- specialist (p. 164)
- voluntary health agencies (p. 165)
- health insurance (p. 166)
- managed care (p. 166)

Focusing on the Main Ideas

In this lesson, you will learn to

- **identify** different types of health care providers.
- **explain** the importance of regular health checkups.
- **apply** the skill of advocacy to raise awareness of health problems.

Reading Strategy

Classifying As you read the lesson, list the different health care providers, groups, and agencies. Find examples of each in your own community.

Quick Write

Explain in a paragraph why you think it's important to have regular medical checkups.

What Is Health Care?

Health care includes *any services provided to individuals or communities that promote, maintain, or restore health.* The health care industry is made up of a number of different health care providers, groups, and agencies. In this lesson, you will learn about the role each of these plays in your health.

Health Care Providers

Imagine you were feeling sick. Your parent or guardian might take you to see a doctor. Your doctor provides you with primary health care. Primary care includes the treatment of illnesses or diseases that do not require hospitalization. Primary care also includes *preventive care* such as regular health checkups and immunization against disease. Preventive care is any action that helps prevent the onset of disease or injury.

Different health professionals can provide primary care. This includes doctors, nurse practitioners, and physicians' assistants. All are trained to answer many health and medical questions and to give regular health checkups. They often work at a hospital, where their patients can receive emergency, surgical, and long-term care.

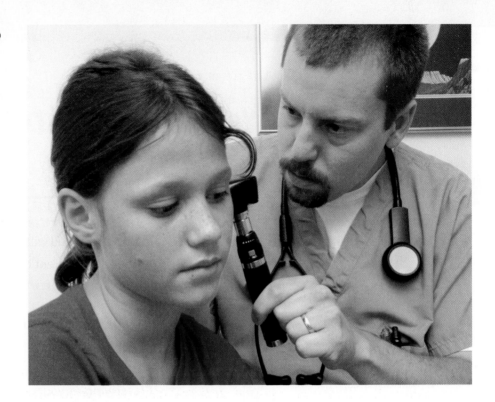

► Regular checkups can help you stay healthy. **Who are some of the different health professionals you could see for a checkup?**

Annual Physical Checkups

Getting regular checkups is one way to prevent health problems and maintain wellness. During a checkup, your health care provider will check your height and weight. He or she will also check your heart and lungs. Your vision and hearing may be tested. You may also receive any immunizations you need. These help your body resist getting certain common childhood diseases, such as measles.

Specialists and Other Health Care Providers

Sometimes the doctor or other health professional you see first will need to refer you to a **specialist** (SPEH·shuh·list). This is *a doctor trained to handle particular health problems*. Some specialists treat specific types of people. Other specialists treat specific conditions or body systems. **Figure 6.10** shows some of these specialists.

Health care today is largely a team effort. It involves more care providers than just your primary doctor and specialists. Think of the many health professionals you see. These probably include a dentist and/or dental hygienist. At school, you probably have a school nurse who can help you. You might see a counselor, either at school or in the community. All of these professionals play a role in keeping you healthy.

Specialist	Specialty
Allergist	Asthma, hay fever, other allergies
Cardiologist	Heart problems
Dermatologist	Skin conditions and diseases
Oncologist	Cancer
Ophthalmologist	Eye diseases
Orthodontist	Tooth and jaw irregularities
Orthopedist	Broken bones and similar problems
Otolaryngologist	Ears, nose, and throat
Pediatrician	Infants, children, and teens

◀ FIGURE 6.10

SOME SPECIALISTS

Different specialists treat different conditions. **Are there other specialties you have heard of?**

Other Sources of Health Care

Your health care doesn't stop with the individuals who treat you personally. There are groups and organizations that contribute to your health. In this country, government agencies oversee the health of communities as a whole. They make sure that our food and water are safe to eat and drink. They also fund research to help treat and cure diseases and improve medical technology.

Other groups that play a role in health care include **voluntary health agencies,** *organizations that work to treat and eliminate certain diseases.* Two examples of these agencies are the American Heart Association and American Cancer Society. These groups are privately run. This means that they receive donations from individuals and groups, and not from the government, to pay for what they do. One of their most important jobs is to educate the public about diseases. They also conduct research to fight diseases.

Reading Check List Name several different types of specialists, and tell what each does.

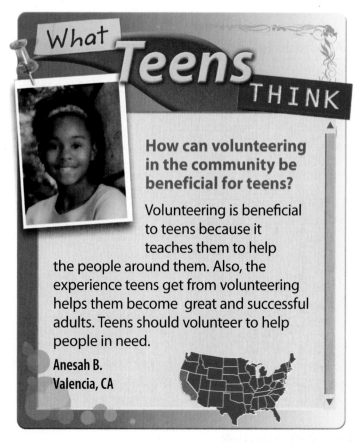

What **Teens** THINK

How can volunteering in the community be beneficial for teens?

Volunteering is beneficial to teens because it teaches them to help the people around them. Also, the experience teens get from volunteering helps them become great and successful adults. Teens should volunteer to help people in need.

Anesah B.
Valencia, CA

Health Skills Activity

Advocacy

Doing Your Part for Community Health

Volunteer health agencies need everyone's help to stamp out disease. How can you help? Here are some suggestions.

- A number of volunteer organizations have local chapters around the country. If there is a chapter in your community, contact them and ask how you can volunteer.
- Take part in a walk or run for a cure. These are held in many places across the country. Walkers or runners find sponsors before the event. Each sponsor donates a sum of money for every mile covered. The money collected from this effort goes toward research.

With a Group

Choose and research a major disease or health problem. Are there any local volunteer organizations for this health problem? Find out what volunteer opportunities they have for teens.

Paying for Health Care

Paying for health care can be difficult, especially if you have an **ongoing** illness. Surgery and hospital stays, for example, can cost thousands of dollars. Many people pay for health care by buying **health insurance.** This is *an insurance policy that covers most health care costs.* These people pay a monthly fee to the health insurance company for the policy. Some employers help their employees pay the monthly fee. When a person goes to the doctor or hospital, their insurance will pay a large part of the health care cost. Health insurance will pay part of the cost of prescription medicines as well. However, health insurance is still very expensive for many Americans and costs continue to rise.

Because of rising costs, there are new options when choosing health insurance. One option is **managed care.** This is *a health insurance plan that saves money by limiting people's choice of doctors.* Patients save money when they visit doctors who participate in the managed care plan. There are many kinds of

Academic Vocabulary

ongoing (ON goh ing) *(adjective)* currently taking place, continuing. *The weather is an ongoing concern for farmers.*

managed care plans. You might have heard of the most common plans: health maintenance organizations (HMOs) and preferred provider organizations (PPOs).

Two types of health insurance offered by the government are Medicaid and Medicare. Medicaid is for people with limited income. Medicare is for adults over the age of 65 and people of any age with certain disabilities.

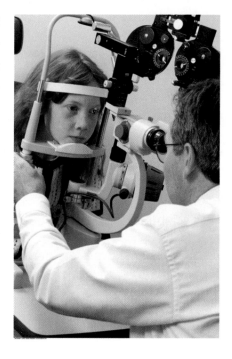

 **Reading Check** Explain
Tell how a patient saves money with a managed care plan.

Vision insurance is one type of health insurance that helps people pay for visits to the eye doctor. **What do you think dental insurance helps people pay for?**

Ge Online

Visit **glencoe.com** and complete the Interactive Study Guide for Lesson 5.

Lesson 5 Review

 After You Read

Review this lesson for new terms, major headings, and Reading Checks.

What I Learned

1. **Vocabulary** Define *health care*.

2. **Describe** Why is it important to have regular health checkups?

3. **Recall** What are some steps the government takes to oversee the health of Americans?

Thinking Critically

4. **Hypothesize** What kinds of information can a patient give to a primary care provider to help solve a health problem?

5. **Evaluate** How do volunteer health agencies contribute to our overall health?

Applying Health Skills

6. **Advocacy** Using the phone directory, make a list of health care resources for your community. Identify the kinds of health care each group offers. Convert your findings into a booklet. Share copies with other students.

Ge Online For more Lesson Review Activities, go to **glencoe.com**.

Lesson 5: Health Care in Your Community **167**

Building Health Skills

What Does Accessing Information Involve?

Accessing information involves finding valid information to make healthy choices. When looking at a source of information, ask yourself these questions:

- Is it scientific?
- Does it give more than one point of view?
- Does it agree with other sources?
- Is it trying to sell something?

Buyer Beware!

Follow the Model, Practice, and Apply steps to help you master this important health skill.

① Model

Read about how Lindsey uses the skill of accessing information to decide which sunglasses to purchase.

Lindsey wanted a pair of sunglasses. In health class, she learned that some advertisements aren't truthful. So when she saw some cool sunglasses in a magazine, she knew she needed more information. First, Lindsey went to a Web site and read that UV protection was important. The Web site ended in *.gov*, so she knew it was a valid source. Next, she went to the mall. She saw several different styles of sunglasses that she liked. Lindsey picked up one style with UV lenses. She also picked up another style she really liked that did not have UV lenses. Lindsey remembered what she had read on that government Web site. She knew that the UV lenses would protect her eyes from potential damage from the sun.

Lindsey knew the government Web site was a valid source she could trust. She felt confident choosing the sunglasses with UV lenses.

168

❷ Practice

Briana wants to choose a product to relieve her sore throat. Read the passage and then practice accessing information skills by answering the questions that follow.

Advertisements often make claims about a product's effectiveness. Briana has a sore throat. She asks her father to help choose a product that would relieve her symptoms. In a newspaper ad, they see a sale on throat lozenges. "Lasts all day," the ad reads. Another product, a throat spray, advertises that it would provide "instant relief." Using what you have learned about accessing information, answer these questions.

1. Are advertisements good sources of information? Why or why not?

2. What additional information might Briana and her father need to make a confident decision?

3. Where could they find valid information about the different products?

❸ Apply

Apply what you have learned about accessing information to complete the activity below.

Working with a group, find three different advertisements for health products. Write down what claim each advertisement makes about the product. Does each claim seem believable? What additional information is needed?

Identify two sources where teens could find valid information about these health products. Explain why these resources are valid.

Self-Check

- Did we find at least three different advertisements for health products?
- Did we name two sources of valid health information?
- Did we explain why these resources are valid?

Observing the Eye

Your eyes can adjust very quickly to different levels of light. The muscles inside the eye change so that more or less light comes in. Most people can also distinguish colors with their eyes. Some, however, are born without the ability to see certain colors. Try this activity to observe how your eyes react to light and color.

What You Will Need

- Mirror
- Pencil or pen
- Paper

What You Will Do

1 Turn off the lights. Sit in the dark for two to three minutes.

2 Turn the lights back on, and quickly look at your eyes in the mirror. Watch what happens in the center of your eyes. Record what you saw.

3 Once your eyes have adjusted to the light, do the color vision test. Look at the circle shown on this page. Can you see a number in the circle? If not, you may have trouble distinguishing between the colors red and green.

Wrapping It Up

As a class, make a chart or graph that compares the results for all students. What do your findings show?

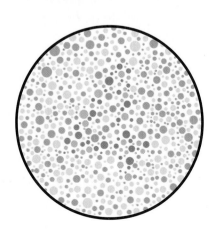

Reading Review

STUDY TO GO Visit **glencoe.com** to download quizzes and eFlashcards for Chapter 6.

FOLDABLES® Study Organizer

Foldables® and Other Study Aids Take out the Foldable® that you created for Lesson 1 and any graphic organizers that you created for Lessons 1–5. Find a partner, and quiz each other using these study aids.

Lesson 1 Your Teeth, Skin, and Hair

Main Idea Your personal hygiene affects all parts of your health triangle.

- Good hygiene includes caring for your teeth, skin, hair, and nails.
- Brushing and flossing your teeth, washing your hair, and keeping your nails clipped are simple tasks that keep you healthy.

Lesson 2 Protecting Your Eyes and Ears

Main Idea Your eyes and ears have important functions.

- You can protect your eyes by wearing safety goggles, reading in a well-lit space, and not sitting too close to the television or computer screen.
- Nearsightedness and farsightedness are two common vision problems.
- The ears carry sound to the brain and help you stay balanced.
- Many ear infections are the result of simple colds in the nose and throat.
- Protecting your ears from loud sounds is the best way to care for them.
- For serious eye and ear problems, special glasses and hearing aids can help.

Lesson 3 Choosing Health Products

Main Idea A smart consumer thinks before he or she buys a product.

- Personal likes and dislikes, the media, and your own experiences all affect your purchases.
- Reading labels, comparison shopping, and spotting false claims are three ways to be a good consumer.

Lesson 4 Using Medicines Responsibly

Main Idea Both prescription and nonprescription medicines must be used with care.

- Always read a medicine's label before you take it.
- A side effect is any reaction to a medicine other than the one intended.
- Tolerance means that the body becomes used to a medicine and it no longer has the same effect.
- It is important that your doctor know about all medicines that you are taking.
- Drug misuse involves using medicines in ways other than those intended.

Lesson 5 Health Care in Your Community

Main Idea Health care is any service provided by a team of health professionals.

- Regular checkups should be part of your overall health care plan and can prevent more serious illnesses from developing.
- Some health organizations work to treat and eliminate certain diseases.

Assessment

 After You Read

HEALTH QUIZ
Now that you have read the chapter, look back at your answers to the Health Quiz in the chapter opener. Would you change any of them? What would your answers be now?

Reviewing Vocabulary and Main Ideas

On a sheet of paper, write the numbers 1–6. After each number, write the term from the list that best completes each sentence.

- acne
- astigmatism
- dermis
- farsightedness
- fluoride
- nearsightedness
- health care
- specialist

Lesson 1 Your Teeth, Skin, and Hair

1. _____ is a substance that fights tooth decay.

2. A condition caused by overly active oil glands is called _____.

3. The thicker inner layer of the skin is known as the _____.

Lesson 2 Protecting Your Eyes and Ears

4. _____ is a condition in which near objects appear clear while those far away look blurry.

5. A misshaped cornea or lens that causes objects to look wavy or blurred is known as _____.

6. _____ is a condition in which faraway objects appear clear while near objects look blurry.

*On a sheet of paper, write the numbers 7–15. Write **True** or **False** for each statement. If the statement is false, change the underlined word to make it true.*

Lesson 3 Choosing Health Products

7. <u>Comparison shopping</u> involves comparing different brands of a product.

8. A <u>unit price</u> is the promise of a refund of your money if the product doesn't work as claimed.

9. The store brand of an item is also known as a <u>generic</u> brand.

Lesson 4 Using Medicines Responsibly

10. <u>Vaccines</u> are medicines that kill or stop the growth of bacteria and other specific germs.

11. When you develop a <u>side effect</u> to a medicine, it no longer has the same effect.

12. Taking more of a medicine than the doctor instructs is an example of <u>drug misuse</u>.

Lesson 5 Health Care in Your Community

13. When a problem is beyond your doctor's training, he or she might suggest that you see a <u>specialist</u>.

14. <u>Voluntary health agencies</u> are organizations that work to help prevent and cure certain diseases.

15. <u>Managed care</u> is a program to help people with limited income get health care.

Go Online Visit **glencoe.com** and take the Online Quiz for Chapter 6.

Thinking Critically

Using complete sentences, answer the following questions on a sheet of paper.

16. **Predict** If you don't treat a hearing problem, how might it affect other areas of your health?

17. **Evaluate** Are consumer skills only good for saving money? Explain.

Write About It

18. **Expository Writing** Imagine that you are writing an article about a volunteer health agency. Explain the kinds of things the volunteer health agency does. Tell how a teen can help.

Applying Technology

Good Hygiene

Use PowerPoint® to create a 10-slide presentation that talks about the importance of good personal hygiene.

- Open a new PowerPoint® project. Choose one of the topics talked about in this chapter.
- Include information on the slides that illustrates good personal hygiene.
- Insert a digital image for each slide.
- Edit your presentation for clarity and content.
- Save your presentation.

Standardized Test Practice

Math

Use the graph to answer the questions.

> **TEST-TAKING TIP**
>
> Make sure you understand the parts of a graph. Read the title. Look at the label next to the vertical (*y*) axis. Look at the label beneath the horizontal (*x*) axis.

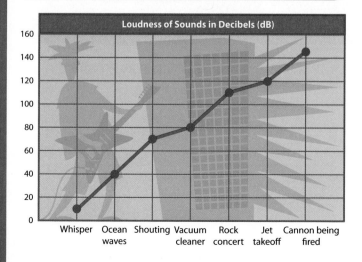

1. If any noise above 85 dB is harmful, then all of the following sounds are harmful *except*
   - **A.** a jet takeoff.
   - **B.** a cannon being fired.
   - **C.** a vacuum cleaner running.
   - **D.** a rock concert.

2. Based on the line graph, which inference can be made?
   - **A.** Two people shouting are likely to be louder than a vacuum cleaner.
   - **B.** Sounds under a whisper are probably too quiet to hear.
   - **C.** Going to the beach can harm your hearing.
   - **D.** Airport ground crews can develop hearing problems.

Chapter Preview

▲ Working with the Photo

Knowing how your body systems work will help you understand how to take care of your body. **Can you name some of the main body systems?**

Start-Up Activities

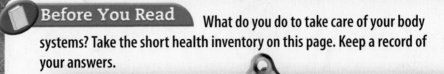

Before You Read What do you do to take care of your body systems? Take the short health inventory on this page. Keep a record of your answers.

HEALTH INVENTORY

1. I wear a helmet when riding my bike.
(a) always   (b) sometimes   (c) never

2. I make sure to include calcium-rich foods in my diet.
(a) always   (b) sometimes   (c) never

3. I drink several glasses of water each day.
(a) always   (b) sometimes   (c) never

4. I take time to stretch after exercising.
(a) always   (b) sometimes   (c) never

FOLDABLES Study Organizer

As You Read Make this Foldable® to help you organize the information on the forms and functions of body systems in Lesson 1. Begin with a plain sheet of 8½" × 11" paper.

1 Fold the sheet of paper along the long axis. Leave a ½" tab along the side.

2 Turn the paper. Fold in half, then fold in half again.

3 Unfold and cut the top layer along the three fold lines. This makes four tabs.

4 Turn the paper vertically, and label the tabs as shown.

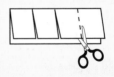

Cells

Tissues

Organs

Body Systems

Write down the definitions of the terms *cells, tissues, organs,* and *body systems,* and list examples of each under the appropriate tab.

G Online Visit **glencoe.com** and complete the eFlashcards to preview Chapter 7 vocabulary terms.

From Cells to Body Systems

Guide to Reading

Building Vocabulary
Write each term below in your notebook. As you come across the term in your reading, write its definition.

- cells (p. 177)
- tissues (p. 177)
- organs (p. 177)
- body systems (p. 177)

Focusing on the Main Ideas
In this lesson, you will learn to

- **identify** the body's building blocks.
- **name** the major body systems and identify their functions.
- **list** ways to care for your body systems.

Reading Strategy
Organizing Information Make a bull's-eye diagram like the one to the right. Show how cells and other "building blocks" of the body relate.

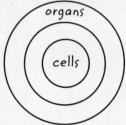

FOLDABLES Study Organizer Use the Foldable® on p. 175 as you read this lesson.

ⓠuick Write

Watch your hand as you form a fist and then release it. Try to name the parts you see working together.

Parts of the Body

Have you ever looked inside a computer? If you have, you know there are many parts that work together. Each part does a separate job. The same is true of your body. Like a computer, your body has a command center. It gives instructions to muscles and joints so that you can raise your arms. It is instructing your eyes to read this page right now!

► FIGURE 7.1

BUILDING BLOCKS OF THE BODY

The body system shown here is the nervous system. What is the most basic building block of the nervous system?

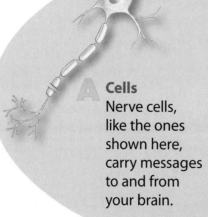

Cells
Nerve cells, like the ones shown here, carry messages to and from your brain.

Tissues
This tissue is made up of nerve cells.

From Cells to Systems

Your body is made up of many different kinds of cells, which **vary** in size and shape. **Cells** are *the basic building blocks of life.* Each cell does a specialized job. Nerve cells, for example, carry messages to and from your brain. Skin cells, on the other hand, are flat and rectangular. This allows them to spread out and cover the surface of your body.

Groups of similar cells that do the same kind of work are called **tissues.** For example, nerve cells such as those shown in **Figure 7.1** come together to form nerve tissue. Tissues come together to form organs. **Organs** are *structures made up of different types of tissues that all work together.* For example, your heart is an organ made up of muscle tissue, nerve tissue, and blood tissue. Organs perform specific jobs. Your brain is an organ that allows you to think and feel. Your stomach is an organ that digests and stores the food you eat. The next level up from organs is body systems. **Body systems** are *groups of organs that perform a body function.* For example, the digestive system breaks down food for energy.

Academic Vocabulary

vary (VAIR ee) *(verb)* to be different. *The organs of the body vary in shape and size.*

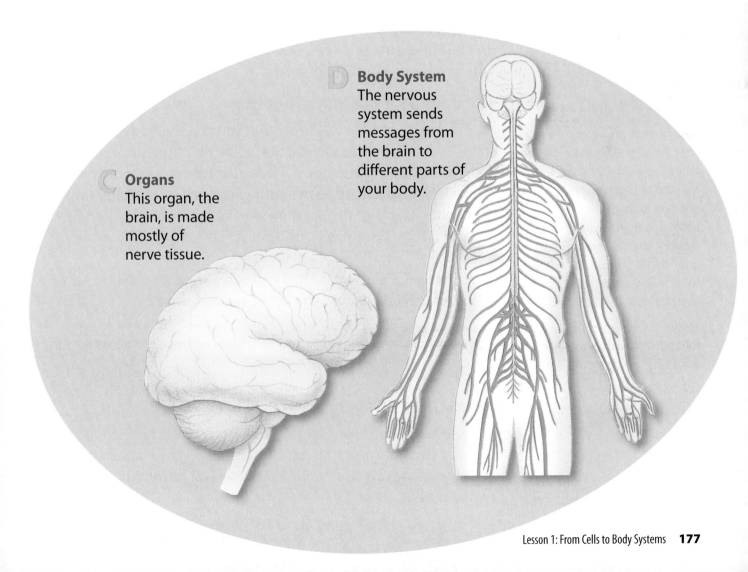

Organs
This organ, the brain, is made mostly of nerve tissue.

Body System
The nervous system sends messages from the brain to different parts of your body.

Main Body Systems and Their Functions

The chart shows the main body systems. **Which of these work together?**

Body System	Jobs
Circulatory system	Brings food and oxygen to cells and takes away cell waste
Digestive system	Breaks down food for energy
Endocrine system	Produces hormones that regulate body functions
Excretory system	Gets rid of body wastes
Muscular system	Allows movement of body parts
Nervous system	Controls all body systems; sends and receives messages; and helps you see, hear, taste, smell, and feel
Reproductive system	Involved in producing *offspring,* or children
Respiratory system	Carries oxygen to blood and removes carbon dioxide
Skeletal system	Provides a hard cage to protect body organs, gives the body structure, and works with the muscular system to allow movement

Connect To... Language Arts

Scientific Word Parts

Many diseases are named after the parts of the body they affect. Take, for example, the word *osteoporosis.* It is a disease that weakens the bones. The word's root, *"osteo"* means "bone." The ending, *"osis"* means "disease of." Other word parts named after the body are:

Optic — Eye

Neur(o) — Nerves or nervous system

Cardi(o) — Heart

Bronch(io) — Lungs

What body system do you think is affected by bronchitis?

The names and functions of the major body systems appear in **Figure 7.2.** This chapter will cover all of these systems except for the endocrine and reproductive systems. Those two systems will be discussed in Chapter 8.

The Body Systems Work Together

The body systems work together to keep the body functioning. For example, the skeletal and muscular systems pair up to support and move the body. They also form a protective shell around organs. The digestive and excretory systems also work as a team. The digestive system breaks down food for energy. The excretory system gets rid of unused food from your body as waste.

Figure 7.3 shows the body systems in action. Notice how all systems relate during the act of running.

 **Reading Check** List Name three body systems, and tell what each does.

Care of the Body Systems

How can you take care of your body systems? The key is healthy living. You've already learned about habits that promote good health and wellness. Here is a summary of some useful ideas.

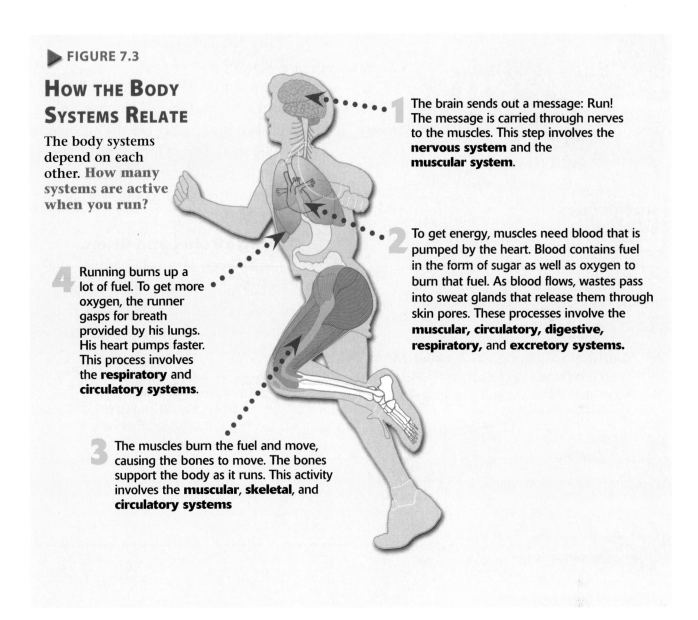

► FIGURE 7.3

HOW THE BODY SYSTEMS RELATE

The body systems depend on each other. **How many systems are active when you run?**

1 The brain sends out a message: Run! The message is carried through nerves to the muscles. This step involves the **nervous system** and the **muscular system**.

2 To get energy, muscles need blood that is pumped by the heart. Blood contains fuel in the form of sugar as well as oxygen to burn that fuel. As blood flows, wastes pass into sweat glands that release them through skin pores. These processes involve the **muscular, circulatory, digestive, respiratory,** and **excretory systems.**

3 The muscles burn the fuel and move, causing the bones to move. The bones support the body as it runs. This activity involves the **muscular**, **skeletal**, and **circulatory systems**

4 Running burns up a lot of fuel. To get more oxygen, the runner gasps for breath provided by his lungs. His heart pumps faster. This process involves the **respiratory** and **circulatory systems**.

- **Eat well.** Following a balanced eating plan will keep your heart and bloodstream healthy. Foods rich in calcium build strong bones. Drinking plenty of water aids your digestive and excretory systems.

- **Get plenty of physical activity.** Teens, should get an hour of physical activity most days. Physical activity makes muscles, bones, and joints stronger. Proper warmups and cooldowns are also important to muscle and bone health. Aerobic activity helps your heart and lungs work more efficiently.

- **Maintain a healthy weight.** This will put less stress on your bones and organs. It will also make it easier for your heart to pump blood throughout your body.

Go Online

Visit **glencoe.com** and complete the Interactive Study Guide for Lesson 1.

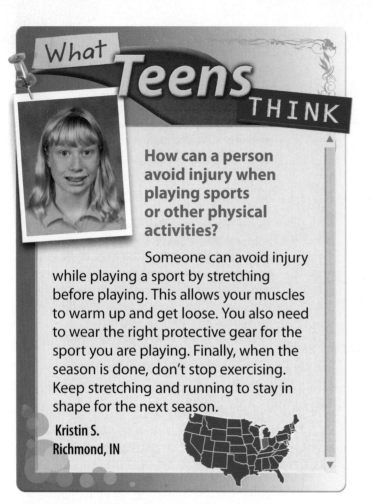

What Teens THINK

How can a person avoid injury when playing sports or other physical activities?

Someone can avoid injury while playing a sport by stretching before playing. This allows your muscles to warm up and get loose. You also need to wear the right protective gear for the sport you are playing. Finally, when the season is done, don't stop exercising. Keep stretching and running to stay in shape for the next season.

Kristin S.
Richmond, IN

- **Play it safe.** Make sure to wear the right gear. A helmet can protect your skull and your brain. Elbow and knee pads will help prevent broken bones. Pay attention to your skill level. For example, if you are just learning how to ski, don't try the most difficult course on the mountain.

- **Avoid alcohol and drugs.** Alcohol can seriously damage the liver and other important organs. Smoking damages the lungs. Drugs of all kinds can damage the nervous system.

Reading Check

Give Examples Name two habits that keep your body systems healthy.

Lesson 1 Review

 After You Read

Review this lesson for new terms, major headings, and Reading Checks.

What I Learned

1. *Vocabulary* Define *tissues*.

2. *Give Examples* What is the function of the circulatory system?

3. *Recall* Name some behaviors that keep the skeletal system healthy.

Thinking Critically

4. *Synthesize* Give an example of a risk a teen might take. Show how this behavior affects one or more body systems.

5. *Analyze* How might an injury to your nervous system affect your muscular system?

Applying Health Skills

6. *Accessing Information* Different types of safety helmets are used for different physical activities. Using reliable print or online resources, research different types of approved helmets. What kind of helmet would be best to wear while riding a bike? How about when you play football?

G⊙ Online For more Lesson Review Activities, go to **glencoe.com.**

Bones and Muscles

Guide to Reading

● **Building Vocabulary**

Write each term below in your notebook. As you come across each term in your reading, write its definition.

- skeletal system (p. 181)
- joints (p. 182)
- muscular system (p. 183)

● **Focusing on the Main Ideas**

In this lesson, you will learn to

- **explain** the parts and functions of the skeletal system.
- **explain** the parts and functions of the muscular system.
- **determine** ways to protect the bones and muscles.

● **Reading Strategy**

Comparing As you read, look for similarities and differences between the skeletal system and the muscular system.

Write a paragraph describing why you think muscles sometimes get sore after exercise or other physical activity.

The Skeletal System

Your bones are living tissue that make up the organs of your **skeletal system.** This is *a body system consisting of bones and the tissues connecting them.* Your bones are like the steel girders that support a skyscraper. They form your body's framework. They protect its soft parts from injury. Your bones also allow you to stand and move, with the help of your muscles. Adults have 206 separate bones in their bodies.

Bones

The bones inside your body are made up of living tissue and cells. Because bone tissue is alive, it is always being destroyed and remade to keep your bones strong. Bones are hard on the outside and have spongy tissue on the inside. This tissue produces blood cells for the circulatory system. Bones also store minerals such as calcium. Calcium strengthens your bones and teeth. When your body needs calcium, the bones release small amounts into the blood. The blood takes the calcium to where it is needed in the body.

▶ Regular physical activity helps keep your bones healthy. **What is another way to strengthen your bones?**

Joints

Joints are *places where one bone meets another*. Different joints move in different ways. Some joints pivot, like your neck. The end of one bone rotates inside a ring formed by another. This joint can move up and down and from side to side. A hinge joint moves in only one direction like a door hinge. Your knee and elbow are examples of hinge joints.

In ball-and-socket joints, the round end of one bone moves inside another's cup-shaped opening. A ball-and-socket joint can move in all directions. Your hip is an example of a ball-and-socket joint. Gliding joints allow one part of a bone to slide over another bone. They also move in a back-and-forth motion. Gliding joints are found in your wrists and ankles. **Figure 7.4** shows the four major types of joints as well as important bones.

Reading Check **Define** What are *joints*?

▼ FIGURE 7.4

THE SKELETAL SYSTEM

Notice the different shapes of different bones. **Which of these bones have joints that pivot? Which have hinge joints?**

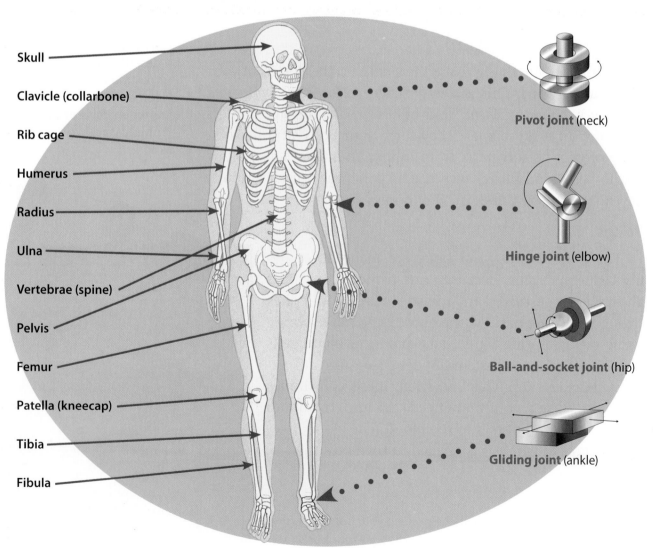

Skull

Clavicle (collarbone)

Rib cage

Humerus

Radius

Ulna

Vertebrae (spine)

Pelvis

Femur

Patella (kneecap)

Tibia

Fibula

Pivot joint (neck)

Hinge joint (elbow)

Ball-and-socket joint (hip)

Gliding joint (ankle)

Health Skills Activity

Practicing Healthful Behaviors

Building Strong Bones

Your body needs plenty of calcium to keep your bones strong. Calcium is a mineral that makes bones hard. As a teen, your body is storing calcium to keep your bones healthy and strong as you get older. By eating calcium-rich foods, you help your body prepare for adulthood. The foods in the picture are all good sources of calcium.

With a Group

Create a plan for a meal that is rich in calcium. Share your meal plan with the other groups so each student in class will have a variety of calcium-rich meals to choose from.

The Muscular System

Your **muscular system** is made up of *all the muscles in your body*. Your muscles move your bones, pump your blood, and move food through your stomach and intestines.

There are three main types of muscles: skeletal, cardiac, and smooth. Skeletal muscles connect to and move your bones. You have this type of muscle in your arms, face, abdomen, back, and legs. They are considered *voluntary muscles* because you are able to control them. You are able to run, for example, by controlling the skeletal muscles in your legs.

Cardiac muscles are **located** only in the heart. They pump blood into and out of your heart. Cardiac muscles are *involuntary*. They move automatically without you having to think about them.

Smooth muscles are found in many of your internal organs. The stomach, intestines, bladder, and blood vessels all have smooth muscles. Like cardiac muscles, smooth muscles are *involuntary* muscles. They slowly contract and relax on their own. **Figure 7.5** on the next page shows important muscle groups of the body.

Academic Vocabulary

located (LOH keyt ed)
(verb) found. *Your heart is located inside your chest.*

 **FIGURE 7.5**

THE MUSCULAR SYSTEM

Muscles do many different jobs in the body. What are the three major types of muscles?

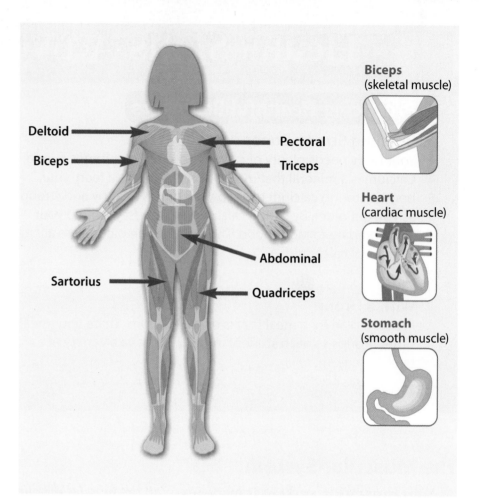

Deltoid

Biceps

Pectoral

Triceps

Abdominal

Sartorius

Quadriceps

Biceps
(skeletal muscle)

Heart
(cardiac muscle)

Stomach
(smooth muscle)

G⊙ Online

Visit glencoe.com and complete the Interactive Study Guide for Lesson 2.

Lesson 2 Review

 After You Read

Review this lesson for new terms, major headings, and Reading Checks.

What I Learned

1. **Vocabulary** What is the *skeletal system*? What does this system do?

2. **Identify** Name the four types of joints. Briefly describe each.

3. **Explain** Tell the difference between voluntary and involuntary muscles.

Thinking Critically

4. **Apply** Juan slipped on the ice. When he stood up, his leg looked fine yet it hurt. Why do you suppose this was the case?

5. **Analyze** Do you think the muscles responsible for activities such as breathing and digesting food are voluntary or involuntary? Are they smooth or skeletal muscles?

Applying Health Skills

6. **Practicing Healthful Behaviors** During most sports, your body parts are frequently in motion. Think of a sport, then list ways to protect the bones and muscles from injury when playing that sport.

G⊙ Online For more Lesson Review Activities, go to **glencoe.com**.

Digestion and Excretion

Guide to Reading

● **Building Vocabulary**
Look for ways the words below are related. Keep these connections in mind as you read the lesson.

■ digestion (p. 185)
■ digestive system (p. 185)
■ excretory system (p. 186)

● **Focusing on the Main Ideas**
In this lesson, you will learn to

■ **explain** the parts and functions of the digestive system.
■ **explain** the parts and functions of the excretory system.
■ **apply** the skill of advocacy to promote ways to care for the digestive and excretory systems.

● **Reading Strategy**
Sequencing Create a flowchart that shows the path of food as your body digests it.

Quick Write

Write a short paragraph explaining how you think digestion and excretion are related.

The Digestive System

As explained in Chapter 4, the foods you eat contain nutrients. Nutrients are substances that nourish and provide energy for the body. *The process by which your body breaks down food into small nutrient particles* is called **digestion.** *The body system that controls this process* is the **digestive** (dy·JES·tiv) **system.** The digestive system has eight main parts, which are shown in **Figure 7.6** on the next page. The arrow shows the order in which the different parts enter into the process of digestion.

The Digestive Process

The digestive process begins in your mouth. When you bite into an apple, for example, your teeth begin grinding the bite of apple into small bits. Chemicals in your saliva (suh·LY·vuh) called *enzymes* (EN·zymz) break down the apple further.

▶ The process of digestion begins in your mouth. **How can eating healthy foods help your digestive system?**

When you swallow, the crushed apple passes into your throat. Muscles contract and relax to push the fruit down the esophagus and into the stomach. The esophagus is a muscular tube that connects the mouth to the stomach. Strong acid, enzymes, and churning muscles in your stomach break down the food particles even further. The food particles move next into the small intestine. There, digestion breaks down the food particles into nutrients that are absorbed into the blood. The blood carries these nutrients throughout the body.

Reading Check **Explain** What are enzymes? What is their role?

The Excretory System

Your **excretory** (EK·skruh·tohr·ee) **system** *gets rid of some of the wastes your body produces and also maintains fluid balance.* The parts of the apple that can't be absorbed through digestion

FIGURE 7.6

THE DIGESTIVE PROCESS

The digestive system involves many different body parts. **Where does this process begin?**

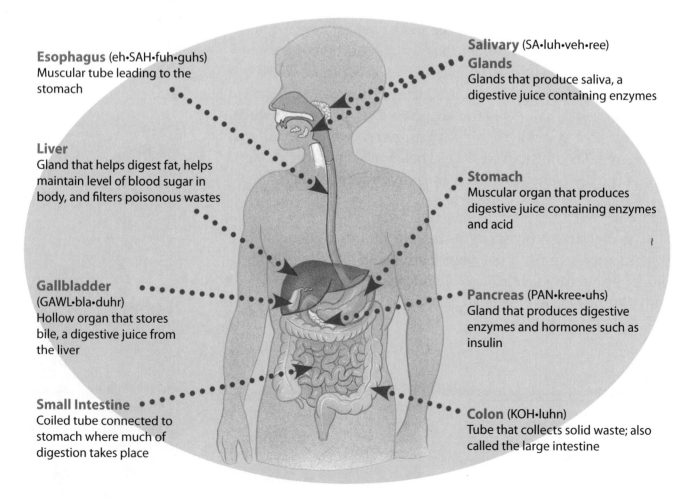

Esophagus (eh·SAH·fuh·guhs)
Muscular tube leading to the stomach

Liver
Gland that helps digest fat, helps maintain level of blood sugar in body, and filters poisonous wastes

Gallbladder
(GAWL·bla·duhr)
Hollow organ that stores bile, a digestive juice from the liver

Small Intestine
Coiled tube connected to stomach where much of digestion takes place

Salivary (SA·luh·veh·ree)
Glands
Glands that produce saliva, a digestive juice containing enzymes

Stomach
Muscular organ that produces digestive juice containing enzymes and acid

Pancreas (PAN·kree·uhs)
Gland that produces digestive enzymes and hormones such as insulin

Colon (KOH·luhn)
Tube that collects solid waste; also called the large intestine

become waste and are excreted, or *removed,* from the body. Your respiratory system and skin are also part of the excretory system. The respiratory system gets rid of carbon dioxide when you exhale. Your skin releases liquid waste and salt in the form of sweat. Your body needs to get rid of wastes to remain healthy. If wastes are not removed, they can build up in the body and damage organs.

Parts of the Excretory System

The major organs of the excretory system are the colon, kidneys, and bladder. Food particles that can't be absorbed in the small intestine are sent to the colon. There, most of the water is removed and absorbed by the body. When the colon fills up, the brain sends a message to the muscles in the colon telling them to contract. This action removes solid waste from the body.

The kidneys have several jobs. They filter the blood, remove water and waste, and maintain the body's fluid balance. When your brain detects too much water in your blood, your kidneys remove the excess water as liquid waste. Liquid waste from the kidneys, or *urine* (YOO·rihn), is stored in the bladder. When the bladder is full, the urine is passed out of the body.

 **Reading Check** **List** Name two organs of the excretory system.

▲ Drinking water helps the digestive and excretory systems function. **What is another health benefit of drinking water each day?**

Visit glencoe.com and complete the Interactive Study Guide for Lesson 3.

Lesson 3 Review

After You Read

Review this lesson for new terms, major headings, and Reading Checks.

What I Learned

1. *Vocabulary* Define *digestion,* and use it in an original sentence.

2. *Recall* Once food is in the throat, how does it reach the stomach?

3. *List* Name two functions of the kidneys.

Thinking Critically

4. *Analyze* Do you think it would take your body longer to digest a large piece of food or one that has been cut into small pieces? Explain.

5. *Hypothesize* What do you think would happen if a person's kidneys were not working properly?

Applying Health Skills

6. *Advocacy* One way to maintain the health of the digestive system is to eat slowly. Research other ways to keep your digestive and excretory systems healthy. Make a list of your findings. Share this list with family members.

 Go Online For more Lesson Review Activities, go to **glencoe.com.**

Heart, Blood, Lungs, and Nerves

Guide to Reading

Building Vocabulary

How are the terms below related? Which terms are muscles? Which terms are body systems?

- circulatory system (p. 188)
- heart (p. 189)
- blood pressure (p. 189)
- respiratory system (p. 191)
- lungs (p. 191)
- diaphragm (p. 191)
- nervous system (p. 192)
- neurons (p. 192)
- spinal cord (p. 192)

Focusing on the Main Ideas

In this lesson, you will learn to

- **explain** how blood moves through the body.
- **understand** how your nervous system controls body functions.
- **analyze** factors in the environment that influence respiratory health.

Reading Strategy

Classifying As you read the lesson, list the parts of each body system discussed. Briefly describe the role of each part.

*Q*uick Write

Take a deep breath. Feel your heart beating in your chest. Write the names of the body systems that make these actions possible.

The Circulatory System

Every modern building has pipes and wires inside the walls that carry water and energy throughout the building. Although these pipes and wires are hidden, each does an important job. The same is true of your body's **circulatory system.** This system *allows the body to move blood to and from tissues.* The blood delivers oxygen, food, and other materials to the cells. It also carries waste products away from the cells. The circulatory system, or *cardiovascular system,* consists of the heart, blood vessels, and blood. See **Figure 7.7** for more information on how the cardiovascular system works.

◀ During exercise, your circulatory system pumps extra blood to and from your body's cells. **Why do your cells need extra blood during exercise or other physical activity?**

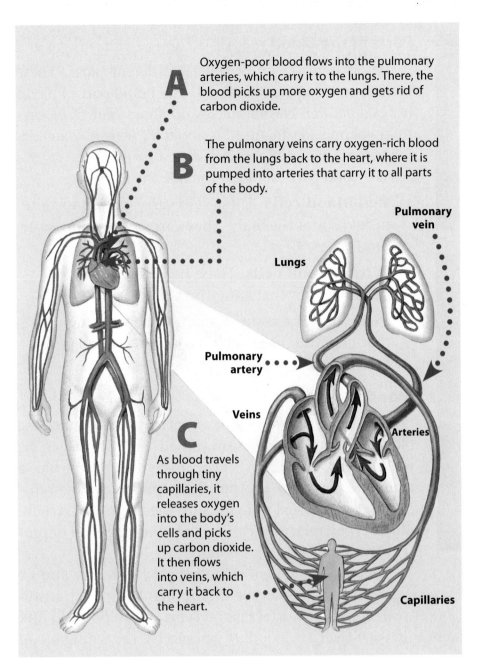

A Oxygen-poor blood flows into the pulmonary arteries, which carry it to the lungs. There, the blood picks up more oxygen and gets rid of carbon dioxide.

B The pulmonary veins carry oxygen-rich blood from the lungs back to the heart, where it is pumped into arteries that carry it to all parts of the body.

Pulmonary vein

Lungs

Pulmonary artery

Veins

Arteries

C As blood travels through tiny capillaries, it releases oxygen into the body's cells and picks up carbon dioxide. It then flows into veins, which carry it back to the heart.

Capillaries

 **FIGURE 7.7**

THE CIRCULATORY SYSTEM

The blood vessels shown in blue carry oxygen-poor blood toward the heart and lungs. The red blood vessels carry oxygen-rich blood from the lungs to the heart. They also carry blood to the rest of the body. **Why are the pulmonary arteries shown in blue?**

Go Online

Topic: Keeping Track of Your Pulse

Visit **glencoe.com** for Student Web Activities that will teach you how to test your heart rate, or pulse.

Activity: Using the information provided at the link above, take your pulse three times a day —when you first get up, at noon before lunch, and before you go to bed—to see when your heart is working hardest.

The Heart: The Body's Pump

The muscle that acts as the pump for the circulatory system is the **heart.** It pushes blood through tubes called blood vessels. There are three different types of blood vessels. *Arteries* carry blood away from the heart. *Veins* return blood to the heart. Between the arteries and veins are tiny blood vessels known as *capillaries* (KAP·uh·layr·eez). The capillaries deliver oxygen and nutrients in the blood directly to the body's cells.

The force of blood pushing against the blood vessel walls is called **blood pressure.** Blood pressure is greatest when the heart contracts, or pushes out blood. It is lowest between heartbeats, when the heart relaxes.

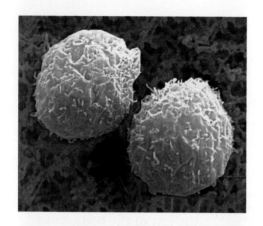

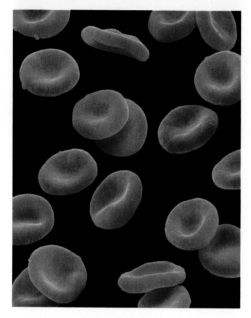

▲ This picture shows blood cells magnified many times. **What does each type of blood cell do?**

Parts of the Blood

Blood is made up of several different parts. These include solids as well as liquid. The liquid part of blood is *blood plasma*. Plasma makes up about half of blood's total volume. Plasma itself is about 92 percent water. Its job is to transport blood cells and dissolve food.

The solid parts of blood include the following:

- **Red blood cells.** These cells carry oxygen to all other cells of the body. They carry away some waste products.

- **White blood cells.** These help destroy disease-causing germs that enter the body.

- **Platelets.** These are small, disk-shaped structures that help your blood clot. Clotting keeps you from losing too much blood when you have a cut.

Blood Types

When a person undergoes surgery, he or she may lose blood during the operation. Blood that is lost can be replaced through a *transfusion*. This is transferring blood from one person to another. Before blood can be transfused, doctors need to make sure the *blood types* match. Blood types are classifications based on the kind of protein the red blood cells contain.

There are four main blood types: A, B, AB, and O. Everyone is born with one type or another. During a transfusion, if you receive the correct blood type, your blood will mix smoothly with the new blood. If you receive the wrong blood type, your blood cells will clump together with the new cells. This can cause serious health problems, even death.

Blood may also contain something called an Rh factor. Blood is either Rh-positive or Rh-negative. People with Rh-positive blood can receive blood from Rh-positive or Rh-negative donors. People with Rh-negative blood can only receive blood from people who are also Rh-negative.

Today, all blood donations are carefully monitored. When a person donates blood, his or her blood type and Rh factor are checked and carefully labeled. The blood is stored in a blood bank until needed.

Reading Check **Identify** Name the main parts of the circulatory system.

The Respiratory System

Your **respiratory system** *enables you to breathe*. Breathing in, or inhaling, brings oxygen into your lungs. Oxygen is needed by the body for survival. The **lungs** are *the main organs of the respiratory system*. When you breathe out, or exhale, the lungs get rid of carbon dioxide gas. The parts of the respiratory system and their functions are shown in **Figure 7.8**.

How You Breathe

Breathing begins with the **diaphragm** (DY·uh·fram). This is *a large muscle at the bottom of the chest*. When you breathe in, the diaphragm contracts. This tightening of the diaphragm allows the lungs to expand and fill with air. When you breathe out, the diaphragm expands. As it enlarges, it pushes on the lungs, forcing out the air.

▼ **FIGURE 7.8**

THE RESPIRATORY SYSTEM

The respiratory system is divided into upper and lower sections. Each performs a different job. In which section are the alveoli found?

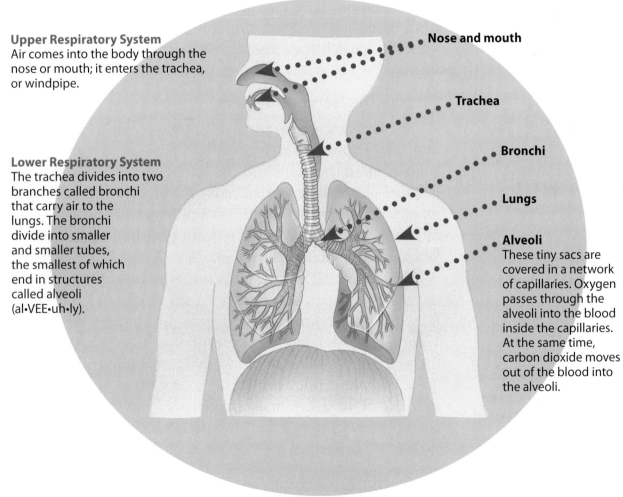

Upper Respiratory System
Air comes into the body through the nose or mouth; it enters the trachea, or windpipe.

Lower Respiratory System
The trachea divides into two branches called bronchi that carry air to the lungs. The bronchi divide into smaller and smaller tubes, the smallest of which end in structures called alveoli (al·VEE·uh·ly).

Nose and mouth

Trachea

Bronchi

Lungs

Alveoli
These tiny sacs are covered in a network of capillaries. Oxygen passes through the alveoli into the blood inside the capillaries. At the same time, carbon dioxide moves out of the blood into the alveoli.

Reading Check **Identify** what are the main parts of the respiratory system? How do they function?

DEVELOPING Good Character

Citizenship

You can demonstrate good citizenship by sharing what you learn about protecting your health with others. For example, encourage family members to protect their brains by always wearing a helmet when riding a bike.

What are some other ways you could promote healthy choices in your family or neighborhood?

Careers for the 21st Century

Doctor

Doctors are health care professionals who treat illnesses and teach people how to stay healthy. Some doctors treat one illness. Other doctors treat all the illnesses that affect a body system. Some doctors also provide basic care. Doctors are in great demand because people are living longer and the population is growing. You can prepare for a career as a doctor by studying the body systems and how they relate to each other.

What skills does a doctor need? Go to *Career Corner* at glencoe.com to find out.

The Nervous System

The **nervous system** is *the control and communication system of the body.* Its command center is the brain. The human brain does several important jobs. It processes thoughts and feelings. It also helps your body process and respond to information it receives from your senses. For example, when you smell fresh-baked cookies, your brain responds to the aroma by telling your tongue to produce saliva.

The brain is made up of billions of **neurons** (NOO·rahnz). These are *cells that carry electrical messages*, the language of the nervous system. There are three types of neurons: sensory neurons, connecting neurons, and motor neurons. Sensory neurons receive information from the outside world. For example, the smell of the fresh-baked cookies would be picked up by sensory neurons in the nose. Connecting neurons take the information picked up by the sensory neurons and pass it on to the motor neurons. The motor neurons send messages to the muscles and glands, telling them how to respond. If you like the smell of fresh-baked cookies, your motor neurons will probably tell your muscles to reach for a cookie, while your glands will produce saliva.

Parts of the Nervous System

The nervous system consists of the central nervous system and the peripheral nervous system. The *central nervous system* is made up of the brain and the spinal cord. The **spinal cord** is *a tube of neurons that runs along the spine.* The brain is made up of many parts. Each part has a different function. The largest part of the brain is the cerebrum (suh·REE·bruhm). This is where thinking takes place.

The *peripheral* (puh·RIF·uh·ruhl) *nervous system* is made up of nerves branching out from the brain and spinal cord. It handles both your voluntary and involuntary movements. Voluntary movements are ones you control. Lifting your arm to throw a ball is a voluntary movement. Involuntary movements are those you cannot control. The beating of your heart is an example of an involuntary movement. The parts of both the central nervous system and the peripheral nervous system are shown in **Figure 7.9**.

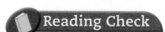 **Reading Check**   **Identify** Name the two main parts of the nervous system.

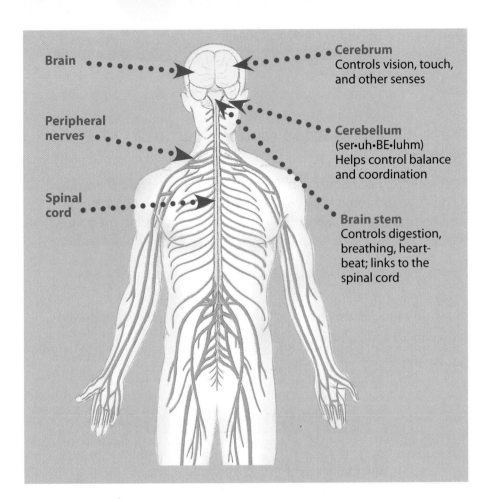

Brain

Peripheral nerves

Spinal cord

Cerebrum
Controls vision, touch, and other senses

Cerebellum
(ser·uh·BE·luhm)
Helps control balance and coordination

Brain stem
Controls digestion, breathing, heartbeat; links to the spinal cord

◀ **FIGURE 7.9**

THE NERVOUS SYSTEM

The central nervous system, shown in yellow, contains the brain and spinal cord. They work together to send messages to the peripheral nervous system, shown in blue. **Which part of the brain controls your sense of smell?**

Go Online

Visit **glencoe.com** and complete the Interactive Study Guide for Lesson 4.

Lesson 4 Review

 After You Read

Review this lesson for new terms, major headings, and Reading Checks.

What I Learned

1. *Recall* What are the three types of blood vessels? What are their functions?

2. *Vocabulary* What is the *diaphragm*?

3. *List* Name two types of neurons, and tell what each does.

Thinking Critically

4. *Analyze* When Nick's father went to give blood, he was tested for his blood type. Why?

5. *Synthesize* Think about the movement of your chest as your lungs take in air. Is this voluntary or involuntary movement? Which part of the nervous system controls this action?

Applying Health Skills

6. *Analyzing Influences* A number of factors in the environment might influence respiratory health. Make a list of these factors and discuss their role in the health of the community.

Why Is It Important to Practice Healthful Behaviors?

When you practice healthful behaviors, you take specific actions to stay healthy and avoid risky behaviors. This will help you prevent injury, illness, disease, and other health problems. Caring for your body systems includes:

- staying physically active
- eating well
- drinking plenty of water
- avoiding harmful substances
- taking care of illnesses
- getting enough rest
- wearing protective gear during sports

Maintaining Healthy Body Systems

Follow the Model, Practice, and Apply steps to help you master this important health skill.

① Model

Read about how Brandon practices healthful behaviors by making a list of helpful habits to keep his bones strong.

The different body systems work together to keep your body functioning properly. As a result, the health of one body system affects the health of others. Brandon knows that keeping his skeletal system healthy is important to his total health. He made a list of healthful habits to keep his bones strong:

1. Eat calcium-rich foods such as milk and yogurt.
2. Avoid tobacco and alcohol.
3. Walk or jog to school whenever I can.
4. Wear a helmet when riding my bike.

② Practice

Read about how Annie can practice healthful habits to benefit her respiratory system.

Annie wants to try out for the cycling club at school. Because cycling requires strong muscles, she wants to develop some healthful habits that will benefit her muscular system. Help Annie by answering the following questions:

1. What are two habits Annie can practice to take care of her muscular system?

2. How will these habits help Annie take care of other body systems?

③ Apply

Apply what you learned about practicing healthful behaviors to complete the activity below.

Working with a group, choose a body system you learned about and create a report explaining how to care for it. Describe why caring for this body system is important. Identify at least four actions to keep this body system healthy. Explain how these actions can benefit your chosen body system. How do these actions keep other body systems healthy? Present your report to the class.

Self-Check
- Did we tell why care of our chosen body system is important?
- Did we identify at least four actions that will benefit our chosen body system?
- Did we explain how these actions keep this body system and other systems healthy?

The Mystery of
SLEEP

You'll spend a third of your life sleeping, but that helps keep your body in shape.

Everyone knows that you can't live without sleep, but no one knows exactly why or precisely how sleep works. Some researchers, such as Dr. Terrence Sejnowski, are working on a theory. He says the brain uses deep slumber to "shut off" so that it can process memories of the day. "It's like when you move out of your house so workers can renovate the kitchen," Dr. Sejnowski says. According to Sejnowski, sleep gives your brain time to refresh itself. In the morning, your brain is ready to go to work.

Scientists such as Dr. Sejnowksi may have different ideas about how sleep works to keep your organs in good working order. All scientists agree, however, that just as eating right and getting enough exercise are important, sleep is something your body needs to keep going strong. During sleep many of your body's major organs and regulatory systems continue to work actively. Some parts of your brain actually increase their activity while you are making zzzz's, and your body produces more of certain hormones that you need.

Did you know that you have an internal biological clock that regulates the timing of sleep? It programs each person to feel sleepy during nighttime hours and to be active during the day. Natural light sets your biological clock to the 24-hour cycle of day and night. And like some clocks, you wind down at the end of the day. That's when your body says it's time to get a good night's rest.

SLEEP TIPS

A good night's sleep can help you do your best in school and at other activities. Use these tips to get the most out of snooze time.

- Set a regular time for bed each night, and stick to it.
- Follow a relaxing bedtime routine, like listening to quiet music or reading a book.
- Don't exercise too close to bedtime.
- Skip anything with caffeine, such as cola drinks, six hours before going to bed.
- Turn off your TV, computer, video game, and other noisy gadgets 30 minutes before bedtime.

Reading Review

Visit **glencoe.com** to download quizzes and eFlashcards for Chapter 7.

FOLDABLES® Study Organizer

Foldables® and Other Study Aids Take out the Foldable® that you created for Lesson 1 and any graphic organizers that you created for Lessons 1–4. Find a partner, and quiz each other using these study aids.

Lesson 1 From Cells to Body Systems

Main Idea Body systems work together to keep your body functioning.

- Cells are the building blocks of life.
- Cells form tissues, tissues form organs, and organs form body systems.
- Body systems include the circulatory system, digestive system, endocrine system, excretory system, muscular system, nervous system, reproductive system, respiratory system, and skeletal system.

Lesson 2 Bones and Muscles

Main Idea The skeletal system is your body's framework and protects your organs from injury.

- Bones allow you to stand and move with the help of muscles.
- Muscles move bones, pump blood, and move food through your stomach and intestines.
- The four major types of joints are pivot joints, hinge joints, ball-and-socket joints, and gliding joints. They allow for different movements of your bones.

Lesson 3 Digestion and Excretion

Main Idea The digestive system and excretory system control the breakdown and removal of food from your body.

- The digestive process begins in your mouth when you first take a bite of food.
- Food that is not absorbed by the body enters the excretory system.
- The major organs of the excretory system are the colon, kidneys, and bladder.

Lesson 4 Heart, Blood, Lungs, and Nerves

Main Idea The heart, blood, lungs, and nerves control how blood moves through your body, how air gets into your lungs, and how you think.

- The circulatory system sends oxygen, food, and other materials through your body.
- The respiratory system enables you to breathe.
- The central and peripheral nervous systems allow your body to get and respond to information from your senses.

After You Read

HEALTH INVENTORY
Now that you have read the chapter, look back at your answers to the Health Inventory on the chapter opener. Is there anything that you should do differently?

Reviewing Vocabulary and Main Ideas

On a sheet of paper, write the numbers 1–6. After each number, write the term from the list that best completes each sentence.

- blood pressure
- body systems
- excretory system
- joints
- muscular system
- nervous system
- organs
- skeletal system
- tissues

Lesson 1 From Cells to Body Systems

1. Structures within the body made of tissues and which carry out specific jobs are called _____.
2. Groups of similar cells that do the same kind of work form _____.
3. Taking care of your _____ is important for good total health.

Lesson 2 Bones and Muscles

4. _____ are places where one bone meets another.
5. The body system consisting of bones and the tissues connecting them is the _____.
6. Your _____ is made up of all the muscles in your body.

On a sheet of paper, write the numbers 7–12. For each phrase, write the letter of the body system that matches.

  a. Circulatory system
  b. Digestive system
  c. Excretory system
  d. Nervous system
  e. Respiratory system

Lesson 3 Digestion and Excretion

7. Eliminates body wastes.
8. Breaks down food for energy.
9. Includes your liver, gallbladder, and stomach.

Lesson 4 Heart, Blood, Lungs, and Nerves

10. Its command center is the brain.
11. Includes blood vessels.
12. Makes breathing possible.

Thinking Critically

Using complete sentences, answer the following questions on a sheet of paper.

13. **Analyze** Which two body systems do you think are most closely related in their functions?
14. **Evaluate** Brainstorm ways of caring for the nervous system.

Go Online Visit **glencoe.com** and take the Online Quiz for Chapter 7.

Write About It

15. Expository Writing Write an article for a health magazine about the factors that can influence a teen's health habits. Explain whether these factors are a positive or negative influence.

16. Descriptive Writing Write a paragraph that describes a behavior that can benefit more than one body system. Explain how this behavior benefits each body system.

Applying Technology

Simple Systems

You and a partner will create an iMovie® clip that shows how a single body system works.

- Choose a body system and write a five-minute script, using the information found in this chapter.
- Rehearse and videotape the script.
- Import the script to a new iMovie® file.
- Edit the clip for accuracy of information and clarity.

Standardized Test Practice

Reading

Read the passage and answer the questions.

Blood pressure is an important measure of heart health. What exactly is blood pressure, and why is it important?

An answer to the first question requires understanding how the heart beats. When you rest, your heart beats about 60 to 70 times a minute. Each time your heart beats, it pumps blood into the arteries. At these moments, your heart is pushing blood. Between beats, your heart relaxes. It does not push blood. Your blood pressure is a measurement of these two states of your heart. It is shown as a fraction, such as 120/80. The top number represents the state of your heart during pushes. The bottom number is your heart when it is not pushing.

A medical professional measures your blood pressure using an instrument called a *sphygmomanometer* (sfig·moh·muh·NOM·i·ter). If your blood pressure is high, your doctor will do other tests to determine why. To lower your blood pressure, the doctor may recommend changes in lifestyle. These include getting regular exercise and eating healthy foods.

TEST-TAKING TIP

When interpreting facts or formulas in a passage, make sure you understand the concepts.

1. The author's purpose includes all of the following *except*
  - **A.** explaining blood pressure.
  - **B.** telling why blood pressure is important as a measure of health.
  - **C.** suggesting ways of keeping your heart healthy.
  - **D.** telling about medications that reduce high blood pressure.

2. Which of the following can be inferred from the passage?
  - **A.** A blood pressure of 120/80 is better than a blood pressure of 120/70.
  - **B.** High blood pressure is a sign of possible heart problems and may require lifestyle changes.
  - **C.** As a teen, your blood pressure should be lower than that of an adult.
  - **D.** Blood pressure cannot be determined in teens.

Growth and Development

Chapter Preview

▲ Working with the Photo

During the teen years, you may take on more responsibility at home. What are some ways to show your parents or guardians that you are ready for more responsibility?

Start-Up Activities

📖 **Before You Read** How much do you know about growth and development during the teen years? Take the short quiz below. Keep a record of your answers.

HEALTH QUIZ Answer *True* or *False* to each of the following questions.

1. Puberty typically starts between the ages of 8 and 14.

2. The human reproductive system is the same for males and females.

3. Each human reproductive cell contains 23 chromosomes.

4. The pancreas regulates the body's growth and development.

ANSWERS: 1. True; 2. False; 3. True; 4. False

FOLDABLES Study Organizer

📖 **As You Read** Make this Foldable® to help you record and organize three changes that are the result of growth and development. Begin with two sheets of 8.5" x 11" paper.

1 Get two sheets of paper and place them 1" apart.

2 Fold up the bottom edges, stopping them 1" from the top edges. This makes all tabs the same size.

3 Crease the paper to hold the tabs in place. Staple along the fold.

4 Turn and label the tabs as shown.

Under the appropriate tab of your Foldable®, record the changes teens go through in all three areas of the health triangle.

Growth & Development
Brings Changes
physical
mental/emotional
social

Go Online Visit **glencoe.com** and complete the Health Inventory for Chapter 8.

Adolescence: A Time of Change

Guide to Reading

● Building Vocabulary
As you read the lesson, write the definition for each of the following terms.
- adolescence (p. 202)
- endocrine system (p. 203)
- puberty (p. 203)

● Focusing on the Main Ideas
In this lesson, you will learn to
- **describe** three kinds of changes you go through during the teen years.
- **identify** the structure and function of the endocrine system.
- **analyze** how a teen is influenced by peers.

● Reading Strategy
Organizing Information Divide a sheet of paper into three columns. Name each column for one of the sides of the health triangle. Write two changes that occur on each side.

FOLDABLES Study Organizer Use the Foldable® on p. 201 as you read this lesson.

*Q*uick Write

Think about ways your body has changed in the past few years. Make a list of some of these changes.

Changes During Adolescence

Look at any group of teens, and you'll probably see big differences between the individuals. One teen may be a head taller than another who is the same age. Some teens may look younger or older than they really are. These differences are caused by the changes teens go through during **adolescence** (a·duhl·EH·suhns). This is *the period between childhood and adulthood*. Although all teens experience these changes, they occur at different times and speeds for everyone. You are just beginning your adolescent years now.

◀ Mood swings are a normal part of adolescence. **What causes mood swings?**

FIGURE 8.1

THE ENDOCRINE SYSTEM

The glands that make up this system perform many different jobs in your body. **Which glands regulate growth?**

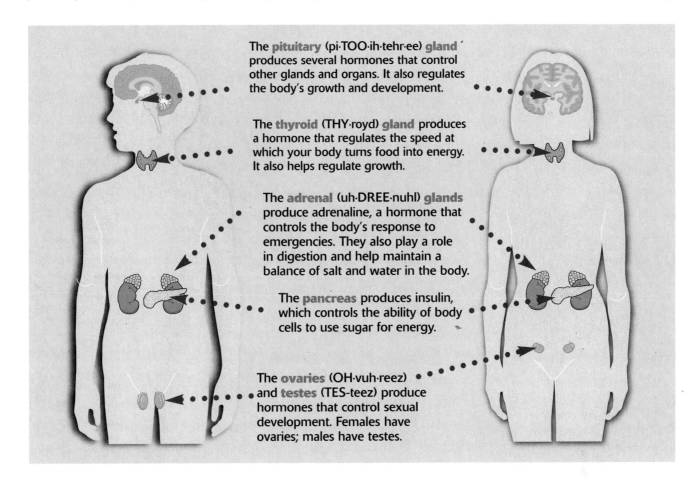

The **pituitary** (pi·TOO·ih·tehr·ee) **gland** produces several hormones that control other glands and organs. It also regulates the body's growth and development.

The **thyroid** (THY·royd) **gland** produces a hormone that regulates the speed at which your body turns food into energy. It also helps regulate growth.

The **adrenal** (uh·DREE·nuhl) **glands** produce adrenaline, a hormone that controls the body's response to emergencies. They also play a role in digestion and help maintain a balance of salt and water in the body.

The **pancreas** produces insulin, which controls the ability of body cells to use sugar for energy.

The **ovaries** (OH·vuh·reez) and **testes** (TES-teez) produce hormones that control sexual development. Females have ovaries; males have testes.

Adolescence brings changes in all three areas of your health triangle. You develop physically, mentally/emotionally, and socially. Many of these changes are caused by *hormones*. As noted in Chapter 2, hormones are chemicals made by the body. Specifically, they are produced in the **endocrine** (EN·duh·krin) **system.** This is *a body system containing glands that regulate growth and other important activities.* **Figure 8.1** describes many important functions of the endocrine system.

Physical Changes

Over the past summer, Phil noticed his voice beginning to change. Acne is appearing on Marie's face. Changes such as these signal the arrival of **puberty** (PYOO·bur·tee). This is *the time when you start developing the physical characteristics of adults of your gender.* Other changes that occur during puberty include the growth of body hair and increased sweating, or perspiration.

PHYSICAL CHANGES DURING ADOLESCENCE

Notice that boys and girls go through some similar changes.
Give an example of a change both boys and girls go through.

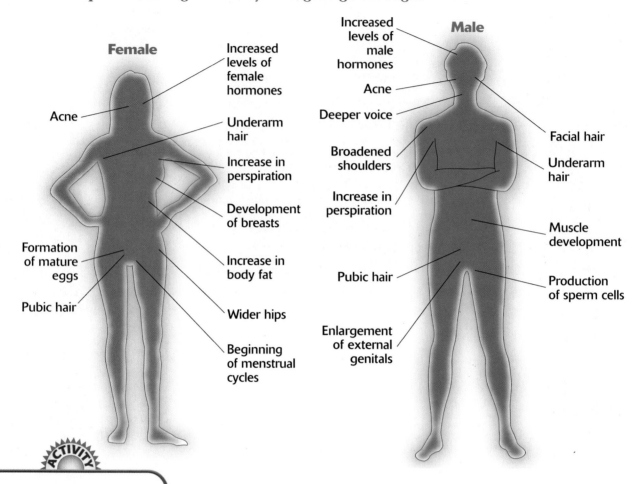

Female

- Increased levels of female hormones
- Acne
- Underarm hair
- Increase in perspiration
- Development of breasts
- Increase in body fat
- Formation of mature eggs
- Pubic hair
- Wider hips
- Beginning of menstrual cycles

Male

- Increased levels of male hormones
- Acne
- Deeper voice
- Facial hair
- Broadened shoulders
- Underarm hair
- Increase in perspiration
- Muscle development
- Pubic hair
- Production of sperm cells
- Enlargement of external genitals

ACTIVITY

Go Online

Topic: Understanding Puberty

Visit **glencoe.com** for Student Web Activities to get answers to questions teens are asking about growth and development.

Activity: Using the information provided at the link above, create a small card that has three resources printed on it where teens can access reliable information on growth and development.

The shape of your body changes, and you grow taller. These and other changes are shown in **Figure 8.2.**

Puberty begins at different times for different people. Typically, it starts between the ages of 8 and 14. During puberty, some body parts may grow faster than other parts. This is especially true of the hands and feet. These changes may make some teens feel awkward or self-conscious. Others, for whom puberty comes later, can feel "left behind." Although these situations can be troubling, remember that they are only temporary.

Mental/Emotional Changes

During adolescence, you begin to think about things in new ways. You learn to appreciate different opinions or points of view. You will begin to identify your own values and beliefs. You will also become aware of how your opinions, decisions, and actions affect others.

Changes in hormones can affect your feelings as well as your thoughts. You may feel strong emotions that you do not always understand. You might be happy one moment and sad the next. These sudden shifts in emotion are called mood swings and are common in adolescence. Talk about your feelings with others. This will help you manage your feelings in a healthy way.

Social Changes

Adolescence brings about changes in the way you relate to others. You become more independent. Your parents may give you more responsibility. For example, you may be asked to help care for a younger **sibling** or to prepare meals.

During this time, your friends may become very important. Like you, they are going through changes and can understand how you feel. As a result, their opinions and actions may influence you without you even knowing it. Choose friends that support you and influence you in a positive way. This will help you make good choices during your teen years.

Academic Vocabulary

sibling (SIB ling) *(noun)* a brother or sister. *Mark has one older sibling and one younger sibling.*

 Reading Check   **Identify** What is puberty?

Visit **glencoe.com** and complete the Interactive Study Guide for Lesson 1.

Lesson 1 Review

 After You Read

Review this lesson for new terms, major headings, and Reading Checks.

What I Learned

1. *Vocabulary* Define *endocrine system*.

2. *Recall* Name two physical changes that occur during puberty.

3. *Identify* What are some social changes that occur during adolescence?

Thinking Critically

4. *Apply* Peter gets teased by some of his peers because he is going through puberty. If you went to school with Peter, how would you teach these peers to respect Peter?

5. *Evaluate* How do you think the changes you experience during puberty help you prepare for adulthood?

Applying Health Skills

6. *Analyzing Influences* Peers can have a strong influence on your actions during adolescence. Give one example of how this can be positive. Give another example of how it can be negative.

Human Reproduction

Guide to Reading

● Building Vocabulary
Create a word web for the terms below. Decide which term belongs in the center.

- reproductive system (p. 206)
- egg cell (p. 206)
- fertilization (p. 206)
- menstruation (p. 207)
- sperm (p. 208)

● Focusing on the Main Ideas
In this lesson, you will learn to

- **identify** the parts and functions of the male and female reproductive systems.
- **explain** how to care for the reproductive system.

● Reading Strategy
Comparing and Contrasting As you read the lesson, compare and contrast the female and male reproductive systems.

*Q*uick Write

Write about what you think teens can do to care for their reproductive systems.

▼ Talking to a trusted adult can help you feel better about the changes you are experiencing. **Who are some adults you could talk to about reproductive health?**

Human Reproduction

So far, all the body systems you've learned about are the same for females and males. The **reproductive system,** however, is different. This is *the body system that makes it possible to create offspring*, or have babies. During puberty, the female and male reproductive systems undergo changes.

The Female Reproductive System

The female reproductive system, shown in **Figure 8.3,** has two main functions. One is to produce, store, and release egg cells. An **egg cell,** also called an *ovum*, is *the female reproductive cell*. The *ovaries* (OH·vuh·reez) are the two female reproductive glands where the eggs are produced, stored, and released. The second function of the female reproductive system is to reproduce, or to create offspring, or children. In order to create offspring, an egg cell must be fertilized. **Fertilization** is *the joining of a female egg cell with a male reproductive cell*. When an egg cell is fertilized, a baby is conceived, and a woman becomes pregnant. The fertilized egg then travels to the uterus (YOO·tuh·ruhs), the organ where the fertilized egg grows into a baby.

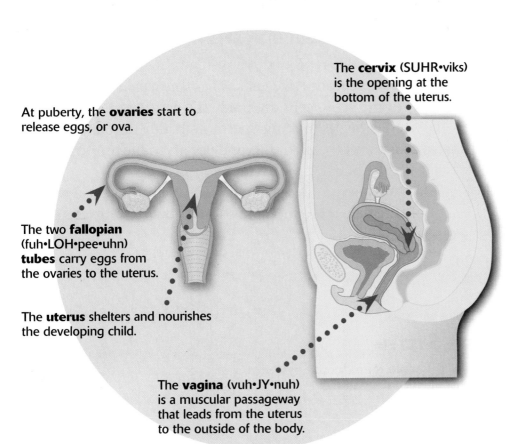

The **cervix** (SUHR•viks) is the opening at the bottom of the uterus.

At puberty, the **ovaries** start to release eggs, or ova.

The two **fallopian** (fuh•LOH•pee•uhn) **tubes** carry eggs from the ovaries to the uterus.

The **uterus** shelters and nourishes the developing child.

The **vagina** (vuh•JY•nuh) is a muscular passageway that leads from the uterus to the outside of the body.

THE FEMALE REPRODUCTIVE SYSTEM

This illustration shows the parts of the female reproductive system. **What is the function of this system?**

Menstruation

Each month, the uterus forms a lining of nutrient-rich blood and tissue to prepare for pregnancy. If an egg is fertilized, it will use the nutrient-rich lining in the uterus. If an egg is not fertilized, the nutrient-rich lining will leave the body during **menstruation** (men•stroo•AY•shuhn). Menstruation occurs when *blood, tissue, and the unfertilized egg flow out of the body.* Some females have heavier menstrual flows than others.

Menstruation is also called a "period." If a female has her period, it means that she has not conceived a child. Females usually get their period once a month. A period can last between three and seven days. Most females get their first period between the ages of 9 and 16. It is common to experience cramps, or soreness in the abdominal area.

During menstruation, females should change their sanitary napkins or tampons several times a day. These items absorb the fluid released during menstruation. How often they are changed in a day depends on how heavy a female's menstrual flow is.

 **Reading Check** **Explain** What is the relationship between conception and the menstrual cycle?

Pediatrician

Pediatricians are medical doctors who care for patients as young as infants and as old as adolescents. They play an important role in helping children grow and develop into healthy adults. There will always be a need for pediatricians as the population grows. You can prepare for a career as a pediatrician by studying human growth and development.

What skills does a pediatrician need? Go to *Career Corner* at **glencoe.com** to find out.

Visit **glencoe.com** and complete the Interactive Study Guide for Lesson 2.

Male Reproductive System

Like the female reproductive system, the male reproductive system makes reproductive cells. *The male reproductive cells* are called **sperm.** These cells are made inside the testes.

The testes begin making sperm cells during puberty. The sperm cells travel through the vas deferens to the urethra where they leave the body.

The testes also produce a hormone that controls the development of the male reproductive system shown in **Figure 8.4.**

Reading Check **Explain** What do the testes do?

▼ FIGURE 8.4

THE MALE REPRODUCTIVE SYSTEM

This illustration shows the parts of the male reproductive system.
What is the job of the male reproductive system?

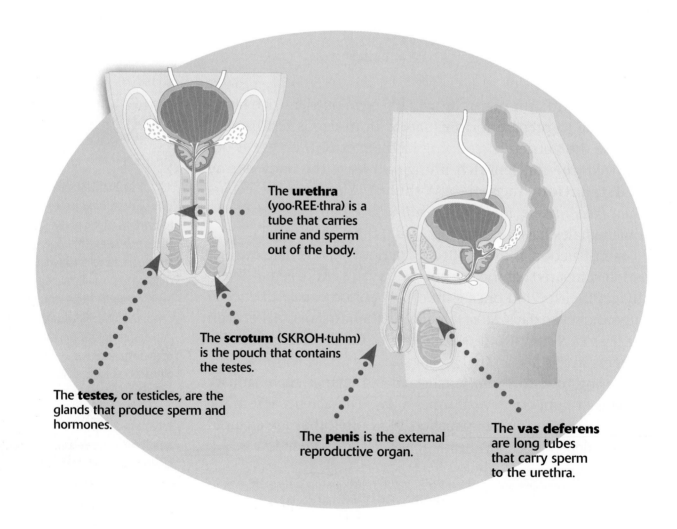

The **urethra** (yoo·REE·thra) is a tube that carries urine and sperm out of the body.

The **scrotum** (SKROH·tuhm) is the pouch that contains the testes.

The **testes,** or testicles, are the glands that produce sperm and hormones.

The **penis** is the external reproductive organ.

The **vas deferens** are long tubes that carry sperm to the urethra.

Health Skills Activity

Practicing Healthful Behaviors

Care of the Reproductive System

Like any body system, the reproductive system needs care. You can protect the health of your reproductive system by practicing the following healthful behaviors:

- Practice good hygiene; this includes showering or bathing regularly.
- Avoid wearing clothing or underwear that is too tight.
- Visit your doctor for regular checkups.
- Practice abstinence to prevent sexually transmitted diseases.
- Males who play contact sports should always wear protective gear.
- If you have questions about your reproductive health, talk to your parent or guardian, your doctor, or another trusted adult.

On Your Own

Make a list of other healthful behaviors you can practice that will help you look and feel your best during adolescence.

Lesson 2 Review

After You Read

Review this lesson for new terms, major headings, and Reading Checks.

What I Learned

1. *Recall* Name two functions of the female reproductive system.

2. *Vocabulary* Define *fertilization*.

3. *Identify* Where in the male reproductive system are sperm made?

Thinking Critically

4. *Compare* How are the female and male reproductive systems similar? How are they different?

5. *Analyze* James will be catcher this year for his baseball team. What special precautions should James take to prevent injury to his reproductive system? Give details to explain your answer.

Applying Health Skills

6. *Advocacy* Caring for your body during puberty is important. With a small group, design and print a pamphlet that explains the kinds of care needed.

Heredity and the Life Cycle

Guide to Reading

Building Vocabulary
Review the terms below. See if you know which term represents a part of another term.

- chromosomes (p. 210)
- genes (p. 210)
- fetus (p. 212)
- prenatal care (p. 212)

Focusing on the Main Ideas
In this lesson, you will learn to

- **explain** how inherited traits are passed along.
- **identify** changes to a developing baby.
- **recognize** stages in the life cycle.

Reading Strategy
Analyzing a Graphic Using the diagram to the right as a guide, describe the stages of development before birth.

The Developing Baby

After 3 months:

After 6 months:

After 9 months:

uick Write

Observe physical traits in your class, such as eye and hair color. Write a short paragraph noting which traits are most common and why you believe this.

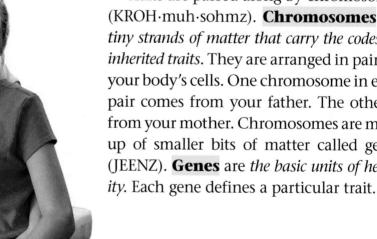

Heredity

Do you remember reading about heredity in Chapter 1? This is the process by which parents pass certain traits to their children. Hair color and body build are two examples of inherited traits. Children may even inherit talents and abilities from parents. The likelihood of developing certain diseases and health problems is also passed along.

Traits are passed along by chromosomes (KROH·muh·sohmz). **Chromosomes** are *tiny strands of matter that carry the codes for inherited traits*. They are arranged in pairs in your body's cells. One chromosome in each pair comes from your father. The other is from your mother. Chromosomes are made up of smaller bits of matter called genes (JEENZ). **Genes** are *the basic units of heredity*. Each gene defines a particular trait.

◀ Parents and their offspring often have similar characteristics because of heredity. **What are some characteristics that can be passed along through heredity?**

Chromosomes and Fertilization

Every type of cell in the human body except one contains 46 chromosomes. That one exception is the reproductive cell. Egg cells and sperm cells each have half the usual number of chromosomes. Each has exactly 23. When these cells unite during fertilization, their chromosomes are joined. The newly fertilized egg cell has 46 chromosomes.

Among each sperm's 23 chromosomes, one alone determines the gender of the fertilized egg cell. This chromosome is represented by the letter *X* or *Y*. If a sperm carries an X chromosome, a female will result. If the sperm has a Y chromosome, a male will result.

Reading Check Define What are *genes*?

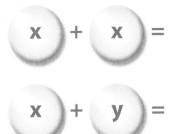

▲ Sperm cells carry either an X or a Y chromosome. Egg cells carry only X chromosomes. **Which of the two unions shown in this illustration will produce a boy?**

Development Before Birth

A female becomes pregnant when one of her egg cells is fertilized by a male sperm cell. Much happens during the first days of pregnancy. The newly fertilized cell travels down the fallopian tube to the uterus. It attaches itself to the wall of the uterus. There, it begins to divide, first into two cells, then into four. This process of doubling, or cell division, continues millions of times. From theses cells, the tissues, organs, and body systems are eventually formed. **Figure 8.5** shows the stages of development from fertilization through birth.

▼ FIGURE 8.5

THE DEVELOPING BABY

After fertilization, it takes about nine months before a baby is born. **About how much does a baby weigh at birth?**

Time	Size	Features	Development
fertilization	microscopic	single cell	undeveloped
3 months after fertilization	about 3 inches long; weighs about 1 ounce	arms, legs, fingers toes, eyes, ears	heart is beating, nervous system is forming; cannot survive outside uterus
6 months after fertilization	about 14 inches long; weighs about 2 pounds	hair, eyebrows, fingernails, toenails	can move and kick, sucks thumb, can hear sounds; might survive outside uterus
9 months after fertilization	18–20 inches long; weights 7–9 pounds	smooth skin, fully developed organs	eyes open and close, fingers can grasp, body organs and systems can now work on their own; ready for birth

In the uterus, the developing baby receives oxygen and nutrients through a tube called the *umbilical cord.* Waste products are also removed through this cord. *The developing unborn baby, from the eighth week until birth,* is known as a **fetus.**

Pregnancy is a time of change for both parents-to-be. Having a child is a joyful event, but it also means added responsibility. Preparations must be made to care for the baby when it arrives and for his or her future. For the mother, changes are taking place in her body that affect her shape, weight, and emotions. Once the baby is born, he or she requires a lot of attention and care. New parents often don't get a lot of sleep and may experience added stress or other emotional changes.

Throughout pregnancy, an expectant mother needs **prenatal care.** This is *special care to* **ensure** *that the mother and her baby remain healthy.* Prenatal care includes eating healthy foods, getting enough rest, and seeing the doctor regularly. The mother-to-be also should avoid using tobacco, alcohol, and other drugs not prescribed by her doctor.

Academic Vocabulary

ensure (en SHUR) *(verb)* to make sure. *Ensure that your growing body gets the nutrients it needs by eating a balanced diet.*

Reading Check

Explain Describe the way a fertilized egg cell divides.

The Life Cycle

Being born is the first step in a lifelong journey full of new experiences and changes. The entire journey is often called the "life cycle." It is divided into six main parts or stages:

- **Infancy.** During their first year of life, infants grow very fast. Babies also grow mentally and emotionally during this time. Infants need loving care and attention.

- **Childhood.** This period lasts from age 1 through 12. During this time, children are busy taking in all sorts of new information. Encouragement and support from others builds positive self-esteem.

- **Adolescence.** Adolescence begins at age 12 and ends around age 18. This is a time of transition from child to adult. Decision making, goal setting, and good communication skills help prepare adolescents for adulthood.

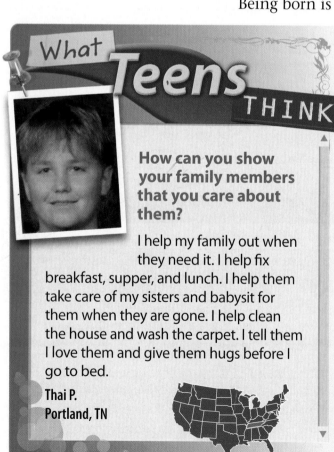

What Teens THINK

How can you show your family members that you care about them?

I help my family out when they need it. I help fix breakfast, supper, and lunch. I help them take care of my sisters and babysit for them when they are gone. I help clean the house and wash the carpet. I tell them I love them and give them hugs before I go to bed.

Thai P.
Portland, TN

- **Young adulthood.** Early adulthood lasts from age 18 until around age 40. Many young adults are busy pursuing an education or training for a career. They may choose to get married and start a family during this time. Working to achieve career and family goals often extends into middle adulthood.

- **Middle adulthood.** This stage begins in the 40s and continues until age 65. People in this life stage may begin looking for ways to contribute to their communities. For example, they may volunteer to coach youth sports or raise money for charity. They may also begin planning for retirement.

- **Maturity.** This stage begins around age 65 when adults are beginning to think of retirement. Retirement gives some people the opportunity to develop new interests or spend more time with family members. Maintaining good health will help you stay active during late adulthood.

 Reading Check **Identify** Name two stages in the life cycle.

Visit **glencoe.com** and complete the Interactive Study Guide for Lesson 3.

Lesson 3 Review

 After You Read

Review this lesson for new terms, major headings, and Reading Checks.

What I Learned

1. *Vocabulary* Define *chromosomes.*

2. *Recall* How many chromosomes are there in most cells of the human body? What is the one exception?

3. *Identify* Name two developments that may take place during early adulthood.

Thinking Critically

4. *Explain* What determines whether a baby will be male or female?

5. *Apply* Yvonne hopes to become a lawyer when she reaches adulthood. What skills can she develop now during her teens to help her achieve her career goals?

Applying Health Skills

6. *Communication Skills* What are the responsibilities of parenthood? Discuss your observations with a parent or trusted adult. Share your findings in an oral report.

What Are Communication Skills?

Communication skills involve learning how to effectively express yourself and understand others.

Speaking Skills

- Think before you speak.
- Use "I" messages.
- Be direct, but avoid being rude or insulting.
- Make eye contact, and use appropriate body language.

Listening Skills

- Use conversation encouragers.
- Pay attention.
- Show empathy.
- Avoid interrupting, but ask questions where appropriate.

Coping with Changes During Puberty

Follow the Model, Practice, and Apply steps to help you master this important health skill.

① Model

Read about how Greg uses communication skills to help his brother, Shaun, cope with adolescence.

Greg: How was school? **(Ask questions.)**

Shaun: Terrible. I felt bad when I saw how much everyone else grew over the summer. I'm the shortest guy in my class! **(Use "I" messages.)** Greg thought a minute, then sat down by Shaun and put a hand on his shoulder. **(Think before you speak. Use appropriate body language.)** You shouldn't be worried that you aren't growing as fast as your friends. Everyone grows at different rates. You'll catch up. Hey, I was the shortest guy in my class until the ninth grade. **(Mirror thoughts and feelings.)** Now look at me. I play basketball.

❷ Practice

Help Selena use communication skills to get help from her mom.

During the school year, Selena began developing acne on her face. At first, it was just a few small blemishes. Then it got worse. Selena wanted to get help from her mom for this problem.

1. What should Selena say and do in her conversation with her mom?

2. Give examples of things that Selena's mom can do to show she's listening to her.

3. In what way does communication help teens cope with adolescence?

❸ Apply

Apply what you have learned about communication skills to complete the activity below.

With a partner, brainstorm problems that teens might experience during puberty. The problem might relate to physical, emotional, or social changes. Write these problems down. Choose one and write a script showing how a teen could use communication skills to talk about this problem. In your script, include behaviors, dialogue, and body language that show good communication skills. Explain how your script would help a teen cope with adolescence.

Self-Check
■ Did we brainstorm problems teens might experience?
■ Did our script show good communication skills?

Building Health Skills

HANDS-ON HEALTH

Looking Ahead

Preparing for adulthood involves behaving in a more mature and responsible way. This activity will give you a chance to do some adult-like thinking and see how you feel about questions that you may face as an adult.

What You Will Need

- Pencil or pen
- Paper

 **What You Will Do**

Number a sheet of paper from 1–10. For each statement below, decide whether you would answer each statement as "always," "sometimes," or "rarely." Then write your answer next to each numbered item.

❶ I try to think through problems, looking at all possible solutions.

❷ I am able to communicate well with my parents or other adults.

❸ I am able to list my four most important beliefs.

❹ I think about the consequences before I act.

❺ I like who I am; I don't try to be something I'm not.

❻ I do some things alone or with friends that I used to do with my family.

❼ I listen to other people's ideas even when they are different than mine.

❽ I am concerned about problems in the world today.

❾ I have one or two close friends with whom I can talk about almost anything.

❿ I think about how my actions affect other people.

Wrapping It Up

When you are finished, look at how many questions you answered "always" and "sometimes." This shows that you are already beginning to think and act in a mature and responsible way. As a class, brainstorm some other ways you can demonstrate mature and responsible behavior.

Reading Review

STUDY TO GO Visit glencoe.com to download quizzes and eFlashcards for Chapter 8.

FOLDABLES Study Organizer

Foldables® and Other Study Aids Take out the Foldable® that you created for Lesson 1 and any graphic organizers that you created for Lessons 1–3. Find a partner, and quiz each other using these study aids.

Lesson 1 Adolescence: A Time of Change

Main Idea During adolescence, all three sides of your health triangle undergo change.

- Adolescence is the period between childhood and adulthood.
- During puberty, your body starts to develop adult characteristics.
- The Endocrine system includes: the pituitary gland, thyroid gland, adrenal glands, pancreas, the ovaries, and the testes.
- During adolescence, you begin to consider the impact of your opinions and decisions.
- You may become more independent and be given greater responsibility.

Lesson 2 Human Reproduction

Main Idea The male and female reproductive systems develop during puberty and make it possible to create offspring, or children.

- The female reproductive system has two functions: to store eggs and to create offspring. If the female egg is not fertilized, menstruation occurs.

- Fertilization is the joining of a female egg cell with a male sperm cell.
- Menstruation occurs when blood, tissue, and an unfertilized egg flow out of the female body.
- The male reproductive system produces sperm, which are stored in the testes.

Lesson 3 Heredity and the Life Cycle

Main Idea Your parents passed certain traits to you like hair color and body build.

- Chromosomes carry the codes for the traits you inherit. You get 23 chromosomes from each parent. Your mother carries two X chromosomes. Your father carries an X and Y chromosome.
- If the father's sperm carries an X chromosome, a female will be conceived. If it carries a Y chromosome, a male will be conceived.
- Prenatal care is special care given by a doctor to a pregnant woman to ensure that both she and her baby remain healthy.
- A developing, unborn baby, from the eighth week until birth is called a fetus.
- A baby takes about nine months to develop.
- The life cycle is divided into six stages: infancy, childhood, adolescence, young adulthood, middle adulthood, and maturity.

 After You Read

HEALTH QUIZ
Look back at your answers to the Health Quiz in the chapter opener. Now that you've read the chapter, have your ideas changed? What would your answers be now?

Reviewing Vocabulary and Main Ideas

On a sheet of paper, write the numbers 1–6. After each number, write the term from the list that best completes each sentence.

- adolescence
- chromosomes
- egg cell
- endocrine system
- genes
- reproductive system
- puberty
- sperm

Lesson 1 Adolescence: A Time of Change

1. _____ is the period between childhood and adulthood.

2. The time when you start developing the physical characteristics of adults of your gender is _____.

3. The _____ is a body system containing glands that regulate growth and other important activities.

Lesson 2 Human Reproduction

4. The body system that makes it possible to create offspring is the _____.

5. The female reproductive cell is known as the _____.

6. The male reproductive cells are known as _____.

Lesson 3 Heredity and the Life Cycle

On a sheet of paper, write the numbers 7–9. Choose the letter of the word or phrase that best completes each statement or question.

7. Which statement about genes is TRUE?
   a. They are made up of chromosomes.
   b. They are tiny strands of matter that carry the codes for inherited traits.
   c. They define particular traits.
   d. They are different for identical twins.

8. Which of the following is part of pre-natal care?
   a. The newly fertilized cell travels down the fallopian tube to the uterus.
   b. The mother-to-be eats healthfully and gets enough rest.
   c. The baby is born.
   d. None of the above.

9. The stage of the life cycle in which many people begin training for a career is
   a. adolescence.
   b. early adulthood.
   c. middle adulthood.
   d. late adulthood.

Go Online   Visit **glencoe.com** and take the Online Quiz for Chapter 8.

Thinking Critically

Using complete sentences, answer the following questions on a sheet of paper.

10. **Analyze** In what ways are emotional and physical changes during adolescence related? Give an example to support your views.

11. **Synthesize** Why do you think the teen years are not a good time for becoming a parent?

Write About It

12. **Persuasive Writing** Write a paragraph persuading teens to use good communication skills to help cope with mood swings.

ACTIVITY
↗ Applying Technology

Gradual Growing

Use Microsoft Word® and the Internet to write an essay about human growth and development during sixth grade.

■ Review the chapter content and create an outline.

■ Using the Microsoft Word® outline format, organize paragraph topics and add sub topics to each paragraph.

■ From the outline, write complete paragraphs. Include details that support facts.

■ Add hyperlinks to key vocabulary words.

■ Edit essay for clarity and punctuation.

Standardized Test Practice

Reading

Read the passage and then answer the questions.

Gregor Mendel was born in 1822 in what is now the Czech Republic. He developed an interest in gardening on his father's farm. As a young man, Mendel studied to become a priest. His teachers noticed his great interest in nature, especially plants. They urged him to become a teacher himself. In 1854, he earned a degree from the University of Vienna and became a teacher. In his spare time, Mendel continued to garden. One day, he noticed differences in pea plants in his garden. Some appeared shriveled, but others did not. Mendel wondered about this. As a result, he tested 28,000 different plants. His experiments led him to identify laws of heredity. Today, Mendel is still considered to be the father of this science.

TEST-TAKING TIP

Cause-and-effect relationships can be determined by word clues. Some of these clues are single words such as *because*. Others are phrases. Examples include *due to* and *as a result*.

1. Gregor Mendel's interest in gardening led to
   A. his becoming a teacher.
   B. his attending the University of Vienna.
   C. his noticing differences in pea plants in his garden.
   D. his returning to his homeland after finishing college.

2. Which best sums up the main idea of the passage?
   A. Most scientific breakthroughs happen by accident.
   B. Gregor Mendel's love of gardening led him to discover the laws of heredity.
   C. Gregor Mendel was a better teacher than a priest.
   D. Gregor Mendel was a better scientist than a teacher.

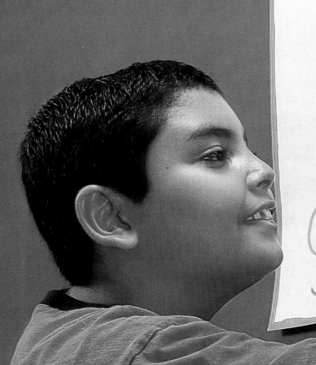

Chapter Preview

▲ *Working with the Photo*

This teen has become an advocate for a smoke-free environment. **What are some ways you can encourage others to say no to tobacco?**

Start-Up Activities

Before You Read Do you know how you and your friends can avoid tobacco products? Answer the Health eSpotlight question below and then watch the online video. Keep a record of your answers.

Health eSpotlight

Avoiding Tobacco

Knowing the damage that tobacco products can do to the body is the first step in helping you and your peers avoid tobacco products. This knowledge can also help teens quit tobacco use. What can you and your friends do to encourage and support other teens who want to stop using tobacco products?

Go to **glencoe.com** and watch the health video for Chapter 9. Then complete the activity provided with the online video.

FOLDABLES Study Organizer

As You Read Make this Foldable® to help you organize information in Lesson 1 on the harmful effects of tobacco. Begin with a plain sheet of 8½″ × 11″ paper.

1 Fold the sheet of paper in half along the short axis.

2 Open and fold the bottom edge up to form a pocket. Glue the edges.

3 Label the cover as shown. Label the pockets "Causes" and "Effects." Place an index card or quarter sheet of notebook paper into each pocket.

List and describe the causes and effects of tobacco addiction on the index cards or sheets of notebook paper cut into quarter sections. Store these cards in the appropriate pocket of your Foldable®.

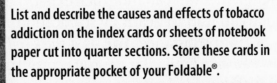

Tobacco Addiction

Go Online Visit **glencoe.com** and complete the Chapter 9 crossword puzzle.

Tobacco: A Harmful Drug

Guide to Reading

● **Building Vocabulary**

Explain how each vocabulary word below is related to tobacco.

■ nicotine (p. 222)
■ carbon monoxide (p. 222)
■ tar (p. 222)
■ emphysema (p. 223)
■ addiction (p. 223)
■ snuff (p. 226)

● **Focusing on the Main Ideas**

In this lesson, you will learn to

■ **identify** how tobacco damages your health.
■ **explain** how tobacco leads to addiction.
■ **practice** the skill of advocacy to inform others about the dangers of tobacco use.

● **Reading Strategy**

Finding the Main Idea Copy the headings from the lesson onto a sheet of paper. After each heading, write a sentence that describes the main idea of each section.

 **FOLDABLES Study Organizer** Use the Foldable® on p. 221 as you read this lesson.

*Q*uick Write

Write a paragraph about the reasons many people choose to remain tobacco free.

▲ More and more locations are displaying this sign. **Why do you think this is happening?**

What's in Tobacco

Tobacco contains a number of harmful chemicals. One of these, **nicotine** (NIH·kuh·teen), is *a drug that speeds up the heartbeat and affects the central nervous system.* It narrows blood vessels to and from the heart. Nicotine is also found in garden insect sprays.

Tobacco smoke contains **carbon monoxide** (KAR·buhn muh·NAHK·syd). This is *a poisonous, odorless gas produced when tobacco burns.* It attaches to red blood cells, preventing them from carrying a full load of oxygen. Carbon monoxide is also an ingredient in car and truck exhaust. Breathing carbon monoxide can lead to death by suffocation.

A third substance, **tar,** is *a thick, oily, dark liquid that forms when tobacco burns.* Tar deposits cover the lining of the lungs. If tar is allowed to build up, breathing problems and lung disease can result.

 **Reading Check**

Identify What are two harmful chemicals found in tobacco and tobacco smoke?

How Tobacco Harms the Body

"How much harm can one cigarette do?" People who ask that question might be surprised by the answer. Just one puff releases harmful chemicals into the mouth, throat, and lungs. It can cause feelings of dizziness. Just one puff can harm both the smoker and anyone around them.

Over time, the effects of tobacco build. Long-term nicotine use is **linked** to heart and lung disease. The tar from tobacco coats the inside of the lungs. It greatly increases the smoker's risks of lung cancer and emphysema (em·fuh·SEE·muh). **Emphysema** is *a disease that occurs when the tiny air sacs in the lungs lose their elasticity, or ability to stretch.* This reduces the amount of oxygen passing from the lungs into the blood. Breathing becomes more difficult for the smoker. Teens who smoke may find it harder to play sports and stay physically active. **Figure 9.1** on the next two pages shows other harmful effects of tobacco use.

Academic Vocabulary

linked (LINKT) *(adjective)* connected to. *Smoking is linked to lung cancer.*

Nicotine and Addiction

Another serious problem related to tobacco use is that nicotine is a powerfully addictive drug. **Addiction** is *the body's physical or mental need for a drug or other substance.* Addiction causes users to depend on the substance in order to feel good. They begin to need the substance just to function normally. Once addicted, quitting becomes extremely difficult. Nicotine addiction is one of the hardest addictions to break. It is as addictive as heroin or cocaine, two widely abused drugs. You will learn more about heroin and cocaine in the next chapter. People who try to break their nicotine addiction may experience unpleasant symptoms. These include shakiness, headache, nervousness, and sleeping problems. Once a person has overcome his or her nicotine addiction, these symptoms will go away and the person will feel much better.

Reading Check **Define** What does *addiction* mean? Use it in a sentence.

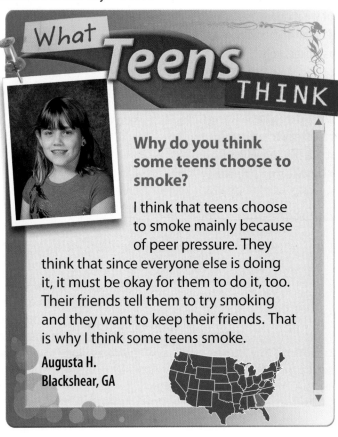

What **Teens** THINK

Why do you think some teens choose to smoke?

I think that teens choose to smoke mainly because of peer pressure. They think that since everyone else is doing it, it must be okay for them to do it, too. Their friends tell them to try smoking and they want to keep their friends. That is why I think some teens smoke.

Augusta H.
Blackshear, GA

THE HARMFUL EFFECTS OF TOBACCO

The chemicals in tobacco harm many parts of the body. How does tobacco harm the blood vessels?

Go Online

Topic: Avoiding the Harmful Effects of Tobacco

Visit **glencoe.com** for Student Web Activities to learn more about what cigarette smoke does to the body and how to help smokers quit.

Activity: Using the information provided at the link above, write a letter to the editor of your local paper talking about what you feel should be done to help make your community smoke free.

Skin

Smoking ages the skin, causing it to wrinkle earlier than a nonsmoker's skin.

Mouth, Teeth, and Throat

Cigarette smoke and smokeless tobacco lead to bad breath and stained teeth. Chemicals in tobacco cause mouth and throat cancers. Smokeless tobacco can cause leukoplakia—white sores in the mouth that can lead to cancer—as well as tooth loss. It also wears away tooth enamel.

Throat • • • • •

Lungs

The tar in cigarette smoke coats the inside of the lungs. This prevents them from working well. Chemicals in tobacco smoke contribute to lung cancer.

Heart

Nicotine increases heart rate and causes blood vessels to become narrower. Narrow vessels make the heart pump harder to move blood through the body. This extra effort raises blood pressure, and can cause a heart attack or stroke.

Fingers

Over time, tobacco use can cause fingers to yellow and stain.

Stomach, Bladder, and Colon

Harmful substances in tobacco smoke can lead to stomach ulcers and bladder and colon cancers. Compared to nonsmokers, smokers are more than twice as likely to get bladder cancer.

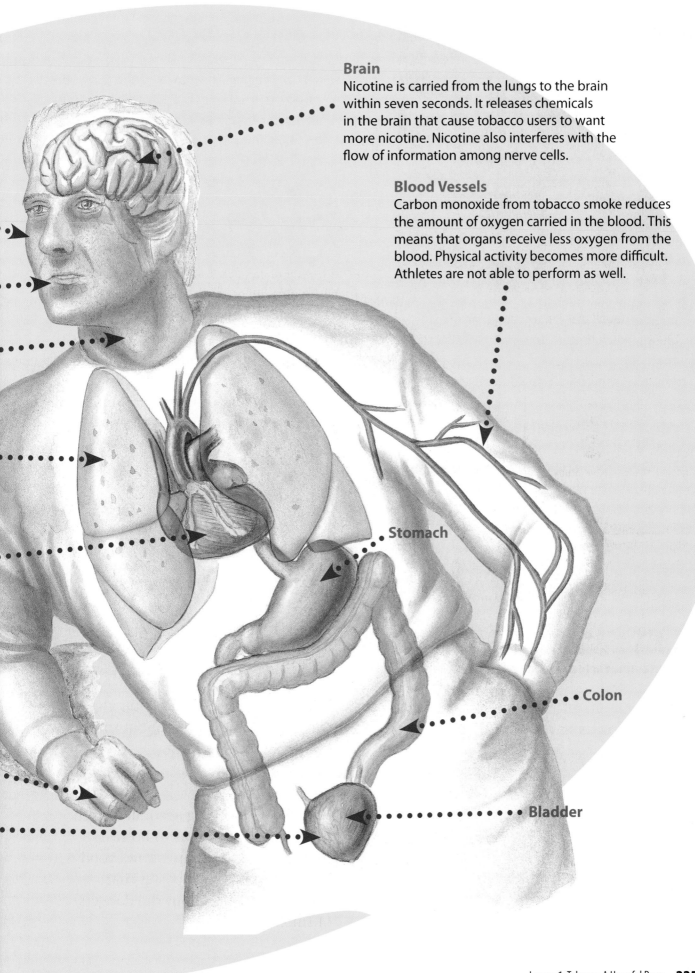

Brain
Nicotine is carried from the lungs to the brain within seven seconds. It releases chemicals in the brain that cause tobacco users to want more nicotine. Nicotine also interferes with the flow of information among nerve cells.

Blood Vessels
Carbon monoxide from tobacco smoke reduces the amount of oxygen carried in the blood. This means that organs receive less oxygen from the blood. Physical activity becomes more difficult. Athletes are not able to perform as well.

Stomach

Colon

Bladder

▲ Fewer baseball players are using smokeless tobacco. **How might this influence fans?**

Other Forms of Tobacco

Cigarettes are not the only delivery system for tobacco. Tobacco smoke is also brought into the body through cigars and pipes. Bidis (BEE·deez)—hand-rolled, flavored cigarettes— are another smoked tobacco product. All do harm to the body.

One form of tobacco some people mistakenly believe to be safe is smokeless tobacco. This product is either chewed in a coarsely ground form or inhaled. **Snuff** is *finely ground tobacco that is inhaled or held in the mouth or cheeks.*

Just like cigarettes, smokeless tobacco products can become habit-forming. In addition, harmful substances in smokeless tobacco can form white spots on your gums and inside your cheeks. These can eventually turn into cancer. Smokeless tobacco also causes bad breath and stains the teeth. Grit and sugar in tobacco can cause cavities and gum disease.

 Reading Check **Explain** What are some physical consequences of tobacco use?

Go Online

Visit **glencoe.com** and complete the Interactive Study Guide for Lesson 1.

Lesson 1 Review

After You Read

Review this lesson for new terms, major headings, and Reading Checks.

What I Learned

1. *List* How does nicotine affect the body?

2. *Vocabulary* What is *emphysema*?

3. *Identify* Name two forms of smokeless tobacco.

Thinking Critically

4. *Analyze* Anne was pressured by a girl at school to try tobacco. "You can quit any time you want," the girl said. How might Anne reply?

5. *Apply* What advice would you give someone who asks you about smokeless tobacco?

Applying Health Skills

6. *Advocacy* Conveying accurate health information and ideas to both individuals and groups shows good citizenship. Create a poster that informs students about the dangers of smoking.

 For more Lesson Review Activities, go to **glencoe.com**.

Teens and Tobacco

Guide to Reading

● Building Vocabulary
Read the terms below. If you have come across these in earlier chapters, review your notebook definitions. If you have not, copy their meanings as they appear in this lesson.

- negative peer pressure (p. 228)
- media (p. 228)

● Focusing on the Main Ideas
In this lesson, you will learn to

- **identify** factors that influence teens to try tobacco.
- **recognize** negative influences on teens to use tobacco.
- **access** reliable information on teens and tobacco use.

● Reading Strategy
Organizing Information Using information from the lesson, create a graphic organizer showing myths and facts about tobacco use.

Facts About Teens and Tobacco

Some teens mistakenly believe tobacco helps them fit in better among their peers. If anything, the *opposite* is true. The Centers for Disease Control and Prevention (CDC) and other organizations report a steady drop in teen tobacco use over the past decade.

Yet despite this positive trend, some teens continue to become first-time smokers. According to the same sources, every day 4,000 young people try their first cigarette. Why do some teens start smoking? **Figure 9.2** summarizes reasons teens give for trying tobacco. It also shows why their beliefs about tobacco use may not be accurate.

Quick Write

Think about influences that might lead some teens to try tobacco. Write a paragraph explaining how a teen can resist these influences.

▶ Friends can influence the choices you make. **Why is it important to choose friends who don't smoke?**

Smoking Cessation Counselor

A smoking cessation counselor is a trained professional who helps people quit smoking. They can provide support through counseling and education. The demand for smoking cessation counselors continues to rise as more people learn about the dangers of tobacco use. If you would like to become a smoking cessation counselor, you should practice your communication skills. You should also study how tobacco affects the body.

What other skills does a smoking cessation counselor need? Go to *Career Corner* at **glencoe.com** to find out.

▼ **FIGURE 9.2**

REASONS FOR TEEN TOBACCO USE AND THE REALITIES

These are some of the reasons teens give for using tobacco. **Are there other reasons or realities you can add to either list?**

Some Teens Believe	In Reality
Smoking makes a person look cool.	Tobacco stains teeth, leads to bad breath, and causes wrinkled skin.
Tobacco makes teens more accepted among their peers.	Between 70 and 80 percent of teens have never tried tobacco. Teens who use tobacco are also more likely to get in fights, carry weapons, and use alcohol and other drugs.
Using tobacco makes teens seem more grown-up.	The number of adult tobacco users is on the decline.
Tobacco won't hurt your health for many years.	Some of tobacco's effects begin with the first use. Tobacco use is habit-forming. Once a person starts using tobacco, it can be very difficult to quit.

Resisting Negative Influences

Many teens decide to try tobacco because they are influenced by others around them. One such influence is **negative peer pressure.** This is *pressure you feel to go along with the harmful behaviors or beliefs of your peers.* A teen whose friends use tobacco is more likely to try it as well.

The same is true of teens with family members who use tobacco. Studies show that teens from homes where tobacco is used are far more likely to start smoking.

Yet another negative influence is the media. The **media** include *the various methods of communicating information, including newspapers, magazines, radio, television, and the Internet.* Several years ago, two government agencies researched the media's influence on teen tobacco use. The study examined 200 popular films and 1,000 popular songs. The findings showed that tobacco was used in more than three-fourths of movies intended for young viewers. The study also showed that nearly a third of pop songs glamorize tobacco use.

Reading Check **Define** What is *negative peer pressure*? What part does it play in tobacco use among teens?

Tobacco Advertising

One especially powerful influence is advertising. Estimates show that the tobacco industry spends $10 billion a year advertising its products. Some of these ads have been proven effective at reaching young people. Another effective method of advertising is "point-of-sale" promotions. These include giveaways and catchy displays near cash registers at stores that sell cigarettes. Recently, cigarette advertisers have even begun to place ads targeted at teens on the Internet.

Visit glencoe.com and complete the Interactive Study Guide for Lesson 2.

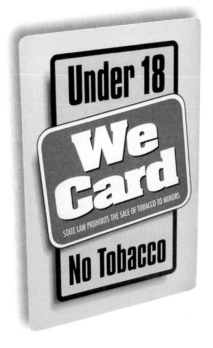

▶ Signs like this are used to help prevent teens from smoking. **Can you think of some other ways to help teens avoid tobacco use?**

Lesson 2 Review

 After You Read

Review this lesson for new terms, major headings, and Reading Checks.

What I Learned

1. *Give Examples* Name two factors that might influence teens to try tobacco.

2. *Vocabulary* Define *media*.

3. *Recall* What are two negative pressures teens might face when it comes to tobacco use?

Thinking Critically

4. *Apply* Identify an example of negative peer pressure to use tobacco. Tell what you could do or say to resist this pressure.

5. *Evaluate* Think about how a cigarette advertisement depicts tobacco use. How might it influence a teen's behavior?

Applying Health Skills

6. *Accessing Information* The lesson mentioned several reliable sources of health information. Gather additional facts or statistics from these or other reliable sources on teen tobacco use. Share your findings with classmates.

Go Online For more Lesson Review Activities, go to **glencoe.com**.

Lesson 2: Teens and Tobacco **229**

Staying Tobacco Free

Guide to Reading

● **Building Vocabulary**
Copy the terms below in your notebook. As you read the lesson, write the definitions for each term.

■ secondhand smoke (p. 232)
■ passive smokers (p. 232)

● **Focusing on the Main Ideas**
In this lesson, you will learn to

■ **demonstrate** ways to say no to tobacco use.
■ **explain** how someone can quit using tobacco.
■ **understand** the rights of nonsmokers.

● **Reading Strategy**
Identifying Problems and Solutions After reading this lesson, state the problem with secondhand smoke. Then think of a solution for how to build a tobacco-free environment.

 uick Write

Write a poem or story about a planet that is smoke free.

▲ Nicotine patches can help a person quit smoking. **What other sources of help are available to those who want to quit smoking?**

Using Refusal Skills

Saying no to tobacco is important, but it is not always easy. Some teens feel pressure from peers to use tobacco. Others see family members smoking and are curious about what it's like.

When faced with real-life pressures, refusal skills can help you say no effectively. Be prepared with some reasons for saying no to tobacco. You can find some examples in **Figure 9.3.** You may be offered tobacco when you least expect it, so it is best to be prepared. Practice saying no in an assertive style, one that shows you are serious, but also shows that you are respectful of others. Speak in a firm voice with your head and shoulders up. This will tell others that you mean what you say.

Kicking the Tobacco Habit

The human body was not designed to inhale smoke of any kind. Some of the damage done by smoking can never be reversed. Once the small airways inside your lungs have been damaged, they cannot repair themselves. Quitting tobacco, however, prevents further damage to the body and will improve a person's overall health.

▼ FIGURE 9.3

SAYING NO TO TOBACCO

If someone offers you tobacco, here are some ways to say no.
What are some other ways of refusing tobacco?

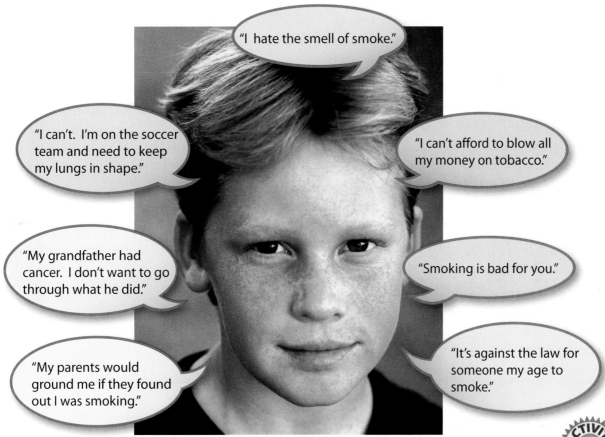

"I hate the smell of smoke."

"I can't. I'm on the soccer team and need to keep my lungs in shape."

"I can't afford to blow all my money on tobacco."

"My grandfather had cancer. I don't want to go through what he did."

"Smoking is bad for you."

"My parents would ground me if they found out I was smoking."

"It's against the law for someone my age to smoke."

One way to quit tobacco use is the cold turkey method. In this method, the user simply stops all use of the tobacco product. This method can be difficult for many people. They need help breaking an addiction to nicotine. One source of help is nicotine replacement therapies (NRTs). These are products to assist a person in breaking a tobacco habit. They include nicotine gums, lozenges, and patches worn on the skin.

Community support groups are another option. Local chapters of the American Cancer Society sponsor programs to help users quit. The American Lung Association and American Heart Association have similar programs. Some schools also now have programs to help teens who want to quit using tobacco.

 **Reading Check** **Give Examples** Identify three ways of saying no to tobacco.

ACTIVITY

DEVELOPING

Good Character

Citizenship

Good citizens look out for the welfare of the community. The term *community* includes more than just your neighborhood. It also includes the environment and the air you breathe. Obeying laws that regulate smoking is one way of showing good citizenship.

What are some other ways of showing good citizenship when it comes to tobacco?

Health Skills Activity

Advocacy

Spreading the Word About Tobacco

You can do your part to help other teens avoid smoking. Here are steps you can take to help your peers help themselves.

- Make colorful posters encouraging teens to avoid using tobacco. Include information on the dangers of tobacco. With permission from school administrators, hang your posters in the hallways at school.

- Create a brochure telling what harmful ingredients are contained in tobacco products and how they damage the body. Distribute your brochure to students and adults in your community.

- Offer to make signs for local retailers that teens frequent, urging teens to say no to smoking. Ask retailers to place these signs in a location where they will be seen.

With a Group

Brainstorm other ways of encouraging students and adults in your community to avoid the risks of tobacco use.

Academic Vocabulary

pollutes (puh LOOTS) *(verb)* to make dirty or unclean. *Cigarette smoke pollutes the air.*

Visit glencoe.com and complete the Interactive Study Guide for Lesson 3.

Tobacco and the Nonsmoker

The dangers of tobacco exist not only for the smoker but for the nonsmoker as well. Tobacco use affects the short-term and long-term health of anyone who is exposed to it.

When a smoker lights up, she or he releases **secondhand smoke.** This is *a mixture of the smoke given off by the burning end of tobacco products and the smoke exhaled by smokers.* Secondhand smoke **pollutes** the air around the smoker. *Nonsmokers who breathe in secondhand smoke* are called **passive smokers.**

Some of the short-term effects of breathing passive smoke include itchy, watery eyes; coughing; and sneezing. Passive smokers can also develop some of the same long-term health problems as smokers. They can develop respiratory problems like asthma, and infections. Passive smokers can also develop heart disease, and even lung cancer. About 3,000 nonsmokers die of lung cancer each year.

Rights of the Nonsmoker

As a nonsmoker, you have the right to breathe air free of tobacco smoke. You have the right to ask people not to smoke around you. For this reason, the federal government has passed laws protecting nonsmokers' rights. Since 1989, it has been illegal to smoke on domestic airplane flights. *Domestic* means "within the country's borders." Many restaurants have set aside specific areas for smokers or banned smoking altogether. The same is true of many offices and factories. Some towns and cities have even banned smoking in certain outdoor locations. These include beaches, children's play areas, and public gardens.

 **Reading Check**

Describe What are the long- and short-term effects of exposure to secondhand smoke?

▶ You can help make your community smoke free. **How can you go about achieving the goal represented by the signs in this picture?**

Lesson 3 Review

 After You Read

Review this lesson for new terms, major headings, and Reading Checks.

What I Learned

1. *Vocabulary* Define *secondhand smoke*. Use it in a sentence.

2. *List* What are two reasons for refusing to use tobacco?

3. *Recall* What have some communities done to protect the rights of nonsmokers?

Thinking Critically

4. *Evaluate* Why do you think it is important to practice refusal skills in advance?

5. *Apply* Tina would like to get her grandfather to stop smoking. When she asked him to stop, he said it was too difficult. What might Tina suggest?

Applying Health Skills

6. *Communication Skills* With classmates, develop a skit showing polite ways to ask a smoker to put out a cigarette. The skit should illustrate ways of asking that are assertive.

Building Health Skills

What Are Refusal Skills?

Refusal skills are strategies that help you say no effectively. If a peer asks you to engage in a risky behavior, remember the S.T.O.P. strategy:

- **Say no firmly.** Be direct and clearly state how you feel. Use direct eye contact and keep your statement short.
- **Tell why not.** Use "I" messages to give your reasons.

- **Offer other ideas.** Suggest an activity that does not involve smoking.
- **Promptly leave.** If you have to, just walk away.

Taking a Stand Against Tobacco

Follow the Model, Practice, and Apply steps to help you master this important health skill.

❶ Model

Read about how Damien uses refusal skills to handle peer pressure.

During the softball game, Elise and Jack showed Damien a cigarette they found on the grass near the center field bleachers. Elise and Jack said someone in the stands must have dropped it. Elise and Jack asked Damien to smoke the cigarette with them after the game. Damien said that he didn't want to smoke **(Say no in a firm voice.)**. He told Elise and Jack that he didn't like to be around cigarette smoke **(Tell why not.)**. He suggested they go to the batting cage after the game **(Offer another idea.)**. When Jack started making chicken noises, Damien decided the conversation was over. He walked away to watch another teammate hit the ball **(Promptly leave.)**.

❷ Practice

Read about how Vivian uses refusal skills with a classmate.

Vivian used refusal skills when a classmate, Jennifer, offered her tobacco. Read the following conversation. Then answer the questions at the end.

Jennifer: Try one of these special flavored cigarettes.

Vivian: No thanks. From what I've read, all cigarettes can affect your health.

Jennifer: You can't believe everything you read.

Vivian: I still don't want one. Let's go play my new computer game instead.

Jennifer: Okay, let's go.

1. Which refusal skills did Vivian use?

2. What words would you use if you were in a similar situation?

❸ Apply

Apply what you have learned about refusal skills when completing the activity below.

With a classmate, develop a situation where a teen feels pressure to use tobacco. Write a conversation between two or more teens. Use all the skills you have learned to show how to refuse tobacco. In your refusal, include reasons why tobacco is an unhealthy choice.

Self-Check

■ Did we use all of the refusal skills?

■ Did we include reasons why tobacco is unhealthy?

Building Health Skills

Across the country, more and more teens are working together to stamp out smoking. They say it's time to...

KICK BUTTS

Did you know that with every puff of a cigarette, a smoker inhales more than 4,000 chemicals? These dangerous substances include ammonia—an ingredient in toilet cleaner, and arsenic—a powerful rat poison.

Scary facts like these have inspired teens all across the United States to take part in Kick Butts Day (KBD), an annual event sponsored by the Campaign for Tobacco-Free Kids. The day, which is run by teens for teens, is about giving young people information to make the right decision about smoking.

A DAY TO TAKE ACTION (AND HAVE FUN!)

"When I found out that tobacco kills 400,000 people each year," says Megan Shaheen, 13, from Washington, D.C., "I knew I had to do something."

Megan heard about KBD from a friend and decided to get involved. Megan especially liked KBD's motto, which is "Stand out, speak up, and seize control."

What does the motto mean to Megan? "It means I can make my opinions known about smoking," she says. "Now I'm going to

speak out to tell my friends and other kids about the dangers of smoking."

Megan's not alone in getting her message heard. For over ten years, thousands of teens have used KBD as a chance to speak up. They get their anti-tobacco messages across through fun activities, such as school and neighborhood carnivals, track meets, and battles of the bands.

SURGEON GENERAL'S WARNING: Smoking Causes Lung Cancer, Heart Disease, Emphysema, and May Complicate Pregnancy

TEENS REACHING TEENS

The good news is youth movements like KBD seem to be working. According to the Campaign for Tobacco-Free Kids, smoking among high school students decreased to 171,000 current smokers.

"Kids talking to kids sometimes works better than adults talking to kids," says Josh Parker, 15, from East Lansing, MI. "The numbers show when we put our minds to something, teens can make a change."

Reading Review

Visit **glencoe.com** to download quizzes and eFlashcards for Chapter 9.

FOLDABLES Study Organizer

Foldables® and Other Study Aids Take out the Foldable® that you created for Lesson 1 and any graphic organizers that you created for Lessons 1–3. Find a partner, and quiz each other using these study aids.

Lesson 1 Tobacco: A Harmful Drug

Main Idea Tobacco is harmful to your health and the health of those around you.

- Tobacco increases your risk of cancer and other serious diseases.
- The nicotine in tobacco causes addiction.
- Addiction is the body's physical or mental need for a drug or other substance.
- Smokers begin to depend on nicotine to feel good and function normally.
- The chemicals in tobacco harm the skin, mouth, lungs, heart, fingers, stomach, bladder, colon, brain, and blood vessels.
- Emphysema is a disease that occurs when the tiny air sacs in the lungs lose their elasticity, or ability to stretch.
- Smokeless tobacco is also harmful and addictive. It can form white spots in the mouth that can turn into cancer. Using smokeless tobacco can form sores in the mouth, stomach, and lungs. It can also cause cancer.

Lesson 2 Teens and Tobacco

Main Idea Many influences cause teens to use tobacco.

- Negative peer pressure can lead teens to try tobacco. They want to feel grown-up or fit in.
- Many teens think that using tobacco has no short-term health effects. This is a myth. Other myths include smoking makes a person look cool, tobacco makes teens more accepted by their peers, and smoking makes teens look more grown-up.
- The media make tobacco use look cool in movies, music, newspapers, magazines, radio, television, and the Internet.
- The tobacco industry uses advertising to target teens.

Lesson 3 Staying Tobacco Free

Main Idea There are several ways to quit tobacco use and stay tobacco-free.

- Refusal skills can help you say no effectively. Remember the S.T.O.P. strategy. **S**ay no firmly. **T**ell why not. **O**ffer another idea. **P**romptly leave.
- Nicotine replacement therapies (NRTs) include nicotine gums, lozenges, and patches.
- "Cold turkey" is a method in which a person simply stops using tobacco.
- Community support groups offer help in quitting tobacco.
- Laws protect nonsmokers' rights to breathe tobacco-free air. Many restaurants either ban smoking or have special seating for smokers. The same is true for many offices, factories, cities, and towns.

Assessment

 After You Read

Health eSpotlight

 VIDEO

Now that you have read the chapter, look back at your answer to the Health eSpotlight question on the chapter opener. What are some additional steps you can recommend to help a friend stop using tobacco products?

Reviewing Vocabulary and Main Ideas

On a sheet of paper, write the numbers 1–5. After each number, write the term from the list that best completes each sentence.

- carbon monoxide
- tar
- addiction
- emphysema
- media
- negative peer pressure
- secondhand smoke
- passive smokers

Lesson 1 Tobacco: A Harmful Drug

1. _____ is a disease in which tiny air sacs in the lungs are damaged and lose their elasticity.

2. _____ is the body's physical or mental need for a drug or other substance.

3. _____ is a thick, oily, dark liquid that forms when tobacco burns.

Lesson 2 Teens and Tobacco

4. Pressure you feel to go along with harmful behaviors or beliefs of your peers is known as _____.

5. Newspapers, radio, television, and the Internet are examples of the _____.

Lesson 3 Staying Tobacco Free

On a sheet of paper, write the numbers 6–10. Choose the letter of the word or phrase that best completes each statement or question.

6. It is illegal in many states for teens to
   a. listen to tobacco advertisements.
   b. use tobacco products.
   c. advocate for a smoke-free environment.

7. *Cold turkey* is
   a. a type of cigarette product in which the tobacco is flavored.
   b. a type of tobacco product that is held in the mouth rather than smoked.
   c. a method of quitting tobacco in which the user simply stops using all such products.

8. Each of the following is a nicotine replacement therapy *except*
   a. nicotine gum.
   b. patches worn on the skin.
   c. group counseling.

9. All of the following statements are true about passive smokers *except*
   a. they are nonsmokers.
   b. they use smokeless tobacco.
   c. they develop some of the same health problems as smokers.

10. Since 1989, it has been illegal to
    a. smoke on domestic airplane flights.
    b. be a passive smoker.
    c. release secondhand smoke into the environment.

Go Online Visit **glencoe.com** and take the Online Quiz for Chapter 9.

Thinking Critically

Using complete sentences, answer the following questions on a sheet of paper.

11. **Evaluate** Why do you think it is difficult for smokers to quit?

12. **Analyze** Why might a teen whose parents use tobacco be more likely to do the same?

Write About It

13. **Personal Writing** Imagine getting a letter from a friend living in another city. In the letter, your friend tells you about a new group of friends who smoke. Your friend is thinking of trying a cigarette, too. Write a letter to your friend giving advice on the dangers of smoking.

⬈ Applying Technology

Tobacco Taboos

Work in pairs to create an iMovie® clip that explains how tobacco is harmful.

- Write a script that highlights the short-term and the long-term consequences of tobacco use. Include a scene that illustrates a teen's refusal of tobacco for health reasons.
- Rehearse and record the script.
- Import the clip into a new iMovie® file.
- Edit the clip for accuracy of information and clarity.
- Save your clip.

Standardized Test Practice

Math

Trends in Smoking Among Young Americans
Use the table to answer the questions.

Year	Percentage of Young Adult Smokers
1965	45.5
1974	37.8
1980	33.3
1985	29.3
1990	24.5
1999	27.9
2002	28.5
2003	23.9
2004	23.6

Source: CDC

1. In which two years did the percent of young adult smokers drop below 24 percent?
   - **A.** 1990 and 2003
   - **B.** 2002 and 2004
   - **C.** 2003 and 2004
   - **D.** 1985 and 1999

2. Which of the following does the table show?
   - **A.** There were just as many young adult smokers in 2003 as there were in 2004.
   - **B.** The percentage of young adult smokers has increased between 1965 and 2004.
   - **C.** The percentage of young adult smokers has decreased between 1965 and 2004.
   - **D.** There are more young adult smokers than middle-aged smokers.

Chapter Preview

▲ *Working with the Photo*

Drugs, including alcohol, can damage your health. **How can you help spread the word about the dangers of alcohol and other drug use?**

Start-Up Activities

Before You Read

Do the media show the real consequences of alcohol and drug abuse? Answer the Health eSpotlight question below and then watch the online video. Keep a record of your answers.

Health eSpotlight

VIDEO

Drugs and the Media

The media, such as television, newspapers, magazines, and the Internet, play a big role in the way we view the impact of drugs in our community. What are some of the media messages about drugs and teen drug use you've seen, read, or heard?

Go to **glencoe.com** and watch the health video for Chapter 10. Then complete the activity provided with the online video.

FOLDABLES Study Organizer

As You Read

Make this Foldable® to record information on alcohol and its harmful effects, presented in Lesson 1. Begin with two sheets of notebook paper.

1 Fold one sheet in half from top to bottom. Cut about 1" along the fold at both ends, stopping at the margin lines.

2 Fold the second sheet in half from top to bottom. Cut the fold between the margin lines.

3 Insert the first sheet through the second sheet and align folds.

4 Fold the bound pages in half to make a booklet, and label the cover as shown. Then label each page as instructed by your teacher.

Take notes on alcohol's harmful effects on the appropriate page of your booklet.

Chapter 10,
Lesson 1:
The Dangers of
Alcohol Use

Go Online

Visit **glencoe.com** and complete the Health Inventory for Chapter 10.

The Dangers of Alcohol Use

Quick Write

Write about a story you have read or heard involving the dangers of alcohol use.

What Is Alcohol?

Have you ever seen food that is spoiled and has mold on it? This change is caused by a chemical reaction. A similar change leads to the creation of alcohol. **Alcohol** (AL·kuh·hawl) is *a substance produced by a chemical reaction in carbohydrates*. Alcohol is a drug. A **drug** is *a substance that changes the structure or function of the body or mind*. Like other drugs, alcohol clouds judgment, making it difficult to think and act responsibly. Over time, alcohol can also cause disease and damage body organs. One of the greatest dangers of using alcohol is that its effects are unpredictable. There is no telling how a person's mind or body might react when he or she has been drinking.

Alcohol's Effects on the Body

Alcohol begins to affect the body systems soon after it is consumed. In the stomach, it increases the flow of acid used for digestion. Over time, the extra acid can cause sores to develop in the stomach lining. These sores are called *ulcers*.

From the stomach, alcohol moves into the bloodstream and causes the blood vessels to expand. More blood passes through the blood vessels, making the body feel warm. As blood flows close to the surface of the skin, the body loses heat. In cold weather, this can cause the body temperature to drop dangerously low before the drinker feels cold.

Consuming alcohol regularly over a long period of time puts a strain on the liver. Heavy drinkers are particularly at risk of developing **cirrhosis** (suh·ROH·sis). This is *destruction and scarring of the liver tissue.* Cirrhosis can lead to death.

Drinking large amounts of alcohol in a short time can lead to alcohol poisoning. The drinker may vomit, become unconscious, or have trouble breathing. If this occurs, the user may be at risk of serious harm or even death.

Alcohol's Effects on the Brain

When alcohol reaches the brain, it slows the body's functions and reaction time. Reaction time is how long it takes a person to respond to a situation. People whose reaction time has been slowed by alcohol are dangerous behind the wheel of a car. They cannot react quickly enough to avoid other vehicles or pedestrians.

Drinking alcohol makes it hard for people to think and speak clearly. They may say or do things they would not normally say or do. A person under the influence of alcohol is more likely to engage in high-risk behaviors.

 **Reading Check** **Explain** How does alcohol affect the brain?

Factors that Influence Alcohol's Effects

Different people react to alcohol in different ways. How a person reacts depends on several factors, including his or her **blood alcohol content (BAC).** This is *a measure of the amount of alcohol present in a person's blood.* It is expressed as a percentage. A BAC of 0.02 percent will cause most people to feel light-headed. A BAC of 0.08 percent interferes with a person's ability to drive a car safely. Police officers use this percentage to determine if a driver is legally drunk. A BAC of 0.40 percent can lead to coma and death.

DEVELOPING Good Character

Being a Responsible Friend

One way of showing you are responsible is by looking out for the well-being of others. Don't let a friend get in a car with a driver who has been drinking. If your friend is using alcohol, urge him or her to get help. Don't hesitate to talk to an adult if your friend is unwilling to reach out. This is not breaking your friend's trust. It is taking the first step in getting your friend the help he or she needs. What are some other ways you can show you are responsible and care about a friend's health?

▼ Drunken driving is a major cause of traffic accidents. **Explain** how alcohol contributes to auto accidents.

Go Online

Visit **glencoe.com** and complete the Interactive Study Guide for Lesson 1.

A number of other factors can influence how alcohol affects an individual. These factors include the following:

- **The person's body weight.** The less a person weighs, the greater the effect the alcohol will have.

- **The person's rate of consumption.** Drinking quickly can overload the liver. When this happens, alcohol builds up in the body and continues to affect the brain and blood vessels.

- **The amount the person consumes.** The size of a drink and the alcohol content will influence its effects. **Figure 10.1** compares the alcohol content of different alcoholic beverages.

- **The amount the person has eaten.** Food slows the absorption of alcohol into the bloodstream. When the stomach is empty, alcohol enters the bloodstream and affects the body much quicker.

- **The presence of other drugs in the person's system.** When you combine alcohol with other drugs, including medicines, they react with each other. This can cause serious harm or even death.

▼ FIGURE 10.1

ALCOHOL CONTENT IN DIFFERENT DRINKS

The three drinks here are different sizes, yet all contain the same amount of alcohol. All have the same effect on the brain and body. **How many ounces of beer would produce the same effect as 4 ounces of wine?**

Liquor 1.5 ounces

Beer 12 ounces

Wine 4 ounces

Teens Who Drink

In the United States, drinking alcohol is illegal for anyone under the age of 21. Teens caught drinking can be arrested. They may also be suspended or expelled from school. Teens who use alcohol risk developing health problems as well. Research has shown that the brains of teenagers continue to develop until the age of 20. Alcohol can affect this development by interfering with the brain's learning and memory functions. When the brain doesn't function properly, it is difficult to do well in school.

In spite of the risks, some teens still choose to drink. Why? Some believe that alcohol helps them relax, fit in, and be accepted by their peers. They might also be influenced by advertising that makes drinking alcohol look "cool." Others feel that drinking helps them escape their problems. In reality, alcohol usually makes problems worse. If you have a problem, talk to a friend or trusted adult.

▲ Finding healthy activities to do with your friends will help you avoid alcohol. **What are some other healthy activities you can enjoy with your friends?**

 **Reading Check** **Explain** How might advertising for alcohol influence teen drinking?

Lesson 1 Review

 After You Read

Review this lesson for new terms, major headings, and Reading Checks.

What I Learned

1. *Vocabulary* Define *alcohol*, and use it in an original sentence.

2. *Recall* Give two examples of how alcohol affects the body.

3. *Identify* What do the letters *BAC* stand for? What does BAC measure?

Thinking Critically

4. *Evaluate* Which of alcohol's effects do you think is the most harmful?

5. *Analyze* Why is a person under the influence of alcohol more likely to engage in other high-risk behaviors?

Applying Health Skills

6. *Goal Setting* Identify some goals you have set for yourself, such as going to college or playing on a sports team. Explain the effects alcohol use could have on these plans.

Alcoholism and Addiction

Guide to Reading

● **Building Vocabulary**
Copy the terms below into your notebook. Define each term as you come across them in your reading.

- tolerance (p. 246)
- alcoholism (p. 247)
- fetal alcohol syndrome (FAS) (p. 248)

● **Focusing on the Main Ideas**
In this lesson, you will learn to

- **describe** the cycle of addiction to alcohol.
- **identify** the health risks of drinking during pregnancy.
- **communicate** ways that teens can reduce stress without using alcohol.

● **Reading Strategy**
Predicting Quickly look at the main headings, figures, and captions. Predict the kinds of information that will be covered.

uick Write

Write a paragraph describing how you think alcoholism might affect a person's life.

Why You Should Avoid Alcohol

Using alcohol carries a number of short- and long-term consequences. People who have been drinking alcohol may do or say things they will regret later. Teens whose judgment has been clouded by alcohol may take part in high-risk behaviors. These include using other drugs, engaging in sexual activity, or riding in a car driven by another drinker.

When used over time, alcohol can damage a person's health. For teens, it also can negatively affect relationships with parents and other family members. It also can affect performance in school and have a lasting effect on a teen's future.

Addiction and Alcoholism

People who use alcohol regularly over a long period of time risk becoming addicted to alcohol. As noted in Chapter 9, addiction is a physical or mental need for a drug. The cycle of addiction is sometimes represented by a downward spiral, as shown in **Figure 10.2.** The spiral shows how addiction to alcohol starts off by having an occasional drink. Soon, drinking becomes a habit. He or she begins drinking larger amounts of alcohol. As time goes on, the person develops a tolerance. **Tolerance** is *a need for increasing amounts of a substance to achieve the same effect.*

If this cycle isn't interrupted, the person develops an addiction to alcohol. A person who is addicted to alcohol suffers from **alcoholism.** This is *a disease in which a person has a physical and mental need for alcohol.* A person with this disease is called an *alcoholic.*

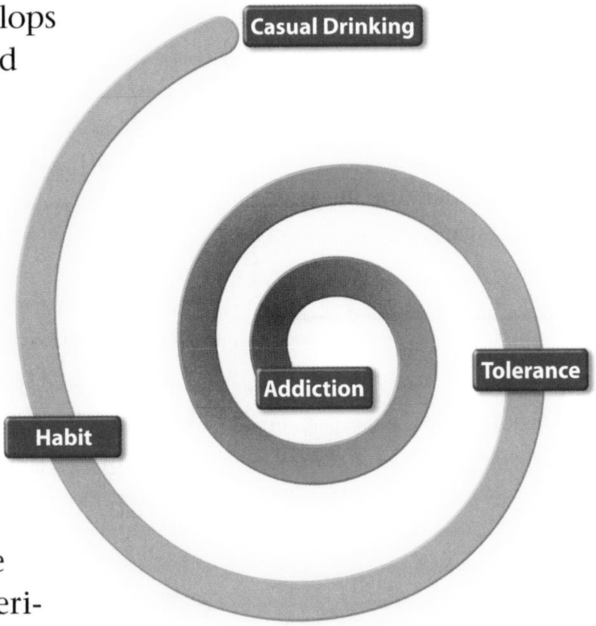

Help for Alcoholics and Their Families

Alcoholism cannot be cured, but it can be treated. Treatment includes cleansing all alcohol from the body. An alcoholic also needs help dealing with the physical and emotional desire to have a drink.

Alcoholism is a problem that affects more than just the alcoholic. It can be a painful experience for family members as well. Children of alcoholics sometimes blame themselves. They believe something they did drove a parent to drink. This is not the case. A child is never to blame for a parent's alcoholism.

When a family member suffers from alcoholism, other family members can try to help. There are community support groups that can help the alcoholic and his or her family. Alcoholics Anonymous (AA) helps people with alcoholism. Al-Anon provides support for family members living with an alcoholic. Alateen, a group within Al-Anon, helps teenage children of alcoholic parents learn to cope with problems at home. Listings for these organizations can be found in phone directories and on the Internet.

Reading Check **Explain** What are two steps in the cycle of addiction?

▲ FIGURE 10.2

SPIRAL OF ADDICTION

The spiral of addiction begins with casual drinking. **Where does the spiral end?**

▶ Help is available for alcoholics and their families. **Name two organizations that can help.**

Visit glencoe.com and complete the Interactive Study Guide for Lesson 2.

Pregnancy and Alcohol

Have you seen warning labels like the one shown on this page? They warn women not to drink alcohol while pregnant. Alcohol consumed during pregnancy passes from the mother into the developing baby's bloodstream. This places the baby at risk of developing **fetal** (FEE·tuhl) **alcohol syndrome (FAS)**. This is *a group of permanent physical and mental problems caused by alcohol use during pregnancy*. Babies with FAS often weigh less than average. They may suffer from birth defects, mental retardation, or learning disabilities that may go unnoticed until they are in school. To protect the health of their babies, pregnant women should completely avoid consuming alcohol.

GOVERNMENT WARNING:
(1) ACCORDING TO THE SURGEON GENERAL, WOMEN SHOULD NOT DRINK ALCOHOLIC BEVERAGES DURING PREGNANCY BECAUSE OF THE RISK OF BIRTH DEFECTS.
(2) CONSUMPTION OF ALCOHOLIC BEVERAGES IMPAIRS YOUR ABILITY TO DRIVE A CAR OR OPERATE MACHINERY, AND MAY CAUSE HEALTH PROBLEMS.

 **Reading Check**   **Define** What do the letters *FAS* stand for? What is FAS?

◀ All alcoholic beverages are required by law to carry the warning label shown here. **What two uses of alcohol does this label warn against?**

Lesson 2 Review

 After You Read

Review this lesson for new terms, major headings, and Reading Checks.

What I Learned

1. *Vocabulary* Explain the connection between *tolerance* and *alcoholism*.

2. *Compare* How are Alateen and Al-Anon similar? How are they different?

3. *Explain* Who is at risk when a pregnant woman drinks? Explain.

Thinking Critically

4. *Analyze* What are some short- and long-term benefits of avoiding alcohol?

5. *Evaluate* Sid was at a party where teens were talking about drinking. He was told that trying alcohol once won't hurt him. Is this statement accurate?

Applying Health Skills

6. *Stress Management* Some people use alcohol to reduce stress. As a class, brainstorm ways that teens can reduce stress without the use of alcohol.

 For more Lesson Review Activities, go to **glencoe.com**.

Lesson 3

What Are Illegal Drugs?

Guide to Reading

● Building Vocabulary
Review the terms below. Write each, along with its definition, in your notebook.

- illegal drugs (p. 249)
- inhalants (p. 249)
- marijuana (p. 250)
- stimulants (p. 250)
- anabolic steroids (p. 251)
- narcotics (p. 251)
- hallucinogens (p. 252)

● Focusing on the Main Ideas
In this lesson, you will learn to

- **identify** the dangers of illegal drugs.
- **explain** the risks of using inhalants and marijuana.
- **identify** the risks of using stimulants, anabolic steroids, narcotics, and hallucinogens.

● Reading Strategy
Identifying Cause-and-Effect Make a two-column chart. In the first column, write the names of the drugs you learned about. In the second, list the effects of these drugs.

Illegal Drugs

Drugs that are made and sold without getting approval from the government are illegal. **Illegal drugs** are *drugs that are made and used purely for their effects.* Anyone who is caught making, selling, or using illegal drugs can be arrested. Punishment can include stiff fines and lengthy jail sentences. Using illegal drugs can damage your health and can even cause death. In this lesson, you will learn about several types of illegal drugs and how they can affect your health.

Inhalants

Inhalants (in·HAY·luhnts) are *substances whose fumes or vapors are inhaled, or breathed in.* Most toxic or poisonous inhalants are common household products like adhesives, lighter fluids, cleaning solvents, and paint. Breathing in these fumes or vapors can cause hallucinations. They can also damage brain cells. Damaging brain cells can make a person lose consciousness and go into a coma. A coma is a deep state of unconsciousness. If the brain has been permanently damaged, a person can die or never wake up from the coma.

Quick Write
Write a list of problems that people might develop from using illegal drugs.

▼ Knowing the facts about illegal drugs can help you avoid using drugs. **What are some ways to get information about illegal drugs?**

Lesson 3: What Are Illegal Drugs? **249**

▶ Talking to a trusted adult can help teens cope with problems without using drugs. **Who are some adults you could turn to for help?**

Careers for the 21st Century

Substance Abuse Counselor

If you are a good listener and like helping people, you should think about a career as a substance abuse counselor. Substance abuse counselors help people who are addicted to alcohol and other drugs. There is a demand for substance abuse counselors because they provide care that other counselors cannot provide. If you are interested in becoming a substance abuse counselor, you should study how drugs and alcohol affect the body.

What skills does a substance abuse counselor need? Go to *Career Corner* **at glencoe.com to find out.**

Marijuana

Marijuana (mar·uh·WAHN·uh) is *an illegal drug that comes from the hemp plant.* Marijuana, also known as *pot* or *weed,* is usually smoked. Using marijuana can increase your heart rate and decrease your energy level. It can interfere with memory and concentration. Users may also experience hallucinations and panic attacks. They may see or hear things that aren't real and feel terrified for no reason. Over time, marijuana can cause brain damage. People who use marijuana and other "gateway" drugs such as tobacco, alcohol, and steroids, are more likely to try other dangerous drugs.

Reading Check **List** Name two gateway drugs.

Stimulants

Stimulants (STIM·yuh·luhnts) are *drugs that speed up the body's functions.* They cause increases in heart and breathing rates. They can also cause loss of coordination, physical collapse, heart failure, and brain damage. Illegal stimulants include cocaine, crack, and methamphetamines.

Cocaine and Crack

One highly addictive illegal stimulant is cocaine (koh·KAYN). Cocaine's effects are unpredictable and very dangerous. Using cocaine even once can cause the user's blood pressure and heart rate to rise to dangerous levels. Cocaine use can also cause feelings of restlessness, anxiety, and loss of appetite. Cocaine is inhaled or injected with a needle. Crack cocaine, or *rock,* is an especially pure and powerful form of cocaine that is heated and smoked.

It has been linked to many deaths. People who use crack cocaine often engage in other high-risk behaviors, such as sexual activity.

Methamphetamine

Another dangerous stimulant whose use has increased in recent years is methamphetamine (meth·uhm·FEH·tuh·meen). Nicknamed *meth* or *crank,* methamphetamine is very addictive. It is available as pills, capsules, powder, and chunks. Effects of the drug include an abnormal or exaggerated level of activity and decreased appetite. Long-term use can damage brain cells, cause breathing problems, and even cause a stroke.

 **Reading Check** **Give Examples** How do stimulants harm the body?

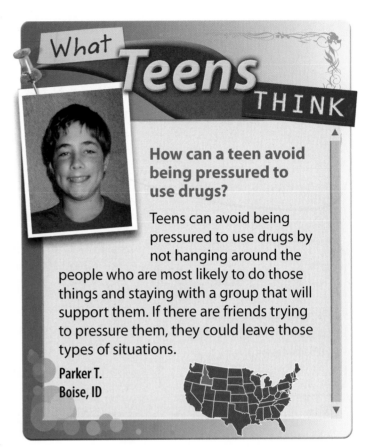

Anabolic Steroids

Some drugs mimic the behavior of chemicals made by the body. One example is **anabolic steroids** (a·nuh·BAH·lik STEHR·oydz), *synthetic drugs based on a male hormone.* Doctors sometimes prescribe steroids to treat certain medical conditions. Some athletes use steroids to increase their body weight and strength. Steroids should never be used for this purpose. Users may become violent and deeply depressed. Steroids can also cause problems in sexual development, liver and brain cancer, and heart attacks.

Narcotics

Narcotics (nar·KAH·tics) are *strong drugs that relieve pain.* Some narcotics are medicines prescribed by doctors. For example, a patient may be given a narcotic after surgery to relieve pain. Some narcotics, however, are illegal.

▶ Responsible teens strengthen their muscles in healthy ways. They steer clear of anabolic steroids. **What are some other physical activities that will build muscle strength?**

Heroin is an illegal narcotic that comes from the Asian poppy plant. It usually appears as a white or brown powder. Its street names include *smack*, *H*, *skag*, and *junk*. Black tar heroin is a kind of heroin produced in Mexico. It is the most common type of heroin used in the Western United States. People who use heroin risk unconsciousness and death. Since it is usually injected, heroin users may also become infected with HIV and hepatitis from shared needles.

Hallucinogens

Hallucinogens (huh·LOO·suhn·uh·jenz) are *illegal drugs that cause the user's brain to create or distort images and to see and hear things that are not real.* As the name suggests, users experience hallucinations. PCP (*angel dust*) and LSD (*acid*) are two very dangerous hallucinogens. Another hallucinogen, called MDMA or ecstasy, is also a stimulant. Use of these drugs can lead to strange and/or violent behavior. Users may become confused or depressed. Long-term use can lead to brain damage.

Reading Check **Identify** What are some risks of using hallucinogens?

Go Online

Visit **glencoe.com** and complete the Interactive Study Guide for Lesson 3.

Lesson 3 Review

After You Read

Review this lesson for new terms, major headings, and Reading Checks.

What I Learned

1. *Vocabulary* Define *inhalant*. Use the word in a sentence.

2. *Recall* What is a street name for crack cocaine? Describe this illegal drug.

3. *List* What are some of the health risks associated with heroin use?

Thinking Critically

4. *Apply* Suppose a friend told you steroids were safe because they are sometimes used as a medicine. How would you respond? Is this valid health information?

5. *Analyze* One day, as Wesley is leaving baseball practice, an older teen offers him some pills. "These will help you hit the ball a mile," the teen says. What advice would you give Wesley?

Applying Health Skills

6. *Analyzing Influences* In pairs, talk about the roles that you think family, peers, and community play in drug use and abuse. Share your opinions with the rest of the class.

Go Online For more Lesson Review Activities, go to **glencoe.com**.

Drug Abuse

Guide to Reading

Building Vocabulary
Copy the terms below into your notebook. Put a checkmark next to the terms you know. Put an *X* next to those you don't know.

- drug abuse (p. 253)
- overdose (p. 253)
- recovery (p. 254)
- withdrawal (p. 254)
- drug rehabilitation (p. 255)

Focusing on the Main Ideas
In this lesson, you will learn to

- **identify** the harmful effects of drug abuse.
- **explain** recovery and withdrawal.
- **describe** treatments for drug addicts.

Reading Strategy
Drawing Conclusions Based on this lesson, list three different ways drug abuse affects your health. Give one example for each of the three sides of your health triangle.

Quick Write

Write about an experience you have had recovering from something, such as a bad cold. What medicines did you take?

What Is Drug Abuse?

Drug abuse is *the use of any drug in a way that is unhealthy or illegal.* Using illegal drugs is a form of drug abuse. Purposely using medicines in ways they were not intended to be used is another form of drug abuse. One medicine that is sometimes abused by teens is a stimulant drug prescribed to treat attention deficit/hyperactivity disorder, or ADHD. Using this drug for any other reason than to treat ADHD is illegal and dangerous. Abuse of this medicine can lead to increased heart rate, high blood pressure, and nervousness. Other possible effects include stroke and seizure.

Harmful Effects of Drug Abuse

People who abuse drugs risk damaging their health and their relationships. Drug abuse can affect all three sides of your health triangle in the following ways.

- **Physical health:** The physical effects of drug abuse can range from sleeplessness and irritability to damage to the body organs. Drug abuse can also cause heart failure and stroke. An **overdose** of drugs—*taking a fatal amount of a drug*—can cause death. It is impossible to tell how much is too much for any given user.

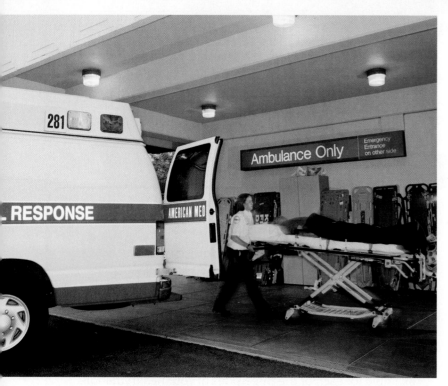

▲ Drug use of any kind is very dangerous. **Why is it risky to try illegal drugs even once?**

- **Mental/emotional health:** Stimulant drugs kill brain cells. These cells continue to die off even after the abuse stops. The brain damage that results can interfere with the user's ability to think. Other drugs cause depression. For teens with low self-esteem, drug-related depression can cause them to think about or commit suicide.

- **Social health:** Teens who abuse drugs may lose interest in school. They may also withdraw from family and friends. Some teens who abuse drugs fall in with a rough crowd. They may become members of gangs, which puts them at risk for being injured in gang-related violence.

Reading Check **List** Name a mental/emotional and a social effect of drug abuse.

Addiction

People who abuse drugs are also at risk for developing an addiction. As noted earlier, addiction is a physical and/or mental need for a drug. There is no telling how many times a person can use a drug before becoming addicted. People with an addiction to a drug can no longer **function** without it. The drug becomes central to their day-to-day life. The addict needs more and more of the drug to feel better.

The Road to Recovery

Recovery begins when a person stops using a drug so the body can cleanse and repair itself. **Recovery** means *to overcome an addiction and return to a mostly normal life.* At the beginning of recovery, the addict may go through withdrawal. **Withdrawal** is *a series of physical and mental symptoms that occur when a person stops using an addictive substance.* Vomiting, hallucinations, and severe anxiety are common withdrawal symptoms. Anyone going through withdrawal needs help from a doctor.

Academic Vocabulary

function (FUNK shun) *(verb)* work. *When Jamie skips breakfast, she feels like her brain can't function.*

Help for Drug Abusers and Their Families

Drug addiction is a disease much like diabetes or heart disease. Like these diseases, treatment for drug addiction requires that sufferers make permanent changes to their behavior. They may also have to change the kinds of medications they take.

Treatment usually includes counseling to help addicts deal with their mental and emotional dependency on drugs. In some cases, **drug rehabilitation** is needed. This is *a process in which a person relearns how to live without the abused drug.* The person is sent to live at a facility for recovering addicts and usually stays from 6 to 12 months.

Because an abuser's family is affected by his or her addiction, they need help, too. Community organizations exist to help families of drug abusers. You will learn more about these in the next lesson.

 **Reading Check** **Define** What is *recovery*?

Go Online

Visit **glencoe.com** and complete the Interactive Study Guide for Lesson 4.

Lesson 4 Review

 After You Read

Review this lesson for new terms, major headings, and Reading Checks.

What I Learned

1. *Describe* Discuss two forms of drug abuse.

2. *Vocabulary* What is an *overdose*? Why are overdoses dangerous?

3. *Explain* What is one form of treatment for drug abuse?

Thinking Critically

4. *Predict* How could drug abuse affect a teen's future?

5. *Analyze* When Alan broke his arm, the doctor prescribed a painkiller. Even after the pain stopped, Alan continued to take the medication. Is he abusing the drug? Why or why not?

Applying Health Skills

6. *Communication Skills* Create a poster that communicates the dangers of drug abuse. You may refer to any of the health problems or other difficulties mentioned in the lesson.

Avoiding Alcohol and Drugs

Guide to Reading

Building Vocabulary
Write the definition of the terms below in your notebook.

- substance abuse (p. 256)
- alternative (p. 258)

Focusing on the Main Ideas
In this lesson, you will learn to

- **demonstrate** the skill of advocacy to explore ways to communicate the dangers of substance abuse.
- **explain** ways to stay substance free.
- **identify** alternatives to substance abuse.

Reading Strategy
Finding the Main Idea Copy the major and minor headings onto a sheet of paper. Leave a space after each heading. Write a sentence after each heading that summarizes its main idea.

Quick Write

Write a brief statement of your long-term goals. Then add another sentence or two explaining how drug use could affect those goals.

Avoiding Substance Abuse

Positive health behaviors include saying no to **substance abuse.** This is *using illegal or harmful drugs, including any use of alcohol, while under the legal drinking age.* Being substance free shows self-control. It means you have taken charge of your life and your health. In this lesson, you will learn healthy ways to avoid using alcohol or other illegal drugs.

▶ Positive peer pressure can help you avoid substance abuse. **What are some benefits of staying substance free?**

Health Skills Activity

Advocacy

Getting SADD About Substance Abuse

Spreading the word about the dangers of substance abuse can save lives. That is why Students Against Destructive Decisions (SADD) was created. SADD is a worldwide organization. It helps students make positive decisions about challenges in their lives.

Members of SADD speak out against the use of alcohol, drugs, or other harmful substances. You can take a stand against substance abuse, too.

With a Group

Explore ways of communicating the dangers of abusing substances. What are some of the different methods organizations such as SADD use to communicate their information to students?

Ways to Stay Substance Free

Teens can be influenced to use alcohol and drugs in several ways. The media often show people enjoying alcohol. You may also see adults around you using alcohol. Your friends or peers may pressure you to use alcohol or other illegal substances.

The best way to avoid being pressured to use illegal substances is to use refusal skills. State your decision clearly and assertively. When you speak assertively, you are letting people know you are serious. If outside pressure is strong, walk away. If it continues, **seek** help from a parent or other trusted adult. Making friends with people who have also chosen not to use drugs will help. They will support your decision and help you avoid situations where drugs and alcohol may be present.

Some teens choose to use alcohol or other drugs to cope with problems. However, alcohol and other drugs will often make problems worse. Instead, talk to a parent, guardian, or other trusted adult. They can help you find positive ways to deal with problems.

Academic Vocabulary

seek (SEEK) (verb) to look for. *Courtney decided to seek more information about the popular acne medicine before she bought it at the drugstore.*

Reading Check **Explain** What kind of influence can peers have on a teen's decision to use alcohol or drugs?

Go Online

Topic: Avoiding Alcohol

Visit **glencoe.com** for Student Web Activities to learn ways to say no to peers who want you to drink.

Activity: Using the information provided at the link above, create an alcohol fact sheet that includes tips for saying no to peer pressure.

Alternatives to Drug and Alcohol Use

When someone offers you drugs or alcohol and you refuse, it is a good idea to suggest a positive alternative. An **alternative** (ahl·TER·nuh·tihv) is *another way of thinking or acting*. Offering a positive alternative allows you to change the subject, redirecting the conversation to another topic. This can help relieve some of the pressure you may be feeling. It also gives you the opportunity to be a positive influence on your friends or other peers. If you are with someone who suggests drinking alcohol, think of something else you both can do. You might suggest getting something to eat or playing a video game instead. **Figure 10.3** shows some other healthful alternatives.

 Reading Check **Define** What is an *alternative*?

 **FIGURE 10.3**

ALTERNATIVES TO SUBSTANCE ABUSE

These are some activities you can enjoy without using alcohol or other drugs. **Can you think of any other positive alternatives to substance abuse?**

- **Have fun at drug-free and alcohol-free events.** Avoid environments where alcohol or other drugs are present. Use positive peer pressure to help others avoid these environments.

- **Improve your talents or skills.** Choose an activity you like, and practice it until you become an expert. Become a great skateboarder, a computer whiz, or the best artist at school.

- **Be part of a group.** Join a sports team, a club, or a community group.

- **Start your own business.** Make yourself available for babysitting, yard work, or other jobs. Let friends and neighbors know.

Help for Families of Substance Abusers

In Lesson 2, you learned about the kinds of support that are available for alcoholics and their families. Similar community resources exist for people with substance abuse problems. They are designed to help a person get his or her life back on track. One organization for families of drug addicts is Nar-Anon. Like Al-Anon, Nar-Anon holds meetings that teach family members how to handle the problems associated with living with an addict.

Go Online

Visit **glencoe.com** and complete the Interactive Study Guide for Lesson 5.

 Reading Check

Give Examples Name one organization that helps families affected by substance abuse.

▶ Support from friends can help you stay substance free. **What resources are available in your community for teens with substance abuse problems?**

Lesson 5 Review

 After You Read

Review this lesson for new terms, major headings, and Reading Checks.

What I Learned

1. *Vocabulary* Define *substance abuse*. Use it in a sentence.

2. *Identify* Name two alternatives to drug abuse.

3. *Recall* What are two ways to stay substance free?

Thinking Critically

4. *Apply* Tell how choosing to be substance free can build character.

5. *Evaluate* How can suggesting a positive alternative to alcohol or drug use help you stay substance free?

Applying Health Skills

6. *Refusal Skills* Think about ways to say no to harmful behaviors. Team up with a classmate. Role-play a situation where you use these strategies to say no to illegal drugs.

Go Online For more Lesson Review Activities, go to **glencoe.com**.

Lesson 5: Avoiding Alcohol and Drugs **259**

What Steps Can You Take to Make Healthy Decisions?

The decision-making process can help you make healthy and responsible choices. The six steps of the decision-making process are:

- State the situation.
- List the options.
- Weigh the possible outcomes.
- Consider your values.
- Make a decision and act on it.
- Evaluate the decision.

Avoiding Drug Abuse

Follow the Model, Practice, and Apply steps to help you master this important health skill.

① Model

Read about how Jason uses the decision-making process to avoid using alcohol.

At Ryan's house, one of the teens suggested that everyone drink some beer. Jason used the decision-making process to help him decide what to do.

1. **State the situation.** I am being pressured to drink beer. I really don't want to do that.

2. **List the options.** I could try the beer. I could just leave. I could say that I would rather play video games.

3. **Weigh the possible outcomes.** I would be breaking my promise to myself that I wouldn't experiment with alcohol or other drugs. Also, we could get caught drinking, which would disappoint my parents. If I just go home, I'll feel left out. If I say I want to stay and play video games, maybe Ryan will back me up.

4. **Consider your values.** Keeping my promise to myself is important. I also don't want to disappoint my parents.

5. **Make a decision and act on it.** I decide to stay and play video games.

6. **Evaluate the decision.** I got to spend time with my friend Ryan. He decided to stay as well.

② Practice

Help Kevin use the decision-making process to avoid using marijuana.

The decision-making process worked well for Kevin. He used it to help him decide whether or not to go to another teen's house. A friend told Kevin that someone was bringing some marijuana over and they could try it.

On your own paper, use the decision-making steps to show how Kevin should make a decision about whether or not to go to the teen's house. If Kevin wanted to spend time with his friends, what are some positive alternatives he could suggest?

③ Apply

Apply what you have learned about decision making when completing the activity below.

With a small group, brainstorm ways teens can stay alcohol and drug free. Choose one of these ideas and write a short story about a teen who makes the choice to stay alcohol and drug free. Show how the teen uses the decision-making process to make this healthy choice.

Self-Check
- Did we brainstorm ways to stay alcohol and drug free?
- Did we use all the decision-making steps in our story?

"Say No to Drugs" Skit

Refusal skills are useful for keeping drugs out of your life. It takes good communication skills to say no in a firm way without offending others. In the activity below, you and your classmates will have a chance to practice refusal skills by creating and acting out a skit.

What You Will Need

■ Pencil and paper

 ### What You Will Do

1 Work with a group of classmates. Think of one-liners teens might use to try to persuade their peers to use drugs. For example, "Just give it a try," or "One time won't hurt."

2 Fold a sheet of paper in half lengthwise to form two columns. In the first column, write your one-liners. Now try to think of ways teens could respond that would allow them to refuse the drug. Write these in the second column.

3 Review your lists. Select the three most persuasive one-liners and the three best refusals. Use these to create a skit to perform for your classmates.

4 After you have finished your performance, pass around a short questionnaire. The questionnaire should ask classmates to tell you what they felt was good and what they thought could be improved in your skit. The questionnaire should conclude by asking them for suggestions on how to improve your refusal strategies.

Wrapping It Up

1 Did your classmates find your refusal statements convincing?

2 If not, what suggestions did they offer for strengthening them?

Reading Review

Visit glencoe.com to download quizzes and eFlashcards for Chapter 10.

FOLDABLES® Study Organizer

Foldables® and Other Study Aids Take out the Foldable® that you created for Lesson 1 and any graphic organizers that you created for Lessons 1–5. Find a partner, and quiz each other using these study aids.

Lesson 1 The Dangers of Alcohol Use

Main Idea Alcohol is a drug that affects a person's ability to think and act responsibly.

- Alcohol has an immediate effect on the body.
- The way alcohol affects the body depends on: body weight, rate of consumption, amount of alcohol consumed, amount eaten before drinking, and if other drugs are in the person's system.
- Alcohol use speeds up the heart rate, harms the liver, and slows the body's functions and reaction time.
- Among reasons teens give for drinking are fitting in with friends or family members who drink, feeling more grown-up, or escaping problems.

Lesson 2 Alcoholism and Addiction

Main Idea Using alcohol regularly over a long period of time can lead to addiction.

- The addiction cycle begins with casual drinking, followed by habit, tolerance, and then addiction.
- If a pregnant woman drinks alcohol, her baby may develop fetal alcohol syndrome.

Lesson 3 What Are Illegal Drugs?

Main Idea Illegal drugs are made and used purely for their effects.

- Inhalants and Marijuana are drugs that can destroy brain cells.
- Marijuana use can cause hallucinations and panic attacks.
- Other types of drugs include stimulants, anabolic steroids, narcotics, and hallucinogens.

Lesson 4 Drug Abuse

Main Idea Drug abuse may harm all sides of the health triangle.

- Drug abuse can lead to brain damage, heart failure, depression, and death.
- Recovery treatments include counseling and drug rehabilitation.
- People who are recovering from a drug addiction may go through withdrawal.

Lesson 5 Avoiding Alcohol and Drugs

Main Idea You can avoid alcohol and drug abuse by using self-control.

- Refusal skills can help you stay substance free.
- Alternatives to drug use include positive activities such as hobbies, sports, and working.

CHAPTER 10: Assessment

After You Read

Health eSpotlight   VIDEO

Now that you have read the chapter, look back at your answer to the Health eSpotlight question on the chapter opener. Do you think that the media show the real mental/emotional and social risks of taking drugs? How might the media help teens stay drug free?

Reviewing Vocabulary and Main Ideas

On a sheet of paper, write the numbers 1–5. After each number, write the term from the list that best completes each sentence.

- alcohol
- alcoholism
- blood alcohol content (BAC)
- cirrhosis
- drug
- fetal alcohol syndrome (FAS)
- tolerance

Lesson 1 The Dangers of Alcohol Use

1. _____, the destruction and scarring of the liver tissue, is a disease that can lead to death.

2. A substance produced by a chemical reaction in carbohydrates is called _____.

3. A(n) _____ is a substance that affects the structure or function of the body or mind.

Lesson 2 Alcoholism and Addiction

4. A need for increasing amounts of a substance to achieve the same effect is called _____.

5. _____ is a disease in which alcohol becomes a force in the drinker's life.

*On a sheet of paper, write the numbers 6–14. Write **True** or **False** for each statement. If the statement is false, change the underlined word or phrase to make it true.*

Lesson 3 What Are Illegal Drugs?

6. Many toxic <u>inhalants</u> are common household products.

7. Cocaine and crack are two examples of <u>hallucinogens</u>.

8. Heroin is a commonly used illegal <u>anabolic steroid</u>.

9. People who use <u>inhalants</u> such as PCP or LSD often show strange and/or violent behavior.

Lesson 4 Drug Abuse

10. The use of any drug in a way that is unhealthy or illegal is an example of <u>drug abuse</u>.

11. Overcoming an addiction and returning to a mostly normal life is called <u>withdrawal</u>.

12. People who need <u>drug rehabilitation</u> are often sent to live at a special facility for recovering addicts.

Lesson 5 Avoiding Alcohol and Drugs

13. Another way of thinking or acting that takes the place of substance abuse is known as <u>tolerance</u>.

14. <u>Al-Anon</u> is an organization that helps families of drug addicts.

Go Online   Visit **glencoe.com** and take the Online Quiz for Chapter 10.

Thinking Critically

Using complete sentences, answer the following questions on a sheet of paper.

15. **Apply** How might a person under the influence of drugs or alcohol put other people at risk?

16. **Synthesize** A friend tells you he plans to use an illegal substance. When you warn him of the dangers, the friend replies, "Lots of kids our age do it." How do you respond?

Write About It

17. **Descriptive Writing** Write a paragraph describing why you think it is important for family members of alcoholics to attend support groups such as Al-Anon and Alateen.

Applying Technology

Preventing Alcohol Abuse

Work in small groups using GarageBand™ or Audacity® to create a podcast that explains the risks and consequences of alcohol abuse.

- Write a three- to five-minute script about a group of students talking about the risks and consequences of alcohol abuse.
- Open a new podcast project. Record your script.
- Insert digital images of alcohol-related accidents or injuries.
- Edit the track for clarity and content.
- Save your track.

Standardized Test Practice

Math

Use the graph to answer the questions.

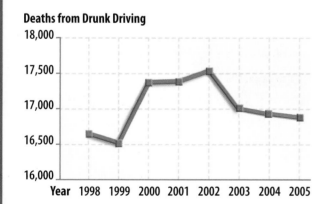

Deaths from Drunk Driving

TEST-TAKING TIP

Estimation will help you eliminate choices in a math problem that are clearly wrong. This will give you more time to find the true answer.

1. Rounding to the nearest thousand, for which 3-year period did deaths total about 51,000?

   A. 1998–2000   **C.** 2003–2005

   B. 2000–2002   **D.** None of the above.

2. In 2003, there were a total 42,643 traffic deaths from all causes. Estimate what percentage of these deaths resulted from drunken driving.

   A. 30   **C.** 40

   B. 35   **D.** 45

Chapter Preview

▲ *Working with the Photo*

Disease-causing germs are so tiny they require a microscope to be seen. **Why is it important for scientists to identify germs that cause disease?**

Start-Up Activities

📖 **Before You Read** Do you know what causes some diseases? Do you know how to prevent them? Take the short quiz on this page. Answer *True* or *False* for each of the following statements. Keep a record of your answers.

HEALTH QUIZ

1. Every disease is caused by a germ.

2. Washing your hands thoroughly helps prevent some diseases from being spread.

3. You can get HIV, the virus that causes AIDS, from shaking hands.

4. Some illnesses, such as heart disease, can result from poor health choices.

ANSWERS: 1. False; 2. True; 3. False; 4. True

FOLDABLES Study Organizer

📖 **As You Read** Make this Foldable® to help you organize the information in Lesson 1 about the four types of disease-causing germs. Begin with a plain sheet of 11" × 17" paper.

1 Fold the short sides of the paper inward so that they meet in the middle.

2 Fold the top to the bottom.

3 Open and cut along the inside fold lines to form four tabs.

4 Label tabs as shown.

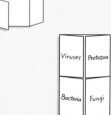

Write down facts about viruses, bacteria, protozoa, and fungi. Give examples of each under the appropriate tab.

G₀ Online Visit **glencoe.com** and complete the Chapter 11 crossword puzzle.

What Causes Disease?

Guide to Reading

● Building Vocabulary

Arrange the terms below into two lists. One list should be labeled *Causes,* the other *Effects.*

- disease (p. 268)
- communicable diseases (p. 268)
- noncommunicable diseases (p. 269)
- pathogen (p. 269)
- viruses (p. 269)
- bacteria (p. 270)
- protozoa (p. 270)
- fungi (p. 270)

● Focusing on the Main Ideas

In this lesson, you will learn to

- **identify** the two main types of disease.
- **recognize** the four common disease-causing organisms.
- **describe** how germs are spread.

● Reading Strategy

Analyzing a Graphic Create a concept map that shows causes of communicable diseases. Use the diagram to the right as a guide.

FOLDABLES Study Organizer Use the Foldable® on p. 267 as you read this lesson.

Write a letter to the editor of your school paper. Discuss ways students can avoid spreading germs.

What Is a Disease?

Angela came home from soccer practice with a cough and sore throat. She was also running a slight fever. Angela's mother gave her some medicine to help relieve her symptoms and told her to rest. A couple of days later, Angela was back on her feet.

Recovering from an illness or disease has not always been so simple. A **disease** (dih·ZEEZ) is *a condition that affects the proper functioning of the body or mind.* The science of fighting disease has come a long way in the past hundred years. Science has made important strides in treating some diseases and preventing others. In this chapter, you'll learn about common diseases and ways to prevent them.

Types of Diseases

There are two main categories of disease. **Communicable** (kuh·MYOO·nih·kuh·buhl) **diseases** are *diseases that can be spread,* such as colds. You can get a communicable disease

from another person, an animal, or an object. In **contrast**, **noncommunicable diseases** are *diseases that do not spread*. Diabetes and cancer are two noncommunicable diseases. You can't catch these diseases from another person.

 **Reading Check** **Define** What is a *noncommunicable disease*? Give an example?

Germs That Cause Disease

Where do communicable diseases come from in the first place? They start with organisms so tiny they can only be seen with a microscope. The popular name for these organisms is *germs*. The scientific name is *pathogens*. A **pathogen** is *a microscopic organism that causes communicable diseases*. Pathogens can be grouped into four main classes: viruses, bacteria, protozoa, and fungi. Within each class are many different *strains*, or subtypes.

Viruses

Viruses (VY·ruh·suhz) are *tiny, nonliving particles that invade and take over healthy cells*. Viruses are so tiny they require a special microscope to be seen. Like bacteria, some strains of viruses are harmless. Others, however, cause serious diseases. For example, AIDS, an immune disorder, and hepatitis, a serious disease of the liver, are caused by viruses. So are the common cold, the flu, and measles.

▲ Taking care of your body can help you recover from a cold quickly. **Which of the two major types of disease is a cold?**

Academic Vocabulary

contrast (KON trast) *(noun)* difference. *Jason chose to compare and contrast two kinds of fish for his life science project.*

Helpful Bacteria

Some bacteria are essential to good health. One helpful strain of bacteria lives inside your body, in your intestines. These bacteria play an important role in breaking down food during digestion. Other helpful bacteria live on your skin and eat dead skin cells.

How can you help maintain the health of your skin and digestive system?

Bacteria

Bacteria (bak·TIR·ee·uh) are *extremely small, single-celled organisms with no cell nucleus.* A nucleus is a cell's control center. Bacteria are everywhere. Some of the diseases they can cause include strep throat and Lyme disease. They can also cause tooth decay. It is important to note that not all bacteria are harmful to humans. Some are even helpful. In fact, we could not live without bacteria.

Protozoa

Protozoa (proh·tuh·ZOH·uh) are *single-celled organisms that have a nucleus.* Some protozoa, called *parasites*, attach themselves to healthy cells. They rob the cell of its nutrients without killing it. Although most protozoa are harmless to humans, some strains can cause disease. One of the most famous and deadly diseases caused by a protozoan is malaria. Malaria is found in tropical regions and spread by a certain kind of mosquito.

Fungi

Fungi (FUHN·jy) are *primitive single- or many-celled organisms that cannot make their own food.* Fungi survive by breaking down other living organisms and absorbing their nutrients. Most fungi are harmless to humans. For example, mushrooms are a fungus and certain kinds are safe to eat. Some strains of fungi, such as molds and yeasts, cause disease, including athlete's foot and ringworm.

 **Reading Check**   **Compare** Identify two similarities and two differences between bacteria and viruses.

▶ These are close-ups of four common pathogens: (clockwise, from top left) viruses, bacteria, fungi, and protozoa. **What are some examples of diseases caused by these organisms?**

How Germs Are Spread

Because germs are so tiny, they can easily be spread. There are four common ways germs are spread. One is by *direct* physical contact with others. Simply shaking hands with someone can pass along germs that are on the skin. Another way is through *indirect* contact. You can pick up germs that travel through the air when people sneeze or cough. Germs can also be spread indirectly by sharing cups, utensils, or other personal items.

A third way germs are spread is by eating or drinking contaminated food or water. Bacteria that cause food poisoning are spread this way. The fourth most common way germs are spread is through contact with animals or insects. Germs can enter your body if you are bitten by a sick animal or disease-carrying insect.

Go Online

Visit **glencoe.com** and complete the Interactive Study Guide for Lesson 1.

Reading Check **List** Name four ways germs are spread.

◄ The West Nile virus is spread by infected mosquitoes. **What are some ways you can protect yourself against mosquito bites?**

Lesson 1 Review

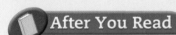
After You Read

Review this lesson for new terms, major headings, and Reading Checks.

What I Learned

1. *Vocabulary* Define *pathogen*. Use the word in a sentence.

2. *Recall* Name a disease caused by a fungus.

3. *Identify* Name four common disease-causing organisms.

Thinking Critically

4. *Explain* What is the difference between a communicable disease and a non-communicable disease?

5. *Apply* At lunchtime, Maria offers Victoria a bite of her sandwich. Victoria remembers that Maria was coughing and sneezing earlier in class. Should Victoria accept the bite of sandwich? Explain your answer.

Applying Health Skills

6. *Decision Making* Imagine you are in school when you begin to feel like you are coming down with a cold. What are your options? What healthy decisions could you make?

Go Online For more Lesson Review Activities, go to **glencoe.com**.

Lesson 1: What Causes Disease? **271**

Communicable Diseases

Guide to Reading

● **Building Vocabulary**

List the terms below in your notebook. Put an X next to those terms that can cause you harm. Put a checkmark next to those that help you.

- contagious (p. 272)
- infection (p. 274)
- immune system (p. 274)
- lymphocytes (p. 274)
- antibodies (p. 274)
- immunity (p. 274)
- vaccine (p. 275)

● **Focusing on the Main Ideas**

In this lesson, you will learn to

- **recognize** ways pathogens are spread.
- **identify** common communicable diseases.
- **demonstrate** healthful behaviors that limit the spread of pathogens.

● **Reading Strategy**

Sequencing Describe the sequence of events that occur when a pathogen enters the body.

Quick Write

Think about the last time you missed school because of an illness. Describe the illness and the steps you took to get better.

Common Communicable Diseases

Can you guess the name of the most common communicable disease? You've probably had it several times. It is the common cold. Colds are responsible for more school absences than any other illness. There are more than 200 different viruses that cause colds. Symptoms include runny nose, sneezing, coughing, sore throat, headache, and mild fever. When these symptoms first appear, you are contagious (kuhn·TA·juhs). **Contagious** means *you can spread the virus to others by direct or indirect contact*. To help prevent this from happening, be sure to cover your mouth and nose when you sneeze or cough.

◀ Sneezing without covering your mouth and nose spreads thousands of pathogens. **What are some other ways pathogens are spread?**

There is no cure for the common cold. To help your body recover, you should rest in bed and drink plenty of fluids. Your parent or guardian may also give you over-the-counter (OTC) medicines that will help with the symptoms. If you have a sore throat for several days, you should see a doctor.

Another communicable disease you are familiar with is influenza (in·floo·EN·zuh). You probably know it as "the flu." Flu symptoms include high fever and joint and muscle aches. Resting and drinking fluids can help you recover faster. Some strains of the flu are serious and may require a doctor's care.

Some other common communicable diseases are listed in **Figure 11.1.** All except hepatitis A are spread through direct or indirect contact. A person gets hepatitis A from food or water containing the virus.

 **Reading Check**   **Define** What does *contagious* mean? Use the word in a sentence.

Your Body's Defenses

In a typical day, your body is exposed to millions of germs, so why aren't you sick all the time? The answer is that your body is protected by its own defense system. This system is like a well-designed fort. It actively protects your health around the clock.

DEVELOPING Good Character

Keep It to Yourself

When you have a cold, take action to prevent spreading your cold to others. Be careful to cover your mouth and nose when you cough or sneeze. Keep as much distance between yourself and others as you can. Avoid sharing cups, utensils, or other personal items. What character traits are you demonstrating when you take steps to prevent spreading communicable diseases?

▼ FIGURE 11.1

COMMON COMMUNICABLE DISEASES

This table lists several common communicable diseases.
What are the symptoms of strep throat?

Disease	Symptoms	Treatment
Mononucleosis	Swollen lymph glands (in neck, underarms, groin), headaches, sore muscles, sore throat, fever, fatigue	Pain relievers, rest, liquids
Hepatitis A, B, and C	Weakness, fatigue, nausea, vomiting, fever, yellowing of eyes, abdominal pain, dark urine	Rest, healthful food choices (medication for types B and C)
Tuberculosis (TB)	Cough, fatigue, persistent fever, night sweats, weight loss	Antibiotics taken over a long period of time
Strep throat	Sore throat, fever, chills, body aches, loss of appetite, nausea, vomiting, swollen tonsils or glands	Antibiotics, soft food, liquids, gargling with salt water

Academic Vocabulary

despite (di SPEYET)
(preposition) in spite of.
Allen went outside to play tennis, despite the rain.

Your Body's First Line of Defense

Your body's defense system has several barriers that work to prevent germs from entering your body. The five major barriers are skin, tears, saliva, mucous membranes, and stomach acid. The skin, your body's largest organ, acts like a wall around the inner organs. Another barrier is formed by body fluids such as tears and saliva. These contain chemicals that kill certain organisms. Your *mucous membranes* are barriers that line the insides of your mouth, throat, nose, and eyes. They are coated with a sticky fluid that traps and destroys germs. Stomach acid kills the germs that make it past the saliva and mucous membranes in your mouth.

Sometimes, **despite** these barriers, germs find a way into your body through a cut or scrape. When this happens, you can develop an **infection.** This is *the result of pathogens or germs invading the body, multiplying, and harming some of your body's cells.* Fortunately, your body is equipped with agents that can fight infection, such as *pyrogen* (PY·ruh·juhn). The release of this chemical triggers a rise in body temperature, or *fever.* The increase in body temperature makes it hard for germs to survive.

Your Immune System

Most of the time, the body's first line of defense is successful in fighting off infections. When it is not, your second line of defense swings into action. This is your **immune** (ih·MYOON) **system,** *a group of cells, tissues, and organs that fight disease.* A key part of the immune system is **lymphocytes** (LIM·fuh·syts), which are *white blood cells that attack pathogens or harmful germs.* Some lymphocytes produce **antibodies.** These are *chemicals produced specifically to fight a particular invading substance.* Antibodies recognize germs that reenter the body and attack and destroy them. This *resistance to infection* is called **immunity.**

 **Reading Check** **Identify** two barriers that protect your body against germs.

Preventing Communicable Diseases

You can help your body prevent disease by avoiding germs. Steer clear of people who you know are sick and get in the habit of washing your hands regularly. Your hands are constantly picking up germs from objects in your environment. When you put your hands to your mouth or nose, these germs can enter your body. Keep a supply of premoistened wipes for your hands when soap and water are not available. You can also fight germs by practicing healthy behaviors. Get enough rest, eat healthy foods, and exercise regularly.

Some communicable diseases can be prevented with vaccines. A **vaccine** (vak·SEEN) is *a dead or weakened pathogen introduced into your body.* This triggers the immune system to make antibodies to fight the pathogen. Because the pathogen is dead or weakened, you don't become ill. Chicken pox, measles, and mumps are much less common in the U.S. because children are vaccinated against these diseases. **Figure 11.2** lists some common vaccines and when they should be taken.

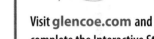

Visit **glencoe.com** and complete the Interactive Study Guide for Lesson 2.

  **List** Name two actions you can take to help your body's defenses.

▼ FIGURE 11.2

VACCINES GIVEN AT DIFFERENT AGES

This table lists the vaccines that help protect against developing certain diseases. **At what ages is the vaccine for measles given?**

Vaccine and the Diseases It Protects Against	Typical Vaccination Schedule
Hep B: hepatitis B	Birth, 2 months, 15–18 months
DTaP: diphtheria, tetanus, pertussis (whooping cough)	2, 4, 6, and 15–18 months; 4–6 years; Td (tetanus and diphtheria toxoid) boosters at 11–12 years; and every 10 years thereafter
Hib: diseases caused by *Hemophilus influenza* type B (Hib) bacteria	2, 4, 6, and 12–15 months
IPV: poliomyelitis	2, 4, and 12–15 months; 4–6 years
PCV: diseases caused by *Streptococcus pneumoniae* bacteria	2, 4, 6, and 12–15 months
MMR: measles, mumps, rubella	12–15 months; 4–6 years
Varicella: chicken pox	15 months; can be given any time after 12 months
Hep A: hepatitis A	2 doses at least 6 months apart, any time between 2 and 18 years; used only in high-risk areas or for high-risk groups

Source: Table based on immunization schedule recommended by the Centers for Disease Control and Prevention, the American Academy of Pediatrics, and the American Academy of Family Physicians

Health Skills Activity

Practicing Healthful Behaviors

Handwashing for Health

One behavior that can help limit the spread of germs is washing your hands thoroughly. Thorough handwashing includes rubbing your hands together for at least 15 seconds using soap and warm water. Be sure to wash the creases in your skin and fingernails where germs can collect. Rinse and dry your hands completely since germs can thrive in moist environments.

Wash your hands after using the restroom and before eating or handling food. Also, avoid touching your mouth and eyes with your hands. This can allow germs to enter your body and make you sick.

On Your Own

Practice this handwashing technique. In the future, remember to use this technique to help your body stay healthy.

Lesson 2 Review

 After You Read

Review this lesson for new terms, major headings, and Reading Checks.

What I Learned

1. *Describe* What is the most common communicable disease? Name other common communicable diseases.

2. *Vocabulary* Define the word *antibodies*, and use it in a sentence.

3. *List* Name a disease that can be prevented with a vaccine.

Thinking Critically

4. *Apply* Why should you avoid sharing an ice cream cone with a friend who has a cold?

5. *Analyze* How does handwashing help protect the health of your school and community?

Applying Health Skills

6. *Advocacy* As a group, create a brochure or flyer informing students of ways they can protect themselves against the spread of communicable diseases. Include a list of common communicable diseases and how they can be transmitted.

Go Online For more Lesson Review Activities, go to **glencoe.com**.

Understanding STDs

Guide to Reading

● **Building Vocabulary**

Copy the terms below into your notebook. As you come across them in your reading, write the definition for each term beside it.

- sexually transmitted diseases (STDs) (p. 277)
- HIV (p. 278)
- AIDS (p. 278)
- abstinence (p. 280)

● **Focusing on the Main Ideas**

In this lesson, you will learn to

- **identify** common STDs.
- **describe** how HIV and other STDs are spread.
- **access** current information on HIV and AIDS.
- **explain** how to protect yourself from STDs.

● **Reading Strategy**

Organizing Information There are many myths and facts about the spread of HIV. As you read, keep a list of both in your notebook.

Sexually Transmitted Diseases

Sexually transmitted diseases (STDs) are *communicable diseases spread from one person to another through sexual activity.* They are also known as *sexually transmitted infections (STIs).* Anyone who is sexually active can get an STD.

You can't tell if someone has an STD just by looking at him or her. It is possible to have an STD but have no visible symptoms or symptoms that come and go. Whether or not symptoms are visible, the person is still contagious and could spread the STD to another person.

STDs can cause serious health problems. They can affect menstrual health and damage the reproductive system. If left untreated, some STDs can prevent a person from being able to have children. Some can even cause death. A person with an STD needs to see a doctor for treatment right away.

▶ Knowing how HIV is and is *not* spread is important. **Why is it important to recognize myths about the spread of this illness?**

**uick Write**

You probably know that HIV, the virus that causes AIDS, is contagious. Make a list of ways you think HIV is spread.

Figure 11.3 lists six common STDs. Be aware that getting one of these diseases does not make a person immune to it. Any time there is contact with a pathogen that causes an STD, the disease can return. It is also important to note that most of these diseases have no vaccines. The only one that does is hepatitis B.

 **Reading Check** **Explain** Why does a person with an STD need to see a doctor?

HIV and AIDS

HIV, which stands for *h*uman *i*mmunodeficiency *v*irus, is *the virus that causes AIDS.* HIV attacks a specific type of lymphocyte called a *T cell.* (See **Figure 11.4.**) The virus replaces the cell's genetic information with its own and then multiplies. The more T cells that are taken over by HIV, the harder it becomes for the body to fight pathogens.

Eventually, the T cell count drops so low that the immune system can no longer protect the body. When this happens, AIDS, or *a*cquired *i*mmuno*d*eficiency *s*yndrome, develops. **AIDS** is *a condition characterized by life-ending infections and a T cell count under 200.*

▼ **FIGURE 11.3**

COMMON STDS

This table identifies common sexually transmitted diseases. **Which STDs cannot be cured with antibiotics?**

STD	Common Symptoms	Treatment
Chlamydia (kluh·MIH·dee·uh)	Pain or burning feeling during urination; unusual discharge from penis or vagina; often has no symptoms (especially in females) but can still be spread	Cured with antibiotics
Gonorrhea (gah·nuh·REE·uh)	Pain or burning during urination; unusual discharge from penis or vagina; abdominal pain; sometimes has no symptoms (especially in females) but can still be spread	Cured with antibiotics
Syphilis (SI·fuh·lis)	Red, wet, painless sores at place where virus enters body, followed by rash and flu-like symptoms; can lead to brain damage and other serious health problems, especially in infants	Cured with antibiotics
Genital warts	Small pink or red bumps in genital area; can increase risk of certain cancers in women	Warts can be removed by a doctor but may return because virus remains in body
Genital herpes (HER·peez)	Itching or pain followed by painful, itchy sores in genital area; symptoms come and go, but virus is still present and able to be spread	Antiviral medication relieves symptoms when sores appear; no cure
Hepatitis B	Weakness, fatigue, nausea, vomiting, fever, yellowing of eyes, abdominal pain, dark urine	Rest, healthful food choices, antiviral medication

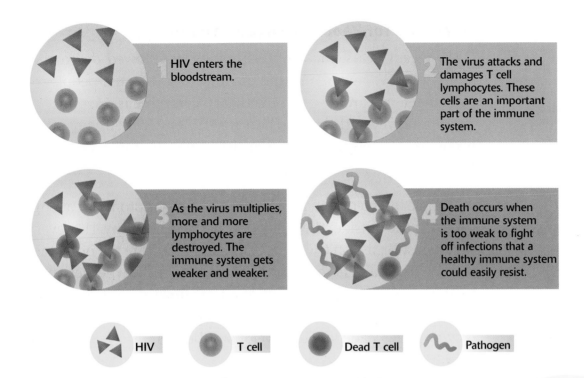

When AIDS weakens the immune system, the body cannot fight off other infections or diseases. Symptoms can include fatigue, frequent long-lasting fevers or cough, and sweating heavily at night. Drugs can delay the onset of AIDS, but there is no cure. People with AIDS will eventually die from diseases that a healthy immune system could have resisted.

How HIV Spreads

HIV is spread through specific body fluids. These include semen, fluid from the vagina, blood, and breast milk. Semen is the fluid that carries sperm.

There are several ways these fluids spread from one person to another. One is by sexual contact. Another is by sharing needles. Drug users can get HIV from a needle already used by an infected person. A pregnant woman with HIV can pass the virus to her developing baby. An infected mother can also spread HIV to her baby when breast-feeding.

HIV spreads *only* through contact with infected body fluids. You cannot get the virus from the air or from mosquito bites. It is not carried in sweat or tears or passed by touching objects, such as toilet seats. You will not get HIV by shaking hands or hugging a person with the virus. At one time, the virus was spread when blood donated by people infected with HIV was used for transfusions. Since 1985, all donated blood in the United States is tested for HIV. Therefore, the risk of getting the virus from a blood transfusion is extremely low.

▲ FIGURE 11.4

HIV IN THE IMMUNE SYSTEM

HIV prevents the immune system from doing its job. **What is the function of the immune system?**

Treatment for People with HIV and AIDS

In recent years, medical technology has slowed down the effects of HIV. New medicines are allowing infected people to live longer. A search for an effective HIV vaccine is ongoing. At present, however, there is no cure for HIV or AIDS. Anyone who becomes infected with HIV is at risk of developing AIDS.

Detecting HIV

People infected with HIV often show no symptoms for a long time. On the outside, they may look perfectly healthy. However, they can still pass on the virus. Laboratory tests are the only way of knowing if a person has HIV. These tests show whether antibodies to the virus are present. If a test shows no antibodies, it should be repeated in three months. A person recently infected may not have had time to develop antibodies.

 **List** Name two ways HIV is spread and two ways it is *not* spread.

Preventing HIV and STDs

HIV infection, AIDS, and other STDs can be prevented. The following are some ways to avoid getting these diseases.

- Choose abstinence. **Abstinence** is *not participating in high-risk behaviors*. These include avoiding sexual contact with another person.

- Avoid sharing needles. This includes the kind of needles used for body piercing. These needles can carry infection into your bloodstream.

- Say no to alcohol and drugs. People who use alcohol or drugs often lose the ability to make wise decisions. They are more likely to engage in risky behaviors.

Getting Help

Teens who think they may have an STD need to take action. They must find out if they are infected. If they are, they need to be treated. The first step in getting help is to talk to a parent or trusted adult. This step is difficult for many teens. They may feel embarrassed or worry that a parent will be angry or disappointed. However, if left untreated, STDs can permanently damage the reproductive system and cause other serious health problems.

Reading Check **Define** What is *abstinence?*

New Strains of HIV

Since HIV first appeared, medical researchers have been developing medications to fight it. At the same time, the virus has been *mutating*. This means it changes itself in ways that make these medications powerless against it. Researchers continue to try to keep up with these new strains of the virus.

Using the Internet or print resources, learn about what steps are currently being taken to fight HIV.

Visit glencoe.com and complete the Interactive Study Guide for Lesson 3.

Health Skills Activity

Accessing Information

Accurate Information on HIV and AIDS

Research on HIV and AIDS is ongoing. New information is being discovered all the time. Knowing where to find it is important. Everyone needs to have up-to-date information on how to prevent HIV infection. Here are some sources you can trust for accurate information.

- **The Centers for Disease Control and Prevention (CDC).** The CDC is the leading federal health information agency.

- **The National Institutes of Health (NIH).** Like the CDC, the NIH is part of the U.S. Department of Health and Human Services. The NIH awards research grants to hospitals and health professionals.

- **National Health Council.** Based in Washington, D.C., this organization is a leader in health advocacy.

With a Group

Locate and contact one of these organizations. Find out what kinds of HIV and AIDS information it offers to teens.

Lesson 3 Review

After You Read

Review this lesson for new terms, major headings, and Reading Checks.

What I Learned

1. *Vocabulary* What do the letters *STD* stand for?

2. *List* What are some ways in which HIV and other STDs are spread?

3. *Recall* Explain the relationship between HIV and AIDS.

Thinking Critically

4. *Evaluate* Why might drinking alcohol increase your risk of getting an STD?

5. *Apply* A teen fears he or she has an STD. Why is it important for this teen to see a health care provider?

Applying Health Skills

6. *Communication Skills* Review the steps in the S.T.O.P. strategy discussed in Chapter 3. Then develop a list of responses to peer pressure to engage in sexual activity.

 **Online** For more Lesson Review Activities, go to **glencoe.com**.

Noncommunicable and Hereditary Diseases

Guide to Reading

Building Vocabulary
Explain how the terms below are related. Write the definitions as you come across the terms in the lesson.

- chronic (p. 283)
- cancer (p. 284)
- tumor (p. 284)
- allergy (p. 285)
- asthma (p. 285)
- diabetes (p. 286)
- insulin (p. 286)

Focusing on the Main Ideas
In this lesson, you will learn to

- **identify** causes of various noncommunicable diseases.
- **develop** behaviors to keep your heart healthy.
- **identify** ways to help prevent diseases like cancer and diabetes.

Reading Strategy
Comparing and Contrasting Create a chart that shows the cause, symptoms, and treatment of four noncommunicable diseases.

Some diseases are not spread from person to person. Name some diseases you know about that you don't catch from someone else. List some reasons why these diseases might develop.

What Causes Noncommunicable Diseases?

Noncommunicable diseases are caused by several different things. One cause is poor health habits. For example, lack of physical activity, being overweight, or eating foods high in fat can lead to heart disease and diabetes. Another cause of noncommunicable disease is a person's environment. Living in a city with heavy smog, for example, can lead to lung disease. A third cause is heredity. Diseases such as allergies or muscular dystrophy can be passed from a parent to a child. Sometimes noncommunicable diseases result from harm done by a communicable disease. An infection from measles, for example, can spread to the brain and cause brain damage.

Some noncommunicable diseases are present at birth. Others develop later in life. One disease that shows up at birth is Tay-Sachs disease, a genetic disorder that destroys the central nervous system. Another noncommunicable disease a person can be born with is congenital heart disease. This is a defect in a heart valve or one of the big blood vessels leading out of the heart.

 **Reading Check**　**Give Examples** Identify two noncommunicable diseases that can be present at birth.

Heart Disease

Heart disease is the number one cause of death in the United States. Heart disease and many other noncommunicable diseases are **chronic** (KRAH·nik), or *long-lasting.* A common cause of heart disease is the narrowing or blockage of blood vessels. This could be brought on by obesity, which you know from Chapter 4 is excess weight. When this happens, the heart has a hard time doing its job and becomes weak. The result can be a heart attack or stroke, which is a destruction of brain tissue caused when the heart can't pump enough blood to the brain.

Heart disease is also caused by high blood pressure, or hypertension (HI·per·tens·shun). This is a condition in which the heart is forced to work unusually hard. High blood pressure can be inherited or caused by stress, kidney problems, or eating too many foods high in fat or cholesterol.

▲ Some noncommunicable diseases are passed on through heredity. **What are some other causes of noncommunicable diseases?**

Heart-Healthy Habits

You can lessen the risk of developing heart disease by practicing some of the following positive health behaviors:

- Stay physically active. Aerobic activity can strengthen your heart and blood vessels. It can also lower blood pressure.

- Maintain a healthy weight. Having less body fat reduces the strain on the heart and blood vessels.

- Eat foods high in fiber and low in salt, fat, and cholesterol.

- Learn to manage stress. Reducing stress can help lower blood pressure.

- Avoid tobacco products. This can lower your risk of stroke, heart attack, and other diseases.

Treating Heart Disease

Heart disease can be treated with medications that widen blood vessels, lower blood pressure, and control a person's heartbeat. When the problem is too serious to be corrected by medication, surgery is recommended. Operations can be done to open blocked arteries or insert devices that regulate the heartbeat. In severe cases, a heart transplant may be needed.

Reading Check **List** Name two positive health behaviors that can reduce the risk of heart disease.

Go Online

Topic: Keeping Your Heart Healthy

Visit glencoe.com for Student Web Activities to learn more about how you can keep your heart strong and healthy.

Activity: Using the information provided at the link above, create a heart health quiz that will help other teens figure out if they are at risk for heart problems.

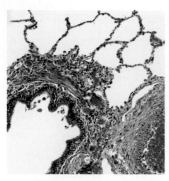

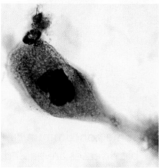

▲ As old cells die, new ones take over. **What happens in the case of cancer?**

Cancer

Sometimes a healthy cell in your body is replaced by one or more abnormal cells. When these cells multiply and destroy the healthy tissue around them, the result is cancer. **Cancer** is *a disease caused by abnormal cells that grow out of control.* Cancer is the second leading cause of death in the United States.

Many cancers start out as a **tumor,** *a mass of abnormal cells.* Some tumors are noncancerous, or benign (bih·NYN). This means they do not spread. Tumors that are cancerous, or malignant (muh·LIG·nuhnt), spread to surrounding tissue. Eventually, cancerous cells from the tumor may spread throughout the body.

Cancer is caused by heredity, exposure to cancer-causing substances, or poor health choices. For example, cigarette smoking accounts for at least 30 percent of all cancer deaths. The most common form of cancer is skin cancer. People who use tanning booths, spend too much time in the sun, or have a family history of skin cancer are more likely to develop skin cancer.

You can lower your risk of getting cancer by taking care of your body. Eat well, stay active, protect your skin with sunscreen, and avoid exposing your body to dangerous substances.

Treating Cancer

When cancer is discovered early, there is a greater chance that the person can be treated successfully. There are seven cancer warning signs. People who notice any of these should see a doctor right away.

- **C**hanges in bowel or bladder habits
- **A** sore that does not heal
- **U**nusual bleeding or discharge
- **T**hickening or lump in the breast or elsewhere
- **I**ndigestion or difficulty swallowing
- **O**bvious changes in a wart or mole
- **N**agging cough or hoarseness

There are four main ways cancer is usually treated: surgery, radiation, chemotherapy, and biologic therapies. Surgery is used to remove tumors. Radiation (ray·dee·AY·shuhn) destroys cancer cells in a specific location. Both of these treatments are most effective when the cancer has not spread. If the cancer has spread, chemotherapy (kee·moh·THEHR·uh·pee) is often used because it travels throughout the body to destroy cancer cells wherever they occur. Biologic treatments work with the body's immune system, stimulating it to fight cancer.

Allergies

When Mike is around cats, he sneezes and his eyes itch. Mike is allergic to cats. An **allergy** is *the body's sensitivity to certain substances.* A substance that causes an allergic reaction is called an *allergen* (AL·er·juhn). Common allergens include the dander in animal hair or fur, dust, pollen, grass, and some molds. People can also have allergies to certain foods, such as peanuts. Allergies are caused by an overreaction of the immune system. The system reacts to allergens as if they were pathogens entering your body.

Simple medical tests can determine if a person has allergies and what he or she is allergic to. Although there is no cure for an allergy, certain medicines can ease the symptoms and even prevent allergic reactions. You can also try to avoid the allergen.

 **Reading Check** **Recall** What seven-letter word forms the warning signs for cancer?

Asthma

A health problem related to allergies is **asthma** (AZ·muh). This is *a chronic disease in which the airways become irritated and swollen.* During an asthma attack, the small airways of the lungs become coated with a thick mucus. It becomes difficult to breathe. If the attack is severe, the person may experience a feeling of suffocation and begin to panic.

Asthma attacks can be triggered by a number of factors. These include allergens, physical activity, and cold or damp air. Smoke from cigarettes and other forms of air pollution can also cause asthma attacks.

Treatment for minor asthma attacks includes inhaling medication that relaxes the airways, making it easier to breathe. Severe attacks may require a visit to the hospital for additional treatment. Most asthmatics regularly take medicine that helps prevent attacks. Avoiding known triggers can also help prevent attacks. Untreated, asthma can lead to permanent lung damage or, in some cases, death.

▼ Animal dander can sometimes trigger an asthma attack. **What are the symptoms of asthma? What are some ways to control it?**

Diabetes

Diabetes (dy·uh·BEE·teez) is *a disease that prevents the body from using the sugars and starches in food for energy.* Diabetes is caused when the body doesn't make or can't use insulin. **Insulin** is *a hormone produced by the pancreas,* which normally moves sugars into cells.

Depending on the specific problem, diabetes is categorized as type 1 or type 2. In type 1 diabetes, the body does not produce insulin at all. In type 2, the body makes insulin but is unable to use it efficiently.

Some symptoms of diabetes are increased thirst, frequent urine production, lack of energy, and blurred vision.

Type 2 Diabetes in Young People

At one time, type 2 diabetes occurred mainly in adults. That has changed. Today, half of all new cases of type 2 diabetes involve young people. This increase is related to the increase in obesity among children and teens. The bar graph in **Figure 11.5** shows a steady increase over a 40-year period. How many percentage points has the obesity rate risen among people your age?

▼ FIGURE 11.5

PERCENTAGE OF OBESE CHILDREN AND TEENS OVER A 40-YEAR TIME PERIOD

The number of obese young people is rising. **What steps can be taken to correct this problem?**

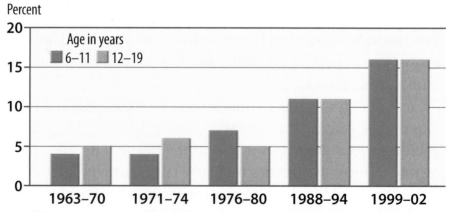

NOTE: Data for 1963–65 are for children 6–11 years of age; data for 1966–70 are for adolescents 12–17 years of age, not 12–19 years. SOURCE: CDC/NCHS, NHES, and NHANES

Treatment for Diabetes

People who have diabetes must be careful to monitor the amount of sugar in their blood. They also need to follow a treatment plan that helps their bodies cope with the disease. Taking insulin, exercising regularly, and watching their weight are all part of a successful treatment plan. Eating foods that help keep an even level of sugar in the blood is also important. Physical exercise lowers blood sugar and pressure, improves the body's ability to use insulin, and helps prevent complications like heart disease. Staying at a healthy weight makes it easier for the body to use the food it takes in.

Developing a good meal plan can help a diabetic decide how much and what kinds of foods to eat. There are several meal plans that have been used successfully to help diabetics manage their blood sugar. They include the Diabetes Food Pyramid, Rate Your Plate, Exchange Lists, and Carbohydrate Counting. Each diabetic must decide which is best with the help of his or her doctor or dietitian.

Visit **glencoe.com** and complete the Interactive Study Guide for Lesson 4.

Reading Check **Compare** How are type 1 and type 2 diabetes similar?

Lesson 4 Review

 After You Read

Review this lesson for new terms, major headings, and Reading Checks.

What I Learned

1. *Vocabulary* What is a *chronic* disease?

2. *Identify* Name a noncommunicable disease triggered by an allergen.

3. *Describe* What are some ways of preventing cancer?

Thinking Critically

4. *Synthesize* Name some ways to keep your heart healthy and lessen the risks of heart disease.

5. *Analyze* Why do you think skin cancer rates have been increasing? What are some ways to prevent skin cancer?

Applying Health Skills

6. *Communication Skills* Some diseases have similar symptoms. How can good communication skills help someone get the right treatment? Make a list of information you think is important to communicate to the doctor when you are sick.

What Is Goal Setting?

Goal setting is a five-step plan for improving and maintaining your personal health. Some goals are easy to reach while others may be more challenging.

The Five Steps of the Goal-Setting Plan

Step 1: Choose a realistic goal and write it down.

Step 2: List the steps that you need to take to reach the goal.

Step 3: Find others, like family, friends, and teachers, who can help and support you.

Step 4: Set checkpoints along the way to evaluate your progress.

Step 5: Reward yourself once you have reached your goal.

Protecting Your Health

Follow the Model, Practice, and Apply steps to help you master this important health skill.

① Model

Read about how Carly uses goal setting to try out for the softball team.

Carly set a goal to try out for the school softball team. By increasing her physical activity, Carly hopes to build up her lung endurance to help her better manage her asthma. Here are the steps Carly is taking to reach her goal.

1. **Make your goal specific.**

   I will try out for the school softball team.

2. **List the steps to reach your goal.**

   I will start practicing for 30 minutes at a time, then gradually build up to 60 minutes as my lungs get stronger.

3. **Get help from others.**

   I will see my doctor to keep my asthma under control. I will ask a friend to practice with me after school.

4. **Evaluate your progress.**

   I will create an activity calendar to keep track of how often I am practicing.

5. **Reward yourself.**

   I will buy a new catcher's mitt with the money I got for my birthday.

② Practice

Read about how Sadie and Megan use goal setting to stay healthy. Then practice goal setting by answering the following questions.

Sadie and Megan got hungry while doing homework at Sadie's house after school. Read their conversation. Use what you know about disease prevention to answer the questions below.

Megan: I'm starving! Do you have any potato chips to snack on?

Sadie: I do, but I would rather eat some fruit. I'm trying to develop good habits to help my body stay healthy.

Megan: That makes sense. What kind of fruit do you have?

1. What is Sadie's new goal?

2. What is one step she is taking to reach this goal?

3. How does Megan's support help Sadie with her goal?

4. How can Sadie evaluate her progress and reward herself for reaching her goal?

③ Apply

Apply what you've learned about goal setting when completing the activity below.

Choose one of the diseases discussed in this chapter. Write a short story about a teen who sets a goal to prevent or manage the disease. Include details about the disease. Describe why it's important to prevent or manage this disease. Explain the steps the teen will take to reach the goal. Share your story with other classmates.

Self-Check

- Did the teen in my story set a specific goal?

- Does my story include details about my chosen disease?

- Does my story show how the teen will reach his or her goal?

Building Health Skills

Don't PANIC!

Ever get a splitting headache or super-bad stomachache and feel convinced you have a deadly disease? Chances are those symptoms aren't life-threatening! So don't worry for no reason. Read this so you don't panic.

POUNDING HEADACHE

WORST NIGHTMARE
Brain tumor!

MORE LIKELY STORY
A migraine or a tension headache—up to 20 percent of all teens experience them regularly.

WHAT TO DO Take acetaminophen or ibuprofen. If headaches occur frequently (once a week), see your doctor, who can evaluate you. Your doctor might prescribe medicine or suggest relaxation methods.

WHEN TO WORRY Get to the emergency room if your headache is severe or accompanied by vomiting, vision changes, high fever, or numbness or tingling in your arms or legs.

HEART FLUTTERS

WORST NIGHTMARE
Heart attack!

MORE LIKELY STORY
Anxiety. When you're tense, stress hormones rise, which may cause your heart to race.

WHAT TO DO If it happens once or twice, don't worry. If it occurs more regularly, get it checked out. The cause could be anything from cold medicine to a thyroid problem.

WHEN TO WORRY See a doctor as soon as possible if your symptoms include shortness of breath or dizziness—that may mean a heart condition.

BELLY PAIN

WORST NIGHTMARE
Appendicitis!

MORE LIKELY STORY
Constipation. This can cause some teens to double over in pain.

WHAT TO DO Drink water (eight glasses a day) and eat fiber-rich foods, such as whole wheat bread.

WHEN TO WORRY Call your doctor right away if the pain is severe or accompanied by fever or vomiting. It could signal anything from food poisoning or a urinary-tract infection to—yes—appendicitis.

STUDY
TO GO

Visit **glencoe.com** to download quizzes and eFlashcards for Chapter 11.

FOLDABLES Study Organizer

Foldables® and Other Study Aids Take out the Foldable® that you created for Lesson 1 and any graphic organizers that you created for Lessons 1–4. Find a partner, and quiz each other using these study aids.

Lesson 1 What Causes Disease?

Main Idea Diseases are caused by bacteria, fungi, protozoa, and viruses.

- There are two basic categories of disease. Communicable diseases are diseases that can be spread. Noncommunicable diseases cannot be spread.

- Germs are spread in four common ways: direct physical contact, indirect contact, contaminated food or water, and contact with infected animals or insects.

Lesson 2 Communicable Diseases

Main Idea The body has several systems that defend against communicable diseases.

- The skin, body fluids, mucous membranes, and stomach acid are the first line of defense against germs.

- The immune system is a group of cells, tissues, and organs that fight disease. It is the second line of defense.

- Vaccines can prevent some communicable diseases.

- You can prevent disease by avoiding germs and washing your hands regularly.

Lesson 3 Understanding STDs

Main Idea Sexually transmitted diseases (STDs) are communicable diseases spread by sexual contact.

- STDs can cause serious health problems and should be treated by a doctor right away.

- HIV is the virus that causes AIDS. It is spread through specific body fluids.

- Abstinence and saying no to alcohol and drug use are ways to avoid getting STDs.

Lesson 4 Noncommunicable and Hereditary Diseases

Main Idea Noncommunicable and hereditary diseases are diseases that cannot be spread.

- Poor health habits, environment, heredity, and harm done by a communicable disease can lead to a noncommunicable disease.

- Many noncommunicable diseases are chronic, or long-lasting.

- Heart disease, cancer, allergies, asthma, diabetes are some common noncommunicable diseases.

- You can keep your heart healthy by being physically active, maintaining a healthy weight, and managing stress.

11 Assessment

After You Read

HEALTH QUIZ

Now that you have read the chapter, look back at your answers to the Health Quiz on the chapter opener. Would you change any of them? What would your answers be now?

Reviewing Vocabulary and Main Ideas

On a sheet of paper, write the numbers 1–6. After each number, write the term from the list that best completes each sentence.

- antibodies
- bacteria
- communicable diseases
- contagious
- immune system
- infection
- noncommunicable diseases
- vaccines
- viruses

Lesson 1 What Causes Disease?

1. _____ are diseases that can be spread, such as colds.

2. Extremely small, single-celled organisms with no cell nucleus are called _____.

3. Tiny, nonliving particles that invade and take over healthy cells are known as _____.

Lesson 2 Communicable Diseases

4. A condition in which pathogens invade the body, multiply, and harm some of your body's cells is known as _____.

5. Your _____ is a group of cells, tissues, and organs that fight disease.

6. Chemicals produced to fight a specific invading substance are called _____.

*On a sheet of paper, write the numbers 7–12. Write **True** or **False** for each statement. If the statement is false, change the underlined word or phrase to make it true.*

Lesson 3 Understanding STDs

7. Another name for STDs is <u>STIs</u>.

8. STDs can damage the <u>circulatory system</u>, making it impossible ever to have children.

9. When a person's T-cell count drops below 200, she or he likely has <u>hepatitis B</u>.

Lesson 4 Noncommunicable and Hereditary Diseases

10. A disease that is <u>chronic</u> continues for a long time.

11. Many cancers start out as masses of abnormal cells called <u>allergens</u>.

12. People with diabetes sometimes need shots of <u>insulin</u>, a hormone produced by the pancreas.

Thinking Critically

Using complete sentences, answer the following questions on a sheet of paper.

13. **Compare and Contrast** In what way are communicable and noncommunicable diseases alike? How are they different?

Go Online Visit **glencoe.com** and take the Online Quiz for Chapter 11.

14. **Evaluate** Explain how a person's environment can contribute to disease.

Write About It

15. **Personal or Descriptive Writing** Write a journal entry describing the last time you were sick with a cold or flu. List some positive health behaviors you can practice to help prevent illness in the future.

16. **Expository Writing** Imagine that you are writing an article about a noncommunicable disease. Identify different factors that can cause this disease. Explain how to reduce the risk of developing a noncommunicable disease.

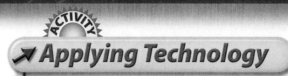

⚡ Applying Technology

Germ Chasers

Use Microsoft Word® to create a cube that explains how germs are spread and how communicable diseases can be prevented.

- Using drawing tools, form a 3-inch square. Copy and paste the square to form a larger square, with 3 squares across and 4 down.
- Inside each square, write 1–2 sentences about a topic in the chapter.
- Click, drag, and drop digital images into each box.
- Save the document.

Standardized Test Practice

Reading

Read the passage and then answer the questions.

Edward Jenner (1749–1823)

Edward Jenner was a keen observer of nature from an early age. This would come in handy in guiding his life's work.

Jenner was born in England in 1749. He studied medicine and became a respected surgeon. During Jenner's time, a disease called smallpox was a leading cause of death. Scientists understood this was caused by a virus; however, no one knew how to prevent it from spreading.

Jenner noticed a similarity between symptoms of smallpox and another disease called cowpox. However, cowpox did not hurt humans. Jenner gave his gardener's son a shot containing a small amount of cowpox virus. Six weeks later, he gave the same person a shot containing smallpox virus. The person did not become sick. The first vaccine had been discovered!

TEST-TAKING TIP

Read the passage carefully once to find out what information it contains. After you read each question, look back at the passage to find the answer.

1. The main idea of this passage is that
   A. Diseases can be deadly.
   B. Smallpox and cowpox are related.
   C. Edward Jenner discovered the first vaccine.
   D. Even the deadliest disease is eventually cured.

2. What trait helped Edward Jenner succeed in his most important life's work?
   A. His refusal to quit when the going got rough
   B. His stubbornness
   C. His powers of observation
   D. His dedication to his wife and family

Safety and the Environment

Chapter Preview

▲ *Working with the Photo*

Taking care of the environment is everyone's responsibility. **How can you help to protect the environment?**

Start-Up Activities

Before You Read Do you practice good safety habits?
Take the short Health Inventory below. Keep a record of your answers.

HEALTH INVENTORY

1. I wear a safety belt when riding in a car.
(a) always (b) sometimes (c) never

2. I look both ways before crossing the street.
(a) always (b) sometimes (c) never

3. I use the proper safety gear when playing sports
or other physical activities.
(a) always (b) sometimes (c) never

FOLDABLES Study Organizer

As You Read Make this Foldable® to help you organize what you
learn in Lesson 1 about personal safety. Begin with a plain sheet of 8½″ × 11″
paper.

1 Fold the sheet of paper from bottom to top, leaving
a 2″ tab at the top.

2 Fold in half from side to side.

3 Unfold and cut along the center fold line of the top
layer only. This will make two tabs.

4 Label as shown.

Think about an injury that you or someone else had.
Briefly describe the injury on the top tab of your Foldable®.
Then, under the appropriate tab, explain why the injury
occurred and what could have been done to prevent it.

Injury:

| Why did it occur? | How could it have been prevented? |

Go Online Visit **glencoe.com** and use the eFlashcards to preview Chapter 12
vocabulary terms.

Personal Safety Habits

Guide to Reading

● **Building Vocabulary**
Describe how the terms below are related. Write the correct definitions as you read them in the lesson.

■ accident (p. 296)
■ accidental injuries (p. 296)
■ accident chain (p. 297)

● **Focusing on the Main Ideas**
In this lesson, you will learn to

■ **identify** the parts of the accident chain.
■ **describe** ways of preventing accidental injuries.
■ **practice** healthful behaviors to develop good safety habits.

● **Reading Strategy**
Identifying Cause-and-Effect List three events that can result in an accidental injury.

FOLDABLES Study Organizer Use the Foldable® on p. 295 as you read the lesson.

Quick Write

Describe some good safety habits you practice at home.

Staying Safe

We all begin learning about safety when we are very young. A toddler who goes near a stove will be warned, "Don't touch! Hot!" Older children are told to look both ways before crossing the street. Learning about safety and practicing behaviors that will keep you safe can help prevent accidents from occurring. An **accident** is *an unexpected event that results in damage or harm*. Every day, thousands of people suffer **accidental injuries.** These are *injuries caused by unexpected events*.

Many accidents happen at or near home. Many involve ordinary, everyday activities, such as riding a bike. Why do accidents happen? How can you reduce your risk of accidental injury? How can you help others stay safe? In the pages ahead, you will find answers to these questions.

Reading Check **Define** What is an *accident*?

◀ Some safety information is learned at an early age. **Why is it important to keep safety in mind as we grow older?**

The Accident Chain

Accidents **occur** because of an **accident chain,** *a sequence of events that often leads to an accidental injury.* **Figure 12.1** illustrates the links in the accident chain. For any accident to occur, three elements must be present. These are *the situation, the unsafe habit,* and *the unsafe act.* To understand the role each of these elements plays, consider Greg's accident:

Academic Vocabulary

occur (uh KUR) *(verb)* happen. *Gwen and Sean were excited about the carnival because it only occurs once a year in their town.*

- **The Situation.** Greg and Maria are throwing a football in their driveway. Maria throws the ball too high and the ball lands on the roof.

- **The Unsafe Habit.** Maria suggests getting a ladder. Greg says he will save time by climbing the tree next to the garage.

- **The Unsafe Act.** To reach the ball, Greg must lean out on a high, narrow branch. The branch snaps under Greg's weight. He falls and breaks his leg.

The three elements leading to Greg's fall and the resulting injury form the accident chain.

▼ FIGURE 12.1

THE ACCIDENT CHAIN

Unsafe habits and acts can lead to accidental injury. However accidents can be avoided. **How could Greg have avoided getting hurt?**

► Wearing the right gear, even at play, can prevent accidental injury. **What sport or activity do you like? What kind of protective gear is worn in this sport or activity?**

Visit **glencoe.com** and complete the Interactive Study Guide for Lesson 1.

How to Prevent Accidental Injuries

You can reduce the risk of accidental injury by practicing positive health behaviors. Many accidents can be prevented by simply breaking the accident chain. By removing or changing any one link, you can stop an accident from happening. Look back at Greg's accident chain.

Greg could have changed the situation. He and Maria could have played ball in a more open area. Greg could have also broken the second link—the unsafe habit. Instead of climbing the tree, he should have waited for the ladder. Finally, Greg could have changed the unsafe action. When he saw he could not reach the ball, he should have stopped trying. He should have climbed back down and gone for the ladder or asked an adult for help.

 **Give Examples** Give an example of how to prevent an injury by breaking the accident chain.

Health Skills Activity

Practicing Healthful Behaviors

Building Safe Habits

As you become more independent, it is important to develop good safety habits. This includes being careful, thinking ahead, and taking precautions. The following are some additional good safety habits:

- Stay away from risky behaviors. Choose not to participate in unsafe activities.
- Resist negative peer pressure. Do not give in to friends who want you to take careless chances.
- Know your limits. Do not attempt to do more than you can do safely. If you just learned how to snowboard, for example, don't go down a hill more difficult than you can handle.
- Wear proper protective gear when playing sports or other physical activities. Before beginning a new sport or activity, find out what protective gear you will need.

On Your Own

Make a list of other safety habits. Explain how these safety habits can prevent accidental injuries. Share your list with the class.

Lesson 1 Review

 After You Read

Review this lesson for new terms, major headings, and Reading Checks.

What I Learned

1. *Vocabulary* What are *accidental injuries*?

2. *List* What three elements must be present for an accident to occur?

3. *Recall* How can many accidents be prevented?

Thinking Critically

4. *Apply* Grant's friend dared him to walk across a narrow 12-foot-high fence. What should Grant do, and why?

5. *Evaluate* Why is it important to know your limitations?

Applying Health Skills

6. *Decision Making* Tina wants to go bike riding with a friend, but she left her helmet in her dad's truck. What are Tina's options? Use the decision-making process to help Tina make a safe decision.

Go Online For more Lesson Review Activities, go to **glencoe.com**.

Lesson 1: Personal Safety Habits   **299**

Lesson 2

Safety at Home and Away

Guide to Reading

Building Vocabulary
Copy the terms below into your notebook. Circle those terms that help you maintain personal safety.

- hazards (p. 300)
- smoke alarm (p. 302)
- fire extinguisher (p. 302)
- pedestrians (p. 303)
- Neighborhood Watch programs (p. 304)

Focusing on the Main Ideas
In this lesson, you will learn to

- **explain** how to prevent accidental injuries in your home.
- **practice** the skill of advocacy to help family members develop a fire escape plan.
- **identify** safety tips and rules of the road.
- **describe** how to be safe in your school and community.

Reading Strategy
Comparing Preview the lesson. Explain ways in which the various safety procedures described are similar. How are they different?

*Q*uick *Write*

List two or three safety rules you follow on your way to and from school.

Safety at Home

Home is a place where everyone should feel safe and comfortable. Yet, homes can contain **hazards,** or *possible sources of harm*. Stairways, for example, can lead to falls. Appliances can cause shocks. Spilled water can cause slips and falls. Sharp tools in the kitchen or garage can lead to cuts. However, these hazards can be avoided. Following safety rules can reduce the risks of home hazards.

 **Explain** Why are safety rules important?

▶ Use a step ladder to reach an item on a high shelf. **How does this safety habit help prevent injury?**

▶ Picking up toys that are left on the stairs can help prevent falls. **What other ways can you help prevent accidents in the home?**

Kitchen Safety

More accidents happen in the kitchen than any other room in the house. Here are some ways to reduce the risk of injury. To avoid cutting yourself, learn to handle knives correctly. Keep your fingers clear of the blade. Don't leave food cooking on the stove unattended, especially if you are home alone. Turn pot handles inward, away from the edge. Keep small children away from the stove. Wipe up any spills right away.

Preventing Falls

To prevent falls, keep stairways well lighted and free of clutter. Keep loose objects off the floor, where they might be tripped over. Rugs should be fastened down firmly. When reaching for items on high shelves, use a sturdy ladder or step stool. Never stand on a chair. Avoid running on wet or waxed floors.

Electrical Safety

In order to avoid electrical hazards, always pull plugs out by the plug itself. Never tug on the cord, which can damage it. If a cord becomes frayed, don't use the appliance until it is repaired. Unused outlets should be covered in homes where there are small children. Keep electrical appliances away from water, and never use them if your skin is wet or if you are in a bathtub.

Gun Safety

If guns are kept in the home, they should always be stored in locked cabinets. Store ammunition separately. Never handle a gun without an adult present. Never play with a gun or point it at a live target.

DEVELOPING Good Character

Safety and Personal Responsibility

Being responsible includes looking out for the well-being of others. You can start doing this at home right now. Pick up an object you see lying on the floor where someone might trip over it. This can prevent someone you care about from being injured.

What other actions can you take to show responsibility for your safety or the safety of others?

Health Skills Activity

Advocacy

Fire Escape Plan

Having an escape plan can help your family prevent injuries or death in the event of a fire. Choose the nearest exit from your home. This may be a first-floor window or a door. Have a back-up exit in case the first is blocked. All family members should know the route to exits from their bedroom. Make sure to have an outdoor meeting place. This is where everyone gathers upon getting out safely. That way, you will know if a member is trapped inside. If this is the case, let the fire department rescue the person. Never go back inside a burning building for any reason.

With a Group

With your family, create an escape plan for your home. Practice your escape plan until every family member knows what to do in the event of a fire.

Careers for the 21st Century

Occupational Safety and Health Specialist

Occupational safety and health specialists keep workers from getting sick or hurt at work. They may teach employees how to use machinery or how to store chemicals. Occupational safety and health specialists are in demand because employees deserve to work in a safe environment. If you would like to become an occupational safety and health specialist, you should work on your personal safety habits.

What skills does an occupational safety and health specialist need?
Go to *Career Corner* at **glencoe.com** to find out.

Fire Safety

To prevent fires, always make sure matches are out before disposing of them. Keep these and cigarette lighters out of reach of small children. Never leave candles burning unattended. In addition, each level of your house should have a **smoke alarm,** *a device that makes a warning noise when it senses smoke.* Replace the batteries in your smoke alarms twice a year to keep them working properly.

It is also a good idea to keep a **fire extinguisher** in the kitchen. This is *a device that releases chemicals that smother flames.* Smother grease fires with a pot lid or baking soda if there is no fire extinguisher. Never use water. Water will cause the burning grease to explode, creating more fire or burning you.

In the event of a major fire, leave the building immediately. Never try to put it out yourself or stop to gather possessions. Every second counts. Make sure your family has an escape route. If your clothes catch fire, remember to *stop, drop, and roll.* First, *stop* moving. If you run, the rush of air will fan the flames. Then *drop* to the floor and *roll* to smother the flames.

 **Reading Check**

Give Examples Give two examples of hazards in the home.

RULES OF ROAD SAFETY

Eighty-three percent of all traffic accidents occur within 20 miles of home. How can you help prevent accidents while riding your bike?

Rules of the Road

- Ride your bike with the traffic flow, and obey traffic rules and signals.
- Never weave in and out of traffic.
- When riding with a friend, ride in single file, not side-by-side.
- Be aware of others. Always watch for cars and pedestrians.
- Be visible to others. Wear bright, reflective clothes. Make sure your bike has lights and reflectors.

Tips for Personal Safety

- When riding in a motor vehicle, use your safety belt.
- When riding a bike, skating, or riding a scooter, use safety gear. These include a helmet, pads, and gloves.
- Don't skate or ride a scooter after dark.
- Avoid riding or skating on wet, dirty, or uneven surfaces.
- Wear pants that won't catch in a bicycle chain.
- Keep your speed under control. When skating, know how to stop and how to fall properly.

Safety on the Road

Safety on the road applies to drivers, passengers, and **pedestrians.** These are *people traveling on foot.* **Figure 12.2** highlights some "rules of the road" and other safety practices.

 **Reading Check** **Give Examples** Name one *do* and one *don't* road safety tip.

Safety at School

Schools should be places for students to learn and develop physical, mental/emotional, and social skills. However, violence can sometimes occur at school. Knowing strategies to prevent violence can help you maintain your personal health and stay safe in school.

Preventing School Violence

Many schools are taking action to prevent violence. Some are using peer mediation and crisis prevention programs. Others are conducting programs that teach students to respect others. Health education classes that teach conflict resolution are helping curb school violence. Many schools

▼ Some schools now have metal detectors to make sure weapons are not brought in. **What would you do if you know someone had a weapon at school?**

▲ Neighborhood Watch programs are one measure for keeping communities safe. **What are some other anti-crime measures?**

Visit glencoe.com and complete the Interactive Study Guide for Lesson 2.

now have police or security officers present. Some schools have metal detectors, to detect weapons brought to school. You can help, too. One way is by never carrying a weapon. Alert school officials if you know, or suspect, someone has a weapon.

Safety in the Community

Schools are not alone in facing crime and violence. Many communities are struggling with the same problems. Some have passed laws against guns. They have also made the punishments for violent crimes stricter. In many areas, people have formed **Neighborhood Watch programs.** These are *programs in which residents are trained to identify and report suspicious activity.* Communities may also try to protect teens by setting curfews. Drug-free zones and after-school and summer programs have also been started.

You can help protect yourself against dangerous situations. Walk with purpose to and from your home. Travel with another person or in a group, whenever possible. Avoid taking shortcuts through unfamiliar or unsafe areas.

Reading Check

Compare How are the actions being taken to make schools safer similar to those that make communities safer?

Lesson 2 Review

After You Read

Review this lesson for new terms, major headings, and Reading Checks.

What I Learned

1. *Recall* Where should smoke alarms be placed in the home?

2. *Describe* What are two ways of making yourself safe when riding your bike?

3. *Vocabulary* What is a *Neighborhood Watch program*?

Thinking Critically

4. *Explain* In what ways is a cluttered room a hazard?

5. *Analyze* Why do you think there is a debate on whether metal detectors should be in schools?

Applying Health Skills

6. *Conflict Resolution* Using the T.A.L.K. strategy, write a dialogue between two teens who are trying to resolve a conflict without using violence.

Go Online For more Lesson Review Activities, go to **glencoe.com**.

Safety Outdoors

Guide to Reading

● **Building Vocabulary**
In your notebook, write the term below. See if you can guess its meaning based on the root *therm-*, which means "temperature."

■ hypothermia (p. 306)

● **Focusing on the Main Ideas**
In this lesson, you will learn to

■ **describe** what you need to know for water safety.
■ **explain** safety when hiking or camping.
■ **practice** decision-making skills to make safe choices.

● **Reading Strategy**
Finding the Main Idea For each main heading in this lesson, write one sentence that states the main idea.

Staying Safe Outdoors

Do you enjoy swimming or boating? How about hiking or camping? These and other outdoor activities are more fun when you "play it safe."

Your environment can affect your personal health. Before scheduling any outing or school field trip, plan ahead. Check the weather forecast and make sure you have the proper safety gear for each activity. Be aware of your skills and abilities. Remember to wear bug protection and sunscreen. It is important to wear sunscreen to protect your skin from the sun's damaging rays, which can cause skin cancer later in life.

Water Safety

Water activities can be a lot of fun. To avoid injury, you should learn and follow water safety rules. Know how to swim well. Good swimmers are less likely to panic in an emergency. Even good swimmers, however, should never swim alone. Use the buddy system. Agree with one or more people to know each other's whereabouts. Go to beaches or pools that have lifeguards. Always know the water depth before entering. Never dive into shallow water.

> **Quick Write**
>
> Write a short paragraph about your favorite outdoor activity. Include two or three sentences on how to be safe when doing this activity.

▼ Water activities can be fun. What can this boy do to protect himself from skin cancer now?

DROWNING PREVENTION

The technique shown below can help you stay afloat in warm water. But in cold water, tread water slowly or float on your back to save energy. **Why is it important to conserve energy while waiting for help?**

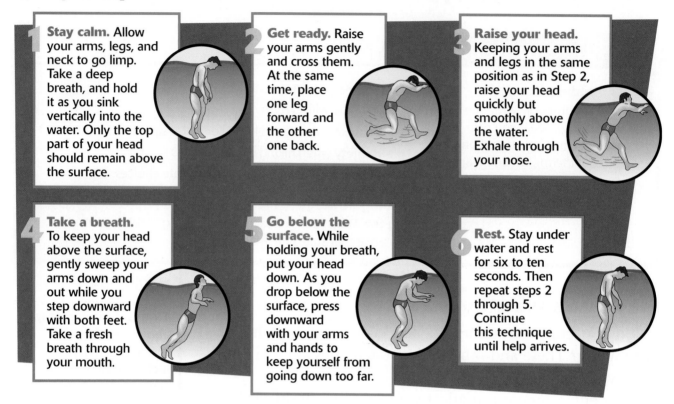

1 Stay calm. Allow your arms, legs, and neck to go limp. Take a deep breath, and hold it as you sink vertically into the water. Only the top part of your head should remain above the surface.

2 Get ready. Raise your arms gently and cross them. At the same time, place one leg forward and the other one back.

3 Raise your head. Keeping your arms and legs in the same position as in Step 2, raise your head quickly but smoothly above the water. Exhale through your nose.

4 Take a breath. To keep your head above the surface, gently sweep your arms down and out while you step downward with both feet. Take a fresh breath through your mouth.

5 Go below the surface. While holding your breath, put your head down. As you drop below the surface, press downward with your arms and hands to keep yourself from going down too far.

6 Rest. Stay under water and rest for six to ten seconds. Then repeat steps 2 through 5. Continue this technique until help arrives.

When boating or waterskiing, wear a life jacket at all times. If the water is cold, wear a wetsuit. This will protect you from developing **hypothermia** (hy·poh·THER·mee·uh). This is *a sudden and dangerous drop in body temperature.* If you ever feel you are in danger of drowning, stay calm. Call for help and use the technique shown in **Figure 12.3.**

Reading Check **Explain** What are some ways to stay safe in the water?

Safety on the Trail

Whether you hike or camp, having the right gear and equipment will help you prevent illness or injury. For hiking, gear should include sturdy, well-cushioned shoes. If shoes are new, break them in a few days before using them to hike. Wearing two pairs of socks can help prevent blisters. Bring enough fresh water and food to last through your trip. Be sure to bring food that won't spoil. You should also wear clothing appropriate for the weather and the season.

◀ Planning out your trip can make it safer and more fun. **What are some specific things you should take on a hike?**

When you go hiking or camping, make sure someone knows your destination and expected date and time of return. Bring a cell phone or walkie-talkie in case of emergency. Other necessary items include a compass and a flashlight to prevent you from getting lost. Bring along extra flashlight batteries, too. Also, bring a first-aid kit in case of minor injuries on the trail.

 Reading Check   **Identify** What safety items should you bring with you on a hike or camping trip?

Visit **glencoe.com** and complete the Interactive Study Guide for Lesson 3.

Lesson 3 Review

 After You Read

Review this lesson for new terms, major headings, and Reading Checks.

What I Learned

1. *Recall* What is the buddy system? Why is it important?

2. *Vocabulary* What is *hypothermia*?

3. *List* Name two ways of staying safe during water activities.

Thinking Critically

4. *Apply* Larissa wants to go on a short hike by herself. What safety advice would you give her?

5. *Analyze* Suppose you are swimming in the ocean when you realize you have gone farther than you should. You don't feel you have enough energy left to swim back. What should you do?

Applying Health Skills

6. *Decision Making* You are looking forward to going out on a friend's boat. The weather forecast is for thunderstorms. Use the decision-making process to help you decide what to do.

Lesson 4

Safety in Severe Weather

Guide to Reading

Building Vocabulary

In your notebook, write what you know about each term below. Correct any definitions as you read the lesson.

- natural disasters (p. 308)
- hurricane (p. 309)
- frostbite (p. 310)
- tornado (p. 310)
- earthquake (p. 311)

Focusing on the Main Ideas

In this lesson, you will learn to

- **identify** types of weather emergencies and natural disasters.
- **recognize** how to prepare for weather emergencies and natural disasters.

Reading Strategy

Comparing and Contrasting As you read, keep notes on the differences between weather emergencies and natural disasters.

Quick Write

Name weather emergencies common in your area. List two or three things your school does to prepare for these emergencies.

Weather Emergencies and Natural Disasters

Different parts of the country are more likely to experience different kinds of weather emergencies. These include thunderstorms, flooding from rains, hurricanes, tornadoes, and earthquakes. These weather emergencies can cause **natural disasters.** These are *events caused by nature that result in widespread damage, destruction, and loss.*

Being prepared for either type of event will reduce the risk of injury. Make sure your family has an emergency kit. **Figure 12.4** shows some items that belong in such a kit. There should be enough supplies to last a family three days.

 **FIGURE 12.4**

EMERGENCY SUPPLY KIT

An emergency supply kit should contain the items shown here. **Does your family maintain a supply kit?**

In some emergencies, you may be instructed to leave your home. If this happens, you should take your supplies with you. You should also bring money and any prescription medicines family members need.

Thunderstorms

Thunderstorms can be frightening sometimes. A *thunderstorm* is a heavy rainstorm accompanied by strong winds, lightning, and thunder. They can occur during any season, though they are more common during warm weather. Lightning is the most dangerous part of a thunderstorm. It is caused by clouds releasing stored-up electrical energy.

Danger from lightning is greatest when you are in or near water. Whenever you see lightning or hear thunder, seek shelter.

If you are indoors, stay there. Do not use the telephone, unless it is a cordless or cell phone. If you are outdoors, look for the nearest building. An alternative is an enclosed metal vehicle with the windows completely shut. If you are in an open field with no shelter nearby, lie down. Wait for the storm to pass. Avoid all metal objects including electric wires, fences, machinery, motors, and power tools. Unsafe places include underneath canopies, small picnic or rain shelters, or near trees.

▲ Lightning carries a deadly electrical charge. **What are some safety rules to follow during an electrical storm?**

Reading Check **Explain** What causes lightning?

Hurricanes

A **hurricane** (HER·uh·kayn) is *a strong tropical windstorm with driving rain.* Hurricanes occur in coastal regions. They can cause high waves, which in turn can produce flooding. Wind speeds during a hurricane can reach or exceed 100 miles per hour. Hurricane-force winds can turn over cars and knock down buildings.

When a hurricane is forecast, windows should be boarded. Outdoor objects should be brought in. Staying alert to TV or radio reports is important. Sometimes residents will be instructed to leave their homes and head inland. It is necessary to follow these safety instructions.

Floods

The most common natural disasters are *floods,* the rising of a body of water and its overflowing onto normally dry land. These can occur almost anywhere. As noted previously, hurricanes can cause floods. Another cause of flooding is heavy rainfall.

▲ Lowland areas or regions with rivers often experience floods. **What actions can you take in the event of a flood?**

Flooding can be especially serious in regions near large bodies of water. Stay tuned to local radio or television stations for reports of rising water. Sometimes there is little or no warning. This is called a *flash flood*. Never walk or ride in a car through floodwater. There is a risk of being swept away. Watch out for downed power lines, which can cause deadly shocks. Floodwaters often pollute tap water. Drink bottled water just in case.

Once the floodwaters go down, make sure that everything that came in contact with the floodwater is cleaned and disinfected. Wear rubber or latex gloves during the cleanup. Throw out all contaminated food. Make sure the water supply is safe before drinking any.

 **Reading Check** **Identify** What other weather emergencies can lead to flooding?

Blizzards

Do you live in an area hit by snow in the winter? If you do, you may experience blizzards. A *blizzard* is a heavy snowstorm accompanied by strong winds. Blizzards make travel difficult, often shutting down roads. Blizzards also make it hard for food and other daily needs to reach consumers. Be careful of downed power lines, which can be dangerous to people on foot.

Blizzards can also lead to "whiteout" conditions. A whiteout is a state where snow falls so rapidly, visibility is significantly reduced. People can become lost or confused. Health risks from being lost in a blizzard include hypothermia, described in Lesson 3. Another health risk is **frostbite,** or *freezing of the skin.* Frostbite can cause severe injury to the skin and sometimes to deeper tissues.

Tornadoes

A **tornado** (tor·NAY·doh) is *a whirling, funnel-shaped windstorm that drops from the sky to the ground.* Most tornadoes occur in the flat central regions of the country. But these disasters can strike anywhere if the weather conditions are right. If a tornado warning is issued for your area, head to a storm cellar or basement. If you don't have a basement or storm cellar, go

Go Online

Visit **glencoe.com** and complete the Interactive Study Guide for Lesson 4.

to a hallway, bathroom, or other inside area without windows. Don't stay in cars or mobile homes. If you are outdoors, look for a ditch and lie down.

 Reading Check **Define** What is a *tornado*?

Earthquakes

An **earthquake** is *the shaking of the ground as rock below the surface moves.* If you are inside when an earthquake hits, stay there. Brace yourself in a doorway. If there is a piece of sturdy furniture, such as a large desk, crawl under. Move away from objects that could fall or shatter. If you are outside during an earthquake, stand in the open. Keep away from buildings, trees, and power lines. After an earthquake, report any odor of gas. An odor might indicate a leak.

▲ What are tornadoes? What should you do if a tornado is headed your way?

Lesson 4 Review

 After You Read

Review this lesson for new terms, major headings, and Reading Checks.

What I Learned

1. *Compare* What is the difference between a weather emergency and a natural disaster?

2. *Vocabulary* What is a hurricane? Where do hurricanes occur?

3. *Identify* Which type of weather emergency can lead to whiteout conditions?

Thinking Critically

4. *Evaulate* How do the media influence community health during a natural disaster or weather emergency?

5. *Analyze* Suppose you are swimming when the sky turns dark. You hear a distant rumble. What should you do to take responsibility for your personal health?

Applying Health Skills

6. *Accessing Information* Do online or library research on how to prepare an emergency supply kit. Write a list of all important supplies that you would need in a severe weather emergency or natural disaster.

 Go Online For more Lesson Review Activities, go to **glencoe.com**.

Lesson 4: Safety in Severe Weather **311**

Lesson 5

First Aid for Emergencies

Guide to Reading

● Building Vocabulary
Make two lists. One should be emergency terms, the other first-aid techniques.

- first aid (p. 312)
- rescue breathing (p. 313)
- cardiopulmonary resuscitation (CPR) (p. 314)
- abdominal thrusts (p. 314)
- poison control center (p. 316)
- first-degree burn (p. 316)
- second-degree burn (p. 316)
- third-degree burn (p. 317)

● Focusing on the Main Ideas
In this lesson, you will learn to

- **name** strategies for responding to injuries.
- **describe** how you can help someone who is bleeding.
- **identify** the universal sign for choking.
- **explain** how to help a burn victim.

● Reading Strategy
Sequencing Choose two of the emergencies described in the lesson. For each, make a flow chart showing the steps in treating the emergency.

*Q*uick Write

List three or four items you would put in a home first-aid kit. Explain why each item is important.

Giving First Aid

Some emergencies are minor. You cut your fingertip and it bleeds. A friend falls while skateboarding and injures his or her knee. These types of injuries should be cleaned with soap and warm water. They can also be wrapped in a breathable bandage. Other emergencies can be life-threatening. Taking immediate action can mean the difference between life and death. Often that includes giving **first aid.** This is *the care first given to an injured or ill person until regular medical care can be supplied.*

Proper training is needed to give first aid. In an emergency, the American Red Cross suggests the following strategy: Check-Call-Care.

- **Check the scene and the victim.** Make sure the area is safe for you and the victim. Move the victim only if he or she is in danger.
- **Call for help.** Call 911 or the local EMS number. *EMS* stands for "emergency medical service."

◄ This boy has fallen off his skateboard. **What can his friend do to treat this injury?**

- **Care for the person until help arrives.** Use the first-aid techniques in this lesson to treat the victim until help arrives.

Life-Threatening Emergencies

How can you tell if an emergency is life-threatening? A victim's life is considered in danger if the person: (1) has stopped breathing, (2) has no heartbeat, (3) is bleeding severely, (4) is choking, (5) has swallowed poison, or (6) has been severely burned. People in these situations need help immediately. Call for help and then begin to treat the victim. Be careful to avoid contact with blood and other body fluids, which can contain viruses. If possible, wear gloves and a face mask when giving first aid. Always wash your hands immediately afterward.

Rescue Breathing and CPR

If you suspect a person has stopped breathing, tap the person and shout, "Are you okay?" If there is no response, call 911. Check the victim for signs of movement and normal breathing. Put your ear and cheek close to the victim's nose and mouth. Listen and feel for exhaled air. Look to see if the chest is rising and falling. If the victim is not breathing, perform **rescue breathing.** This is *a substitute for normal breathing in which someone forces air into the victim's lungs.* **Figure 12.5** shows how to perform rescue breathing on an adult or older child. Special rescue breathing techniques are used for infants and children. If you are planning to babysit, contact the American Red Cross for training on infant and child rescue breathing.

Academic Vocabulary

substitute (SUHB sti toot) *(noun)* a person or thing acting in place of another. *Margarine is often used as a substitute for butter.*

▼ **FIGURE 12.5**

RESCUE BREATHING TECHNIQUE

When a victim is not breathing, first call 911. Then begin rescue breathing if the person has a pulse. **How can you determine if a victim has stopped breathing?**

1 Point the victim's chin upward by gently lifting it up with your fingers and tilting the head back. The airway will now be open. If you have a sterile breathing mask, place it over the victim's mouth and nose.

2 Pinch the victim's nostrils shut. Take a breath and cover the victim's mouth with your own, forming a tight seal. Exhale for one second. Make sure the victim's chest rises.

3 Watch for the victim's chest to fall, and listen for air flowing from the lungs. Give the victim a second breath. If the victim begins breathing normally, stop.

Often, when a person stops breathing, the heart also stops beating. When this happens, the person needs **cardiopulmonary resuscitation (CPR).** This is *a rescue measure that attempts to restore heartbeat and breathing.* Only people who have been trained should perform CPR.

 **Reading Check** **Define** What is *CPR?*

First Aid for Severe Bleeding

Severe bleeding from an injury can be a serious problem. When treating a victim with severe bleeding, take precautions to limit touching another person's blood. Wear gloves if possible and always wash your hands afterward.

First aid for severe bleeding begins with lying the victim down. Apply direct, steady pressure to the wound, by pressing down firmly with a clean cloth. If necessary, add more cloth without removing the first cloth.

Once the bleeding has slowed or stopped, secure the cloth with a bandage or strips of gauze or other material. This helps prevent infection. If the victim needs professional medical treatment, leave the bandages in place. Get the person medical help quickly.

First Aid for Choking

Choking is a life-and-death emergency. It is a condition that occurs when a person's airway becomes blocked. A choking victim can die in minutes because air cannot get to the lungs. The universal sign for choking is grabbing the throat between the thumb and forefinger. Knowing this gesture can help you identify a choking victim. It can also help you alert someone in the event you are choking. A person who is choking may gasp for breath. He or she may be unable to speak. The person's face may turn red, then bluish.

For an adult or child, first aid for choking begins with a question. Ask, "Are you choking?" If the victim nods or is unable to speak, give the person five blows to the back. To give back blows, stand slightly behind the victim. Place your arm diagonally across the victim's chest. Lean the victim forward and strike the victim between the shoulder blades five times. If the back blows do not dislodge the choking object, give five **abdominal thrusts.** These are *quick upward pulls into the diaphragm to force out the object blocking the airway.* This technique is illustrated in **Figure 12.6.**

If an infant is choking, position the infant on his or her abdomen along your forearm. Brace your arm against your thigh. Support the infant's head with your hand and point the head down. Using the heel of your hand, give the infant up to five blows between the shoulder blades. If the object is still stuck, turn the victim on his or her back. Support the shoulders and neck with one hand. With the other hand, place two fingers in the middle of the infant's breastbone. Press quickly up to five times. Alternate five back blows and five chest thrusts until the object comes out. If the child becomes unconscious, call 911. For more detailed instructions on helping a choking infant, consult a first-aid manual.

Suppose you are choking and no one is around to help. If this happens, don't panic. Instead, make a fist and thrust it quickly into your upper abdomen. This will force out the object blocking your airway. You can also try pushing your abdomen against the back or arm of a chair.

 Reading Check Explain Describe first aid for a choking infant.

▼ **FIGURE 12.6**

ABDOMINAL THRUSTS

Use these steps to help a victim who is choking. If the person can talk or cough or you can hear breathing, don't do anything. **Why might it be dangerous to perform abdominal thrusts on a person who is not choking?**

1 Stand behind the victim. Wrap your arms around his or her waist, and bend the victim slightly forward. Place your fist slightly above the person's navel.

2 Hold your fist with your other hand, and press it hard into the abdomen with an upward thrust. Give five back blows and then five abdominal thrusts until the object is coughed up.

First Aid for Poisoning

If you think someone has swallowed poison, get professional help. Call 911, EMS, or your local **poison control center.** This is *a community agency that helps people deal with poisoning emergencies.* The inside cover of your telephone book usually lists the phone number of the center. When you call, you will be given directions on how to treat the victim.

While waiting for help to arrive, keep the person warm and breathing. Look for extra traces of poison around the victim's mouth. Remove these with a damp, clean cloth wrapped around your finger. Make sure to save the container of poison. Show it to the ambulance team. Tell them all you know about what happened.

Some cases of poisoning are caused by contact with a poisonous plant. Poison ivy, poison oak, and poison sumac are three such plants. Contact with these plants can cause redness, itching, and swelling. Most of these injuries can be easily treated at home using soap and water, rubbing alcohol, and over-the-counter creams. For severe cases, see a doctor for treatment.

 **Reading Check** **List** Give two ways poisons can enter the body.

First Aid for Burns

Different kinds of burns require different treatments. A **first-degree burn**, or superficial burn, is *a burn in which only the outer part of the skin is burned and turns red.* Cool the burned area with cold water (not ice) for at least 20 minutes. Wrap the burned area loosely in a clean, dry dressing.

Second-degree burns are more serious. A **second-degree burn**, or partial-thickness burn, is *a serious type of burn in which the damaged area blisters or peels.* Cool the burn in cold water (not ice) for at least 20 minutes and elevate the burned area. Wrap loosely with a clean, dry dressing. Do not pop blisters or peel loose skin. Call your doctor.

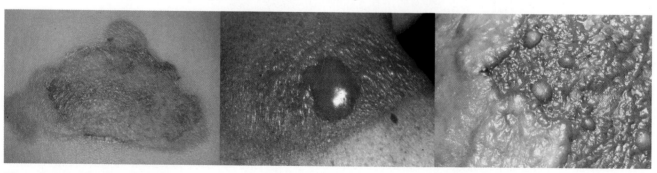

First-degree burn   **Second-degree burn**   **Third-degree burn**

A **third-degree burn**, or full-thickness burn, is *a very serious burn in which deeper layers of skin and nerve endings are damaged.* Call 911 immediately. Only a medical professional should treat third-degree burns. Do not try to remove burned clothing. Cool the affected area and then cover with a clean cloth until help arrives.

First Aid for Breaks and Sprains

A break in a bone is called a *fracture.* If you suspect someone has a fracture, start by asking questions. Ask if the person heard a snap or whether touching the injured area hurts. If you're not sure, treat the person as though they have a broken bone. First, call 911 or EMS. If there is bleeding, apply pressure with a clean cloth. Do not attempt to straighten the injured part. Avoid moving the person.

A sprain occurs when a joint is stretched or twisted or has torn ligaments. Sprains are often sports-related. To treat a sprain use the P.R.I.C.E. formula outlined in Chapter 5 (see page 134).

 Reading Check **Explain** How do you treat a fracture?

Visit **glencoe.com** and complete the Interactive Study Guide for Lesson 5.

 **Lesson 5 Review**

After You Read

Review this lesson for new terms, major headings, and Reading Checks.

What I Learned

1. *Recall* What is the universal sign for choking?

2. *List* Briefly give the steps in controlling severe bleeding.

3. *Vocabulary* What's the difference between a *first-* and *second-degree burn*?

Thinking Critically

4. *Evaluate* What steps can be taken to reduce poisoning risks in homes with small children?

5. *Apply* Ken and Phil see an older adult collapse to the ground. Using the Check-Call-Care strategy, show how Ken and Phil should respond to this emergency.

Applying Health Skills

6. *Stress Management* Emergency situations are often very stressful. With classmates, discuss strategies for reducing stress while dealing with a medical emergency.

Lesson 6

Protecting Your Environment

Guide to Reading

Building Vocabulary
Write each term in your notebook. Add a definition for each as you come across the term in your reading.

- environment (p. 318)
- pollute (p. 318)
- fossil fuels (p. 319)
- ozone (p. 319)
- smog (p. 319)
- acid rain (p. 319)
- recycling (p. 320)
- conservation (p. 321)
- biodegradable (p. 321)

Focusing on the Main Ideas
In this lesson, you will learn to

- **identify** the causes of air, water, and land pollution.
- **describe** what happens to garbage after it is thrown away.
- **explain** how you can help protect the environment.

Reading Strategy
Organizing Information Create a chart that shows the causes for the three types of pollution.

uick Write

Your school is part of your environment. Explain how you can help take care of your school environment.

The Health of the Environment

The **environment** is *the sum total of your surroundings.* It includes living things such as people, plants, and animals. It also includes nonliving things such as homes, buildings, cars, and other things we use each day. All living things are affected by the health of the environment.

Unfortunately, the way people live can pollute the environment. **Pollute** (puh·LOOT) means *to make unfit or harmful for living things.* Pollution affects the air we breathe, the water we drink, and the land we live on.

Air Pollution

Some air pollution is caused by natural events. For example, gases and ash from erupting volcanoes pollute the air. The main cause of air pollution, however, is the

◄ People who care about nature want to protect it.
What can you do to help protect nature?

burning of **fossil** (FAH·suhl) **fuels.** These are *coal, oil, and natural gas.* They are used to power motor vehicles, run factories, and heat homes and buildings.

Air pollution can cause physical problems such as watery eyes, headaches, dizziness, and breathing difficulties. It also causes other environmental problems. One of these is damage to the ozone (OH·zohn) layer. **Ozone** is *a special form of oxygen.* It naturally occurs in the earth's upper atmosphere. The ozone layer is needed to shield the earth from the sun's harmful rays.

Another problem related to air pollution is **smog.** This is *a yellow-brown haze that forms when sunlight reacts with impurities in car exhaust.* Over long periods, breathing smog can cause serious damage to your lungs. Still another problem is **acid rain.** This is *rainfall that contains air pollution from the burning of fossil fuels.* Over time, acid rain can destroy large forests, wildlife, and plants.

 **Reading Check** **Identify** Name two environmental problems caused by air pollution.

Water Pollution

Some water pollution is caused directly by the dumping of waste materials. Indirect causes include poisonous wastes buried in landfills and chemical fertilizers used in farming. Harmful substances from both can leak down through the soil and into the *ground water.* This is water that runs deep under the surface. Other causes of water pollution are accidental, such as oil spills from tanker ships. This pollution damages beaches and harms wildlife.

No matter what the cause, the cost to the environment is great. Harm to the water supply endangers all living things. People can become sick when they drink polluted water. Eating fish that have absorbed wastes and chemicals can lead to illness. In some parts of the world, unclean water spreads deadly diseases. Two of these are cholera (KAH·luh·ruh) and typhoid. These illnesses threaten whole communities.

Connect To...
Science

Alternate Energy Sources

Scientists are busily working at developing alternate energy sources that can be used in place of fossil fuels. Two examples are solar energy—energy from the sun—and wind energy.

Research how these alternate energy sources can improve the environment and your personal health.

▼ The damage to this sculpture was done by acid rain. **What causes acid rain?**

Teens THINK

What can teens do to help protect the environment?

Teens can help the environment by planting all kinds of plants. Plants provide oxygen and more plants sprout up from those plants. We can also pick up trash when we see it. We can clean up the dead branches in the woods. By taking the dead branches away, new plants will grow. Removing the dead stuff will also help prevent fires from spreading faster. These are just a few things we can do to help our environment.

Jake F.
Monument, CO

Land Pollution

Communities that produce large amounts of trash build landfills to bury their wastes. Special linings are designed to prevent pollution from leaking into ground water.

Hazardous wastes include paints, acids, and chemicals used to kill insects. All can cause serious illnesses and environmental damage. Nuclear wastes, the chemicals left over from nuclear power plants, are especially dangerous. They take tens of thousands of years to break down naturally and become harmless. Most communities have approved locations where you can safely dispose of hazardous wastes.

Exhausting Natural Resources

Trees are cut down to make paper and lumber. Removing too many trees upsets the balance of nature. By upsetting this balance, the lives of all living things are endangered.

Another resource we are exhausting is our energy sources. The earth's fossil fuel supplies are not endless. Some day they will run out. Current usage rates are making that happen sooner rather than later.

Environmental protection agencies set and enforce regulations for air, water, and other natural resources. But individuals can help the environment, too.

 **Reading Check**   **Identify** What services are provided by environmental protection agencies?

 **G Online**

Visit **glencoe.com** and complete the Interactive Study Guide for Lesson 6.

How Can You Help?

"What can one person do?" The answer is *plenty*—especially if you are willing to take positive action. For starters, you can create less trash. One way is by reusing as many items as possible. Another is by **recycling.** This means *recovering and changing items so they can be used for other purposes.* Find out where there are recycling centers in your community.

Another solution is **conservation,** *the saving of resources.* When you buy new items, look for ones with the least packaging. This will conserve resources and create less trash to throw away.

Conserve energy at home by turning off electric lights and appliances when not in use. Keep windows closed while the heat or air conditioning is on. Towel or air dry dishes instead of heat drying them in a dishwasher.

Conserve water by using less of it. Turn the water off while you brush your teeth. Take shorter showers. Protect our water supply by using cleaning supplies that are biodegradable (by·oh·di·GRAY·duh·buhl). **Biodegradable** means *capable of breaking down naturally without causing pollution.* Don't dump detergents and cleaning supplies down the drain. They only end up in our rivers, lakes, and oceans.

Advocacy

Set a positive example for others. Urge others to carpool to cut down the number of cars on the road. Having fewer cars on the road means less exhaust in the air from motor vehicles and less fuel consumption.

 **Reading Check** **Explain** What will happen to the environment if you dump detergents down the drain?

G⊚ Online

Topic: Protecting the Environment

Visit glencoe.com for Student Web Activities to learn more about environmental issues and what you can do to help.

Activity: After studying the information provided at the link above, choose an environmental issue that is important to you. Create a brochure that explains the issue and how teens can help.

Lesson 6 Review

 After You Read

Review this lesson for new terms, major headings, and Reading Checks.

What I Learned

1. *Vocabulary* What is *ozone*? Why is it important?

2. *Recall* How does burying wastes in landfills cause water pollution?

3. *List* What are two ways of conserving water?

Thinking Critically

4. *Analyze* How does properly disposing of hazardous waste affect your environment as well as your personal health?

5. *Synthesize* What kind of effect do products that use a lot of packaging have on the environment?

Applying Health Skills

6. *Advocacy* One way to help maintain the environment is to become an advocate. With a group, brainstorm different ways to spread the word about the importance of conservation. Which methods do you think would be most effective?

What Are Advocacy Skills?

Advocacy skills involve taking action in support of a cause. An advocate is someone who works to bring about a change.

Ways to Take Action

- Write letters to government leaders or magazine and newspaper editors.
- Collect signatures from people in your community.
- Organize activities in your school or neighborhood.
- Volunteer with a group that shares your feelings. If no group exists, start your own group.
- Contact local radio or television stations to see if they will give your cause airtime.

Reduce Waste

Follow the Model, Practice, and Apply steps to help you master this important health skill.

❶ Model

Read about how Justin uses advocacy skills to suggest ways his family can help protect the environment.

When Justin learned about ways to protect the environment, he wanted to take action within his own family. He decided to speak with his mom. Read a part of their conversation below.

Justin: We've been studying the environment in school. I would like our family to do more to protect the earth. **(Take a clear stand on an issue.)**

Mom: What do you have in mind?

Justin: Well, I've noticed things in our trash that could still be useful. We can look carefully at every item before throwing it away. If it is something that someone else might use, we can give it to charity. We can also do a better job of recycling and using fewer disposable items, like paper plates. **(Be convincing.)**

Mom: Those are great ideas! I'm glad you care about the environment. **(Persuade others to make healthy choices.)**

② Practice

Read about how Colin uses advocacy to help his school learn to recycle.

Colin wants to help his school learn to recycle and reuse items. He made a list of suggestions, which included using both sides of every piece of paper before it is thrown into the recycle bin. He also suggested starting a recycling program for printer cartridges and old computers.

1. With a group, write a letter to your school's administrators. In your letter, convince them to adopt Colin's suggestions and two other suggestions that your group has come up with.

2. Share your letter with other groups in your class. How is your response similar to or different from theirs?

③ Apply

Apply what you have learned about advocacy when completing the activity below.

Develop a 30-second public service announcement to persuade other teens to reduce, reuse, and recycle. In your announcement, explain why protecting the environment is important. Describe at least three actions students should take to ensure a healthier world.

Self-Check
- Did I explain why environmental protection is important?
- Did I describe three actions students should take?
- Is my announcement persuasive and convincing to teens?

Building Health Skills

Are You Earth-Friendly?

How do you rate as a friend of the environment? Take this conservation inventory to find out.

What You Will Need

- Pencil or pen
- Paper

 What You Will Do

1 Write the letters *a-j.* on your paper.

2 Write yes or no for each statement:

   a. I take quick showers.

   b. I turn off lights and appliances that are not in use.

   c. I keep windows closed when the heat or air conditioning is on.

   d. I don't let the water run when I'm brushing my teeth.

   e. I recycle products whenever possible.

   f. I bring my own bags to the store.

   g. I find new ways to use old items.

   h. I put litter in trash containers.

   i. I encourage my family to carpool.

   j. I walk or ride my bicycle whenever possible instead of asking for a ride.

Wrapping It Up

Give yourself 1 point for each yes answer. Add up your score to see how you rate.

3 or fewer:	Energy Eater
4 to 7:	Average Earth Friend
8 or more:	Conservation Star

List ways you can improve your rating.

CHAPTER

Reading Review

Visit glencoe.com to download quizzes and eFlashcards for Chapter 12.

FOLDABLES Study Organizer

Foldables® and Other Study Aids Take out the Foldable® that you created for Lesson 1 and any graphic organizers that you created for Lessons 1–6. Find a partner, and quiz each other using these study aids.

Lesson 1 Personal Safety Habits

Main Idea You start to learn personal safety habits at a young age.

- The accident chain has three parts: the situation, the unsafe habit, and the unsafe act.
- Many accidents can be prevented by breaking the accident chain, practicing healthful behaviors, and making good decisions.

Lesson 2 Safety at Home and Away

Main Idea Following safety rules can keep you safe both at home and away from home.

- Your home may be filled with many potential safety hazards, such as stairs or appliances.
- It is a healthy practice to have a fire safety plan, a fire extinguisher, and a working smoke alarm.
- Safety procedures should be obeyed on the road, in school, and in your community.

Lesson 3 Safety Outdoors

Main Idea Safety precautions make outdoor activities more fun.

- Safety rules for the water include: never swim alone, go to pools and beaches that have lifeguards, and always know water depth before swimming.
- Always have the right gear and equipment for your outdoor activities.
- Cell phones or walkie-talkies can help you communicate in an emergency.

Lesson 4 Safety in Severe Weather

Main Idea You can prepare for a severe weather emergency or natural disaster by having an emergency kit.

- Weather emergencies include thunderstorms, hurricanes, floods, blizzards, tornadoes, and earthquakes.
- Your kit should contain enough food, water, and first-aid supplies to last for three days.

Lesson 5 First Aid for Emergencies

Main Idea Proper training is needed to give first aid.

- The Check-Call-Care strategy stands for: check the scene and the victim, call for help (dial 911 or your local emergency number), care for the victim until help arrives.

Lesson 6 Protecting Your Environment

Main Idea The health of the environment impacts the health of all living things.

- Air, water, and land pollution compromise the health of our surroundings.
- Recycling and conservation have a positive impact on the environment.

12 Assessment

 After You Read

HEALTH INVENTORY
Now that you have read the chapter, look back at your answer to the Health Inventory on the chapter opener. Have your ideas changed? What would your answers be now?

Reviewing Vocabulary and Main Ideas

On a sheet of paper, write the numbers 1–5. After each number, write the term from the list that best completes each sentence.

- abdominal thrusts
- accident
- accident chain
- accidental injuries
- biodegradable
- hazard
- Neighborhood Watch program
- pedestrians

Lesson 1) Personal Safety Habits

1. _____ are injuries caused by unexpected events.

2. A(n) _____ is an unexpected event that results in damage or harm.

3. The situation, the unsafe habit, and the unsafe act are all parts of the _____.

Lesson 2) Safety at Home and Away

4. A loose floor rug that someone might trip on is an example of a _____ in the home.

5. Some communities try to protect teens by developing a _____.

*On a sheet of paper, write the numbers 6–13. Write **True** or **False** for each statement below. If the statement is false, change the underlined word or phrase to make it true.*

Lesson 3) Safety Outdoors

6. Knowing how to <u>swim</u> is an important part of water safety.

7. A <u>first-aid kit</u> comes in handy for treating minor injuries on the trail.

Lesson 4) Safety in Severe Weather

8. <u>Earthquakes</u>, the most common natural disaster, can happen almost anywhere.

9. Whirling, funnel-shaped windstorms, or <u>hurricanes</u>, occur mostly in the flat central regions of the country.

Lesson 5) First Aid for Emergencies

10. A life saving technique for a victim whose heart has stopped beating is <u>abdominal thrusts</u>.

11. A <u>first-degree</u> burn is very serious because deeper layers of skin and nerve endings are damaged.

Lesson 6) Protecting Your Environment

12. Recovering and changing items so they can be used for other purposes is called <u>pollution</u>.

13. Cleaning supplies that are <u>biodegradable</u> break down naturally without causing pollution.

Go Online   Visit glencoe.com and take the Online Quiz for Chapter 12.

Thinking Critically

Using complete sentences, answer the following questions on a sheet of paper.

14. **Analyze** Sara is skating with her friends. They decide to race. Sara notices a crack in the ice in the distance. What safety tips might she give her friends?

15. **Describe** In what ways can the skill of advocacy make your community safer?

Write About It

16. **Descriptive Writing** Write a paragraph discussing some of the positive health behaviors you can practice to help protect the environment.

Applying Technology

Protect Our Earth

Work in pairs to develop a PowerPoint® project that demonstrates the importance of environmental safety.

- Collect 20 digital images of textbook illustrations and classmates demonstrating personal safety.
- Import the images into your computer.
- Write a script about one of the topics discussed in this chapter.
- Open a new PowerPoint® project with 20 slides. Select the slide layout that has both an image and text box, side-by-side.
- Import one image and the text that goes with it on each slide.
- Save your project.

Standardized Test Practice

Math

Use the following information to answer the questions about safety in the event of lightning.

Earth is struck by lightning approximately 100 times every second. A formula exists for estimating how close a lightning strike is.

1. When you see the flash, begin counting seconds. If no clock is available, count *one one-hundred, two one-hundred,* and so on.

2. When you hear the sound of thunder, stop counting.

3. Each 5 seconds you counted is equal to about 1 mile.

Whenever lightning is within 7 miles of your location, seek shelter. If it is within 10 miles, continue to monitor the track of the storm. To do this, repeat the process for the next lightning flash. If the number is smaller, the storm is headed your way. Take cover.

TEST-TAKING TIP

To solve a math problem, be sure you understand the type of problem. Make sure you understand what you are being asked to do.

1. If you see lightning, count to 22, and then hear thunder,
   A. the lightning is 22 miles away.
   B. the lightning is 2.2 miles away.
   C. the lightning is 5.4 miles away.
   D. the lightning is 4.2 miles away.

2. A camper sees lightning and counts to 41, then hears thunder. Which statement is NOT true?
   A. The lightning is more than 8 miles from the camper's location.
   B. The camper should count again after the next flash.
   C. The camper should seek shelter at once.
   D. The camper is in no immediate danger but is not totally safe.

▶ Reading: What's in It for You?

What role does reading play in your life? There are many different ways that reading could be part of what you do every day. Are you on a sports team? Perhaps you like to read the latest news about your favorite team or find out about new ways to train for your sport. Are you interested in music or art? You might be looking for information about ways to create songs or about styles of painting. Are you enrolled in an English class, a math class, or a health class? Then your assignments probably require a lot of reading.

Improving or Fine-Tuning Your Reading Skills Will:

- ◆ **Improve your grades**
- ◆ **Allow you to read faster and more efficiently**
- ◆ **Improve your study skills**
- ◆ **Help you remember more information**
- ◆ **Improve your writing**

▶ The Reading Process

Good reading skills build on one another, overlap, and spiral around just like a winding staircase goes around and around while leading you to a higher place. This Reading Guide will help you find and use the tools you'll need before, during, and after reading.

Strategies You Can Use

- ◆ **Identify, understand, and learn new words**
- ◆ **Understand why you read**
- ◆ **Take a quick look at the whole text**
- ◆ **Try to predict what you are about to read**

- ◆ **Take breaks while you read and ask yourself questions about the text**
- ◆ **Take notes**
- ◆ **Keep thinking about what will come next**
- ◆ **Summarize**

▶ Vocabulary Development

Vocabulary skills are the building blocks of the reading and writing processes. By learning to use a number of strategies to build your word skills, you will become a stronger reader.

Use Context to Determine Meaning

The best way to increase your vocabulary is to read widely, listen carefully, and take part in many kinds of discussions. When reading on your own, you can often figure out the meanings of new words by looking at their **context**, the other words and sentences that surround them.

> **Tips for Using Context**
>
> **Look for clues such as:**
>
> A synonym or an explanation of the unknown word in the sentence:
> *Elise's shop specialized in millinery, or hats for women.*
>
> A reference to what the word is or is not like:
> *An archaeologist, like a historian, deals with the past.*
>
> A general topic associated with the word:
> *The cooking teacher discussed the best way to braise meat.*
>
> A description or action associated with the word:
> *He used the shovel to dig up the garden.*

Predict a Possible Meaning

Another way to determine the meaning of a word is to take the word apart. If you understand the meaning of the **base,** or **root,** part of a word, and also know the meanings of key syllables added either to the beginning or end of the base word, you can usually figure out what the word means.

Word Origins Since Latin, Greek, and Anglo-Saxon roots are the basis for much of our English vocabulary, having some background in languages can be a useful vocabulary tool. For example, *astronomy* comes from the Greek root *astro*, which means "relating to the stars." *Stellar* also has a meaning referring to stars, but it's from Latin. Knowing root words in other languages can help you figure out meanings, word sources, and spellings in English.

Prefixes and Suffixes A prefix is a word part that can be added to the beginning of a word. For example, the prefix *semi* means "half" or "partial," so *semicircle* means "half a circle." A suffix is a word part that can be added to the end of a word. Adding a suffix often changes a word from one part of speech to another.

Using Dictionaries A dictionary gives the meaning or meanings of a word. Look at the example on the next page to see what else a dictionary can offer.

Thesauruses and Specialized Reference Books A thesaurus gives synonyms and sometimes antonyms. It is a useful tool to expand your vocabulary. Remember to check the exact meaning of words in a dictionary before you use a thesaurus. Specialized dictionaries such as *The New American Medical Dictionary* and *Health Manual* list terms that are not always included in a general dictionary. You can also use online dictionaries.

Glossaries Many textbooks have a condensed dictionary. This kind of dictionary offers an alphabetical listing of vocabulary words used in the text along with definitions.

Dictionary Entry

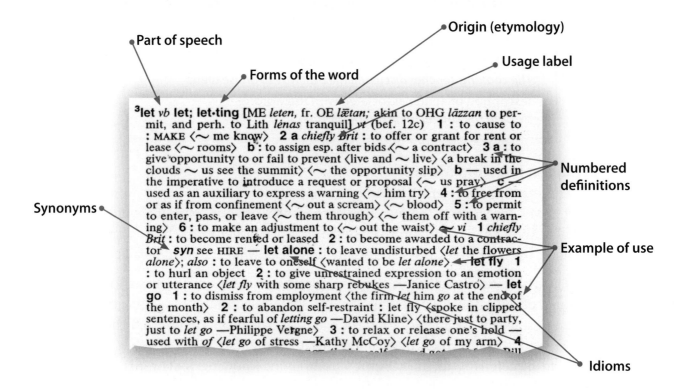

By permission. From *Merriam-Webster's Collegiate® Dictionary, Eleventh Edition©* 2005 by Merriam-Webster, Incorporated (www.merriam-webster.com)

Recognize Word Meanings Across Subjects Have you learned a new word in one class and then noticed it in your reading for other subjects? The word might not mean exactly the same thing in each class, but you can use the meaning you already know to help you understand what it means in another subject area. For example:

Math After you multiply the two numbers, explain how you arrived at the **product.**

Science One **product** of photosynthesis is oxygen.

Health The **product** of a balanced diet and regular exercise is a healthy body.

▶ Understanding What You Read

Reading comprehension means understanding or gaining meaning from what you have read. Using a variety of strategies can help you improve your comprehension and make reading more interesting and more fun.

Read for a Reason

To get the greatest value from what you read, you should **establish a purpose for reading.** In school, you have many reasons for reading. Some of them are to

- learn and understand new information.
- find specific information.
- review before a test.
- finish an assignment.
- prepare to write.

As your reading skills improve, you will notice that you use different strategies to fit the different reasons for reading. If you are reading for fun, you might read quickly, but if you read to gather information or follow directions, you might read more slowly. You might also take notes, develop a graphic organizer, or reread parts of the text.

Draw on Personal Background

Drawing on your own background is also called activating prior knowledge. Before you start reading a text, ask yourself questions like these:

- What have I heard or read about this topic?
- Do I have any personal experiences that might connect to this topic?

Using a KWL Chart A KWL chart is a good device for organizing information you gather before, during, and after reading. In the first column, list what you already **know,** then list what you **want** to know in the middle column. Use the third column when you review and assess what you **learned.** You can add more columns to record places where you found information and places where you can look for more information.

K (What I already know)	W (What I want to know)	L (What I have learned)

Adjust Your Reading Speed Your reading speed is an important factor in how well you understand what you are reading. You will need to change your speed depending on the reason you are reading.

Scanning means running your eyes quickly over the material to look for words or phrases. Scan when you need specific information.

Skimming means reading a section of text quickly to find its main idea. Skim when you want to determine what the reading is about.

Reading for detail involves careful reading while paying attention to the structure of the text and to your own understanding. Read for detail when you are learning about new ideas or when you are following directions. It is also important when you are getting ready to analyze a text.

▶ Techniques to Understand and Remember What You Read

Preview

Before beginning a selection, it is helpful to **preview** what you are about to read.

> **Previewing Strategies**
>
> Read the title, headings, and subheadings of the selection.
>
> Look at the illustrations and notice how the text is set up.
>
> Skim the reading: Take a quick look at the whole thing.
>
> Decide what the main idea might be.
>
> Predict what the reading will be about.

Predict

Have you ever read a mystery, decided who was the criminal, and then changed your mind as more clues were offered? You were changing your predictions based on the information you had available. Did you smile when you found out you guessed the criminal? You were checking your predictions.

As you read, take educated guesses about story events and outcomes; that is, **make predictions** before and during reading. This will help you focus your attention on the text, and it will improve your understanding.

Determine the Main Idea

When you look for the **main idea,** you are looking for the most important sentences in a text. Depending on what kind of text you are reading, the main idea can be found at the very beginning (news stories in a newspaper or magazine) or at the end (scientific research document). Ask yourself:

- What is each sentence about?
- Is there one sentence that is more important than all the others?
- What idea do details support or point out?

Taking Notes

Cornell Note-Taking System There are many methods for note taking. The **Cornell Note-Taking System** is a well-known method that can help you organize what you read. To the right is a note-taking activity based on the Cornell Note-Taking System.

Graphic organizers Using a graphic organizer will help you remember and hold on to new information. You might make a **chart** or **diagram** that helps you organize what you have read. Here are some ways to make graphic organizers:

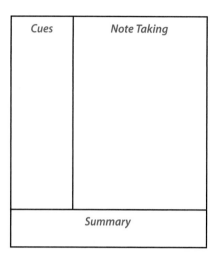

Venn diagrams When mapping out a comparison-and-contrast text structure, you can use a Venn diagram. The outer parts of the circles will show how two characters, ideas, or items contrast, or are different. The overlapping part in the middle will compare two things, or show how they are alike.

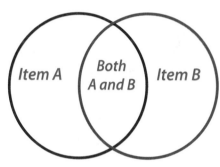

Flow charts To help you track the order of events, or cause and effect, use a flow chart. Arrange ideas or events in their logical, step-by-step order. Then draw arrows between your ideas to show how one idea or event flows into another.

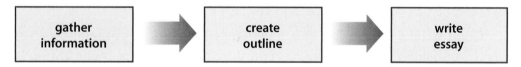

Visualize

Try to form a picture in your mind of scenes, characters, and events as you read. Use the details and descriptions the author gives you. If you can picture, or visualize, what you read, it will be more interesting and you will remember it better.

Question

Ask yourself questions about the text while you read. Ask yourself about the importance of the sentences, how they relate to one another, if you understand what you just read, and what you think is going to come next.

Clarify

If you feel you do not understand the meaning of what you read (through questioning), try these ideas:

What to Do When You Do Not Understand

- ◆ Reread confusing parts of the text.
- ◆ Make diagrams that show how pieces of text, ideas, and sentences connect to each other.
- ◆ Look up new words.
- ◆ Talk about the text to yourself.
- ◆ Read the text over again.

Review

Take time to stop and review what you have read. Use your note-taking tools (graphic organizers or Cornell notes charts). Also, think about what you've written in your KWL chart.

Monitor Your Comprehension

Continue to check your understanding by using the following two strategies:

Summarize Pause and tell yourself the main ideas of the text and the key supporting details. Try to answer the following questions: Who? What? When? Where? Why? How?

Paraphrase Pause, close the book, and try to retell what you have just read in your own words. It might help to pretend you are explaining the text to someone who has not read it and does not know the material.

▶ Understanding Text Structure

Good writers do not just put together sentences and paragraphs; they organize their writing with a certain purpose in mind. That organization is called text structure. When you understand and follow the way a text is set up, it is easier to remember what you are reading. There are many ways text may be structured. Watch for **signal words.** They will help you follow the text's organization (also, remember to use these ideas when you write).

Compare and Contrast

This structure shows similarities and differences between people, things, and ideas. This is often used to show that things that seem alike are really different, or vice versa.

Signal words: similarly, more, less, on the one hand / on the other hand, in contrast, but, however

Cause and Effect

Writers use the cause and effect structure to show why something takes place and to look at what happens because of certain actions.

Signal words: so, because, as a result, therefore, for the following reasons

Problem and Solution

Sometimes writers organize text around the question "how?" To do this, they state a problem and then present answers for the reader to think about.

Signal words: how, help, problem, obstruction, overcome, difficulty, need, attempt, have to, must

Sequence

Sequencing tells you in which order to think about ideas or facts. Examples of sequencing are:

Chronological order tells you the order in which events take place.

Signal words: first, next, then, finally

Spatial order describes the way things are arranged in space (to describe a room, for example).

Signal words: above, below, behind, next to

Order of importance lists things or thoughts from the most important to the least important (or the other way around).

Signal words: principal, central, main, important, fundamental

▶ Reading for Meaning

It is important to think about what you are reading to get the most information out of the text and to gain an understanding of what the text is saying. This will also help you to remember the key points and will guide you to form your own thoughts about what you've read.

Interpret

Interpreting is asking yourself, "What is the writer really saying?" and then using what you already know to answer that question.

Infer

Writers do not always say exactly everything they want you to understand. By providing clues and details, they sometimes imply certain concepts. An inference involves using your reason and background to develop ideas on your own. These ideas are based on what an author implies or suggests. What is most important when making inferences is to be sure that you have correctly based your guesses on details from the reading. If you cannot point to a place in the text to help back up your inference, you may need to go back and think about your guess again.

Draw Conclusions

A conclusion is a general statement you can make and explain with reasoning, or with details from a text. If you read a story describing a sport where five players bounce a ball and throw it through a high hoop, you may conclude that the sport is basketball.

Analyze

Persuasive nonfiction is a text that presents facts and opinions that lead to a conclusion. To understand this kind of text, you need to look at statements and examples to see if they connect to the key ideas. An informational text, like a textbook, gives information instead of opinions. To understand this kind of text, you need to notice how ideas are put together to find the key points.

Hint: Use your graphic organizers and notes charts.

Distinguish Facts and Opinions

This is one of the most important reading skills you can learn. A fact is a statement that can be shown to be true. An opinion is what the writer believes. A writer may support opinions with facts, but an opinion cannot be proven. For example:

Fact: California produces fruit and other agricultural products.

Opinion: California produces the best fruit and other agricultural products.

Evaluate

Would you take seriously an article on nuclear fission if you knew a comedy actor wrote it? If you need true and correct information, you need to find out who wrote what you are reading and why. Where did the writer get the information? Is the information one-sided? Can you show that the information is true?

▶ Reading for Research

You will need to think about what you are reading while you read in order to research a subject. You also may need to develop an interesting and fitting **question** that you can study on your own. Be sure to find the right kind of information from many different sources, including print material, and nonprint material. Then you will need to determine key ideas so that you can **organize** the information in a way that fits your readers. Finally, you should **draw conclusions** that connect to your research question. This may lead you to other areas for study.

Locate Appropriate Print and Nonprint Information

In your research, try to use many different sources. This will help you see information in different ways, and will help your project to be interesting and fairly presented.

Literature and Textbooks These texts include any book used for learning or gathering information.

Book Indices A book index, or a bibliography, is an alphabetical listing of books. Some book indices list books on certain subjects; others are more general. Other indices have an array of topics or resources.

Periodicals Magazines and journals are issued regularly, such as weekly or monthly. One way to find information in magazines is to use the *Readers' Guide to Periodical Literature*. This guide can be found in print form in most libraries.

Technical Manuals A manual is a guide or handbook intended to give instruction on how to do a task or operate something. A vehicle owner's manual might give information on how to use and take care of a car.

Reference Books Reference books include encyclopedias and almanacs, and are used to find specific pieces of information.

Electronic Encyclopedias, Databases, and the Internet There are many ways to find information using your computer. Infotrac, for instance, acts as an online reader's guide. The Internet or encyclopedias on CD-ROM can easily provide information on most subjects.

Organize and Convert Information

As you gather information from different sources, taking careful notes, you will need to think about how to **synthesize** the information. This means you will have to join the pieces of information together to make a whole text. You will also need to change it to a form that will fit your audience and will meet the requirements of the assignment.

1. First, ask yourself what you want your readers to know.
2. Then, think about a pattern of organization, a structure that will best show your key ideas. You might ask yourself the following questions:
   - When comparing items or ideas, what graphic aids can I use?
   - When showing the reasons something happened and the results of certain actions, what text structure would be best?
   - How can I briefly and clearly show important information to my readers?
   - Would an illustration or even a cartoon help to make a certain point?

Glossary

The Glossary contains all the important terms used through-out the text. It includes the **boldfaced** terms in the "Building Vocabulary" lists at the beginning of each lesson, which also appear in the text and illustrations.

The Glossary lists the term, the pronunciation (in the case of difficult terms), the definition, and the page on which the term is defined. The pronunciations here and in the text follow the system outlined below. The column headed "Sound" shows the spelling used in this book to represent the appropriate sound.

Pronunciation Key

Symbol	As In	Sound	Example
ă	hat, map	a	abscess (AB·ses)
ā	age, face	ay	atrium (AY·tree·uhm)
a	care, their	eh	capillaries (KAP·uh·lehr·eez)
ä, ŏ	father, hot	ah	biopsy (BY·ahp·See)
ar	far	ar	cardiac (KAR·dee·ak)
ch	child, much	ch	barbiturate (bar·BI·chuh·ruht)
ĕ	let, best	e	vessel (VE·suhl)
ē	beat, See, city	ee	acne (AK·nee)
er	term, stir, purr	er	nuclear (NOO·klee·er)
g	grow	g	malignant (muh·LIG·nuhnt)
ĭ	it, hymn	i	bacteria (bak·TIR·ee·uh)
ī	ice, five	y	benign (bi·NYN)
		eye	iris (EYE·ris)
j	page, fungi	j	cartilage (KAR·tuhl·ij)
k	coat, look, chorus	k	defect (DEE·fekt)
ō	open, coat, grow	oh	aerobic (ehr·OH·bik)
ô	order	or	organ (OR·guhn)
ò	flaw, all	aw	palsy (PAWL·zee)
oi	voice	oy	goiter (GOY·ter)
ou	out	ow	fountain (FOWN·tuhn)
s	say, rice	s	dermis (DER·mis)
sh	she, attention	sh	conservation (kahn·ser·VAY·shuhn)
ŭ	cup, flood	uh	bunion (BUHN·yuhn)
u	put, wood, could	u	pulmonary (PUL·muh·nehr·ee)
ü	rule, move, you	oo	attitudes (AT·i·toodz)
w	win	w	warranty (WAWR·uhn·tee)
y	your	yu	urethra (yu·REE·thruh)
z	says	z	hormones (HOR·mohnz)
zh	pleasure	zh	transfusion (trans·FYOO·zhuhn)
ə	about, collide	uh	addiction (uh·DIK·shuhn)

Abdominal thrusts Quick upward pulls into the diaphragm to force out the object blocking the airway. (page 314)

Abstinence (AB·stuh·nuhns) Not participating in high-risk behaviors. (page 44)

Abuse (uh·BYOOS) A pattern of mistreatment of another person. (page 71)

Accident An unexpected event that results in damage or harm. (page 296)

Accident chain A sequence of events that often leads to an accidental injury. (page 297)

Accidental injuries Injuries caused by unexpected events. (page 296)

Acid rain Rainfall that contains air pollution from the burning of fossil fuels. (page 319)

Acne A skin condition caused by overly active oil glands. (page 148)

Addiction The body's physical or mental need for a drug or other substance. (page 223)

Adolescence (a·duhl·EH·suhns) The period between childhood and adulthood. (page 202)

Adrenaline A hormone that prepares the body to respond to stress. (page 47)

Advocacy Taking a stand to make a difference. (page 38)

Advocate Encourage other people to live healthy lives. (page 15)

AIDS A condition characterized by life-ending infections and a T-cell count under 200. (page 278)

Alcohol (AL·kuh·hawl) A substance produced by a chemical reaction in carbohydrates. (page 242)

Alcoholism A disease in which a person has a physical and mental need for alcohol. (page 247)

Allergen A substance that causes an allergic reaction. (page 285)

Allergy The body's sensitivity to certain substances. (page 285)

Alternative (ahl·TER·nuh·tihv) Another way of thinking or acting. (page 258)

Anabolic steroids (a·nuh·BAH·lik STEHR·oydz) Synthetic drugs based on a male hormone. (page 251)

Antibiotics (an·tih·by·AH·tiks) Kill or stop the growth of bacteria and other specific germs. (page 160)

Antibodies Chemicals produced specifically to fight a particular invading substance. (page 274)

Anxiety Feelings of uncertainty or worry over what may happen. (page 46)

Anxiety disorder A serious emotional problem that keeps a person from functioning normally. (page 51)

Assertive Making your wants and needs known in a positive, active manner. (page 66)

Asthma (AZ·muh) A chronic disease in which the airways become irritated and swollen. (page 285)

Astigmatism (ah·STIG·muh·tizm) A misshaped cornea or lens causing objects to look wavy or blurred. (page 152)

Attitude What you believe or feel about someone or something. (page 11)

Bacteria (bak·TIR·ee·uh) Extremely small, single-celled organisms with no cell nucleus. (page 270)

Behavior The way you act in the many different situations and events in your life. (page 11)

Biodegradable (by·oh·di·GRAY·duh·buhl) Capable of breaking down naturally without causing pollution. (page 321)

Blood alcohol content (BAC) A measure of the amount of alcohol present in a person's blood. (page 243)

Blood pressure The force of blood pushing against the blood vessel walls. (page 189)

Body image How you view your body. (page 109)

Body language Facial expressions, eye contact, gestures, and posture. (page 63)

Body systems Groups of organs that perform a body function. (page 177)

Calorie A unit of heat that measures the energy available in foods. (page 100)

Cancer A disease caused by abnormal cells that grow out of control. (page 284)

Carbohydrates (kar·boh·HY·drayts) Sugars and starches contained in foods. (page 95)

Carbon monoxide (KAR·buhn muh·NAHK·syd) A poisonous, odorless gas produced when tobacco burns. (page 222)

Cardiopulmonary resuscitation (CPR) A rescue measure that attempts to restore heartbeat and breathing. (page 314)

Cells The basic building blocks of life. (page 177)

Character The way you think, feel, and act. (page 36)

Cholesterol (kuh·LES·tuh·rawl) A waxy chemical our bodies produce and need in small amounts. (page 106)

Chromosomes (KROH·muh·sohmz) Tiny strands of matter that carry the codes for inherited traits. (page 210)

Chronic (KRAH·nik) Long-lasting. (page 283)

Circulatory system Allows the body to move blood to and from tissues. (page 188)

Cirrhosis (suh·ROH·sis) Destruction and scarring of the liver tissue. (page 243)

Communicable (kuh·MYOO·nih·kuh·buhl) **diseases** Diseases that can be spread. (page 268)

Communication The clear exchange of ideas and information. (page 15)

Compromise A skill in which each side gives up something in order to reach an agreeable solution. (page 83)

Conflicts Disagreements in ideas, beliefs, or interests. (page 81)

Consequences Results. (page 16)

Conservation The saving of resources. (page 321)

Consumer Someone who buys products or services. (page 155)

Contagious (kuhn·TA·juhs) When one can spread a virus to others by direct or indirect contact. (page 272)

Cooldown Gentle activity to slow down after exercise. (page 131)

Cooperation Working together for the common good. (page 75)

Coupons Slips of paper that save you money on certain brands. (page 158)

Culture The collected beliefs, customs, and behaviors of a group. (page 9)

Cumulative (KYOO·myuh·luh·tiv) **risk** The addition of one risk factor to another, increasing the chance of harm or loss. (page 17)

Cuticle (KYOO·ti·kuhl) A nonliving band of outer skin. (page 150)

Dandruff Flaking of the outer layer of dead skin cells. (page 149)

Decisions Choices that you make. (page 16)

Dehydration A condition caused by too much water loss. (page 134)

Depression An emotional problem marked by long periods of hopelessness and despair. (page 51)

Dermis The thicker inner layer of the skin. (page 147)

Diabetes (dy·uh·BEE·teez) A disease that prevents the body from using the sugars and starches in food for energy. (page 286)

Diaphragm (Dy·uh·fram) A large muscle at the bottom of the chest. (page 191)

Digestion The process by which your body breaks down food into small nutrient particles. (page 185)

Digestive (dY·JES·tiv) **system** The body system that controls the digestion process. (page 185)

Disease (dih·ZEEZ) A condition that affects the proper functioning of the body or mind. (page 268)

Drug A substance that changes the structure or function of the body or mind. (page 242)

Drug abuse The use of any drug in a way that is unhealthy or illegal. (page 253)

Drug misuse Taking medicine in a way that is not intended. (page 162)

Drug rehabilitation A process in which a person relearns how to live without the abused drug. (page 255)

 E

Earthquake The shaking of the ground as rock below the surface moves. (page 311)

Eating disorder Extreme eating behavior that can seriously damage the body. (page 110)

Egg cell The female reproductive cell. (page 206)

Emotions Feelings such as joy, love, anger, or fear. (page 41)

Empathy The ability to identify and share another person's feelings. (page 74)

Emphysema (em·fuh·SEE·muh) A disease that occurs when tiny air sacs in the lungs lose their elasticity, or ability to stretch. (page 223)

Endocrine (EN·duh·krin) **system** A body system containing glands that regulate growth and other important activities. (page 203)

Endurance (en·DER·uhns) The ability to keep up a physical activity without becoming overly tired. (page 123)

Environment (en·VY·ruhn·muhnt) The sum total of your surroundings. (page 9)

Epidermis The thinner outer layer of the skin. (page 147)

Excretory (EK·skruh·tohr·ee) **system** Gets rid of some of the wastes your body produces and also maintains fluid balance. (page 186)

Exercise Planned, structured, repetitive physical activity that improves or maintains physical fitness. (page 125)

 F

Family The basic unit of society. (page 67)

Farsightedness The ability to see objects at a distance while close objects look blurry. (page 152)

Fats Nutrients found in fatty animal tissue and plant oils. (page 95)

Fertilization The joining of a female egg cell with a male reproductive cell. (page 206)

Fetal (FEE·tuhl) **alcohol syndrome (FAS)** A group of permanent physical and mental problems caused by alcohol use during pregnancy. (page 248)

Fetus A developing, unborn baby from the eighth week until birth. (page 212)

Fiber The tough, stringy part of raw fruits, raw vegetables, whole wheat, and other whole grains. (page 95)

Fire extinguisher A device that releases chemicals that smother flames. (page 302)

First aid The care first given to an injured or ill person until regular medical care can be supplied. (page 312)

First-degree burn A burn in which only the outer part of the skin is burned and turns red. (page 316)

F.I.T.T. principle A method for safely increasing aspects of your workout without injuring yourself. (page 128)

Flexibility The ability to move body joints through a full range of motion. (page 124)

Fluoride (FLAWR·ahyd) A substance that fights tooth decay. (page 146)

Fossil (FAH·suhl) **fuels** Coal, oil, and natural gas. (page 319)

Fraud Deliberately trying to trick consumers into buying a product or service. (page 158)

Friendship A special type of relationship between people who enjoy being together. (page 73)

Frostbite Freezing of the skin. (page 135)

Fungi (FUHN·jy) Primitive single- or many-celled organisms that cannot make their own food. (page 270)

 G

Gang A group whose members often use violence or take part in criminal activity. (page 84)

Generic (juh·NEHR·ik) Products that imitate name-brand products but are sold in plain packages. (page 158)

Genes (JEENZ) The basic units of heredity. (page 210)

Goal Something you hope to accomplish. (page 20)

Guarantee A promise to refund your money if the product does not work as claimed. (page 157)

Habit A pattern of behavior that you follow almost without thinking. (page 7)

Hallucinogens (huh·LOO·suhn·uh·jenz) Illegal drug that causes the user's brain to create or distort images and to see and hear things that are not real. (page 252)

Hazards Possible sources of harm. (page 300)

Health A combination of physical, mental/emotional, and social well-being. (page 4)

Health care Any services provided to individuals or communities that promote, maintain, or restore health. (page 163)

Health insurance An insurance policy that covers most health care costs. (page 166)

Health skills Skills that help you become and stay healthy. (page 12)

Heart The muscle that acts as the pump for the circulatory system. (page 189)

Heat exhaustion An overheating of the body that can result from dehydration. (page 134)

Heredity The process by which biological parents pass traits to their children. (page 8)

HIV The virus that causes AIDS. (page 278)

Hormones (HOR·mohnz) Powerful chemicals, produced by glands, which regulate many body functions. (page 41)

Hurricane (HER·uh·kayn) A strong tropical windstorm with driving rain. (page 309)

Hygiene (HY·jeen) The action you take to improve or maintain your health. (page 144)

Hypothermia (hy·poh·THER·mee·uh) A sudden and dangerous drop in body temperature. (page 306)

Illegal drugs Drugs that are made and used purely for their effects. (page 249)

Immune (ih·MYOON) **system** A group of cells, tissues, and organs that fights disease. (page 274)

Immunity Resistance to infection. (page 274)

Infection The result of pathogens or germs invading the body, multiplying, and harming some of your body's cells. (page 274)

Inhalants (in·HAY·luhnts) Substances whose fumes or vapors are inhaled, or breathed in. (page 249)

Insulin A hormone produced by the pancreas. (page 286)

Joints Places where one bone meets another. (page 182)

Lifestyle activities Physical activities that are part of your day-to-day routine or recreation. (page 121)

Long-term goal A goal that you hope to achieve within a period of months or years. (page 21)

Loyal Faithful. (page 74)

Lungs The main organs of the respiratory system. (page 191)

Lymphocyte (LIM·fuh·syt) A white blood cell that attacks pathogens or harmful germs. (page 274)

Managed care A health insurance plan that saves money by limiting people's choice of doctors. (page 166)

Marijuana (mar·uh·WAHN·uh) An illegal drug that comes from the hemp plant. (page 250)

Media The various methods of communicating information, including newspapers, magazines, radio, television, and the Internet. (page 10)

Medicines Drugs used to treat, cure, or prevent diseases or other medical conditions. (page 159)

Menstruation (men·stroo·AY·shuhn) Blood, tissue, and the unfertilized egg flow out of the body. (page 207)

Minerals (MIN·uh·ruhls) Elements in foods that help your body work properly. (page 96)

Mood disorder A serious emotional problem where a person's mood goes from one extreme to another. (page 51)

Muscular system All the muscles in your body. (page 183)

MyPyramid food guidance system A system designed to help Americans make healthful food choices. (page 98)

Narcotics (nar·KAH·tics) Strong drugs that relieve pain. (page 251)

Natural disaster An event caused by nature that results in widespread damage, destruction, and loss. (page 308)

Nearsightedness The ability to see objects close to you while distant objects look blurry. (page 152)

Negative peer pressure Pressure you feel to go along with the harmful behaviors or beliefs of your peers. (page 228)

Neglect The failure of parents to provide their children with basic physical and emotional care and protection. (page 71)

Negotiation (neh·GOH·shee·AY·shuhn) The process of talking about a conflict and deciding how to reach a compromise. (page 83)

Neighborhood Watch programs Programs in which residents are trained to identify and report suspicious activity. (page 304)

Nervous system The control and communication system of the body. (page 192)

Neurons (NOO·rahnz) A cell that carries electrical messages. (page 192)

Nicotine (NIH·kuh·teen) A drug found in tobacco that speeds up the heartbeat and affects the central nervous system. (page 222)

Noncommunicable diseases Diseases that do not spread. (page 269)

Nurture To fulfill physical, mental/emotional, and social needs. (page 69)

Nutrients (NOO·tree·ents) Substances in food that your body needs to carry out its normal functions. (page 94)

Nutrition (noo·TRIH·shun) The process of taking in food and using it for energy, growth, and good health. (page 94)

Obese Significantly overweight. (page 109)

Organs A structure made up of different types of tissues that all work together. (page 177)

Overdose Taking a fatal amount of a drug. (page 253)

Over-the-counter (OTC) medicines Medicines available without a written order from a doctor. (page 159)

Ozone (OH·zohn) A special form of oxygen. (page 319)

P

Passive smokers Nonsmokers who breathe in secondhand smoke. (page 232)

Pathogen A microscopic organism that causes communicable diseases. (page 269)

Pedestrian A person traveling on foot. (page 303)

Peer mediation (mee·dee·AY·shuhn) A process in which a specially trained student listens to both sides of an argument to help the people reach a solution (page 83)

Peer pressure The influence that people your age may have on you. (page 76)

Peers Friends and other people in your age group. (page 9)

Physical abuse Involves the use of physical force. (page 71)

Physical activity Any kind of movement that causes your body to use energy. (page 120)

Physical fitness The ability to handle everyday physical work and play without becoming tired. (page 121)

Plaque (PLAK) A soft, colorless, sticky film containing bacteria that grows on your teeth. (page 145)

Poison control center A community agency that helps people deal with poisoning emergencies. (page 316)

Pollute (puh·LOOT) To make unfit or harmful for living things. (page 318)

Prejudice (PREH·juh·dis) An opinion or fear formed without having facts or firsthand knowledge. (page 82)

Prenatal care Special care to ensure that the mother and her baby remain healthy. (page 212)

Prescription (prih·SKRIP·shuhn) **medicines** Medicines sold only with a written order from a doctor. (page 159)

Prevention Practicing health and safety habits to remain free of disease and injury. (page 12)

P.R.I.C.E. Protect, rest, ice, compress, and elevate. (page 134)

Proteins (PROH·teenz) Nutrients that provide the building blocks your body needs for growth. (page 95)

Protozoa (proh·tuh·ZOH·uh) Single-celled organisms that have a nucleus. (page 270)

Puberty (PYOO·bur·tee) The time when you start developing physical characteristics of adults of your gender. (page 203)

R

Recovery To overcome an addiction and return to a mostly normal life. (page 254)

Recovery heart rate How quickly your heart rate returns to normal right after exercise is stopped. (page 130)

Recycling Recovering and changing items so they can be used for other purposes. (page 320)

Refusal skills Ways of saying no. (page 78)

Reinforce Support. (page 33)

Relationship A connection you have with another person or group. (page 62)

Reliable Dependable. (page 74)

Reproductive system The body system that makes it possible to create offspring. (page 206)

Rescue breathing A substitute for normal breathing in which someone forces air into the victim's lungs. (page 313)

Resilience The ability to work through and recover from disappointment. (page 34)

Respiratory system Enables you to breathe. (page 191)

Resting heart rate The number of times your heart beats per minute when you are relaxing. (page 129)

Risk The chance of harm, or loss. (page 16)

Role model A person whose success or behavior serves as a good example for others. (page 39)

 S

Saturated (SAT·chur·ay·tuhd) **fats** Fats found in many animal products such as butter, meat, and cheese. (page 106)

Second-degree burn A serious type of burn in which the damaged area blisters or peels. (page 316)

Secondhand smoke A mixture of the smoke given off by the burning end of tobacco products and the smoke exhaled by smokers. (page 232)

Self-concept The view you have of yourself. (page 32)

Self-esteem A measure of how much you like and respect yourself. (page 34)

Sexual abuse Any mistreatment of a child or adult involving sexual activity. (page 71)

Sexually transmitted diseases (STDs) Communicable diseases spread from one person to another through sexual activity. (page 277)

Short-term goal A goal that you plan to accomplish in a short time. (page 21)

Side effect Any reaction to a medicine other than the one intended. (page 160)

Skeletal system A body system consisting of bones and the tissues connecting them. (page 181)

Smog A yellow-brown haze that forms when sunlight reacts with impurities in car exhaust. (page 319)

Smoke alarm A device that makes a warning noise when it senses smoke. (page 302)

Snuff Finely ground tobacco that is inhaled or held in the mouth or cheeks. (page 226)

Sodium A mineral that helps control the amount of fluid in your body. (page 107)

Specialist (SPEH·shuh·list) A doctor trained to handle particular health problems. (page 164)

Sperm The male reproductive cells. (page 208)

Spinal cord A tube of neurons that runs along the spine. (page 192)

Sports gear Sports clothing and safety equipment. (page 132)

Stamina (STA·mih·nuh) Your ability to stick with a task or activity for a long period of time. (page 123)

Stimulants (STIM·yuh·luhnts) Drugs that speed up the body's functions. (page 250)

Strength The ability of your muscles to exert a force. (page 123)

Stress Your body's response to changes around you. (page 45)

Substance abuse Using illegal or harmful drugs, including any use of alcohol, while under the legal drinking age. (page 256)

Suicide The deliberate act of taking one's own life. (page 51)

Sunscreen A cream or lotion that filters out some UV rays. (page 147)

Tar A thick, oily, dark liquid that forms when tobacco burns. (page 222)

Target heart rate The level at which your heart and lungs receive the most benefit from a workout. (page 130)

Tartar When plaque hardens into a shell on your teeth and cannot be brushed away. (page 145)

Technology The use of scientific ideas to improve the quality of life. (page 10)

Third-degree burn A very serious burn in which deeper layers of skin and nerve endings are damaged. (page 317)

Tissues Groups of similar cells that do the same kind of work. (page 177)

Tolerance The ability to accept other people as they are. (page 82)

Tolerance A need for increasing amounts of a substance to achieve the same effect. (page 246)

Tornado (tor·NAY·doh) A whirling, funnel-shaped windstorm that drops from the sky to the ground. (page 310)

Trans fats Fats that start off as oils and are made solid through processing. (page 106)

Tumor A mass of abnormal cells. (page 284)

Unit price Cost per unit of weight or volume. (page 157)

Vaccine (vak·SEEN) A dead or weakened pathogen introduced into your body. (page 275)

Vaccines Medicines that protect you from getting certain diseases. (page 160)

Values Beliefs you feel strongly about that help guide the way you live. (page 18)

Violence The use of physical force to harm someone or something. (page 84)

Viruses (VY·ruh·suhz) Tiny, nonliving particles that invade and take over healthy cells. (page 269)

Vitamins (VY·tuh·muhnz) Nutrients that help regulate body functions. (page 96)

Voluntary health agencies Organizations that work to treat and eliminate certain diseases. (page 165)

Warm-up Gentle activity that prepares your body for exercise or sport. (page 130)

Wellness A state of well-being, or total health. (page 7)

Withdrawal A series of physical and mental symptoms that occur when a person stops using an addictive substance. (page 254)

Glosario

A

Abdominal thrusts/presiones abdominales Movimientos en los que se ejerce una presión hacia arriba sobre el diafragma, para desalojar un objeto que obstruye la vía respiratoria.

Abstinence/abstinencia No participar en conductas de riesgo para la salud.

Abuse/abuso Patrón de maltrato a otra persona.

Accident/accidente Evento inesperado que resulta en algún daño.

Accident chain/accidente en cadena Secuencia de sucesos que muchas veces termina en un daño accidental.

Accidental injuries/herida accidental Herida causada por sucesos inesperados.

Acid rain/lluvia ácida Lluvia contaminada debido a la quema de combustibles fósiles.

Acne/acné Afección de la piel causada por la actividad excesiva de las glándulas sebáceas.

Addiction/adicción Necesidad física o mental del cuerpo de consumir una droga u otra sustancia.

Adolescence/adolescencia Período de vida entre la niñez y la adultez.

Adrenaline/adrenalina Hormona que prepara el cuerpo para responder el estrés.

Advocacy/promoción Tomar una posición para hacer una diferencia.

Advocate/Defensor Animar a la gente a vivir vidas sanas.

AIDS/SIDA Condición caracterizada por infecciones que terminan con la vida y cuenta de células T por debajo de 200.

Alcohol/alcohol Sustancia producida por una reacción química en carbohidratos.

Alcoholism/alcoholismo Enfermedad en la cual una persona tiene necesidad física y mental de alcohol.

Allergen/alergeno Sustancia que causa una reacción alérgica.

Allergy/alergia Sensibilidad del cuerpo a ciertas sustancias.

Alternative/alternativa Modo distinto de pensar o actuar.

Anabolic steroids/esteroides anabólicos Drogas sintéticas basadas en una hormona masculina.

Antibiotics/antibióticos Medicina que mata o detiene el crecimiento de bacterias y otros gérmenes específicos.

Antibodies/anticuerpos Sustancias químicas producidas específicamente para combatir una sustancia invasora determinada.

Anxiety/Ansiedad Sentimiento de incertidumbre o preocupación sobre lo que pueda pasar.

Anxiety disorder/Trastorno de ansiedad Serio problema emocional que evita que una persona funcione normalmente.

Assertive/Firme Dispuesto a defenderte de una manera positiva.

Asthma/asma Enfermedad crónica en la cual las vías respiratorias se irritan e hinchan.

Astigmatism/astigmatismo Córnea o lente deformado que causa que los objetos se vean ondulados o borrosos.

Attitude/actitud Lo que crees o sientes sobre alguien o algo.

B

Bacteria/bacterias Organismo de una sola célula sin núcleo, extremadamente pequeño.

Behavior/Comportamiento Forma en la cual actúas en diferentes situaciones y eventos en tu vida.

Biodegradable/biodegradable Que se descompone naturalmente, sin causar contaminación.

Blood alcohol content (BAC)/concentración de alcohol en la sangre Medida de la cantidad de alcohol presente en la sangre de una persona.

Blood pressure/presión arterial Fuerza que ejerce la sangre sobre las paredes de los vasos sanguíneos.

Body image/imagen corporal Cómo ves tu cuerpo.

Body language/lenguaje corporal Expresiones faciales, contacto visual, gestos y postura.

Body systems/sistema del cuerpo Grupo de órganos que ejecuta una función del cuerpo.

Calorie/caloría Unidad de calor que mide la energía disponible en los alimentos.

Cancer/cáncer Enfermedad causada por células anormales cuyo crecimiento está fuera de control.

Carbohydrates/hidratos de carbono Azúcares y almidones contenidos en los alimentos.

Carbon monoxide/monóxido de carbono Gas tóxico e inodoro que produce el tabaco al quemarse.

Cardiopulmonary resuscitation (CPR)/ resucitación cardiopulmonar Medida de primeros auxilios que intenta restaurar el ritmo cardiaco y la respiración.

Cells/células Bloques de estructura básica de la vida.

Character/carácter Manera en que piensas, sientes y actúas.

Cholesterol/colesterol Substancia química cerosa que el cuerpo produce y necesita en pequeñas cantidades.

Chromosomes/cromosomas Filamentos minúsculos de materia que llevan los códigos de rasgos heredados.

Chronic/crónico De larga duración.

Circulatory system/aparato circulatorio Sistema del cuerpo que mueve la sangre desde y hacia los tejidos.

Cirrhosis/cirrosis Destrucción y cicatrización del tejido del hígado.

Communicable diseases/enfermedad contagiosa Enfermedad que se puede propagar.

Communication/comunicación Intercambio claro de ideas e información.

Compromise/acuerdo Habilidad en la cual cada lado deja algo para llegar a una solución.

Conflicts/conflictos Desentendimientos en ideas, creencias o intereses.

Consequences/consecuencia Resultado.

Conservation/conservación Protección de los recursos naturales.

Consumer/consumidor Persona que compra productos o servicios.

Contagious/contagioso Capaz de propagarse a otros por contacto directo o indirecto.

Cooldown/recuperación Actividad suave para desacelerarse después de hacer ejercicios.

Cooperation/cooperación Trabajar juntos por el bienestar común.

Coupons/cupones Boletas de papel que te permiten ahorrar dinero en ciertas marcas.

Culture/cultura Conjunto de creencias, costumbres y comportamientos de un grupo.

Cumulative risk/riesgo acumulativo Adición de un riesgo a otro aumentando la posibilidad de daño o pérdida.

Cuticle/cutícula Banda de piel externa sin vida que rodea las uñas de las manos y los pies.

Dandruff/caspa Descamado de la capa externa de las células muertas de la piel del cuero cabelludo.

Decisions/decisión Opciones que eliges.

Dehydration/deshidratación Condición causada por mucha pérdida de agua.

Depression/depresión Problema emocional marcado por largos períodos de desesperación.

Dermis/dermis La capa más gruesa y profunda de la piel.

Diabetes/ diabetes Enfermedad que le impide al cuerpo utilizar los azúcares y almidones de los alimentos para crear energía.

Diaphragm/diafragma Músculo grande ubicado en la parte inferior del pecho.

Digestion/digestión Proceso por el cual el cuerpo deshace la comida en pequeñas partículas nutrientes.

Digestive system/aparato digestivo Sistema del cuerpo que controla el proceso digestivo.

Disease/enfermedad Condición que afecta el funcionamiento propio del cuerpo o la mente.

Drug/droga Toda sustancia que altera la estructura o el funcionamiento del cuerpo o de la mente.

Drug abuse/abuso de drogas Uso de cualquier droga en una forma no saludable o ilegal.

Drug misuse/mal empleo de drogas Tomar medicinas sin cumplir con las indicaciones.

Drug rehabilitation/rehabilitación de las drogas Proceso por el cual una persona vuelve a aprender cómo vivir sin el abuso de una droga.

E

Earthquake/terremoto Sacudimiento de la tierra mientras la capa de roca por debajo de la superficie terrestre se mueve.

Eating disorder/trastorno de la alimentación Comportamiento alimenticio extremo que puede dañar seriamente el cuerpo.

Egg cell/óvulo Célula reproductora del cuerpo femenino.

Emotions/emociones Sentimientos.

Empathy/empatía Habilidad de identificar y compartir los sentimientos de otra persona.

Emphysema/enfisema Enfermedad que ocurre cuando los pequeños sacos de aire en los pulmones pierden elasticidad o capacidad de estirarse.

Endocrine system/sistema endocrino Sistema del cuerpo que contiene glándulas que regulan el crecimiento.

Endurance/resistencia Habilidad de mantener una actividad física sin cansarse demasiado.

Environment/medio Suma total de tus alrededores.

Epidermis/epidermis La capa externa y más delgada de la piel.

Excretory system/sistema excretor Sistema del cuerpo que elimina algunos de los desechos producidos en el cuerpo y que mantiene el equilibrio de los líquidos.

Exercise/ejercicio Actividad física planeada, estructurada y repetitiva que mejora o mantiene el buen estado físico.

Family/familia Unidad básica de la sociedad.

Farsightedness/hipermetropía Capacidad de ver claramente los objetos a la distancia, mientras los objetos cercanos se ven borrosos.

Fats/grasas Nutrientes que se encuentran en tejido animal graso y aceites de plantas.

Fertilization/fertilización Unión de una célula reproductora femenina con una célula reproductora masculina.

Fetal alcohol syndrome (FAS)/síndrome de alcoholismo fetal Conjunto de problemas físicos y mentales permanentes causados por el consumo de alcohol de la madre durante el embarazo.

Fetus/feto Niño en desarrollo desde las ocho semanas hasta el nacimiento.

Fiber/fibra Parte dura y resistente de frutas crudas, vegetales crudos, trigo entero y otros granos.

Fire extinguisher/extintor de incendios Dispositivo que suelta productos químicos que sofocan las llamas.

First aid/primeros auxilios Cuidados que se dan a una persona herida o enferma, durante una emergencia hasta que se obtiene asistencia médica regular.

First-degree burn/quemadura de primer grado Quemadura en que sólo la capa exterior de la piel se quema y enrojece.

F.I.T.T. principle/principio F.I.T.T. Método para aumento seguro de los aspectos de tu entrenamiento sin dañarte a ti mismo.

Flexibility/flexibilidad Habilidad de mover las articulaciones del cuerpo a través del arco completo de movimiento.

Fluoride/fluoruro Sustancia que combate las caries.

Fossil fuels/combustible fósil Estos son carbón, aceite y gas natural.

Fraud/fraude Engaño o estafa deliberada.

Friendship/amistad Tipo especial de relación entre personas que disfrutan el estar juntas.

Frostbite/congelación Congelamiento de la piel.

Fungi/hongos Organismos primitivos de una o mas células que no pueden producir su propio alimento.

Gang/pandilla Grupo en el cual los miembros, muchas veces, utilizan la violencia para ser parte en actividad criminal.

Generic/genérico Productos que imitan productos de marca pero que se venden en paquetes simples.

Genes/genes Unidades básicas de la herencia.

Goal/meta Algo que esperas lograr.

Guarantee/garantía Promesa de que en caso de que el producto no sirva como se ha dicho tu dinero te será devuelto.

Habit/hábito Patrón de conducta que sigues casi sin pensarlo.

Hallucinogens/alucinógeno Droga ilegal que causa que el cerebro de la persona que la use cree imágenes distorsionadas.

Hazards/peligro Posible fuente de daño.

Health/salud Combinación de bienestar físico, mental, emocional y social.

Health care/cuidado médico Cualquier servicio proporcionado a individuos o comunidades que promueve, mantiene y les hace recobrar la salud.

Health insurance/seguro médico Póliza de seguro que cubre la mayor parte de los costos del cuidado de la salud.

Health skills/habilidades de salud Habilidades que te ayudan a estar y mantenerte saludable.

Heart/corazón Músculo que funciona como una bomba para el aparato circulatorio.

Heat exhaustion/agotamiento por calor Recalentamiento del cuerpo que resulta en deshidratación.

Heredity/herencia Proceso por el cual los padres biológicos pasan rasgos a los hijos.

HIV/VIH Virus que causa el sida.

Hormones/hormonas Sustancias químicas potentes producidas por las glándulas que regulan muchas funciones del cuerpo.

Hurricane/huracán Tormenta tropical fuerte con vientos y lluvia torrencial.

Hygiene/higiene Acciones tomadas para mejorar y mantener tu salud.

Hypothermia/hipotermia Descenso repentino y peligroso de la temperatura del cuerpo.

Illegal drugs/drogas ilegales Drogas que son hechas y usadas sólo por sus efectos.

Immune system/sistema inmunológico Grupo de células, tejidos y órganos que combaten las enfermedades.

Immunity/inmunidad Resistencia a un agente infeccioso.

Infection/infección Resultado de la invasión, multiplicación y daño celular de un agente patógeno en tu cuerpo.

Inhalants/inhalante Sustancia cuyos vapores se inhalan para producir alucinaciones.

Insulin/insulina Hormona producida por el páncreas.

Joints/articulaciones Lugares donde los huesos se unen con otros huesos.

Lifestyle activities/actividades de vida diaria Actividades físicas que son parte de la rutina diaria o recreación.

Long-term goal/meta a largo plazo Meta que esperas lograr en un período de meses o años.

Loyal/leal Fiel.

Lungs/pulmones Órganos principales del aparato respiratorio.

Lymphocytes/linfocito Glóbulo blanco que ataca a los agentes patógenos.

Managed care/cuidado controlado Plan de seguro médico que ahorra dinero al limitar la selección de doctores de las personas.

Marijuana/mariguana Droga ilegal que proviene de la planta del cáñamo.

Media/medios de difusión Diversos métodos de comunicación de información que comprenden los periódicos, revistas, radio, televisión e internet.

Medicines/medicina Droga que se usa para curar o prevenir enfermedades u otras afecciones.

Menstruation/menstruación Sangre, tejidos y óvulos no fertilizados que son expulsados del cuerpo.

Minerals/minerales Elementos en los alimentos que ayudan al cuerpo a trabajar adecuadamente.

Mood disorder/trastorno del humor Serio problema emocional en el cual el humor de una persona cambia de un extremo al otro.

Muscular system/sistema muscular Todos los músculos de tu cuerpo.

MyPyramid food guidance system/ pirámide alimenticia Sistema diseñado para ayudar a los americanos a tomar decisiones alimenticias saludables.

Narcotics/narcóticos Drogas fuertes que calman el dolor y desaceleran las funciones del cuerpo.

Natural disasters/desastre natural Evento causado por la naturaleza que resulta en daños extensos, destrucción y pérdida.

Nearsightedness/miopía Capacidad de ver claramente los objetos cercanos, mientras los objetos lejanos se ven borrosos.

Negative peer pressure/presión negativa de compañeros Presión que sientes de seguir comportamientos que causen daño o creencias de tus compañeros.

Neglect/abandono Falla de los padres de proveer a sus niños con protección y cuidado físico y emocional básico.

Negotiation/negociación Proceso de hablar sobre un conflicto y decidir cómo llegar a un acuerdo.

Neighborhood Watch programs/programa de vigilancia vecinal Programa en el cual los residentes están entrenados para identificar y reportar actividades sospechosas.

Nervous system/sistema nervioso Sistema de control y comunicación del cuerpo.

Neurons/neurona Célula que transporta mensajes eléctricos.

Nicotine/nicotina Droga que acelera el ritmo cardiaco y afecta al sistema nervioso central.

Noncommunicable diseases/enfermedad no contagiosa Enfermedad que no se propaga.

Nurture/criar Satisfacer las necesidades físicas, emocionales, mentales y sociales de una persona.

Nutrients/nutrientes Substancias en los alimentos que tu cuerpo necesita para desarrollar las funciones normales.

Nutrition/nutrición Proceso de consumir alimentos y utilizarlos como energía, crecimiento y buena salud.

Obese/obeso(a) Sobrepeso excesivo.

Organs/órgano Estructura formada por diferentes clases de tejidos que ejecutan una función específica.

Overdose/sobredosis Consumir una cantidad de droga mortal.

Over-the-counter (OTC) medicines/ medicina sin receta Medicina que se puede adquirir sin receta de un médico.

Ozone/ozono Forma especial del oxígeno.

Passive smokers/fumadores pasivos No fumadores que respiran el humo de segunda mano.

Pathogen/patógeno Organismo microscópico que causa enfermedades contagiosas.

Pedestrians/peatón Persona que se traslada a pie.

Peer mediation/ mediación de compañeros Proceso en el cual un estudiante especialmente capacitado escucha los dos lados de un argumento para ayudar a las personas a llegar a un acuerdo.

Peer pressure/presión de pares Influencia que tu personas de tienen sobre ti misma edad.

Peers/compañeros Amigos y otras personas de tu grupo de edad.

Physical abuse/mal trato físico Implica el uso de fuerza física.

Physical activity/actividad física Cualquier movimiento que cause que el cuerpo use energía.

Physical fitness/buen estado físico Capacidad de llevar a cabo trabajos físicos y juegos cotidianos sin sentirte cansado.

Plaque/placa bacteriana Película blanda, incolora y pegajosa que contiene bacterias que se reproducen en los dientes.

Poison control center/centro de control de venenos Agencia de la comunidad que ayuda a personas con emergencias relacionadas con venenos.

Pollute/contaminar Hacer algo impropio o dañoso para las cosas vivientes.

Prejudice/prejuicio Opinión o miedo formado sin tener hechos ni conocimiento de primera mano.

Prenatal care/cuidado prenatal Cuidado especial para asegurar que el bebé y la madre se mantengan saludables.

Prescription medicines/medicina bajo receta Medicina que puede venderse sólo con receta escrita por un médico.

Prevention/prevención Mantener hábitos de salud y seguridad para estar libre de enfermedades y lesiones.

P.R.I.C.E. Protege, descansa, hiela, comprime, y eleva.

Proteins/proteínas Nutrientes que proveen los bloques de estructura que el cuerpo necesita para crecer.

Protozoa/protozoarios Organismos de una sola célula con núcleo.

Puberty/pubertad Tiempo en el cual comienzas a desarrollar las características físicas de adultos de tu género.

Recovery/recuperación Superar una adicción y regresar a tener una vida mayormente normal.

Recovery heart rate/ritmo cardiaco de recuperación Qué tan rápido tu corazón regresa a lo normal después de haber parado el ejercicio.

Recycling/reciclaje Recuperar y cambiar un objeto para usarlo con otro propósito.

Refusal skills/habilidades de rechazo Formas de decir que no.

Reinforce/refuerza Ayuda, apoyo.

Relationship/relación Conexión que tienes con otra persona o grupo.

Reliable/confiable De fiar.

Reproductive system/aparato reproductor Sistema del cuerpo que hace posible tener descendientes o hijos.

Rescue breathing/respiración de rescate Método que reemplaza la respiración normal en el cual otra persona le llena los pulmones de aire a la víctima.

Resilience/capacidad de recuperación Habilidad de sobrepasar y recuperarte de una decepción.

Respiratory system/aparato respiratorio Aparato del cuerpo que permite la respiración.

Resting heart rate/ritmo cardiaco de descanso Número de veces que el corazón late por minuto cuando estás relajado.

Risk/riesgo Posibilidad de daño o pérdida.

Role model/modelo, ejemplo Persona cuyo éxito o comportamiento sirve de buen ejemplo para otros.

Saturated fats/grasas saturadas Grasas que se encuentran en muchos productos animales como mantequilla, carnes y queso.

Second-degree burn/quemadura de segundo grado Tipo de quemadura grave en la que se forman ampollas o se despelleja la piel quemada.

Secondhand smoke/humo secundario Mezcla del humo producida por quemar productos de tabaco y por el humo que exhalan los fumadores.

Self-concept/autoconcepto Percepción que tienes de ti mismo.

Self-esteem/autoestima Medida de cuánto te quieres y te respetas a ti mismo.

Sexual abuse/abuso sexual Cualquier maltrato a un niño o un adulto que implique actividad sexual.

Sexually transmitted diseases (STDs)/ enfermedades de transmisión sexual (ETS) Enfermedades contagiosas pasadas de una persona a otra a través de la actividad sexual.

Short-term goal/meta a corto plazo Meta que planeas lograr en un corto período de tiempo.

Side effect/efecto colateral Toda reacción a una medicina diferente de la que se procura.

Skeletal system/sistema osteoarticular Sistema del cuerpo que consiste de huesos y y tejidos que los conectan.

Smog/smog Neblina de color amarillento-café que se forma cuando la luz solar reacciona con las impurezas en el gas de los escapes de los automóviles.

Smoke alarm/alarma contra incendios Aparato que emite un ruido de emergencia cuando detecta humo.

Snuff/rapé Tabaco molido finamente que es inhalado o mantenido en la boca o las mejillas.

Sodium/sodio Mineral que ayuda a controlar la cantidad de líquido en tu cuerpo.

Specialist/especialista Doctor capacitado para atender problemas específicos de la salud.

Sperm/espermatozoides Células reproductivas masculinas.

Spinal cord/médula espinal Conducto de neuronas que se encuentra a lo largo de la columna vertebral.

Sports gear/accesorios deportivos Ropa para deportes y equipo de seguridad.

Stamina/vigor, energía Habilidad de poder realizar y mantener una actividad por largos períodos de tiempo.

Stimulants/estimulante Substancia que acelera las funciones del cuerpo.

Strength/fuerza Capacidad de tus músculos para ejercer una fuerza.

Stress/estrés Respuesta de tu cuerpo a los cambios que ocurren a tu alrededor.

Substance abuse/abuso de sustancias Consumo de drogas ilegales o nocivas, incluso el consumo del alcohol en cualquiera de sus formas antes de la edad legal para beber.

Suicide/suicidio Acto deliberado de quitarse la propia vida.

Sunscreen/bloqueador solar Crema o loción que filtra algunos rayos UV.

Tar/alquitrán Líquido espeso, aceitoso y oscuro que forma el tabaco al quemarse.

Target heart rate/ritmo cardiaco meta Nivel deseado en el cual tu corazón y tus pulmones reciben mayor beneficio de tu entrenamiento.

Tartar/sarro Materia dura que se forma cuando la placa bacteriana se acumula en los dientes.

Technology/tecnología Uso de ideas científicas para mejorar la calidad de vida.

Third-degree burn/quemadura de tercer grado Quemadura muy grave que daña las capas más profundas de la piel y las terminaciones nerviosas.

Tissues/tejidos Grupos de células similares que tienen la misma función.

Tolerance/tolerancia Habilidad para aceptar a otras personas tal como son.

Tolerance/tolerancia Necesidad de aumentos de cantidades de una sustancia para conseguir el mismo efecto.

Tornado/tornado Tormenta en forma de torbellino que gira en grandes círculos y que cae del cielo a la tierra.

Trans fats/grasas trans Grasas que empiezan como aceites y se convierten en sólidos a través de varios procesos.

Tumor/tumor Masa de células anormales.

Unit price/precio por unidad Costo por unidad de peso o volumen.

Vaccine/vacuna Germenes patógenos débiles o muertos introducidos en el cuerpo.

Vaccines/vacunas Medicinas que protegen de ciertas enfermedades.

Values/valores Creencias importantes para ti que te ayudan a guiar la forma en que vives.

Violence/violencia Uso de fuerza física para hacer daño a alguien o a algo.

Viruses/virus Pequeñas partículas sin vida que invaden y toman control de las células saludables.

Vitamins/vitaminas Nutrientes que ayudan a regular las funciones del cuerpo.

Voluntary health agencies/agencias de salud voluntarias Organizaciones que trabajan para tratar de eliminar algunas enfermedades.

Warm-up/precalentamiento Actividad moderada que prepara tu cuerpo para hacer ejercicio o deporte.

Wellness/bienestar Estado de bienestar total.

Withdrawal/síndrome de abstinencia Una serie de síntomas físicos y mentales que ocurren cuando una persona deja de consumir una sustancia adictiva.

Index

Photo Credits

Cover: Cretas (bl), Getty Images (t), Index Stock (br)

Richard Anderson **xv**; Glencoe/McGraw-Hill **xvi**; age fotostock/CORBIS **2–3**; Tim Fuller Photography **5**(t); Tim Fuller Photography **5**(r); Tim Fuller Photography **5**(c); Tim Fuller Photography **5**(l); Tim Fuller Photography **6**; Tim Fuller Photography **8**; Michael Newman/Photo Edit **9**; Tim Fuller Photography **12**; Tim Fuller Photography **14**; Tim Fuller Photography **15**; Tim Fuller Photography **16**; Tim Fuller Photography **18**; Tim Fuller Photography **19**; Tim Fuller Photography **20**(r); Tim Fuller Photography **20**(l); Tim Fuller Photography **21**(t); Tim Fuller Photography **21**(tc); Tim Fuller Photography **21**(bc); Tim Fuller Photography **22**; Photodisc **24**; Jonathan Nourok/Photo Edit **25**; Jose Luiz Pelaez/CORBIS **26**; Getty Images **30–31**; Getty Images **32**; Getty Images **33**; Getty Images **34**; Getty Images **36**; Tim Fuller Photography **38**; Getty Images **39**; Getty Images **42**; Getty Images **43**; Masterfile **45**; Getty Images **46**; Getty Images **50**; Getty Images **51**; Getty Images **52**; Getty Images **53**; Masterfile **54**; LWA-Dann Tardif/CORBIS **55**; image 100/Getty Images **56**; Ed Imaging **60–61**; Tim Fuller Photography **62**; Tim Fuller Photography **63**; Tim Fuller Photography **67**; Tim Fuller Photography **69**; Tim Fuller Photography **70**; Tim Fuller Photography **71**; Tim Fuller Photography **73**; Tim Fuller Photography **74**; Tim Fuller Photography **75**; Tim Fuller Photography **76**; Chris Collins/CORBIS **78**; Tim Fuller Photography **79**; Tim Fuller Photography **81**; Tim Fuller Photography **84**; Tim Fuller Photography **85**; Picture Partners/Alamy **86**; Tim Fuller Photography **87**; David Young-Wolf/Photo Edit **92–93**; Tim Fuller Photography **94**; Brian Leatart/Getty Images **95**(t); Nathan Benn/CORBIS **95**(m); Joaquim Vila/age fotostock/Superstock **95**(b); Tim Fuller Photography **97**(tl); Tim Fuller Photography **97**(r); Tim Fuller Photography **97**(bl); Spencer Grant/Photo Edit **98**; Tim Fuller Photography **106**(l); Tim Fuller Photography **106**(r); Tim Fuller Photography **109**; Tim Fuller Photography **110**; Tim Fuller Photography **111**; Noel Hendrickson/Masterfile **112**; Tim Fuller Photography **113**; A. Huber/U. Starke/zefa/CORBIS **114**; Larry Del Gordon/Getty Images **118–119**; Tim Fuller Photography **123**; Ron Chapple/Getty Images **123**(b); Tim Fuller Photography **125**; Tom Stewart/CORBIS **126**; Tim Fuller Photography **129**; Tim Fuller Photography **133**; Tim Fuller Photography **134**; CORBIS **135**; Tay Rees/Getty Images **136**; Tim Fuller Photography **137**; rubberball/Getty Images **142–143**; Tim Fuller Photography **147**; Amy Etra/Photo Edit **150**(l); Alamy Images **150**(m); Alamy Images **150**(r); Tim Fuller Photography **154**; Tim Fuller Photography **155**; Tim Fuller Photography **159**; Michael Newman/Photo Edit **160**; Robin Nelson/Photo Edit **164**; Ariel Skelley/Masterfile **167**; Tim Fuller Photography **168**; Tim Fuller Photography **169**; Ariel Skelley/Masterfile **170**; Tim Fuller Photography **174–175**; Rudi Von Briel/Photo Edit **181**; Tim Fuller Photography **183**; Thinkstock/Getty images **185**; Tim Fuller Photography **187**; Tim Fuller Photography **188**; Dr. Fred E. Hossler/Visuals Unlimited **190**(t); Andrew Syred/Getty Images **190**(b); Dana White/PhotoEdit **194**; Tim Fuller Photography **195**; Sean Justice/CORBIS **200–201**; Tim Fuller Photography **202**(l); Tim Fuller Photography **202**(r); Tim Fuller Photography **206**; Tim Fuller Photography **210**; Tim Fuller Photography **214**; Tim Fuller Photography **215**; David Young Wolff/Photo Edit **216**; Tim Fuller Photography **220–221**; Tim Fuller Photography **222**; Internationals Photos **226**; Tim Fuller Photography **227**; Tony Freeman/Photo Edit **229**; PR Inc. **230**; Tim Fuller Photography **233**; Tim Fuller Photography **234**; Michael Newman/Photo Edit **235**; Kayte M. Deioma/Photo Edit **240–241**; SuperStock **243**; SuperStock **245**; CORBIS **247**; Tim Fuller Photography **249**; Tim Fuller Photography **250**; Tim Fuller Photography **251**(t); Tim Fuller Photography **251**(b); Ryan McVay/Photodisc Red **254**; Index Stock **256**; Tim Fuller Photography **258**(b); Tim Fuller Photography **259**; Tanya Constantine/Getty Images **260**; Ron Fehlig/Masterfile **261**; Tim Fuller Photography **262**; Tim Fuller Photography **266–267**; Tim Fuller Photography **269**(l); Tim Fuller Photography **269**(r); Science Photo Library **270**(tr); Getty Images **270**(bl); Getty Images **270**(tl); Getty Images **270**(br); PR Inc. **271**; Lester V. Bergman/CORBIS **272**; Tim Fuller Photography **277**; Tim Fuller Photography **283**; Dr. Gladden Willis/Visuals Unlimited **284**(t); Dr. Gladden Willis/Visuals Unlimited **284**(b); Tim Fuller Photography **285**; LWA-Dan Tardiff/CORBIS **288**; Tim Fuller Photography **289**; Bobbe LeLand/Getty Images **294–295**; Tim Fuller Photography **296**; Tim Fuller Photography **298**; Tim Fuller Photography **300**; Tim Fuller Photography **301**; Alan Schein Photography/CORBIS **303**(t); Don Tremain/Photodisc Green **303**(b); S. Meltzer/PhotoLink/Photodisc Green **304**; Index Stock **305**; SuperStock **307**; Tim Fuller Photography **308**; Douglas E. Walker/Masterfile **309**; Patti McConville/Getty Images **310**; Carsten Peter/Getty Images **311**; Tim Fuller Photography **312**; Lester V. Bergman/CORBIS **316**(l); Dr. P. Marazzi/Science Photo Library **316**(m); St. Stephen's Hospital/Science Photo Library **316**(r); Tom Stewart/CORBIS **318**; Science Photo Library **319**; Tim Fuller Photography **322**; Anton J. Geisser/age fotostock **323**; Tim Fuller Photography **324**